(and even if they don't)

**TIMELESS WISDOM FOR
TRANSFORMING CONFLICTS INTO
CONFIDENCE & CONNECTION**

SVEN MASTERSON

COPYRIGHT

What to Do When the Aliens Arrive (and Even If They Don't): Timeless Wisdom for Transforming Conflict into Confidence & Connection

Copyright © 2024 **Sven Masterson**

All rights reserved. No part of this publication may be reproduced, distributed, or transmitted in any form or by any means, including photocopying, recording, or other electronic or mechanical methods, without the prior written permission of the publisher, except in the case of brief quotations embodied in critical reviews and certain other noncommercial uses permitted by copyright law.

For permission requests, write to the publisher at:

Sven Masterson, LLC
320 Gold Ave. SW Ste. 620
Albuquerque, NM 87102 USA
sven@svenmasterson.com

First Edition | First Printing, 2024

Library of Congress Cataloging-in-Publication Data

Names: Sven Masterson, author.

Title: *What to Do When the Aliens Arrive (and Even If They Don't): Timeless Wisdom for Transforming Conflict into Connection* / Sven Masterson and Steve Horsmon

Description: First Edition. | Albuquerque: Sven Masterson, LLC, 2024. | Includes bibliographical references and index.

Identifiers: ISBN 979-8-9921098-3-2 (eBook) | ISBN 979-8-9921098-4-9 (Paperback)

Subjects:

- LCSH: Fear—Psychological aspects. | Anxiety—Psychological aspects. | Interpersonal relations. | Conflict management. | Self-help.
- BISAC: FAMILY & RELATIONSHIPS / Conflict Resolution. | SELF-HELP / Personal Growth / Self-Esteem.
- Classification: LCC HQXXXX .M37 2024 | DDC 306.8—dc23

Cover design by Sven Masterson

DEDICATION

TO THOSE WHO CARRY THE LIGHT: A BEACON IN EVERY INVASION

For my children,
I don't know what kind of material wealth I'll leave you when I'm gone. That's the truth. But what I hope to give you is this: a life so full of what matters—love, courage, and a sense of enough—that it spills over into your own.
Take it. Drink deeply. Live fully. And when the storms come, may you know you have everything you need to rise, rebuild, and thrive–including my total acceptance and unconditional love.
In the great words of Robert Munsch...

I'll love you forever,
I'll like you for always,
As long as I'm living,
My baby you'll be.

—Dad
Acts 17:28

CONTENTS

Prologue   1
Introduction   5

PRELUDE: THE STAGE IS SET
UNCERTAINTY, CONFUSION & THE CALL TO AWARENESS

1. What's Going On?   11
   The Nature of Fear and Uncertainty
2. When Fear and Confusion Reign   17
   How Deception Thrives in Uncertainty
3. The Alien Invasion Begins   25
   How the Forces of Fear and Deception Seized Our World
4. The Battle Plan   31
   Charting The Path From Invasion to Liberation

PART ONE
THE INVASION UNMASKED
EXPOSING THE TACTICS THAT KEEP YOU SMALL

5. The First Wave Of Attack   47
   Fear & Anxiety Unleashed
6. The Second Wave Of Attack   55
   Longing & Insecurity in the Crossfire
7. The Exploit of Critical Infrastructure: 65
   Dependency and Control
8. The War for Your Worth   73
   How Fear and Disconnection Hijack Your Self-Worth
9. Stories We Tell Ourselves   79
   The Propaganda of the Invaders
10. The Crippling Blow   85
    Disconnection from Self and Others - the Silent Killer
11. The Invaders' Masterstroke   93
    Shame, the Stealth & Sneaky Operative
12. The Latent Saboteur   101
    Judgment—The Original Lie

PART TWO
THE TURNING POINT
CHOOSING TO RISE

13. No Cavalry Coming   113
    Embracing the Truth That Change Begins with You
14. Breaking Free From the Alien Mind Trap   123
    Escaping the Roles That Keep You Stuck
15. How PAPA Changes Everything   135
    Choosing Your Path in the Heat of Battle
16. Intercepting & Interrogating the Invaders   153
    Challenging Assumptions to Reclaim Your Sovereignty
17. The Empowerment Offensive   163
    Transforming Reactive Roles Into Sources of Strength
18. Decoding the Signals   173
    Using Emotions as Guides to Freedom
19. The Alien Code   183
    Deciphering Emotional Messages to Reclaim Your Power
20. Strongholds of Sovereignty   195
    Fortifying Your Inner World Against Alien Threats
21. Retreat to the Redoubt of Renewal   207
    Building Your Sanctuary of Supported Sovereignty
22. Dismantling the Shame Machine   219
    The Four Strategies for Freedom
23. Hobbling the Doomsday Device   235
    Ending The Judgment Fuels Destruction
24. Reclaiming the Ground From The Enemy   245
    Restoring What the Invaders Took: Rebuilding Worth and Purpose
25. The Freedom & Liberation Protocol   255
    Removing the Masks & False Identities That Keep You Bound
26. Restoring Sovereignty   265
    Bold Decisions and the Power of Choice
27. Fortify Our Stronghold   275
    Building Boundaries That Protect and Empower

PART THREE
THE COUNTEROFFENSIVE
RECLAIMING YOUR POWER & BIRTHRIGHT

28. Defeating Judgment   289
    The First Wave of Reclamation
29. Reclaiming Self-Acceptance   299
    The Fall of Shame
30. Defeating The Illusions   309
    Waking Up To Being Human

31. Inside-Out Living *The Art of Reclaiming Your Reality From The Matrix of Alien Deception*	317
32. Breaking the Walls of Disconnection *Reclaiming Yourself, Your Tribe, and Your Humanity*	329
33. Self-Sourcing Strength *Reclaiming Your Power From And Drawing From The Wellspring Within*	339
34. Fortress of Confidence *Turning Insecurity Into Bold Security*	349
35. The Liberation of Story: Writing Your Truth *Transforming the lies into a story of freedom, liberation and strength.*	357
36. Sowing Seeds of Liberation *Spreading Truth and Building a Better World*	365
37. Faith & Courage *The Antidotes To The Alien Infection*	373
38. The Planet Reclaimed *Thriving in Authenticity and Abundance*	385
39. Next Steps *Living the Transformation*	393

PART FOUR
THE GREAT UNCOVERING
MY PERSONAL JOURNEY FROM ALIENATION TO EMPOWERMENT

40. From Fear to Flourishing *My Journey of Transformation*	407
41. Debugging the Alien Code *Unmasking Fear, Shame, and the Systems That Keep Us Powerless*	417
42. The Genesis Code *Unlocking Humanity's Original Design*	425
43. The Forbidden Fruit *The Weight of Judgment and the Love That Protects*	433
44. The Serpent's Trap *Humanity's First Drama Triangle*	441
45. From Fig Leaves to Freedom *Reclaiming Connection After the First Judgment*	449
46. The First Steps Into Exile *The Creator's Plan from the Garden to the Exodus*	457
47. The Exodus Of The Alienated *The Journey from Dependency to Empowerment*	465
48. Ministry of Life *Restoring Dignity and Freedom Through the Law*	473
49. The Radical Rest *Finding Freedom from Shame, Striving, and Endless To-Do Lists*	485

50. The Second Adam *Yeshua's Life as the Embodiment of Connection, Love, and Freedom*	493
51. Forgiveness Unveiled *A Journey from Judgment to Freedom Through Yeshua's Life, Death, and Resurrection*	507
52. The Rescue That Wasn't *Salvation as Connection, Not Escape*	523
53. The Creator's Boundaries *Gravity, Grace, and the Patterns of the Universe*	535
54. Who Are the Wicked? *Understanding the Creator's Justice and Wrath*	543
55. Repentance & Deliverance *From Fear to Flourishing*	553
56. The Cosmic Family *From Hired Hands to Beloved Sons*	567
57. Mission Recalibrated *An Invitation to Flourish and Co-Create*	575
58. The Breath Within *Our Co-Pilot in Creation*	583
59. Ground Zero *The Unshakable Love That Holds Us Steady*	597
60. The Wellspring *Drinking Deeply from the Source of Love*	605
61. The Resistance Begins with You *How to Reject Fear-Based Narratives and Embrace Empowerment*	615
The Power of Discernment	623
Conclusion: Living Free, No Matter What	627

PART FIVE
APPENDIX

62. The Mathematical Miracle of Your Existence	633
63. From DRAMA To CREATOR *Tools for Discernment and Empowerment*	635
Epilogue	641

Join the Conversation	643
About Sven Masterson	645
Acknowledgments	647
Special Thanks	649
Extra Special Thanks	651
Also by Sven Masterson	653
A Note to Readers	655
End Notes	657

PROLOGUE
THE FIRST INVASION

I'LL ADMIT IT RIGHT UP FRONT: THIS IS AN UNUSUAL BOOK. I ALSO want to say this book isn't really about aliens. And yet, in some ways, it absolutely is.

Let me explain.

Aliens are both a symbol and a metaphor—a playful, attention-grabbing hook to explore something far deeper. Fear, anxiety, deception, conflict, and the uncertainty of the unknown—they're the real invaders. Aliens just make the stakes feel bigger and more cinematic. After all, what better way to dive into life's biggest questions than with a thought experiment straight out of a blockbuster?

But my fascination with "what if" scenarios didn't start with aliens. It started with the Cold War.

I grew up in the 1980s, a time when the specter of nuclear war loomed large over every childhood. Duck-and-cover drills, headlines about mutually assured destruction, and whispered fears about "the Russians" were part of the cultural landscape. All my schools had "Fallout Shelter" signage, and the threat of imminent nuclear annihilation was part of our daily routine. Add to that the evangelical tradition I was raised in—a tradition that waited expectantly for Armageddon, The Rapture, and the Apocalypse—and you could say I had a front-row seat to a jumbo-sized bucket of buttery fear and salty, existential angst. Quite a lot for a little guy to stomach.

These fears, though unsettling, were strangely captivating. They opened the door to curiosity, and, at times, excitement. What if the invasion—whatever form it took—wasn't just a disaster, but an unveiling? What if it revealed truths about who we are, what we're capable of, and how we can fight back?

This fascination crystallized in a moment I'll never forget: the first time my family brought home a VCR. The very first movie we watched on it was *Red Dawn*, the first-ever PG-13 film—a movie that made an indelible mark on me. Set against the backdrop of an invasion, it was equal parts terrifying and thrilling. Here were kids my age—ordinary teenagers—who found themselves on the frontlines of an unimaginable war. They were scared, overwhelmed, and outmatched, but they found their courage. They fought back.

Red Dawn became one of those stories I carried with me, a reminder that fear and uncertainty don't have to define us. Even in the face of overwhelming odds, there's room for bravery, connection, and resilience.

It wasn't just global fears that shaped me. There were smaller, more personal ones, too. As a kid, I dealt with early thyroid health challenges that left me feeling different and fragile. I was bullied from the first to eighth grade, carrying the all-too-familiar anxieties about fitting in, being good enough, and surviving the gauntlet of adolescence. Conflict—whether with others, with myself, or with the world at large—was a constant companion.

This is the backdrop of my story—and maybe yours, too. Fear and conflict often feel like invaders. They barge into your life, disrupt your sense of stability, and demand your attention. They whisper lies about your worth, capability, and future. But here's the truth: the invasion is also an opportunity. It's a chance to see the lies for what they are, to reclaim your agency, and to begin rebuilding something stronger.

Which brings me back to aliens.

I could have chosen anything as a metaphor for this book:

nukes, pandemics, grid collapses, financial implosions, or even the zombie apocalypse. But aliens? Aliens are universal. To me, they're the ultimate "what if." (Okay, they might be tied with nukes. But if the nukes start falling, who will have time to go online and look for a book about it?)

What if beings from another world landed tomorrow? What if everything we thought we knew about reality got turned upside down? What if we found ourselves in the middle of the kind of global chaos that only seemed possible in the movies?

Here's the thing: you don't need actual aliens to feel that kind of disruption. Every one of us faces moments that make us question everything we thought we knew. Fear and conflict have a way of landing in our lives like an invasion, leaving us scrambling to figure out what to do next.

This book is about that scramble—and how to stop it. It's about reclaiming your agency and power, even when the world (or your mind) feels like it's falling apart. It's about uncovering the truth beneath the lies, the courage beneath the fear, and the connection beneath the disconnection.

In short, it's about thriving when everything feels impossible.

So buckle up. Whether or not aliens ever land, we're about to tackle the invaders already in your life—and chart a path to freedom, peace, and abundance.

Oh, and one last thing: **Wolverines!** *(if you know, you know.)*

INTRODUCTION

RECLAIMING YOUR HEART, MIND, COMMUNITY, AND PLANET

Imagine waking up one day to find the world as you know it turned upside down, not by a natural disaster, a nuclear war, or even an alien invasion that arrived with flashing lights and ominous spacecraft. No, the attack I'm talking about was far more subtle, far more insidious. It wasn't just "out there" on the news or in distant cities. It was inside—within our thoughts, our beliefs, and our sense of self.

We've been under attack for as long as humanity has existed. Fear, shame, dependency, judgment—these are the weapons of the invaders, sowing disconnection and despair. These forces masquerade as protectors or even saviors, promising security, worth, and love if we play their game. But the truth? They thrive on our suffering and keep us trapped in cycles of longing, seeking, and grasping for external validation. Their power lies in keeping us blind to the fact that the battle is happening at all.

This is not a story about aliens—not really. But it is a story about an invasion. It's a story about how I came to recognize these forces at work in my own life, tearing me apart from the inside out. And it's about how I—and how you—can fight back.

WHY THIS BOOK?

You're holding this book because something inside you recognizes that the world you've been living in doesn't quite fit. Maybe you're overwhelmed by fear and anxiety. Maybe you feel disconnected—from others, from yourself, or from something greater. Maybe you're stuck in patterns of dependency or insecurity, longing for a way out but unsure where to begin.

I wrote this book for people dear to me, and I wrote it for you—not as a guru or guide who has it all figured out, but as someone who has been there. Someone who has walked through the valley of disconnection, despair, and alienation and found a way to reclaim life on the other side.

This is a battle plan, but it's not about winning against others. It's about liberation—about reclaiming your power, your worth, and your connection to yourself, others, and the Creator. It's about thriving in the face of forces that would have you live small, afraid, and disconnected.

STAGES OF TRANSFORMATION

This book is structured to guide you through a progression—a way of moving from unconscious suffering to conscious thriving. Along the way, you'll encounter three pivotal shifts:

1. **Acute Pain (or Inspiration):** This is the wake-up call, the moment you realize something has to change. For some, it's a crisis. For others, it's a sudden, clear, intoxicating vision of what life *must* be.
2. **The Decision Point:** Here lies the most significant turning point. Do you continue the same patterns that led to this pain, or do you choose a new path? This is where fear tries to keep you stuck, but it's also where courage begins.

3. **Supported Repetitive Growth:** Transformation isn't a one-time decision. It's built through daily practice, deliberate action, and the support of others on the same journey.

This process isn't linear. It's a cycle, a rhythm that we move through repeatedly as we grow. Each step forward brings you closer to the life you're meant to live—one of authenticity, connection, and abundance.

WHAT YOU'LL FIND INSIDE

This book unfolds in four parts:

1. **The Invasion Unmasked:** We begin by identifying the forces at work—the fear, shame, dependency, and judgment that keep us trapped in suffering.
2. **The Turning Point:** Here, we explore what it means to reclaim agency, face shame, and begin making empowered choices.
3. **The Counteroffensive:** This is where we reverse the damage, reclaiming the ground lost to the invaders and building a life of security, love, and purpose.
4. **The Great Uncovering:** For those who are curious about the spiritual dimension of this journey, this section delves into my personal faith reconstruction, offering insights and reflections for those on similar paths.

YOU ARE THE HERO

This book isn't just a guide—it's a mirror. As you read, you'll find tools, insights, and stories to help you on your journey, but ultimately, the hero of this story is you. No one else can walk this path for you. No one else can claim your power, make your choices, or live your truth.

But you're not alone. This book is a companion, a map, and a reminder that the battle is not the end—it's the beginning.

Welcome to the counteroffensive. Let's reclaim your planet together.

COMING UP NEXT

As we proceed, we'll explore how these invaders—fear, shame, dependency, and deception—operate and how they infiltrate our lives, often without us realizing it. We'll also uncover the tools to resist them: clarity, connection, and courage. These are not just abstract concepts but practical, actionable principles you can use to reclaim your life and step into freedom. Let's begin by asking a vital question: What's going on?

PRELUDE: THE STAGE IS SET

UNCERTAINTY, CONFUSION & THE CALL TO AWARENESS

CHAPTER ONE
WHAT'S GOING ON?
THE NATURE OF FEAR AND UNCERTAINTY

EVERY SO OFTEN, THE WORLD HANDS US A MOMENT THAT LEAVES US shaken and scrambling to make sense of it. For some, it's personal—a relationship ending out of nowhere, the sudden loss of a loved one, or a diagnosis that changes everything. For others, it's global—a pandemic, a natural disaster, or the kind of headline that sounds like science fiction. In recent years, we've seen an increasing number of those: unexplained aerial phenomena (UAPs), classified briefings to Congress about mysterious objects in the sky, and even public statements from military officials admitting they don't know what's flying around our world.

If you've paid attention to the news, you know these events aren't just whispered rumors. They're on mainstream networks, discussed in government hearings, and acknowledged by trusted institutions. Some reports involve military encounters with objects that defy the laws of physics. Others describe drones or unidentified craft near sensitive installations, raising questions about espionage—or something else entirely.

It's the kind of story that leaves us unsettled. And if tomorrow brought undeniable evidence of extraterrestrial life—or something masquerading as such—what would you feel? What would you do? What *could* you do?

SVEN MASTERSON

This book doesn't claim to have all the answers. But it does offer a way to face these questions—not just about aliens, but about any crisis—with clarity, strength, and a sense of purpose. Whether the invaders are metaphorical (as they so often are) or one day literal, the tools and perspectives we'll explore together are designed to help you navigate fear and uncertainty, whatever shape they take.

WHEN THE METAPHOR MIGHT STOP BEING A METAPHOR

Let's be honest: the idea of an alien invasion feels, for most people, like the stuff of movies. And yet, as I write this, the news is filled with stories of unexplainable phenomena in our skies. Pilots report strange encounters. Intelligence officials hint at capabilities far beyond human technology. Whistleblowers allege secret programs and hidden truths. The details are murky, and skepticism is warranted, but one thing is certain: our world is wrestling with questions it hasn't faced before.

Here's the thing about the unknown: it's disorienting. Even if the explanation for UAPs turns out to be terrestrial—drones, advanced technology, or misidentified objects—the mere possibility of something greater shakes our foundations. And if, someday, the metaphor of this book stops being a metaphor, if something truly other reveals itself to humanity, it will test us in ways we can barely imagine.

But here's what's important: this book is not just about aliens. It's about fear, uncertainty, and how we respond to them. The principles you'll find here apply whether the "invasion" is global and dramatic, like the sudden confirmation of extraterrestrial life, or deeply personal, like a phone call that changes your life forever. The tools we'll discuss are universal because fear and uncertainty, while they may take many forms, always seek to destabilize us in the same ways.

WHAT HAPPENS WHEN FEAR TAKES OVER?

When the skies darken with mystery—or when your own world is turned upside down—fear is often the first wave of attack. It whispers questions that cut to the core of our human vulnerability: *What does this mean? Am I safe? Will things ever go back to normal?*

These questions aren't just intellectual; they're visceral. They ignite a cascade of emotions—anxiety, confusion, even panic—that can leave us grasping for certainty, for rescue, for someone to tell us what to do. This is where our need for understanding becomes both a strength and a potential vulnerability. In moments of crisis, our search for meaning can drive us to wisdom—or to deception.

Think about a personal crisis: a breakup you didn't see coming, a sudden loss, or the realization of a terrible illness. Those moments don't just leave us grieving; they leave us searching. We want explanations. We want control. We want reassurance that things will be okay. And in that desperate search, we sometimes accept easy answers or false narratives, simply because they soothe the chaos in our minds.

Now imagine that same dynamic playing out on a global scale. Imagine waking up to undeniable evidence of an alien presence—or the appearance of one. Would you know what to believe? Would you trust your instincts, your leaders, your faith? Or would fear paralyze you, leaving you vulnerable to the loudest, most confident voices, whether they speak truth or lies?

NAVIGATING THE UNKNOWN

The purpose of this book is to prepare you—not just for the unimaginable, but for the very real challenges we all face. Life will always bring uncertainty, whether in the form of strange lights in the sky or the sudden collapse of something you thought was secure. And while you can't control what happens, you can choose how you respond.

Here's what I hope you'll take from this chapter as we begin this journey together:

1. Fear Is a Signal, Not a Sentence

Fear isn't inherently bad. It's your mind's way of alerting you to something important. But fear only serves you when you recognize it for what it is: a signal to pay attention, not a verdict on your ability to cope. The tools in this book will help you interpret fear without letting it dominate you.

2. The Unknown Doesn't Have to Be the Enemy

When life presents us with the unexplainable, our first instinct is often to fight against it, to demand answers and certainty. But what if the unknown isn't an enemy to be defeated, but a challenge to be met with curiosity and courage? The discomfort of not knowing is where growth begins.

3. Connection Is Your Greatest Resource

Crises, whether personal or global, often isolate us, making us feel like we're alone in our fear and uncertainty. But that's a lie. You're not alone. Connection—to yourself, to others, and to something greater—can anchor you in even the most turbulent times. This book will explore how to strengthen those connections and why they're essential to navigating the unknown.

WHAT'S GOING ON?

The question at the heart of every crisis—*What's going on?*—is a powerful one. It's not just about facts; it's about meaning. It's about finding your footing when the world feels like it's slipping away. Whether you're facing the possibility of extraterrestrial life, the loss of a relationship, or a sudden health scare, that question will echo in your mind. This book exists to help you answer it—not with false certainty, but with the tools and perspectives you need to navigate the uncertainty with strength, clarity, and connection.

So what's going on? That's what we're here to explore.

Fear is the first wave of attack, but it's not the invaders' only weapon. Once fear takes hold, it opens the door to deception—a force that thrives on our need for certainty and control. Understanding deception is the next step in reclaiming your agency and breaking free from the invaders' grip."

COMING UP NEXT: THE POWER OF DECEPTION

In the next chapter, we'll explore why fear and uncertainty make us especially vulnerable to deception—and how you can build resilience against it. Whether the "invasion" is personal, global, or extraterrestrial, understanding the tactics of deception is your first step to reclaiming agency and truth.

REFLECTION QUESTIONS

1. How do you typically respond to moments of uncertainty or fear? Do you try to control the situation, or do you withdraw?
2. Think of a time when you faced an unexpected personal crisis. What helped you navigate it, and what made it harder?
3. What would it look like to embrace the unknown in your life with curiosity and courage, rather than fear?
4. How might fear be signaling something important in your life right now? How can you acknowledge it without letting it take control?

CHAPTER TWO
WHEN FEAR AND CONFUSION REIGN
HOW DECEPTION THRIVES IN UNCERTAINTY

When the world feels uncertain and confusion takes hold, deception thrives. Whether it's the swirl of misinformation following a global event, the subtle manipulations in a toxic relationship, or the lies we tell ourselves in moments of doubt, deception feeds on fear and disorientation. Confusion creates gaps in our understanding, and deception eagerly fills them, offering easy answers or comforting illusions in exchange for clarity, agency, and truth.

This isn't just a phenomenon of global upheaval; it plays out in conflicts of every scale. Consider marriage trouble, factions at work, polarizing politics, election cycles, or even wars. In each scenario, confusion fuels fear, mistrust spreads, and false narratives take root. The tools of deception are universal, whether wielded by a controlling partner, a divisive politician, or (for a playful example) invading aliens in a Red Dawn-style scenario.

And yes, even in the event of a global alien invasion. Whether the crisis is personal, political, or planetary, deception thrives in moments of fear, confusion, and disorientation. It exploits our natural search for stability, twisting our vulnerabilities into opportunities for control. This chapter explores why crises make us so susceptible to manipulation, how deception operates, and how you can resist its pull.

DECEPTION THRIVES IN UNCERTAINTY AND CONFUSION

In times of uncertainty—whether personal, societal, or global—we crave stability and clarity. This isn't a weakness; it's human nature. Our brains are wired to seek patterns and meaning, to make sense of the unknown so we can act with confidence. But when answers don't come easily, confusion leaves us vulnerable to deception.

Fear as a Gateway

Fear narrows our focus, turning our attention toward perceived threats and potential saviors. When we're afraid, we're more likely to accept simple explanations or promises, even if they're untrue, because they offer relief from the discomfort of not knowing.

In a struggling relationship, fear of rejection might lead you to believe your partner's coldness is entirely your fault, even if the reality is more complex. At work, fear of losing your job might push you to align with a toxic faction, just to feel secure. On a national level, fear drives political polarization, with each side scapegoating the other. And in a full-blown alien invasion? Fear might make us trust the first leader who offers a solution, no matter how flawed it is.

Crisis Drives Dependency

When fear takes over, crises amplify our dependency on external sources of guidance. In personal crises, this might mean turning to someone who seems to offer comfort or solutions, even if their intentions are self-serving. On a larger scale, people often look to leaders, institutions, or charismatic figures who claim to have all the answers.

Think about election cycles, where leaders exploit fears to position themselves as the sole solution. Or consider the *Red Dawn* invasion scenario—when the world seems to crumble, communities often consolidate around those who promise safety, even if it comes at a cost. Dependency breeds vulnerability, and deception thrives on that dynamic.

The Illusion of Certainty

Deception often thrives because it offers what we think we need most: certainty. It fills the void created by ambiguity with narratives that seem plausible—or at least comforting. But the certainty it provides is an illusion, a carefully crafted narrative designed to pacify our fears while distracting us from asking deeper questions.

Whether it's a manipulative partner claiming to know what's best for you, a conspiracy theory offering a simple explanation for a complex world, or a global leader promising salvation during an alien attack, the pattern is the same. Certainty feels like safety, but when it's built on deception, it's just another trap.

HOW DECEPTION OPERATES

Deception works through strategies that exploit our emotions—especially fear, insecurity, and shame. Understanding these tactics is the first step in resisting them.

Creating a Scapegoat

Deception often involves pointing to an external enemy—a person, group, or concept to blame for our pain or fear. This tactic simplifies complex problems and directs our energy outward, keeping us from examining the true source of our discomfort.

In a relationship, this might mean blaming your partner entirely for the conflict, rather than reflecting on your own contributions. Politically, it could mean scapegoating another nation or group for societal struggles. And in something like *Red Dawn* or an alien invasion? Scapegoating becomes a survival tactic, with people latching onto enemies—real or imagined—to channel their fear.

Overpromising Rescue

Deceivers often position themselves as the only solution to our crisis. Whether it's a manipulative partner in a toxic relationship or a global figure during a societal upheaval, the promise is the same: "Only I can fix this."

The danger here is dependency. When we place all our hope in a rescuer, we surrender our agency, forgetting that true resilience comes from within. Whether in a marriage or during a supposed alien invasion, the result is the same—disempowerment disguised as salvation.

Sowing Division

Deception thrives on isolation and division. By pitting us against one another, it weakens the connections that could otherwise help us discern truth and resist manipulation.

This is as true in families and workplaces as it is in politics or hypothetical global crises. In *Red Dawn,* the invaders benefit from turning communities against themselves. And if aliens ever did invade? Sowing mistrust among humans would be their most effective strategy.

Using Partial Truths

The most effective lies often contain elements of truth. By weaving in facts or plausible ideas, deception gains credibility and becomes harder to unravel. Whether it's a half-truth told by a controlling partner, a distorted political narrative, or a conspiracy about aliens, the presence of some truth makes the deception more believable.

WHY WE'RE VULNERABLE

Deception isn't just an external force—it also preys on the stories we carry within ourselves.

The Pull of Insecurity

Crises bring our insecurities to the surface. In moments of doubt, we may question our worth or ability to handle the situation, making us more likely to accept narratives that validate those fears.

The Influence of Shame

Shame whispers that we're not enough, that we need someone or something else to save us. It disconnects us from our inner wisdom, making us easy targets for manipulation.

The Desire for Belonging

When crises isolate us, we long for connection. This longing can make us susceptible to groupthink or charismatic leaders who promise unity—often at the cost of truth.

BUILDING RESILIENCE AGAINST DECEPTION

Resisting deception begins with cultivating clarity, connection, and courage. These tools help us navigate fear and uncertainty without losing our agency or authenticity. Here are four key steps to building resilience:

1. Clarity: Know Yourself and Your Values

Deception thrives on confusion. Reflect on your values, boundaries, and the kind of life you want to build. When you're grounded in your identity, you're less likely to be swayed by external pressures.

Ask yourself: Does this narrative align with my values? Am I reacting out of fear or strength?

2. Connection: Strengthen Your Relationships

Deception isolates; connection protects. Seek out relationships that encourage honesty, self-reflection, and mutual respect. A trusted community can act as a mirror, helping you see through manipulative tactics and reconnect with your inner wisdom.

Practical step: Share your uncertainties with trusted people who challenge and uplift you.

3. Clear Thinking: Examine the Messenger and Their Motives

Deception often relies on the credibility of the messenger, so it's essential to ask: *Who is delivering this message? What do they stand to gain?* Consider whether the messenger's motives align with your best interests or if they're exploiting fear to achieve their own goals. Later, in Part 2, we'll explore tools and frameworks to sharpen this kind of discernment, helping you recognize manipulative dynamics and resist their pull.

4. Courage: Embrace the Unknown

Deception feeds on our discomfort with uncertainty. By learning to sit with the unknown and act in alignment with your truth, you reclaim your power. Courage isn't the absence of fear; it's the decision to act in alignment with your values, even when fear is present.

Mantra to practice: "I can face the unknown with curiosity and strength."

A CRISIS OF TRUTH

Whether it's personal heartbreak, workplace factions, an election cycle, or the surreal possibility of extraterrestrial contact, moments of crisis are also moments of choice. Will we give in to fear and the seductive simplicity of deception, or will we rise above it, reclaiming our agency and our truth?

Deception may be powerful, but it is not invincible. This book's tools—clarity, connection, clear thinking, and courage—can help you see through manipulation and transform fear into resilience. Whether the crisis is as personal as a breakup or as monumental as alien contact, the principles remain the same.

REFLECTION QUESTIONS

1. Can you think of a time when fear or uncertainty led you to believe a false narrative? What factors made it convincing?
2. How does fear influence your decision-making? What helps you regain clarity in moments of doubt?
3. Who in your life acts as a mirror, helping you stay grounded and discerning?

CHAPTER THREE
THE ALIEN INVASION BEGINS
HOW THE FORCES OF FEAR AND DECEPTION SEIZED OUR WORLD

THE INVASION DIDN'T START WITH SHIPS

THE INVASION DIDN'T START WITH THE SUDDEN ARRIVAL OF otherworldly ships or shimmering beams of light from the sky. No, this invasion began far more subtly and insidiously—a slow creep of shadows whispering into the depths of our hearts and minds. It wasn't an assault on cities or nations but on us as individuals and as a collective, targeting our most vulnerable places: our sense of self, our connection to one another, and our relationship with the Creator.

> *Throughout this book, you'll find notes like this one. These are personal reflections and stories that provide deeper context and share how the ideas in this book have played out in my life. They're meant to offer a more personal touch and help you see how these concepts can be applied in real-world situations.*
>
> *My first note is to explain my use of "The Creator" and "faith." I often use "The Creator" because it's the most authentic way for me to describe my perspective and experi-*

ences. However, you don't need to share my view to find value in this book. The insights I share are for anyone seeking clarity, growth, and connection, regardless of beliefs or background.

When I talk about faith, I mean something broader than its purely religious connotations. Faith, as I use it here, is about how we choose to look at the uncertain and unknown future. It's an optimistic, confident, and expectant lens—believing that good is possible and that we can navigate whatever lies ahead. In many ways, faith is the opposite of fear, which also looks at the unknown future but with negative expectations. I see faith and fear are two sides of the same process—both rooted in how we choose to perceive and anticipate what's to come.

It's tempting to think of alien invasions as fictional tales or metaphorical musings, but this book treats the concept as an opportunity for exploration—a lens through which to understand the most primal and profound conflicts of our shared human experience. Isn't that how fear, shame, and deception often feel? Like stealthy invaders, creeping in when we least expect it, shaping our actions and beliefs before we even realize they're there. They come from nowhere, slipping into our thoughts, warping our perceptions, and leaving us wondering how we ever let them in.

For me, the invasion didn't look like shimmering lights or sudden chaos. It started subtly—a creeping sense of unworthiness, the slow erosion of trust in myself and others. At first, I didn't even recognize it for what it was. But over time, the signs became clearer, and I had to confront the ways fear and shame were shaping my life.

This is the story of that invasion—and the counter-offensive we're about to launch.

A DIFFERENT KIND OF APOCALYPSE

In the popular imagination, an apocalypse is often synonymous with destruction. But its true meaning is much more profound: The word *apocalypse* comes from the Greek *apokálypsis*, which means "unveiling" or "revealing." What if the crises we face aren't just about loss but also about clarity? What if they pull back the curtain on truths we might otherwise have ignored?

This invasion brought its share of destruction, but it also exposed us to truths about ourselves, truths we might have buried beneath layers of avoidance or fear.

The invaders' strategy was precise. They sought to undermine us by targeting our core needs: security, connection, and meaning. Fear was their vanguard, and anxiety was their first wave of attack. Next came shame, a stealthy weapon that eroded our self-worth, convincing us to hide behind masks and facades. Dependency followed, exploited as critical infrastructure, persuading us that our well-being could only be sourced externally—through the approval of others, success, or possessions.

This invasion didn't just attack us individually; it fractured our communities, pitted us against one another, and sowed seeds of distrust. The goal wasn't just to conquer—it was to leave us so disoriented and alienated from ourselves that we wouldn't even consider resistance.

THE TURNING POINT

This isn't just a story about being invaded—it's a story about reclaiming the planet, about turning their weapons of fear, shame, and dependency against them. It's about the journey from victim to victor, from helplessness to empowerment.

Every invasion brings its moment of choice. We can surrender, giving ourselves over to the invaders' lies, or we can resist. Resistance begins with one critical realization: the invaders are not omnipotent. Their power lies in deception, and like all lies, their strength crumbles when confronted with truth.

The invaders' goal is to keep us stuck in unconscious suffering, where their lies go unchallenged. But every crisis brings an opportunity for transformation. In the next chapter, we'll explore the universal pattern that leads from suffering to thriving—a journey that begins with awareness and grows through deliberate action.

This book is our guide to the counter-offensive. It's not about ignoring the invaders or pretending they don't exist—it's about recognizing them, dismantling their lies, and reclaiming our lives. It will help us uncover the tactics the invaders used, not just in our own lives but in the broader patterns of humanity. It will show us how to break free from the lies that have held us captive, rediscover our authentic selves, and rebuild our lives on a foundation of truth, connection, and courage.

> For me, this invasion became the backdrop for my most personal apocalypse—my personal "Unveiling," one that unraveled and then re-wove the fabric of my life, beliefs, relationships, and identity. I didn't just face the invaders; I had to confront the ways I'd been complicit in their presence.
>
> This journey wasn't easy. It meant staring down fears I'd long ignored, peeling back layers of shame, and questioning beliefs I had clung to for years. My faith, in particular, underwent a radical transformation—what some might call a deconstruction but what I now see as a reconstruction. While this book is not primarily about faith, I've included the highlights of that journey in a separate section for those interested.

WHY THIS STORY MATTERS

This isn't just my story. It's ours. These invaders—fear, shame, deception—are universal enemies, ones we all encounter in some form or another. They don't need flying saucers to wreak havoc; they already exist in the judgments we internalize, the connections we sever, and the lies we believe.

This book isn't a tale of escapism or science fiction; it's an invitation to transformation.

As we begin, I ask us to consider this: What lies have the invaders planted in our lives? Where have fear, shame, or dependency taken root? And what would it feel like to finally expel them, reclaim our sovereignty, and thrive in authenticity, connection, and abundance?

The counter-offensive begins here.

Let's begin.

REFLECTION QUESTIONS

1. When in our lives have we felt the "alien invasion" of fear, shame, or dependency?
2. What aspects of our identity or lives do we suspect have been shaped by these forces?
3. Are we ready to confront the invaders and reclaim our lives?
4. Think about a time when you felt 'invaded' by fear or shame. What did that experience reveal about your deeper needs?

CHAPTER FOUR
THE BATTLE PLAN
CHARTING THE PATH FROM INVASION TO LIBERATION

THE ALIEN INVASION TYPICALLY FOLLOWS A PATTERN

INVASION STORIES ALWAYS FOLLOW A PATTERN. WHETHER ALIENS TEAR through our cities or life throws us into a storm of conflict, the chaos might look different, but the process is the same. There's an initial shock, a period of painful struggle, a deliberate choice to fight back, and a time when thriving becomes second nature if we stick with it. It's not just how humanity survives an apocalypse—it's how we survive anything.

This same pattern—chaos, struggle, choice, and thriving—is universal. It manifests in alien invasions and relationships, careers, health crises, and any time life feels overwhelming. Recognizing this pattern can help us navigate our "invasions" with clarity and courage.

In this chapter, I want to share how this universal pattern—these four stages—has manifested in my life, especially during one of the most difficult periods of my marriage. But first, let's break down the stages themselves. Recognizing them can help us navigate any alien invasion or personal crisis we might be facing.

The Four Stages of Experience

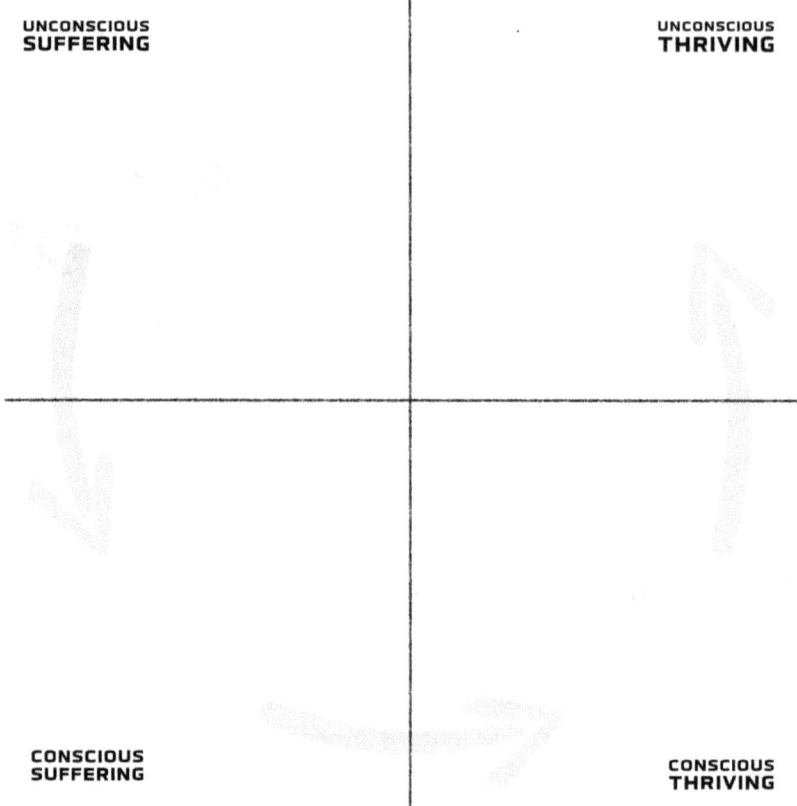

The Four Stages of Our Experience

Let's start with how this plays out in the most dramatic scenario: an alien invasion. Picture the moment the ships arrive—the chaos, the uncertainty, the fear. We wake up one morning to the news that ships have appeared in the sky, and suddenly, everything feels chaotic. The world as we know it is turned upside down. But even in this situation, the journey from fear to thriving follows the same universal pattern:

Stage 1: Unconscious Suffering—The Frog in the Pot Stage

This stage doesn't begin with explosions or overt chaos. It starts quietly, subtly, as life becomes a simmering pot of low-key suffering. The enemy's saboteurs have already infiltrated, planting seeds of disconnection, dependency, and externalized self-worth long before the first wave of fear arrives. Like the proverbial frog in the boiling pot, we don't notice the temperature rising—we're too busy adjusting to the discomfort, convincing ourselves it's normal.

- **Alien Invasion Example:** Before the ships appear, strange things begin to happen: power outages, odd news reports, and people withdrawing from each other. We feel uneasy, but we ignore it, writing it off as "just life." Meanwhile, the invaders are quietly setting the stage for full-scale chaos.
- **The Pandemic:** During the pandemic, many of us didn't realize how disconnected we'd become from one another until isolation forced us to confront it. We'd adjusted to small disconnections without noticing the cumulative impact.
- **Real-Life Example:** In a relationship, this might manifest as growing emotional distance, small unresolved misunderstandings, and unspoken resentments that build over time. It feels normal because it happens so gradually, but the disconnection is already taking root.

Stage 2: Conscious Suffering—The Clarity Stage

When the invasion becomes undeniable, the boiling pot is tipped over, and chaos erupts. In this stage, we start to see what's really going on, including our own role in the mess. This awareness hurts, but it's the first step toward change.

- **Alien Invasion Example:** You realize that hiding in fear isn't sustainable and that blaming others for the crisis doesn't help. You begin to confront the reality of the situation.

- **The Pandemic:** As the crisis became undeniable, people faced hard truths about their relationships, work, and mental health. The clarity was painful but necessary for change.
- **Real-Life Example:** In a marriage, this might mean acknowledging the emotional distance and realizing that avoidance and blame aren't solutions.

Stage 3: Conscious Thriving—The Rebuilding Stage

In this stage, we make deliberate choices to create new patterns. It's hard work, but this is where transformation happens.

- **Alien Invasion Example:** You gather with a group of survivors, each taking on specific roles to support the group. Trust begins to grow, and hope is reignited.
- **The Pandemic:** Conscious thriving began when people started actively rebuilding—reaching out to loved ones, finding new ways to connect, and prioritizing what mattered most.
- **Real-Life Example:** You and your partner start having difficult conversations, seeking understanding instead of blame, and rebuilding trust step by step.

Stage 4: Unconscious Thriving—The Freedom Stage

Hard work pays off, and we navigate life with confidence and grace. Thriving becomes our natural state.

- **Alien Invasion Example:** Over time, you adapt to the new reality, finding ways to thrive despite the ongoing challenges. Your courage inspires others, and together, you rebuild.
- **The Pandemic:** For those who embraced the lessons of that time, the growth became second nature—stronger

relationships, clearer priorities, and a renewed sense of purpose.
- **Real-Life Example:** Your relationship becomes stronger and more resilient. The trust and connection you've built sustain you through future challenges.

MAPPING SUFFERING TO THRIVING

The Suffering-to-Thriving progression outlines the emotional cascade that keeps us stuck—and the deliberate steps that lead to freedom. It's a journey from unconscious suffering to the fulfillment of unconscious thriving, and it starts with understanding where the invaders have taken hold.

I know how difficult it can be at first to consider that fear, especially in the face of something as overwhelming as an alien invasion, a job loss, or a divorce, might not be as external as it seems. The very idea that fear is rooted in a mental landscape—shaped by judgments and beliefs rather than just the circumstances themselves—can feel counterintuitive, even head-scratching. Everyone feels this resistance at first. It's natural to believe that fear comes directly from what's happening *to* us rather than what's happening *within* us.

But I invite you to stick with me. Over the years, I've helped countless people move through this discomfort to see how recognizing the mental roots of fear doesn't minimize its impact—it empowers us to navigate it. Together, we'll explore this concept and its profound implications for facing any kind of upheaval, whether personal or global. My goal is to help you see not only that this understanding is possible, but how it can be life-changing.

THE PATH FROM FEAR AND SUFFERING TO FAITH AND THRIVING

The Descent ("Suffering")

The descent into suffering begins with something few of us easily recognize: a choice—whether conscious or unconscious—to align with judgment. This decision initiates a cascading series of reinforcing steps that deepen disconnection and fear.

One reason this is so difficult to recognize is that our choices to judge become automated over time through learning and conditioning. Take, for example, my own experience with snakes. Somewhere in my childhood, I learned a terrified, fearful response to them. Perhaps it was something I saw on TV, a reaction I picked up from someone else, or simply a natural association with danger. Over time, this response became ingrained to the point where encountering a snake would automatically trigger fear. I don't remember consciously choosing this fear—it felt like it "just happened."

But as I began to explore these concepts, I started to understand that there was, in fact, a choice buried within that automated response. Living on my homestead in Pennsylvania, where I regularly encounter snakes, I've used this understanding to reframe my reaction. I no longer react to snakes with fear but with curiosity and interest. How? By uncovering my choice in the matter—realizing that my judgment of snakes as "dangerous" or "scary" was not absolute truth but a learned belief I could examine and change.

This relationship between judgment and automated responses is echoed in concepts like Cognitive Behavioral Therapy (CBT), which teaches us to identify and challenge automatic thoughts and beliefs that drive emotional reactions. Much like CBT, this approach emphasizes the power of recognizing and revising the mental patterns that shape our experience.

Understanding that fear stems from a choice to judge—often made so quickly and unconsciously that it feels involuntary—can help us reclaim our ability to respond intentionally. This is the key to breaking free from automated cycles of suffering and moving toward a state of thriving.

WHAT TO DO WHEN THE ALIENS SHOW UP (AND EVEN IF THEY DON'T)

Choice

Judgment

Shame

Disconnection

Externalized Self-Worth

Dependency

Insecurity

Anxious Uncertainty

Fear & Suffering

The Descent: How Choosing Judgment Leads to Fear & Suffering

1. **Choice → Judgment:** Every descent begins with a moment of choice. This step reflects the decision—whether intentional or automatic—to believe a narrative of judgment. You choose to accept or internalize a voice, either your own or someone else's, that tells you you're not enough, not worthy, or not capable. This judgment becomes the lens through which you view yourself and the world.
2. **Judgment → Shame:** Judgment plants the belief that your worth is conditional, flawed, or insufficient. This belief takes root as shame—a persistent sense of inadequacy and unworthiness that begins to define your identity.
3. **Shame → Disconnection:** Shame creates distance—from yourself, your loved ones, and your sense of purpose. You withdraw emotionally and spiritually,

losing trust in your ability to connect meaningfully with yourself or others.

4. **Disconnection → Externalized Self-Worth:** As disconnection deepens, you stop seeing your inner self as a source of value and well-being. Instead, you externalize your self-worth, tying it to others' approval, achievements, or possessions. This externalized self-worth becomes a fragile foundation for your identity.

5. **Externalized Self-Worth → Dependency:** Once self-worth is externalized, you grow dependent on external sources to feel stable, validated, and secure. You rely on others' perceptions, behaviors, or circumstances to define your sense of self, weakening your internal foundation.

6. **Dependency → Insecurity:** Dependency breeds insecurity because the external sources you depend on are beyond your control. You constantly fear they might disappear or fail to meet your needs, leaving you vulnerable and unsupported.

7. **Insecurity → Anxious Uncertainty:** Insecurity fuels anxious uncertainty—a relentless focus on the unknown and the uncontrollable. This state keeps you obsessing over potential losses, worst-case scenarios, and imagined threats, making it impossible to relax or trust in your ability to cope.

8. **Anxious Uncertainty → Fear:** Anxious uncertainty culminates in fear, the loudest and most immediate symptom of the descent. Fear paralyzes you, narrowing your focus to survival and keeping you from taking meaningful action.

9. **Fear → Stagnation:** Fear solidifies into stagnation, where growth feels impossible. You resign yourself to a life defined by avoidance, smallness, and suffering. This final step ensures the cycle of suffering continues, keeping you stuck and powerless.

THE TURNING POINT: CHOICE

AT THE HEART of the journey lies a choice rooted in a change of understanding. It's the pivot point where we decide whether to remain stuck in judgment and shame or begin the work of transformation.

The Ascent ("Thriving")

The ascent to thriving begins with choice and moves through a series of deliberate steps:

> Faith & Thriving
> Calm Confidence
> Security
> Self-Sourcing
> Internalized Self-Worth
> Connection
> Self-Acceptance
> Unconditional High Regard
> **Choice**

The Ascent: How Choosing Unconditional High Regard Leads to Faith & Thriving

1. **Choice → Unconditional High Regard:** Replacing judgment with empathy, warmth, and kindness—both for yourself and others.
2. **Unconditional High Regard → Self-Acceptance:** Letting go of shame by embracing your inherent worth.

3. **Self-Acceptance → Connection:** Rebuilding trust and intimacy with yourself and those around you.
4. **Connection → Internalized Self-Worth:** Anchoring your sense of value within yourself rather than seeking it externally. Internalized self-worth emerges as you recognize that your inherent value is not contingent on external validation or achievements. This step strengthens your identity, enabling you to trust your inner voice and resilience.
5. **Internalized Self-Worth → Self-Sourcing:** Developing internal strength and validation, drawing upon your internalized self-worth to sustain and energize you. This step empowers you to rely on your inner resources for stability and fulfillment rather than depending on others for approval.
6. **Self-Sourcing → Security:** Feeling stable and confident, even in the face of uncertainty.
7. **Security → Calm Confidence:** Trusting yourself, others, and the process of growth.
8. **Calm Confidence → Faith:** Acting boldly in alignment with your values, even when fear lingers.
9. **Faith → Thriving:** Reaching a state where connection, purpose, and fulfillment become second nature.

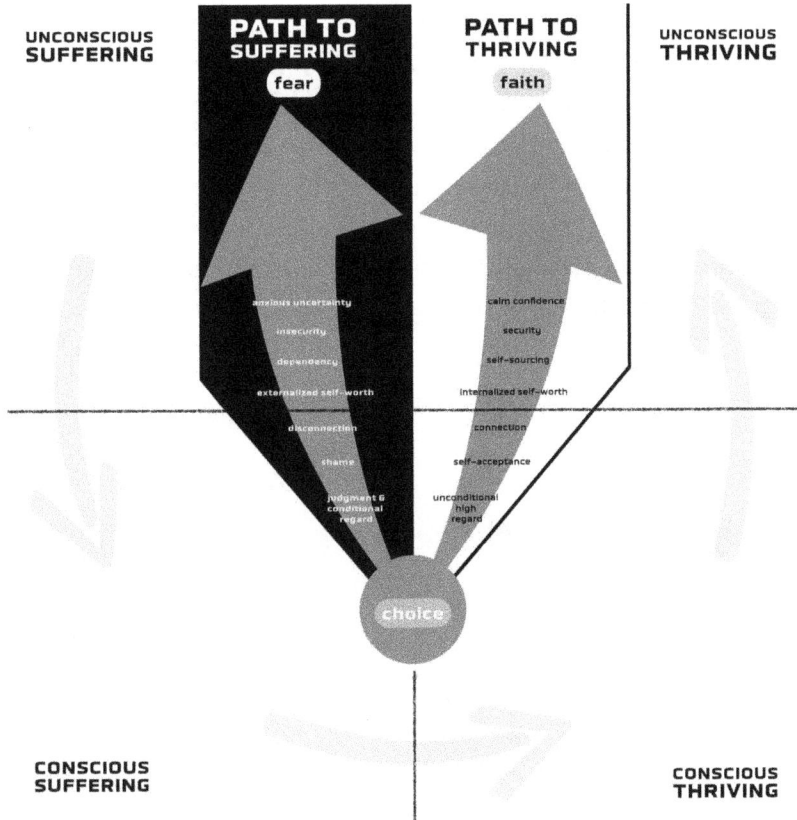

THE MAIN TAKEAWAY: THERE IS A PATH FROM SUFFERING TO THRIVING

The stages are universal, but growth is intentional. Every crisis, whether alien invaders or personal struggles, has the potential to follow this path. The good news is that if we're willing to do the work, thriving is possible—even amid an alien invasion.

COMING UP NEXT: THE INVASION UNMASKED

In the next section, we'll dive deeper into the tactics the invaders use to destabilize and manipulate. You'll learn how fear and shame are wielded as tools of control, and how they mask the truth of your strength, connection, and resilience. By exposing these strategies, you'll begin to see the first cracks in their illusion of power.

Fear, shame, and deception are the invaders' first wave, but they are not invincible. By recognizing their tactics and understanding the stages of transformation, you're already taking the first steps toward reclaiming your life. In the next section, we'll unmask the strategies of the invaders in greater detail, equipping you with the tools to resist, rebuild, and thrive.

REFLECTION QUESTIONS

1. Where do you see yourself in the four stages of experience right now?
2. What would it look like to choose growth in your current situation?
3. Which word pair (suffering/thriving, disconnection/connection) best describes your challenge?
4. Which stage of transformation resonates most with your current experience? What would moving to the next stage look like for you?

PART ONE
THE INVASION UNMASKED
EXPOSING THE TACTICS THAT KEEP YOU SMALL

THE INVASION WITHIN

An alien invasion isn't fought in a single day, and the fallout isn't contained in a single moment. The attacks leave scars—not just on the world they devastate but also on the people who survive them. The first step to reclaiming our lives—to rebuilding from the chaos—is to face the reality of the war we've been living through.

Part 1 begins with that first sobering truth: the invaders have been here all along. They didn't just arrive yesterday; they've been working quietly, behind the scenes, wearing down our defenses. The fear, anxiety, shame, dependency, and disconnection we've felt weren't random. They were weapons deployed with precision, designed to keep us small, powerless, and lost. Their strategies were subtle but deliberate—planting seeds of doubt, erecting walls of shame, and feeding cycles of fear that disconnect us from our truest selves.

But this is not a book about defeat. **This is a book about revolution.**

Revolutions don't begin with swords drawn or fists raised; they begin with clarity. To win this war, we must first understand how it was waged against us. We'll need to see the invaders' tactics for what they are and recognize the ways they've shaped our lives. More importantly, we'll need a battle plan—a clear map to guide us out of the chaos. That's where the four stages of experience come in: from unconscious suffering, where the invaders thrive in the shadows, to conscious awareness, where their tactics are laid bare. From intentional action, where we rebuild layer by layer, to thriving—a state of peace, connection, and abundance that feels natural.

This process isn't automatic. The first stages—suffering—are easy; life drags us through them whether we like it or not. But moving beyond suffering into thriving takes courage, humility, and choice. This is where the real battle begins. Together, we'll dismantle the alien strategies layer by layer, tracing the path from suffering to thriving. Whether we think of it as moving from unhappiness to joy, disconnection to connection, or incompetence to confidence, the path forward is the same. And it's waiting for us.

The journey we're about to take won't sugarcoat the damage, nor will it promise quick fixes or superficial remedies. Instead, it will give us the tools to reclaim our power, layer by layer. We'll learn to recognize the invaders' lies for what they are, break free of the traps they've set, and rebuild what was taken.

In Part I, we'll shine a spotlight on the invaders themselves—their tactics, their weapons, and the strategies they use to keep us stuck. From fear and judgment to shame and dependency, we'll peel back the layers of their deception to reveal the truths they've worked so hard to obscure. We'll also introduce the framework—the four stages—that will serve as our map for navigating this war. These aren't just steps; they're our lifeline for facing whatever "alien invasion" life throws our way.

WHAT TO DO WHEN THE ALIENS SHOW UP (AND EVEN IF THEY DON'T)

Are you ready to face the invasion? To take back what's been stolen and reclaim the part of yourself that's been lost? If so, the journey begins now. The battle plan is ours for the taking.

CHAPTER FIVE
THE FIRST WAVE OF ATTACK
FEAR & ANXIETY UNLEASHED

Fear is the mind-killer. Fear is the little-death that brings total obliteration." – Frank Herbert, *Dune*

THE INVADERS' FIRST STRIKE: FEAR

FEAR IS THE INVADERS' OPENING GAMBIT. THEY USE IT TO KEEP US powerless. Whether it's alien ships blotting out the sky or that gnawing worry that keeps us awake at night, fear is their weapon of choice to destabilize, overwhelm, and confuse us. It's the first wave of attack, creating chaos and leaving us too frozen to respond. And let's be honest—it works.

Fear doesn't need to be big to be effective. It can start small, like a flicker of unease that something isn't quite right. It whispers worst-case scenarios, planting seeds of anxiety that grow until they choke out our peace. Fear thrives on uncertainty, and when we're unsure of what's coming next, it's easy to fall into its trap. That's why fear is the first tool of the invaders. It's disorienting, paralyzing, and incredibly effective at keeping us small.

SVEN MASTERSON

THE ROLE OF ANXIOUS UNCERTAINTY

At its core, fear feeds on anxious uncertainty—the desperate, futile desire to make the uncertain certain. It's the need to know what the future holds, to predict the outcome of events, or to control how others will behave. But no one has that capacity. Life is inherently uncertain, and no amount of overthinking, worrying, or planning can change that. Yet, anxious uncertainty thrives because it isn't just about the future—it's about us.

Anxious uncertainty is the fruit of a low view of self. When we lack confidence in our worth, resilience, and trustability, the future feels threatening. It's not just a fear of what might happen—it's a fear that the version of us who encounters it will not be able to cope. This is where shame and low self-worth reveal themselves as the true roots of anxious uncertainty.

The anxiety we feel about the future is often a disguised flavor of uncertainty about who we are in the present. We're not just afraid of what might happen—we're scared we won't be enough to handle it. This masked uncertainty about ourselves masquerades as fear about what lies ahead. When we lack confidence in our ability to adapt, grow, and overcome, we obsess over controlling what's beyond our reach because we don't trust ourselves to manage what's within it.

The lens of today shapes how we view everything. When we look to the past, we see it filtered through the lens of who we believe ourselves to be today. The same is true of the future. If we see ourselves as lacking, unworthy, or incapable, we project those beliefs onto the future and anticipate failure, rejection, or catastrophe. Anxious uncertainty is a mirror reflecting how we see ourselves today more than it is a reflection of actual future risks.

FEAR AS A WEAPON

Think of the invasion metaphor. The first wave of an alien attack is about overwhelming the population—not just with destruction but with the psychological shock of realizing the world we knew is gone. Similarly, when fear strikes in our lives, it's not just about the immediate situation—it's about what that fear represents.

Fear tells us three lies:

1. You're not safe.
2. You're not enough.
3. You're alone.

It creates a narrative of insufficiency and isolation, leaving us vulnerable to deeper forms of suffering. Fear often carries anxiety in its wake, a kind of hyper-alertness that keeps us scanning for threats that might not even be there. It tricks us into thinking it's helping—keeping us on our toes, preparing us for the worst—but all it really does is exhaust and immobilize us.

When fear goes unchecked, it leads to emotional paralysis. We start avoiding risks, stepping back from opportunities, and shrinking into a shell where we feel safe but deeply unsatisfied. That's exactly what the invaders want: to keep us small, quiet, and contained.

THE CASCADE OF ENEMY TACTICS THAT LEAD TO FEAR

Fear doesn't operate in isolation—it's the final symptom of a deeper chain reaction. At its core, fear is a product of unresolved emotions and disconnections that build on each other, layer by layer. By the time fear reaches the surface, it feels overwhelming, but its roots lie much deeper.

This chain reaction unfolds as follows:

1. **Choice → Judgment:** Every descent begins with a moment of choice. This step reflects the decision—whether intentional or automatic—to believe a narrative of judgment. We choose to accept or internalize a voice, either our own or someone else's, that tells us we're not

enough, not worthy, or not capable. This judgment becomes the lens through which we view ourselves and the world.

2. **Judgment → Shame:** Judgment plants the belief that our worth is conditional, flawed, or insufficient. This belief takes root as shame—a persistent sense of inadequacy and unworthiness that begins to define our identity.

3. **Shame → Disconnection:** Shame creates distance—from ourselves, our loved ones, and our sense of purpose. When we believe we're fundamentally unworthy, we start withdrawing emotionally and spiritually. We stop trusting ourselves as a source of wisdom or well-being. Instead, we isolate ourselves from the very support and connection we need to thrive.

4. **Disconnection → Externalized Self-Worth:** As disconnection deepens, we stop seeing our inner selves as a source of value and well-being. Instead, we externalize our self-worth, tying it to others' approval, achievements, or possessions. This externalized self-worth becomes a fragile foundation for our identity.

5. **Externalized Self-Worth → Dependency:** Once self-worth is externalized, we grow dependent on external sources to feel stable, validated, and secure. We rely on others' perceptions, behaviors, or circumstances to define our sense of self, weakening our internal foundation.

6. **Dependency → Insecurity:** Dependency breeds insecurity because the external sources we depend on are beyond our control. We constantly fear they might disappear or fail to meet our needs, leaving us vulnerable and unsupported.

7. **Insecurity → Anxious Uncertainty:** Insecurity fuels anxious uncertainty—a heightened state of vigilance and worry rooted in the fear of the unknown. We begin

obsessing over potential losses, imagining worst-case scenarios, and trying to predict or control what cannot be guaranteed.
8. **Anxious Uncertainty → Fear:** Finally, fear emerges as the culmination of this chain reaction. It's the loudest and most immediate symptom, but it's just the surface layer of a much deeper web of judgment, shame, disconnection, and externalized self-worth.

WHY THIS MATTERS

Each step in this chain reaction feeds the next, creating a cycle that deepens fear's hold over time. When self-worth is externalized, we lose trust in our inner strength and begin relying on unstable sources for our sense of value. This leaves us vulnerable to insecurity, enmeshment, and the exhausting vigilance of anxious uncertainty. Recognizing and addressing these steps is the first move in dismantling fear and reclaiming our sense of agency.

HOW TO BEGIN DISMANTLING FEAR

1. **Name It:** Fear thrives on vagueness. When you name it —give it words, and pin it down—it starts to lose its power. Ask yourself, "What exactly am I afraid of?" Be specific.
2. **Challenge It:** Fear loves worst-case scenarios, but they're rarely true. Ask yourself:
    - Is this fear based on a real threat or an imagined catastrophe?
    - What evidence do I have that this will actually happen?
    - How often has fear been exaggerated or been wrong before?

3. **Take a Small Step:** Fear says, "You can't handle this." Action proves otherwise. You don't have to conquer the whole mountain at once—just take one step forward. Courage is built one small action at a time.

When we consistently do this, fear's grip weakens. We start to see it as a tactic, not the truth.

MAIN TAKEAWAY: FEAR IS JUST THE BEGINNING

Fear isn't the enemy—it's just a tool the invaders use to keep us small. Recognizing it as a weapon and learning to challenge it is the first step toward regaining control. Fear doesn't have to define us, but it does invite us to grow.

COMING UP NEXT: THE SECOND WAVE OF ATTACK

After exposing fear and anxiety as the invaders' initial assault, we'll explore the deeper forces they exploit—our natural longing for connection and the insecurities that twist it into endless seeking. You'll learn how this trap keeps us chasing external solutions and how recognizing our inherent worth can help us break free.

COMMON RESPONSES

"Yeah, but my fear feels so real—it's not just in my head."

It makes sense that your fear feels real; fear is incredibly convincing, especially when it taps into something deep within us. I hear you. But here's the thing: fear's strength isn't about reality—it's about perception. By naming and examining your fear, you're not dismissing it; you're taking the first step in seeing it for what it truly is. You've faced tough things before, and this fear isn't bigger than the strength already in you.

"Yeah, but I've tried to overcome fear before, and it always comes back."

That's a real and valid frustration. Fear does tend to resurface, like waves on the shore. But just like the shore isn't defeated by the waves, you can weather it. Each time you face fear, even in small ways, you build resilience. Progress isn't about erasing fear forever—it's about learning to respond differently each time it appears. You've already proven you can grow stronger.

"Yeah, but what if I fail? What if my fear is right?"

It's brave of you to even voice that worry. Here's something to consider: failure is just information—it's not a verdict on your worth. And fear being "right" doesn't mean you're doomed; it means you've identified something to navigate. Failure can teach, refine, and guide you toward success. The you who faces failure is also the you who learns and rises again.

"Yeah, but uncertainty is terrifying—I can't function without control."

I get that. Uncertainty can feel like standing in quicksand. But you don't have to control everything to move forward. Think about the moments in your life where you embraced uncertainty, even for a moment—like trying something new or trusting someone. Those moments likely led to growth. You don't need to eliminate uncertainty; you just need to remind yourself that you've managed it before.

"Yeah, but what if I'm not strong enough to handle the future?"

It's natural to doubt our strength when we're looking at an uncertain horizon. But strength isn't about having all the answers right now—it's about showing up, one step at a time. The fact that you're reflecting, asking questions, and seeking growth proves there's more strength in you than you might see today. You've made it this far; you're capable of handling what comes next.

REFLECTION QUESTIONS

1. What fears have been keeping you small or stuck in your life?
2. What narrative does your fear keep telling you? How can you challenge it?
3. What small, courageous step can you take today to begin dismantling fear's hold on you?

CHAPTER SIX
THE SECOND WAVE OF ATTACK
LONGING & INSECURITY IN THE CROSSFIRE

Your task is not to seek for love, but merely to seek and find all the barriers within yourself that you have built against it. – Rumi

LONGING: THE INVADERS' FAVORITE VECTOR OF ATTACK

ONCE THE INVADERS ESTABLISH THEIR FOOTHOLD WITH FEAR AND anxiety, their next move is equally insidious. They exploit the deep, unspoken hunger within us—the longing for connection, belonging, and fulfillment. They know that longing, when paired with insecurity and disconnection, becomes the perfect trap—a bait that keeps us chasing external solutions while leading us further from ourselves.

Longing is not the enemy. It's a natural part of being human. But when longing arises from a place of disconnection, it becomes overloaded with neediness, leading us into patterns of insecurity, shape-shifting, and ultimately the creation of an even more false self. This chapter explores the nature of longing, the ways it can lead us astray, and how to transform it into a path back to connection and authenticity.

THE NATURE OF LONGING

Longing is the echo of our deepest desires:

- To be seen and valued.
- To be loved without condition.
- To feel significant, capable, and whole.

These desires are not wrong. In fact, they reflect the best parts of our humanity. But when longing is experienced from a place of disconnection—from ourselves, our inherent worth, and a sense of unshakable value—it becomes overcharged and distorted.

Instead of desiring others to share life with, we seek them as a remedy for our disconnection from ourselves. This creates an unhealthy dynamic where the connection we seek becomes not a mutual experience but a means to address the emptiness we feel inside. We begin to depend on others to bridge the gap left by our disconnection, setting the stage for insecurity, fear, and a false self.

DISCONNECTION AMPLIFIES LONGING

When we are disconnected from ourselves and a source of immutable, unchangeable value and worth, our natural longings become overwhelmed with neediness. In this state, longing stops being a healthy desire for connection and instead becomes a frantic search for validation, safety, or approval. This shift leads to:

1. Connection as a Remedy for Disconnection

When disconnected from ourselves, we attempt to use connection with others to remedy our inner void. The danger, however, is that as long as we remain disconnected from ourselves, we cannot fully receive or utilize the connection we find with others. Instead of feeling secure in the relationship, we interpret their acceptance or rejection of us as a reflection of our value.

2. Insecurity and Shape-Shifting

This dynamic creates tremendous insecurity. We begin to shape-shift, molding ourselves into what we think others want, in an attempt to gain their approval and feel safe. This pattern fosters the creation of an even more false self—a version of ourselves designed to please or appease others rather than reflect our authentic identity.

3. Pain in Connection

Paradoxically, connection becomes painful. Rather than soothing our longing, it exacerbates our disconnection. Because we lack internal grounding, we place the weight of our self-worth on how others perceive us. Their acceptance temporarily soothes us, but their rejection (real or perceived) can feel devastating. This cycle deepens the disconnection, reinforcing the neediness and fragility of our longing.

THE PARADOX OF CONNECTION

While disconnection from ourselves makes longing dangerous, the paradox is that we also seem to remedy our self-rejection through supportive relationships with others. The key difference lies in the type of connection we seek and the environment it creates. Relationships and communities that offer unconditional high regard—a safe, judgment-free zone—can provide the support we need to begin the work of overcoming judgment and shame and reconnecting with ourselves.

1. Unconditional High Regard

In relationships where unconditional high regard is present, we are given the space to rediscover our worth without fear of rejection or judgment. This might occur in the safety of a one-on-one relationship like marriage, friendship, or mentorship, or within a larger community oriented around support and growth.

2. Healing Through Relationship

These connections create an environment where we feel seen and valued as we are, rather than for what we do or how we perform. This allows us to gradually shift our reliance away from external validation and toward internal grounding. While the work of reconnection is ultimately personal, the support of others can provide the stability and perspective needed to begin.

SEEKING THE MIRAGE

When longing is coupled with insecurity and disconnection, we start seeking external solutions that appear to offer fulfillment but ultimately leave us emptier than before:

- **Relationships:** Hoping a romantic partner will fix our loneliness or validate our worth.
- **Success:** Believing a promotion, award, or accolade will finally make us feel enough.
- **Possessions:** Chasing material markers of status or accomplishment to prove we've arrived.
- **Physical appearance:** Striving to meet an ideal as a means of gaining approval or significance.

These pursuits are like drinking salt water when you're thirsty—they momentarily relieve our thirst but ultimately leave us more parched. When driven by disconnection, they distract us from the deeper work of self-reconnection.

BREAKING FREE: THE PATH TO HEALTHY LONGING

To break free from the distortions of longing, we must address its root causes: disconnection, insecurity, and the false self. Here's how to begin:

1. Recognize the Overcharged Longing

Notice when your longing feels heavy with neediness or insecurity. Ask yourself: "Am I seeking connection as an experience or as a remedy for my disconnection?"

2. Reconnect to Yourself

Spend time identifying your needs, desires, and boundaries. Begin to reconnect with your authentic self through journaling, mindfulness, therapy, or time in nature.

3. Seek Unconditional Support

Surround yourself with relationships and communities that offer unconditional high regard. Use these safe spaces to explore and challenge the judgments and shame that have fueled your disconnection.

4. Challenge the False Self

Notice when you're shape-shifting or abandoning parts of yourself to gain approval. As a step toward reclaiming your true identity, begin practicing authenticity, even in small ways.

5. Practice Internal Validation

Remind yourself that your worth is not conditional. Affirm your value daily: "I am enough, just as I am."

. . .

For years, I sought connection to fix the disconnection I felt within myself. I believed relationships, success, or validation could fill the void. But the harder I chased, the further I felt from peace. It wasn't until I began reconnecting with my inherent worth and sought relationships built on unconditional high regard that I found the space to heal. As I worked to release the false self I had created, I discovered a connection with myself that transformed how I experienced connection with others.

THE MAIN TAKEAWAY: CONNECTION BEGINS WITHIN

LONGING IS A BEAUTIFUL, human experience, but when driven by disconnection, it becomes distorted and destructive. Reclaiming connection begins with ourselves—rebuilding the bridge that disconnection tore down and surrounding ourselves with relationships that nurture, rather than deplete, our authenticity and worth.

COMING UP NEXT: DEPENDENCY EXPOSED - HOW THE INVADERS USE CONTROL TO KEEP YOU STUCK

In the next chapter, we'll examine how invaders leverage your dependence on external validation and systems to create a stronghold. We'll discover why this dependency feels inescapable and explore the first steps toward reclaiming your power by building an internal locus of control.

WHAT TO DO WHEN THE ALIENS SHOW UP (AND EVEN IF THEY DON'T)

COMMON RESPONSES

"Yeah, but I can't just stop wanting connection or love."

You're right—longing for connection isn't something to stop. It's natural and good. But here's the key: when you rely solely on others to meet that longing, it becomes fragile. Others can support and enhance your sense of worth, but they can't replace your own acceptance of yourself. Start offering yourself what you crave from others—patience, compassion, and acceptance—and you'll find your connections outside become more enriching and less desperate.

"Yeah, but people can't always offer unconditional support."

That's true; others can't always show up perfectly. But here's the important part: when you learn to offer yourself unconditional support, external relationships become less about filling a void and more about sharing fullness. You're not asking others to carry what only you can carry for yourself. This shift doesn't mean others won't let you down, but it does mean their imperfections won't shatter you.

"Yeah, but what if I don't know who my authentic self is?"

That uncertainty is common, especially when we've spent years living for others' approval. Start by practicing unconditional acceptance of wherever you are right now, even if you feel lost. Tell yourself: "It's okay not to have all the answers yet." This creates a space where self-discovery can unfold naturally. The journey to your authentic self becomes possible only when you stop judging yourself for not being there already.

"Yeah, but I've been shape-shifting for so long—how can I even stop?"

That's a powerful realization, and stopping the habit of shape-shifting is a process. The first step is to offer yourself the unconditional support you've been trying to earn from others. Say to yourself: "I see you. I value you as you are." This will feel unfamiliar at first, but over time, it gives you the foundation to step out of false roles and into your true self. The stability you create within becomes your anchor.

"Yeah, but what if reconnecting with myself doesn't fill the void?"

That's a valid concern. Here's the truth: no external solution will fill the void if you're not offering yourself unconditional acceptance. When you reconnect with yourself, you're not trying to erase the void but to heal your relationship with it. You're saying: "Even if I feel incomplete at times, I'm still whole, still worthy, still enough." This shift transforms longing from desperation into a deep and gentle desire for connection that enriches rather than depletes you.

REFLECTION QUESTIONS

1. In what ways has disconnection shaped your experience of longing?
2. How does insecurity or the false self influence the connections you seek?
3. Who in your life offers unconditional high regard? How might you lean into that support?
4. What is one step you can take this week to reconnect with your authentic self?

CHAPTER SEVEN
THE EXPLOIT OF CRITICAL INFRASTRUCTURE:
DEPENDENCY AND CONTROL

Freedom is what you do with what's been done to you. – Jean-Paul Sartre

DEPENDENCY: THE INVADERS' STRONGEST HOLD

IN THE AFTERMATH OF FEAR, ANXIETY, AND THE RELENTLESS SEEKING born from our insecurity, the invaders strike at our most vulnerable point: our dependency on external sources of power. This is the phase where they gain their strongest foothold—not by force, but by persuasion. They convince us that we are powerless without something—or someone—outside of ourselves.

Like an invading force cutting off a city's access to resources, the invaders sever us from our internal wellspring of agency and convince us that we must depend on external systems, validation, or people for our survival. In this chapter, we explore how dependency develops, why it keeps us stuck, and how reconnecting with our internal locus of control is key to liberation.

SVEN MASTERSON

WHAT IS DEPENDENCY?

Dependency is the belief that our well-being, identity, or happiness is tied to something outside of ourselves:

- A partner's love and approval.
- A job title or financial status.
- The validation of friends, family, or society.
- The stability of external systems like governments, institutions, or even religious organizations

Dependency isn't inherently bad. In fact, we are all born utterly dependent. As infants, we rely entirely on others for survival, love, and care. But life is a process of maturing—a journey where we gradually exchange dependency for autonomy and agency. Along the way, we learn to stand, walk, tie our shoes, brush our teeth, fry an egg, make toast, and much more. Each step is a marker of growth, a step toward greater self-reliance.

This doesn't mean we don't need support, but support is different from dependency. Support is having people assist me while I write this book, while dependency is having them write it for me. Healthy support involves connection, collaboration, and mutuality—leaning on others without surrendering our autonomy or sense of self. Dependency becomes a trap when it stagnates, keeping us tethered to external sources for identity or security rather than fostering growth and self-agency.

Of course, some of us may find ourselves in exceptional circumstances where dependency is unavoidable—due to illness, injury, or other limitations—but those situations are not what we're talking about here. The kind of dependency we're addressing in this chapter is the unnecessary kind, the kind rooted in self-limiting beliefs that keep us stuck, small, and reliant on external validation long after we should have outgrown it.

The invaders masterfully exploit this unnecessary dependency. They whisper, "You're nothing without them," planting seeds of doubt that grow into tangled webs of insecurity. Like a city under siege, we come to believe we can't survive without the systems, relationships, or approvals that have taken us hostage.

THE EXTERNAL LOCUS OF CONTROL

Psychologists describe an external locus of control as the belief that our lives are shaped primarily by external factors—luck, circumstances, or other people—rather than our own actions. This mindset fosters dependency and leaves us feeling powerless.

For years, we may have lived with an external locus of control. Perhaps we believed that if we could just do enough, be enough, or earn enough approval, we would finally feel whole. Our sense of worth might have been tied to roles we played, the admiration of others, or the stability of external systems. But no matter how much we achieved, it never felt like enough because we were looking for power in all the wrong places.

THE PRICE OF DEPENDENCY

Dependency takes a heavy toll:

1. **Loss of autonomy:** We become beholden to the very things we believe sustain us. This might look like staying in toxic relationships, enduring unfulfilling jobs, or clinging to outdated beliefs because we fear what will happen if we let go.
2. **Heightened anxiety:** When our sense of security is external, we're constantly on edge, fearing its loss.
3. **Manipulation and control:** Dependency makes us easy targets for manipulation—whether by individuals, societal systems, or even our own internal narratives.
4. **Erosion of identity:** When our worth is tied to external sources, we lose touch with our core identity.

The invaders know this. They exploit our dependency to keep us tethered, making us believe we can't survive without their systems or approval. And as long as we buy into this lie, we remain stuck, unable to reclaim our power.

HOW DEPENDENCY KEEPS US STUCK

Dependency thrives on fear and insecurity. The invaders perpetuate it with lies like:

- "You'll never make it on your own."
- "You need this job, relationship, or status to survive."
- "If you lose their approval, you'll be nothing."

In our own lives, we've likely seen how deeply dependency can root itself. Perhaps we've relied on external validation—whether from a spouse, friends, or colleagues—to feel valuable. We may have believed that if we could just meet everyone's expectations, we would finally feel at peace. Piece by piece, we've given away our power, and the invaders are more than happy to take it.

THE FIRST STEPS TO RECLAIMING POWER

Breaking free from dependency doesn't mean rejecting all external support. It means shifting from an external to an internal locus of control—recognizing that while we can't always control circumstances, we can control our responses, decisions, and beliefs. Here's how to start:

1. **Recognize the lies:** Begin by identifying the narratives that keep us dependent. Ask ourselves: "What am I afraid of losing, and why?"
2. **Reconnect with our agency:** Realize that we always have choices, even in difficult circumstances. Our power lies in our ability to decide and act.

3. **Build internal validation:** Practice affirming our worth independently of external achievements or approval. Journaling, mindfulness, and therapy can help.
4. **Set healthy boundaries:** Begin to untangle our identity from the roles, relationships, or systems we've relied on for validation.

These steps aren't about shutting others out—they're about reclaiming what's been ours all along: our agency, worth, and power.

> One of the most pivotal moments in my journey was realizing how much I depended on external approval to feel worthy. I was bending over backward to meet others' expectations, neglecting my own needs and values.
>
> The breakthrough came when I started asking, "What do I want? What do I need?" Those questions were harder to answer than I expected because I had spent so long ignoring them. For the first time, I allowed myself to envision a life where I wasn't tethered to others' perceptions. It was terrifying but liberating.
>
> Gradually, I began making decisions based on my values and desires rather than the fear of disappointing others. Each step was a reclamation of my power, and with each step, I felt the invaders' hold on me weaken.

THE MAIN TAKEAWAY: POWER COMES FROM WITHIN

DEPENDENCY TRAPS us by making us believe that our worth, happiness, and security lie outside of ourselves. Reclaiming our power starts with recognizing this lie and reconnecting to the truth: our agency, worth, and resilience reside within.

COMING UP NEXT: THE POWER OF YOUR INNER NARRATIVE - REWRITING THE STORIES THE INVADERS PLANTED

Our dependency is reinforced by the stories we tell ourselves, often seeded by judgment and fear. In the next chapter, we'll reveal how to identify these harmful narratives, challenge their validity, and replace them with truths that reflect our inherent value and potential.

COMMON RESPONSES

"Yeah, but I can't let go of my dependency without losing what makes me feel safe."

That fear is valid. Dependency feels like safety because it's familiar, but true safety doesn't come from clinging to something outside of ourselves. It comes from building trust in your ability to navigate life's uncertainties. Start small—ask yourself, "What's one thing I can try standing on my own for today?" With each step, you'll find that safety wasn't something external; it's something you've been carrying all along.

"Yeah, but I've been dependent for so long, I don't know where to start."

It's okay to feel overwhelmed—dependency is a tough habit to break. Start with one small step: reflect on a choice you can make for yourself, no matter how minor. Every moment you honor your own desires or boundaries is a step toward reclaiming your agency. You don't have to do it all at once; just one decision can begin to shift the tide.

"Yeah, but what if I let go of dependency and end up completely alone?"

That's a deep and real fear. But letting go of dependency doesn't mean isolation—it means building relationships based on mutual respect and authenticity. As you connect more deeply with yourself, you'll find that the connections you build with others become richer and more meaningful. You're not replacing others' presence; you're redefining its purpose in your life.

"Yeah, but I've tried to stand on my own before, and I failed."

That experience is tough, and it's understandable to feel hesitant. But every effort teaches us something, even if it doesn't turn out as we hoped. What if standing on your own doesn't mean doing it perfectly but simply trying again? Your worth isn't tied to whether you succeed immediately —it's in the courage to keep showing up for yourself. Each attempt is a victory.

"Yeah, but aren't we supposed to need each other?"

Absolutely. Healthy interdependence is part of being human. But there's a big difference between needing support and relying on others for your <u>identity</u> or <u>worth</u>. True connection happens when we show up as whole, autonomous individuals—not when we hand others the keys to our sense of self. Needing others doesn't diminish you; it enriches you, but only when your foundation is solid within yourself.

REFLECTION QUESTIONS

1. What external sources do you currently rely on for your sense of worth or security?
2. How does dependency show up in your relationships, career, or self-perception?
3. What's one small decision you can make this week that affirms your agency?
4. How would your life change if you shifted from an external to an internal locus of control?

CHAPTER EIGHT
THE WAR FOR YOUR WORTH
HOW FEAR AND DISCONNECTION HIJACK YOUR SELF-WORTH

You have been criticizing yourself for years, and it hasn't worked. Try approving of yourself and see what happens. – Louise Hay

---

DEPENDENCY AND DISCONNECTION

DEPENDENCY IS A FOOTHOLD FOR THE INVADERS, BUT IT DOESN'T exist in isolation. Beneath dependency lies a deeper, more insidious truth: our reliance on external sources stems from a disconnection from ourselves. When we lose touch with our inherent worth and stop seeing ourselves as the source of our stability, value, and identity, we begin to externalize these. This shift leads directly to dependency.

The invaders masterfully exploit this dynamic. They sever our internal connection and then convince us that we must look outward for validation, approval, and security. This is the trap of externalized self-worth: believing that who we are is determined by how others see us, what we achieve, or what we have.

WHAT IS EXTERNALIZED SELF-WORTH?

Externalized self-worth is the belief that your value and identity are determined by external factors. When disconnection leaves a void in our sense of self, we turn outward to fill it, tying our worth to:

- **How others perceive us:** Their approval becomes a proxy for our value.
- **What we achieve:** Success or productivity determines whether we feel worthy.
- **What we possess:** The material markers of worth—money, status, appearance—become our identity.

This creates a fragile sense of self. If these external sources shift, diminish, or disappear, our entire sense of worth collapses.

THE ROOT CAUSE: DISOWNING AND DISCONNECTION

Externalized self-worth doesn't happen by accident. It grows out of disconnection—the belief, seeded by judgment and shame, that we are inherently unworthy or insufficient. This disconnection severs us from:

- **Our internal value:** We stop trusting that our worth is inherent, not conditional.
- **Our inner compass:** We lose sight of our needs, desires, and boundaries.
- **Our authentic self:** We become performers, molding ourselves to fit others' expectations.

In this state, the invaders' whispers grow louder: *You'll never be enough without their approval* or *If you don't achieve, you're nothing.* These lies keep us tied to external validation, reinforcing dependency.

THE COSTS OF EXTERNALIZED SELF-WORTH

Living with externalized self-worth comes at a steep price. The more we rely on others to define our value, the more we lose touch with ourselves. Over time, this dynamic leads to:

1. **Emotional fragility:** External sources of worth are unpredictable, leaving us anxious and unstable.
2. **Perfectionism:** We constantly strive to meet impossible standards to feel enough.
3. **Enmeshment:** The lines between our identity and others' perceptions blur, making it difficult to distinguish what's ours from what belongs to them.
4. **Chronic dissatisfaction:** External validation never fills the void created by disconnection, leaving us perpetually seeking more.

THE INVADERS' EXPLOITATION OF EXTERNALIZED SELF-WORTH

The invaders know that as long as our worth depends on external factors, we are easy to manipulate. They plant lies like:

- *"If they don't love you, you're unlovable."*
- *"Your value depends on what you achieve."*
- *"Without their approval, you're nothing."*
- *"You must do more to earn their love."*

These narratives keep us tethered to their systems of control, ensuring we never look inward for the validation and strength already within us.

For years, I believed my value was tied to how others saw me. I worked tirelessly to earn their approval, molding myself into the version of me I thought they wanted. But no matter how hard I tried, it never felt like enough.

The breakthrough came when I realized that I had no idea what I wanted. My identity was so wrapped up in external validation that I couldn't see myself clearly. The journey back to myself wasn't easy, but it started with small steps: asking what I needed, setting boundaries, and practicing kindness toward myself. Gradually, I began to see that my worth didn't depend on others—it was mine all along.

THE MAIN TAKEAWAY: WORTH COMES FROM WITHIN

Externalized self-worth is the hidden cause of dependency. It keeps us tethered to others for validation, making us vulnerable to manipulation and control. Reclaiming our worth begins with reconnecting to ourselves, breaking the agreements that reinforce limiting beliefs, and challenging the narratives that insist our value lies outside of us.

COMING UP NEXT: THE LIES THAT LINGER

The stories we tell ourselves reinforce dependency and externalized self-worth. These false narratives, planted by the invaders, shape how we see ourselves and the world. In the next chapter, we'll learn how to identify and rewrite these harmful stories, replacing them with truths that reflect our inherent value and potential.

COMMON RESPONSES

"Yeah, but I don't even know how to start reconnecting with myself."

That's a brave admission, and it's okay to feel unsure about where to begin. Reconnection isn't about finding all the answers at once; it's about taking small, intentional steps. Start by asking yourself, "What do I enjoy? What feels good to me?" Spend time with those questions, even if the answers come slowly. Each step toward self-awareness is a step toward self-worth.

"Yeah, but if I stop relying on external validation, won't I lose my motivation?"

It's natural to feel that way when we've tied our drive to external sources for so long. But imagine what it would be like to be motivated by genuine passion and purpose, rather than the fear of not being enough. Reconnecting with your worth doesn't mean losing motivation—it means shifting to a healthier, more sustainable kind that aligns with your authentic self.

"Yeah, but I feel like I'll disappoint people if I stop meeting their expectations."

That's a tough spot to be in, and it shows how deeply you care. But meeting others' expectations at the cost of your own well-being isn't true connection—it's performance. You can care about others without abandoning yourself. It's okay to take small steps toward honoring your needs while communicating with kindness and clarity. The people who truly value you will understand.

"Yeah, but my worth has always been tied to what I achieve— how can I just let that go?"

Letting go doesn't mean abandoning your ambitions or achievements; it means no longer letting them define you. You are valuable not because of what you do, but because of who you are. Start by celebrating yourself for reasons that have nothing to do with accomplishment—your kindness, resilience, or courage. Over time, you'll see that your worth is already complete.

"Yeah, but what if I don't feel worthy, no matter what I do?"

That's a hard place to be, and it's okay to feel that way right now. Worth isn't something you have to earn—it's something you uncover. It might take time to see, but your worth has been there all along, waiting for you to notice. Start by practicing small acts of self-compassion—treating yourself as you would a dear friend. You don't have to feel worthy to begin the journey; just begin.

REFLECTION QUESTIONS

1. Where do you currently tie your sense of worth to external factors?
2. How does externalized self-worth affect your relationships, career, or self-perception?
3. What narratives or agreements about your worth might you need to break?
4. What is one small step you can take this week to practice internal validation?

CHAPTER NINE
STORIES WE TELL OURSELVES
THE PROPAGANDA OF THE INVADERS

Be careful how you are talking to yourself, because you are listening. – Lisa M. Hayes

THE LIES THAT LINGER

Some nights, the silence in our home felt heavier than any argument could. I'd sit on the couch, staring at the TV but barely registering what was on the screen. Zelda would be a few feet away, scrolling through her phone or lost in her own thoughts. We weren't yelling, but the space between us felt like a canyon I couldn't cross.

I told myself, *This is just how marriage is after a few years.* But deep down, I didn't believe that. The real story running through my mind was far darker: *She doesn't love you anymore. You're not enough—not attractive enough, not successful enough, not interesting enough.*

It wasn't just her silence that hurt. It was what I thought it meant: *I'm not worth engaging with.*

But here's the deal—Zelda wasn't actually saying those things.

SVEN MASTERSON

The invaders in my mind were. I had internalized their messages long before I even met her.

THE PROPAGANDA MACHINE

The invaders don't conquer us through brute force. They don't need to when they can feed you stories—subtle, persistent narratives undermining our confidence, worth, and identity.

These stories don't announce themselves as lies. They disguise themselves as observations or "truths" about who you are:

- *You're a failure if you don't meet everyone's expectations.*
- *You're unlovable because of your past mistakes.*
- *You'll only be happy if you achieve [insert impossible standard here].*

Like propaganda* during wartime, these narratives are designed to keep you off balance and under control. And the worst part? They come from within, making them harder to identify and resist.

WHERE DO THESE STORIES COME FROM?

If you dig into the origins of these stories, you'll often find they were planted early—by well-meaning parents, teachers, friends, or even yourself. A throwaway comment like, "Why can't you be more like your brother?" or "You're such a daydreamer" can snowball into an internal script that defines your reality.

For me, the stories started young:

- *You're too sensitive; toughen up.*
- *You'll never be as good as [insert comparison].*

---

* **Propaganda:** A systematic dissemination of biased or misleading information, typically used to promote a particular agenda or perspective.

- *Stop being a burden.*

Over time, those stories became my framework for interpreting the world and my place in it. They influenced how I saw myself, how I interacted with others, and what I believed was possible.

BREAKING FREE FROM THE STORIES

Recognizing the lies is the first step toward liberation. But breaking free requires more than awareness; it demands rewriting the narrative.

Here's what that process looked like for me:

1. **Identifying the Lies:** I started by listing the recurring stories in my head: *You're not enough, you're unlovable, and you'll never be successful.*
2. **Questioning Their Validity:** I asked myself, "Is this actually true? Where's the evidence?"
3. **Replacing Them with Truths:** This part felt awkward at first, like trying to speak a new language. But I began to tell myself:
   - *You are enough, just as you are.*
   - *You are capable of love and connection.*
   - *Your success or appearance doesn't determine your worth.*

The stories we tell ourselves aren't just words—they're the lenses through which we see the world. Changing the story changes the view.

For years, I had been living as a man defeated by his own propaganda. But the more I rewrote my narrative, the more I saw glimmers of hope, clarity, and self-acceptance. It didn't happen overnight, but with time, I started to believe a new story: I am enough! I am worthy of love! I am capable of building a life I don't need to escape from!

This changed <u>everything</u> for me, and it continues to do so.

THE MAIN TAKEAWAY: RECLAIMING THE NARRATIVE

The stories you tell yourself shape your reality. If you want to change your life, start by changing the story. Recognize the lies, challenge them, and replace them with empowering truths. This is how you weaken the invaders' hold and begin reclaiming your freedom. This is how you weaken the invaders' hold and begin reclaiming your freedom.

COMING UP NEXT: DISCONNECTION AS A SILENT KILLER - REBUILDING THE BRIDGES TO YOURSELF AND OTHERS

False narratives set the stage for isolation, leaving you disconnected from yourself and those around you. In the next chapter, uncover the devastating impact of disconnection and how vulnerability and honesty are key to rebuilding meaningful relationships and reclaiming your true self.

COMMON RESPONSES

> "Yeah, but these stories feel true—they've been with me for so long."

Of course, they feel true; they've been part of your mental landscape for years, maybe even decades. But just because something feels true doesn't mean it is. Imagine looking through a pair of glasses with smudged lenses—your view might feel accurate, but it's distorted. Start small: question just one story and see if you can clean the lens a bit. You might be surprised at how your perspective shifts.

"Yeah, but what if I can't tell the difference between the lies and the truth?"

That's completely understandable—when lies have been with us for so long, they blend into the background. A good way to start is by asking, "Would I say this to someone I love?" Often, the lies we accept for ourselves would sound absurd if spoken to someone else. Let that kindness you'd offer a friend guide you toward a clearer understanding of the truth.

"Yeah, but rewriting my story feels fake, like I'm lying to myself."

It can feel that way at first—like trying to write with your non-dominant hand. But consider this: the old stories were also written by repetition. You're not lying to yourself now; you're choosing a narrative that supports your growth. With time and practice, these empowering truths will feel just as natural as the old ones, but with a much kinder outcome.

"Yeah, but I've tried to rewrite my story before, and it didn't work."

I hear you, and it's discouraging when efforts don't seem to stick. But rewriting your story isn't about one grand rewrite—it's about consistent, deliberate edits. Each time you catch a lie and replace it with truth, you're making progress. The change happens gradually, like water shaping stone, but it's happening. Be patient with yourself; this is a process, not an event.

"Yeah, but some of these stories came from people I trusted. Doesn't that make them true?"

It's so hard when the lies come from people we love or respect. But remember, people project their own fears and limitations onto others, often without meaning harm. Just because someone said it doesn't make it true for you. You have the right to examine those stories, keep what serves you, and let go of what doesn't. You're not dishonoring them by seeking your own truth—you're honoring yourself.

REFLECTION QUESTIONS:

1. What are the recurring stories you tell yourself about your worth, capabilities, or relationships?
2. Where do you think these stories originated? Who or what planted them?
3. How might your life change if you replaced these stories with empowering truths?
4. What's one small step you can take today to rewrite your narrative?

CHAPTER TEN
THE CRIPPLING BLOW
DISCONNECTION FROM SELF AND OTHERS - THE SILENT KILLER

The greatest thing in the world is to know how to belong to oneself.
– Michel de Montaigne

THE ALIEN INVADERS DON'T JUST STRIKE FEAR INTO OUR HEARTS OR manipulate us with stories—they drive us apart. Their ultimate goal is disconnection. Once isolated, we become vulnerable, divided, and ripe for further attacks. If fear is the first wave and manipulation is the second, disconnection is the silent killer.

THE LONELINESS WITHIN

Disconnection often begins long before we realize it. It doesn't always look like being alone. For many, it happens in the middle of crowded rooms, bustling family dinners, or marriages that feel distant despite proximity. It's the sense that no one truly sees you for who you are—or worse, that they wouldn't love you if they did.

I know this pain well... unfortunately. In the darkest seasons of my life, surrounded by family and friends, I felt completely alone. Shame had driven a wedge between me and others. It whispered that I wasn't enough, that I was fundamentally flawed, and that if people really knew me, they would reject me. So, I began to withdraw—sometimes physically, but nearly always at least emotionally. I put up walls to protect myself, but those walls also kept me from feeling truly connected. This just fed the story more, making it self-fulfilling.

This disconnection wasn't just with others. Shame had also severed me from myself. I couldn't look in the mirror without hearing the invaders' voice: You're awkward and weird-looking. You're ugly. You're not attractive enough. Who'd ever want to be with you? You're not successful enough. You're not enough. I didn't even know who I was anymore, only who I was trying to be.

THE ANATOMY OF DISCONNECTION

Disconnection is both a cause and a consequence of shame. When we feel unworthy, we withdraw to protect ourselves from rejection, but that withdrawal feeds our loneliness and reinforces the belief that we are unlovable. It's a vicious cycle.

Think about the invaders in an alien invasion story. What's their first move after the initial attack? They divide and isolate. They cut communication lines, disable power grids, and separate communities. Without connection, people are easier to manipulate and control, and this makes it easier to lead them to feel powerless, defeated, and hopeless. That's precisely how shame operates within us. It cuts the lines of connection, leaving us stranded and vulnerable.

HOW SHAME TARGETS CONNECTION

Shame doesn't just happen—it's planted. It grows in the soil of our insecurities and blossoms when we compare ourselves to others. Shame abounds anywhere that comparison exists. These days, social media is one of the alien invaders' greatest tools, allowing us to curate perfect versions of our lives while secretly feeling unworthy behind the screen. We scroll through highlight reels of others' achievements, relationships, and adventures, all the while feeling the weight of our own perceived failures and shortcomings.

But shame doesn't just thrive online. It shows up in our most intimate relationships. In my marriage, shame turned conversations into battlegrounds. I was so afraid of being "found out" as inadequate that I became defensive, withdrawing emotionally while projecting blame outward. Zelda also felt the disconnection, and though neither of us realized it at the time, we were both fighting battles with shame that left us feeling alone—even when we were together. Oh, what a gut-wrenching and tragic delusion this becomes!

BREAKING THROUGH DISCONNECTION

The antidote to disconnection isn't just proximity or time spent together; it's vulnerability. And vulnerability, as terrifying as it sounds, is the one thing the invaders can't stand. Why? Because vulnerability is a courageous expression of truth. It's letting someone in on what's going on inside of us. When we let someone see the parts of ourselves we're most ashamed of, we begin to rebuild the broken lines of connection.

For me, this started with a simple but terrifying act: admitting that I didn't have it all together. I began sharing my fears, doubts, and shame—not with everyone but with a trusted few. It wasn't easy. It was mortifying! Vulnerability is the equivalent of standing unarmed in front of an alien warship. But instead of being destroyed, the warship began to retreat. Vulnerable connection was the ultimate weapon against the invaders.

THE POWER OF RECONNECTION

Reconnection doesn't happen all at once. It's a slow process of undoing the "alien technology" of shame and fear. It means reaching out when everything in you wants to withdraw. It means listening without judgment when someone shares their pain. It means risking rejection to find real intimacy.

> As I began to reconnect—with myself, Zelda, and trusted friends—I started to see the invaders for what they were: deceivers and manipulators. They had told me that I was unworthy, that no one would love the real me, and that I had to hide to survive. But the truth was this: Connection wasn't just possible—it was necessary for my survival, and fortunately, it was also not as scarce as I'd been led to believe, but was ample—if I'd just be willing to tell the truth about myself.

THE MAIN TAKEAWAY: RECONNECTION IS THE KEY TO RESISTANCE

Disconnection is the invaders' ultimate weapon but also their greatest weakness. When we reconnect—with ourselves and others—we dismantle their control. Vulnerability is the bridge that spans the chasm of shame, allowing us to rebuild the relationships that shame tried to destroy.

COMING UP NEXT: SHAME UNVEILED - HOW IT TURNS YOU INTO YOUR OWN WORST ENEMY

Disconnection paves the way for shame, the invaders' stealthiest and most corrosive weapon. Next, you'll learn how shame infiltrates your life, convinces you to self-sabotage, and how practicing self-compassion can dismantle its hold and restore your sense of worth.

COMMON RESPONSES

"Yeah, but being vulnerable feels too risky—I might get hurt."

It's true—vulnerability does carry risk. But ask yourself this: What's the cost of staying disconnected? While rejection is painful, disconnection often hurts more in the long run. Vulnerability isn't about sharing everything with everyone; it's about letting the right people see your truth. Start small, with someone you trust, and remember—you're taking a risk for the possibility of something profoundly healing.

"Yeah, but no one would really understand me if I opened up."

I hear you, and it can feel that way when shame convinces us we're alone in our struggles. But the truth is, your experiences—though unique—are not incomprehensible. The right people, those who care about you, won't need to have lived your exact story to understand your feelings. Connection often begins when someone sees your willingness to be honest and meets it with empathy.

"Yeah, but I've tried to connect before, and people let me down."

That pain is valid, and it's hard to trust again after being hurt. But connection isn't about finding people who never let us down—it's about finding those who show up even when things aren't perfect. Each attempt at connection teaches us something about who to trust and how to protect our boundaries while staying open. It's okay to move slowly, but don't let past hurt rob you of future connection.

"Yeah, but I wouldn't even know where to start reconnecting with myself."

That's completely okay—reconnection with yourself doesn't have to be a grand gesture. Start by asking small, gentle questions: "What am I feeling right now?" or "What do I need in this moment?" Spending time doing something that brings you peace or joy can also help. Reconnection isn't about perfection; it's about showing up for yourself in little ways and watching them add up.

"Yeah, but the people I want to connect with might reject me."

That fear is real, and rejection hurts. But connection isn't about convincing others to accept you—it's about finding those who value the real you. If someone can't meet you in your vulnerability, that's not a reflection of your worth but of their readiness. Each act of vulnerability helps you discover who's truly safe and builds the courage to try again, even if it feels hard.

REFLECTION QUESTIONS:

1. When do you feel most disconnected from others? From yourself?

WHAT TO DO WHEN THE ALIENS SHOW UP (AND EVEN IF THEY DON'T)

2. How has shame influenced your ability to be vulnerable or open with others?
3. What relationships in your life could benefit from more honesty and vulnerability?
4. Who are the "trusted few" in your life with whom you can begin to reconnect?

CHAPTER ELEVEN
THE INVADERS' MASTERSTROKE
SHAME, THE STEALTH & SNEAKY OPERATIVE

What if I fall? Oh, but my darling, what if you fly? – Erin Hanson

SHAME'S INFILTRATION: HOW IT GETS INSIDE

OF ALL THE WEAPONS IN THE ALIEN INVADERS' ARSENAL, SHAME IS THE most insidious. Fear and deception may create chaos and weaken our defenses, but shame works differently. It doesn't just attack—it takes over. Shame convinces us that we are the problem, turning our minds into battlegrounds and pitting us against ourselves. Once shame takes root, we become our own worst enemy, leaving the invaders free to wreak havoc while we focus inward, doubting our worth, withdrawing from connection, and questioning our ability to fight back.

Imagine an invasion in which the aliens don't just bombard cities or unleash terrifying creatures. Instead, they plant seeds of self-doubt in every mind, whispering, "You're not enough. You'll never be enough." The whispers grow louder until the people begin to destroy themselves from the inside out, isolating themselves from one another, sabotaging their own lives, and letting the invaders' work go unchallenged.

This is how shame operates. Unlike fear, which feels sharp and immediate, shame is a slow, insidious burn. It embeds itself in the stories we tell ourselves, shaping how we see the world and our place in it. Fear says, "You might fail." Shame says, "You are a failure." Fear warns of external threats, but shame undermines from within.

At first, recognizing shame can feel overwhelming. For most of us, shame doesn't announce itself clearly—it sneaks into our thoughts in subtle ways. It disguises itself as self-criticism, humility, or motivation to improve. It takes time and effort to realize that these whispers aren't helping—they're holding us back. The good news is that by the end of this book, you'll have the tools to expose shame for what it is and begin breaking free from its hold.

THE CYCLE OF SHAME

Shame isn't passive. It feeds on itself, creating a vicious cycle that's hard to escape. The more it takes hold, the harder it becomes to resist its grip. Here's how the cycle of shame typically unfolds:

1. **Judgment:** Shame often begins with a moment of judgment—by ourselves or others. Perhaps we make a mistake at work, someone criticizes us, or we fail to meet a goal we set for ourselves. Shame seizes on these moments, interpreting them as proof that we are fundamentally flawed.
2. **Isolation:** Shame drives us to withdraw in response to judgment. We don't want others to see our perceived flaws, so we build walls, hide our true selves, or wear masks to fit in. This isolation deepens our disconnection from others and from ourselves.
3. **Reinforcement:** The more isolated we become, the more shame convinces us that we are alone, unworthy,

and beyond redemption. This sense of disconnection reinforces the shame, creating a loop that grows harder to break with each turn.

This cycle isn't unique to personal struggles—it can also affect groups, workplaces, and entire societies. Shame, wherever it takes root, creates division, mistrust, and paralysis. It's one of the invaders' most effective strategies for keeping us disconnected and disempowered.

I lived with those whispers for years. I've heard them in the quiet moments when my thoughts turned inward: You're not good enough. You're not strong enough. You're not successful enough. You'll never measure up. You have no value. You are a mistake. Over time, these whispers grew louder, shaping the way I interacted with the world. Shame convinced me that I wasn't just flawed—I was fundamentally broken and, thus, unwanted.

THE POWER OF SHAME'S LIES

SHAME IS UNIQUELY destructive because it doesn't just criticize our actions—it attacks our identity. Where fear warns of a specific danger, shame creates a general sense of inadequacy. It whispers lies like:

- "You're not good enough."
- "You'll never measure up."
- "You're worthless."
- "You have no value."
- "No one cares about you."

These whispers become the lens through which we view

ourselves and the world, shaping how we act, connect, and respond to challenges. Over time, shame convinces us to avoid risks, suppress our true selves, and stay small, safe, and unseen.

Perhaps the most devious lie shame tells is that it's the only way to motivate improvement. It suggests that if we stop listening to its whispers, we'll stop growing, succeeding, or caring about others. In reality, shame does the opposite—it keeps us stuck in fear, limiting our ability to grow or thrive.

WHY SHAME IS SO EFFECTIVE

Shame's power lies in its subtlety. Most people don't recognize it as a force separate from themselves; instead, they accept its whispers as truth. This is why shame is so effective at undermining our ability to resist fear and deception. When we believe shame's lies, we become disconnected—from ourselves, from others, and from the truth of our worth.

Shame thrives in silence. It wants us to keep our struggles hidden, to believe that we are the only ones feeling this way. It isolates us, convincing us that no one else could understand or accept us if they truly knew what we were struggling with. This isolation makes us easy targets for further manipulation, whether from external invaders or our own internalized fears.

THE TURNING POINT: RECOGNIZING THE LIES

Although shame is a powerful weapon, its strength lies in deception. Once we begin to see shame for what it is—a lie—it starts to lose its grip. Shame tells us that our worth is tied to our actions, appearances, or achievements. But the truth is that our worth is inherent. It doesn't come from what we do or how others see us.

If you're skeptical of this idea, I get it. I've been there too. It's not easy to confront shame's lies, especially when they've been part of your internal narrative for years. But I hope this book will help you begin that process. As we move through Parts 2 and 3, we'll explore practical ways to recognize shame's lies, disrupt the cycle, and replace shame with connection, courage, and compassion.

For now, take this first step: Start noticing when shame speaks. Pay attention to the whispers that tell you you're not enough. Recognizing these lies is the beginning of breaking free.

COMING UP NEXT: JUDGMENT UNDER THE MICROSCOPE

Shame's power comes from its ability to take root in judgment. Whether it's judgment from others or judgment we place on ourselves, it creates the perfect environment for shame to grow. In the next chapter, we'll dive deeper into the role of judgment, exploring how it fuels fear, shame, and disconnection—and how we can begin to loosen its grip.

COMMON RESPONSES

"Yeah, but what if the whispers of shame are actually true?"

I hear you—that's the hardest part of shame. It's so convincing that it feels like truth. But ask yourself: Is shame offering you clarity or keeping you stuck? The truth about you isn't found in shame's whispers—it's found in the way you show courage, kindness, and resilience every day. The real truth about you is that you are enough, even when it doesn't feel like it.

"Yeah, but isn't shame sometimes necessary to keep us humble?"

It's a common belief, but humility and shame are not the same thing. Humility comes from a place of strength and self-awareness, allowing us to see our worth alongside our imperfections. Shame, on the other hand, attacks our very sense of worth. Letting go of shame doesn't make you arrogant—it makes you free to grow, connect, and show compassion to yourself and others.

> "Yeah, but I've been living with shame for so long—I don't know any other way."

That's a heavy burden to carry, and it's no wonder it feels daunting to imagine life without it. But here's the truth: You've been stronger than shame this whole time—it's just convinced you otherwise. Even a small step toward recognizing its lies is proof of your strength. You don't have to leave shame behind all at once—just one step at a time.

> "Yeah, but I feel like I deserve the shame I feel."

I want to acknowledge how real and deep that feeling can be. Shame wants you to believe that your mistakes or struggles define you, but they don't. What you deserve isn't shame—it's growth, forgiveness, and compassion. You are not your mistakes; you are the person learning and growing through them. That's worth celebrating, not condemning.

> "Yeah, but what if people really do reject me if they see the real me?"

That fear is real, and rejection hurts. But hiding doesn't protect you—it isolates you and reinforces shame. Vulnerability doesn't mean revealing everything to everyone—it's about finding safe spaces where you can be seen and accepted. The right people won't reject you for being real; they'll draw closer, because your courage to be authentic invites deeper connection.

REFLECTION QUESTIONS

1. What are some of the lies Shame has told you about yourself?
2. How has shame influenced your decisions or relationships?
3. Who could you trust to share your struggles with, and how might that help?
4. How does recognizing shame as a lie change the way you see it?

CHAPTER TWELVE
THE LATENT SABOTEUR
JUDGMENT—THE ORIGINAL LIE

> We can never judge the lives of others, because each person knows only their own pain and renunciation. It's one thing to feel that you are on the right path, but it's another to think that yours is the only path. – Paulo Coelho

THE FIRST ACT OF JUDGMENT

IF SHAME IS THE INVADERS' MOST POWERFUL WEAPON, JUDGMENT IS the foundation on which their strategy is built. Without judgment, shame wouldn't have fertile ground to grow. Judgment is the original lie, the first wedge that separates us from ourselves, others, and the life we're meant to live.

Imagine an alien invasion so clever, so diabolical, that it begins not with bombs or armies but with a whisper: *This is wrong. You're wrong.* The invaders don't need to force you into submission. Instead, they plant a seed of judgment and let it take root. Before long, you're policing yourself, questioning your every thought and action, and turning away from others who seem different or threatening.

This process mirrors the ancient story of Adam and Eve, who, after gaining the "knowledge of good and evil," took that new "knowledge" and judged themselves as broken and unworthy. They hid in shame, convinced they were no longer lovable as they were. The tragedy of their story isn't just that it happened—it's that it keeps happening. Every human seems to repeat this experience, often beginning in the early years of life.

> *I've watched with sadness as each of my children has traversed this awful path of judgment, disowning themselves and the resulting shame. Each one entered this world so full of delight and seemingly limitless curiosity, joy, and wonder. Watching them encounter the world's constant barrage of arbitrary evaluations has been heartbreaking. No matter how much I have tried to shield them, they, like all of us, have internalized the lie that they needed to be something "better," "different," or "more" to be enough. Comparisons are endless, and as Theodore Roosevelt said, "Comparison is the thief of joy."*

THE NATURE OF JUDGMENT

Judgment is so pervasive in our world that it feels almost inevitable. It's woven into the way we think, relate to others, and understand ourselves.

But here's the key: judgment isn't built on objective truth—it's a story we construct, shaped by our perceptions, past experiences, and the interpretations we attach to them.

When we perceive the world, we don't see objective reality. Our senses gather raw information, but what we experience as "real" is a filtered version of that information, colored by our emotions, memories, and learned patterns. Someone's critical look might simply reflect their bad day, but through the lens of judgment, we interpret it as confirmation of our unworthiness.

Over time, these judgments become automatically embedded in our mental landscape. That's because anything we learn to do, our brains learn to automate and optimize. This means when we start saying, "I screwed up" or "I'm bad at this," or we hear things like, "your suck at soccer," our brain will learn to build these judgments into optimized, automatic responses we often label "beliefs." We rarely stop to question the validity of these thoughts and beliefs because they feel so real. But they're not—they're constructs reinforced by repetition and the stories we learn from others and eventually begin to teach ourselves.

THE ALIEN LIE: YOU'RE INCOMPLETE

The invaders' lie is simple yet devastating: *You're not whole. You're missing something.* Judgment convinces us that we're not enough as we are. It tells us that to be worthy, we need to be better, smarter, richer, thinner, more attractive, more successful—always *more*.

This lie keeps us on a hamster wheel of striving and performing, forever seeking something outside ourselves to fill the void. But the truth is, we've never been incomplete. The alien lie blinds us to the fact that our worth is inherent, not something we need to earn or prove.

Judgment doesn't just harm us individually—it fractures our relationships and communities. It separates us from one another, breeding suspicion, comparison, and conflict. We judge others just as harshly as we judge ourselves, creating cycles of disconnection and mistrust.

HOW JUDGMENT CONVINCES US

What makes judgment so powerful is how convinced we are of its accuracy. We mistake our perceptions—those interpretations colored by past pain, fear, and insecurity—for objective truth. We believe the critical voice in our head, the one that tells us we're not enough, is offering us valuable insight rather than perpetuating the invaders' lies.

Here are some examples of how this plays out:

1. **Judging Ourselves:** "I'm such a failure. Why can't I get this right?"
2. **Judging Others:** "Why are they so difficult? They're the problem."
3. **Judging Life:** "This isn't fair. Life shouldn't be this hard."

In each case, judgment creates separation—between ourselves and our worth, between us and others, and between us and life itself.

THE COSTS OF JUDGMENT

Judgment isn't just a mental habit; it's a barrier to wholeness. It creates:

- **Disconnection:** Judgment cuts us off from ourselves, others, and the truth of our worth.
- **Isolation:** We withdraw to avoid the pain of judgment, creating a vicious cycle of loneliness and shame.
- **Distorted Perception:** Judgment skews our view of reality, making it hard to see clearly or act with wisdom.
- **Emotional Exhaustion:** The mental energy required to maintain judgmental narratives drains us, leaving us anxious and depleted.

JUDGMENT AND THE ROOTS OF SHAME

Every act of shame begins with *judgment*. We judge ourselves for our mistakes, flaws, and failures. We judge others for not meeting our expectations. And we judge life itself as being messy, unpredictable, and painful.

This cycle of judgment and shame is self-reinforcing. Judgment fuels shame, and shame keeps us locked in judgment. It's a pattern that feels inescapable—but it's not.

> *I spent years caught in the grip of judgment. It wasn't always obvious—I wasn't the kind of person who pointed fingers or criticized others openly. But inside, I was relentless. I judged myself for not being good enough, not doing enough, or being the kind of person I thought I should be. Every time I fell short, I reinforced the story that I was fundamentally broken.*

WE'LL ADDRESS THIS TOGETHER

In Parts 2 and 3, we'll explore powerful ways to break free from judgment and shame. You'll discover tools to challenge your perceptions, reframe the stories you tell yourself, and reconnect with your inherent worth. For now, recognize this: judgment is not reality. It's a filter we've been taught to apply, and it can be unlearned.

The invaders want you to stay trapped in their cycle, believing the lies of judgment and shame. But you don't have to. The choice to see differently—to question judgment and uncover the truth—is the beginning of freedom.

THE MAIN TAKEAWAY: JUDGMENT IS THE FOUNDATION OF SUFFERING

Judgment is the original lie that separates us from our inherent worth and from one another. It convinces us to see the world through a distorted lens, one that reinforces shame and disconnection. By recognizing judgment's pervasiveness and how it shapes our perceptions, we take the first step toward dismantling its power.

COMING UP NEXT: RISING ABOVE THE LIES - CHOOSING TO BEGIN THE COUNTEROFFENSIVE

Judgment creates a cycle of suffering, but the turning point begins with choice. In Parts 2 and 3, we'll explore how to break free from the hold of judgment, reframe your perceptions, and reclaim your worth. For now, let this truth take root: judgment is not reality, and freedom is possible.

COMMON RESPONSES

"Yeah, but isn't judgment necessary to make sense of the world?"

It's natural to think that judgment helps us navigate life, and in some cases, discernment is necessary. But judgment, as this chapter explores, isn't about understanding—it's about condemning. Discernment seeks truth with compassion, while judgment separates us from it. You can see clearly without harshly labeling yourself, others, or life itself.

"Yeah, but if I stop judging myself, won't I lose my drive to improve?"

It's easy to believe that self-criticism fuels growth, but the truth is, shame and judgment often paralyze us more than they motivate. Real growth comes from curiosity, self-compassion, and a willingness to learn. When you approach yourself with kindness, you'll find a far more sustainable and empowering source of motivation.

"Yeah, but some people deserve to be judged for their actions."

It's understandable to feel that way when people hurt us or act

WHAT TO DO WHEN THE ALIENS SHOW UP (AND EVEN IF THEY DON'T)

unjustly. But judgment, as this chapter explains, often keeps us locked in resentment and disconnection. You can hold others accountable without carrying the weight of judgment—it's about separating their actions from your peace. Accountability and judgment are not the same thing.

> "Yeah, but my judgments feel so automatic—I can't just turn them off."

That's absolutely true—judgment has likely been part of your mental landscape for a long time. But the goal isn't to turn off the judgmental thoughts we experience but to change how we respond to them; it's to begin noticing them and choosing a different response than our automatic, knee-jerk reactions. Awareness is the first step toward change. Each time you catch yourself judging, you create a small opening for curiosity and compassion to take root.

> "Yeah, but I've been judged so much by others—how can I stop doing it to myself?"

Being judged by others leaves deep scars, and it makes sense that this would shape how you see yourself. But consider this: the judgments you've endured don't define you—they reflect others' limited perceptions. Choosing to release self-judgment is a way of reclaiming your story and refusing to let others' opinions control your life.

REFLECTION QUESTIONS

1. What judgments have you held about yourself that have shaped your identity?
2. How has judgment influenced your relationships with others?

3. What would change if you approached yourself and others with curiosity instead of criticism?
4. How can you begin to notice when your perceptions are shaped by judgment rather than objective reality?

PART TWO
THE TURNING POINT
CHOOSING TO RISE

An invasion isn't just a series of attacks—it's a test of resilience, strategy, and spirit. In Part 1, we uncovered the invaders' weapons: fear, shame, judgment, dependency, and disconnection. We've seen how they infiltrate our minds, erode our confidence, and turn us against ourselves. It's a sobering reality. But as bleak as it may seem, this is not the end of the story.

Every invasion brings its turning point—a moment of choice.

This is the point in every great story where the heroes face their darkest hour but find the courage to rise. They choose to stop running, stop hiding, and stop living as victims of the invasion. Instead, they resolve to fight back, to reclaim their lives and their world.

That moment of choice isn't just for the heroes on the screen—it's for us, too. The invaders may have struck the first blow, but you hold the power to decide what happens next. And that power lies in choice.

THE CHALLENGE OF CHOICE

Choice is the pivotal moment that shifts the tide. It's the turning point where suffering begins to transform into thriving. But if choice were easy, wouldn't we all have made it already? Why does it feel so hard to change direction, especially when the stakes are high?

One reason is the power of the invaders' lies. Fear whispers that it's safer to stay where we are. Shame tells us we're not capable of something better. Judgment insists we don't deserve it. These voices grow loudest when we stand at the edge of transformation, convincing us that staying stuck is the only option.

Another reason is the way habits and patterns take root in our minds. The invaders' strategies—especially judgment and dependency—don't just create pain; they condition us to live within its boundaries. Over time, these patterns become so familiar that breaking free feels impossible, even when we sense the harm they're causing.

Finally, choice is difficult because it demands something profound: responsibility. To choose differently is to take ownership of your life, to acknowledge that while you may not control the circumstances you face, you do have power over how you respond to them. This can feel overwhelming, especially if you've spent years believing otherwise.

THE PROMISE OF CHOICE

Yet, as daunting as it may feel, choice is also incredibly liberating. It's the doorway through which resilience, growth, and freedom become possible. Every small step you take toward reclaiming your agency weakens the invaders' hold, setting the stage for transformation.

In Part 2, we'll explore what it takes to make that choice. We'll delve into the tools and mindsets that empower you to confront fear, challenge shame, and disrupt the cycle of judgment. We'll also uncover why choice feels so difficult and how to overcome the resistance that keeps you stuck.

Most importantly, we'll begin your counter-offensive—the process of reclaiming your life, step by step. You'll learn how to replace the invaders' lies with truth, rebuild your sense of self, and reconnect with the courage and clarity that have been within you all along.

YOUR TURNING POINT

This is your moment of choice. The invaders may have infiltrated your mind and eroded your confidence, but they cannot take away your ability to decide what happens next. It's not about being fearless or having all the answers—it's about being willing to take the first step, even in the face of uncertainty.

In the chapters ahead, we'll walk this path together. You'll discover how clarity, courage, and deliberate action can turn the tide, transforming suffering into thriving and reclaiming the freedom, connection, and empowerment that are your birthright.

This is your turning point. Are you ready to rise?

CHAPTER THIRTEEN
NO CAVALRY COMING
EMBRACING THE TRUTH THAT CHANGE BEGINS WITH YOU

The cave you fear to enter holds the treasure you seek. – Joseph Campbell

NO ONE IS COMING

For many of us, life feels like a slow, agonizing descent into despair. We wait for someone or something to come along and pull us out of the mess we find ourselves in. Maybe it's a job, a partner, a sudden windfall, or divine intervention. We look around at our suffering and think, "Surely, someone will save me. Surely, this can't be how the story ends."

The reality is this: no one is coming.

This is a brutal, sobering truth that is both terrifying and liberating. It's terrifying because it means there will be no cavalry charging over the hill to rescue us. It's liberating because it also means the solution doesn't depend on something or someone outside of us. This is the moment when the battle turns. The power to change our lives is already within us. The question is, are we ready to stop waiting and start acting?

A LOOK BACK: THE JOURNEY THROUGH PART 1

In Part 1, we uncovered how the invaders disarmed us layer by layer, attacking from the outside in:

1. **Judgment** planted the first seeds, introducing the idea that we are not enough. It created the framework for self-condemnation, convincing us that our flaws defined us and setting the stage for shame to flourish.
2. **Shame** took root, whispering that our worth was tied to our failures. It eroded our sense of self, leading us to hide, withdraw, and disconnect from our authentic selves and others.
3. **Disconnection** spread, severing our connections with ourselves, our loved ones, and even our sense of purpose. It left us isolated and vulnerable to external control, amplifying the belief that we were powerless.
4. **Externalized Self-Worth** emerged as a natural response to disconnection. Cut off from our internal sense of value, we began looking outward for validation, tying our worth to how others perceived us, our achievements, or our material possessions. This fragile and conditional sense of worth deepened our vulnerability.
5. **Dependency** reinforced the illusion, tethering our sense of security, worth, and identity to external sources like relationships, achievements, or societal validation. This false reliance kept us trapped in cycles of fear and unworthiness.
6. **Insecurity** took hold as the external sources of self-worth proved unstable and unpredictable. This constant fragility created confusion between our identity and the actions or perceptions of others, leaving us emotionally vulnerable and hyper-aware of external threats.
7. **Anxious Uncertainty** flourished, preying on the instability bred by dependency and insecurity. With

every external source of validation feeling fragile or conditional, it heightened our sense of insecurity, leaving us constantly scanning for threats and obsessing over the unknown.
8. **Fear** took over, paralyzing us and cementing the invaders' hold. It convinced us to stay small, reactive, and stuck, perpetuating the cycle of suffering and silencing any possibility of reclaiming our agency.
9. **Suffering & Stagnation** became the end result, as fear and anxiety drained us of the courage and hope needed to move forward. We found ourselves resigned to a life of avoidance, disconnected from purpose, growth, or thriving.

If you felt seen in those chapters, it's because I've been there too. I've lived that life of stagnation and waiting—waiting for my marriage to fix itself, for my career to feel fulfilling, for someone to tell me I was enough. I spent years hoping external solutions would cure internal pain, only to find myself more entrenched in suffering.

And that's the harsh truth: external rescue is a deadly myth.

THE ALLURE OF RESCUE

Let's be honest—waiting for someone to save us is comforting. It lets us off the hook. We don't have to face the terrifying unknown or take responsibility for our own lives.

This isn't just about fairy tales or superhero movies; it's baked into our culture. We grow up hearing stories about knights in shining armor, daring rescues, and divine interventions that set everything right. We internalize the idea that if we just hold on long enough, someone or something will save us.

But here's the harsh truth: while it's true that others can help, no one can do the work of saving *you* but *you*–because *you* are the one who has been deceived into giving these alien invaders residence within. Only *you* can evict them.

RESCUE VS. SUPPORT

It's critical to understand the difference between *rescue* and *support*. Just because no one is coming doesn't mean that we are completely alone or that there is no one to walk alongside us. Support is real and available, but it's not the same as rescue.

- **Rescue** implies that someone will parachute into our story, take over our individual sovereignty*, fix everything for us, and free us from the need to experience transformation. Rescue is about *avoidance*—it's an escape hatch that sidesteps the messy, painful, but ultimately necessary process of growth. It keeps us dependent, passive, waiting–and stuck.
- **Support,** on the other hand, honors our autonomy. It provides encouragement, guidance, and resources while respecting that the work of transformation must be ours. Support can hold space for our struggle, offer wisdom from those who've walked similar paths, and remind us that we're not alone. But it cannot—and should not—take over the responsibility of our healing or growth.

Recognizing this distinction is vital because waiting for rescue leaves us in a state of powerlessness, while embracing support allows us to draw strength from others without surrendering one's agency.

---

* **Sovereignty:** In this context, sovereignty refers to the idea of having full control and authority over one's own life, thoughts, and actions.

FAITH IN THE BIGGER PICTURE

Those with some religious worldviews may have felt tension in recognizing this truth. Some people get kinda angry hearing me say these things, thinking I am peddling a message that violates some core ideas of their faith. Their response is something like, "yeah, but... doesn't faith promise rescue, salvation, and intervention?" If that's you, take a deep breath and keep reading. Lean into this discomfort and keep reading. If you're grappling with these questions, know this: In Parts 4-5, I will explore the faith dimension of rescue and "salvation" in tremendous depth. For now, understand this: waiting for divine rescue without personal action misses the point. Even the most sacred texts emphasize *faith* and *power* as inseparable from choice, action, and partnership with the divine.

Part 2 *isn't* about rejecting faith but explaining the fullness of what it means to truly live by a faith that I believe you'll find empowering. This faith requires us to take the steps that only we can take. It's about stepping into the truth that transformation requires our *participation*. Hopefully, by the end of this book, whatever faith you have will be strengthened and more alive than ever!

THE COST OF WAITING

The cost of believing that an external rescue will happen without our choice, action, and participation is that our lives will stall. We become stuck in patterns of fear, dependency, and self-abandonment. We surrender our agency, telling ourselves it's not our job to fix things, and the clock keeps ticking. The pain doesn't go away; it grows.

- We wait for our partner to change, and the relationship deteriorates.
- We wait for our boss to recognize our value, and the promotion never comes.

- We wait for our feelings of shame to vanish, and instead, they deepen.
- We wait to win the lottery so we can feel financially free.
- We wait for the aliens to stop attacking the planet so we can return to life as we used to know it.

Waiting for someone else to fix things doesn't make life better; it just makes us more entrenched in the very suffering we're trying to escape.

THE DRAMA TRIANGLE: A HIDDEN TRAP

Before we can fully embrace the journey of transformation, we need to understand one of the most pervasive dynamics that keeps us stuck: the *Drama Triangle*. In the next chapter, we'll explore how this framework of Victim, Persecutor, and Rescuer roles traps us in cycles of disempowerment. These roles feed the myth of external rescue and reinforce the very suffering we're trying to escape.

Understanding the Drama Triangle is crucial because it reveals the deeper patterns of how we relate to ourselves and others. Once you see these patterns for what they are, you'll have the tools to dismantle them and begin stepping into the Empowerment Dynamic—a framework that restores your agency and helps you move from survival to thriving.

> *I know what it feels like to wait for rescue, to hold onto the hope that someone—or something—will swoop in to make it all better. As a kid, bullied and struggling with self-worth, I prayed desperately for God to step in, to silence the bullies, to fix my family's struggles, to change the face staring back at me in the mirror to no longer have acne and crooked teeth. When prayers weren't answered, or changes didn't come, I felt abandoned, unworthy, and*

WHAT TO DO WHEN THE ALIENS SHOW UP (AND EVEN IF THEY DON'T)

unseen.

That pattern didn't stop in childhood; it followed me into adulthood. You'd think I would have grown out of it as I got older, but instead, it just changed shape. I clung to the belief that if I just waited long enough, change would come. In fact, I even called that 'optimism' or 'hope' at times, but in reality, it was 'wishing'. Whether it was waiting for my marriage to magically heal, for God to reveal His 'plan' in the midst of my struggles, or for someone else to validate my worth, I kept expecting rescue. But waiting for a rescuer <u>didn't</u> bring peace—it <u>deepened</u> my pain. I've since learned that the answers I was searching for were never 'out there' somewhere—they were <u>inside</u>, waiting for <u>me</u> to claim them. But that realization didn't come easily, and the road to it was filled with moments of raw frustration, disillusionment, and doubt.

MAIN TAKEAWAY: THE POWER TO CHANGE IS ALREADY WITHIN YOU

The truth that no one is coming to save you is both sobering and liberating. It calls us to stop waiting for external rescue and start reclaiming our power. While support is essential, true transformation requires our active participation. By embracing this truth, we can break cycles of dependency and take the first courageous steps toward living a life of agency, freedom, and purpose.

COMING UP NEXT: CHOOSING A NEW PATH

Now that we've embraced the liberating truth that no one is coming to save us, the next step is to confront the true battlefield: our mind. The invaders' strongest weapon isn't external force—it's the thought patterns and beliefs they've implanted within us. In the next chapter, we'll explore how fear, shame, and judgment have shaped your inner narrative and kept you stuck. Most importantly, we'll begin to learn how to identify and disarm these invasive thoughts, reclaiming our mental sovereignty and rewriting the stories that define our lives.

COMMON RESPONSES

"Yeah, but I don't have the strength to do this on my own."

It's okay to feel that way. Starting this journey doesn't mean you have to be strong all at once. It's about taking one small step at a time. Strength isn't something you start with—it's something you build along the way. Remember, you're not as alone as you think; support is there, but the first step begins with you.

"Yeah, but isn't it normal to expect help from others?"

Yes, it's absolutely normal to need support. But this chapter isn't about rejecting help—it's about letting go of the myth of total rescue. Support can walk beside you, but transformation comes when you take ownership of your journey. You're not waiting for someone to fix it all; you're learning to lead your own way forward.

"Yeah, but what if I fail without rescue?"

Failure is scary, but it's also part of growth. Every step, even the ones that don't go as planned, teaches you something valuable. Waiting for rescue keeps you stuck in fear, but taking action—imperfect as it may be—opens the door to possibility. You've already faced so much; this is just another step forward.

WHAT TO DO WHEN THE ALIENS SHOW UP (AND EVEN IF THEY DON'T)

"Yeah, but isn't it selfish to focus on saving myself?"

It's not selfish—it's essential. When you take responsibility for your own life, you're not just helping yourself; you're creating space to show up authentically for others. You can't pour from an empty cup. By reclaiming your power, you model courage and agency for those around you.

"Yeah, but I've been waiting for so long—I don't know where to start."

That's okay. Waiting feels safe because it's familiar, but starting doesn't have to be overwhelming. Pick one small area of your life where you've felt stuck and take one step—no matter how small—toward change. Action doesn't need to be perfect to be powerful.

REFLECTION QUESTIONS

1. Where in your life have you been waiting for external rescue? How has that served you?
2. What fears arise when you consider that no one is coming to save you?
3. What small step can you take today to begin reclaiming your agency?
4. How might embracing this truth lead to greater freedom and possibility in your life?

CHAPTER FOURTEEN
BREAKING FREE FROM THE ALIEN MIND TRAP
ESCAPING THE ROLES THAT KEEP YOU STUCK

The moment you take responsibility for everything in your life is the moment you can change anything in your life. – Hal Elrod

THE DRAMA TRIANGLE: A HIDDEN TRAP

THE DRAMA TRIANGLE, INTRODUCED BY DR. STEPHEN KARPMAN, IS A mental and relational trap that keeps us stuck in cycles of disconnection, blame, and emotional entanglement. Its power lies in its subtlety—operating in the background of our relationships, thoughts, and even societal structures. At its core are three roles: Victim, Persecutor, and Rescuer. These roles create toxic dynamics that feel inescapable, convincing, and all too real.

This chapter explores how the Drama Triangle operates, why we fall into it, how it appears at every level of society, and why stepping out of it is so difficult. Additionally, we'll uncover the psychological motivations that drive each role, revealing how this dynamic feeds on deep insecurities and unmet needs.

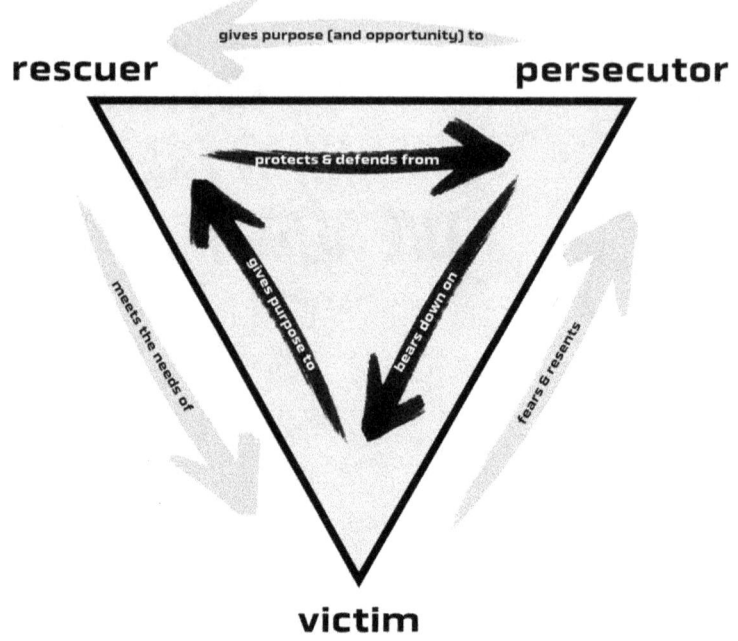

The Drama Triangle

HOW THE DRAMA TRIANGLE WORKS

At its heart, the Drama Triangle is a framework of disempowerment. It operates like an invisible play, with scripts and roles that we assume unconsciously. Sometimes, we cast ourselves into the roles, and other times, we are cast into them by others. The result is relational chaos, emotional suffering, and a profound sense of disconnection. Here's how the roles function:

The Victim: The Entry Point

The Victim role is where the Drama Triangle often begins. In this role, we feel **stuck**, powerless, trapped, and unable to meet our own needs, wants, and desires. The Victim believes that their circumstances are controlled entirely by external forces—other people, systems, or even their own limitations.

The Victim's inner narrative often sounds like this:

- "This isn't fair."
- "Why does this always happen to me?"
- "I can't do anything about it."
- "I can't _____ because you _____."

While hardship and suffering are real, the Victim's role is defined not by circumstances but by their belief in personal helplessness. The Victim's primary coping mechanism is blame, which externalizes their sense of powerlessness. Blame may be directed at others, a situation, or even themselves, reinforcing the perception that they are at the mercy of forces beyond their control.

The Persecutor: The Villain Causing the Victimhood

Once we assume the Victim role, the next step is assigning blame. Enter the Persecutor—the person, group, or situation we hold responsible for our suffering. Persecutors may be real or imagined, but the Victim perceives them as the villains who must change for their suffering to end.

From the Persecutor's perspective, this role often emerges as a defensive response to the Victim's blame. Feeling targeted or accused, the Persecutor may begin to see themselves as a Victim in their own counter-drama triangle. To protect themselves, they may focus on proving their superiority or "rightness" over the Victim, believing this will restore their sense of safety or control. This defensiveness often exacerbates the conflict, escalating the cycle.

Judgment fuels the Persecutor role. The Victim judges the Persecutor as cruel or unfair, while the Persecutor judges the

Victim as irrational or overly dependent. This mutual blame traps both parties, reinforcing disconnection and hostility.

The Rescuer: The False Savior Who Can Make It All Better

The Rescuer role might seem positive at first glance, but it's just as disempowering. The Rescuer steps in to "save" the Victim, often at the expense of their own well-being or boundaries. They take on the responsibility of fixing the Victim's situation, perpetuating the idea that the Victim cannot solve their own problems.

From the Rescuer's perspective, this role is often driven by insecurity. Rescuers derive their sense of worth and value from being needed by others. Their attempts to "help" are often rooted in a subconscious belief that their own worth is conditional—tied to their ability to solve problems or make others happy. This insecurity-based attempt to feel valuable inadvertently reinforces the Victim's dependence while depleting the Rescuer's emotional and mental energy.

When the Rescuer inevitably falls short—because no one can meet another person's needs perfectly—the Victim may reframe them as a Persecutor, setting the stage for deeper conflict. Meanwhile, the Rescuer may begin to feel resentment, frustration, or burnout, further straining the relationship.

Why the Drama Triangle Feels Like Reality

The Drama Triangle doesn't rely on physical barriers or advanced tactics—it works by distorting perception. It creates a powerful illusion that the roles are objective realities rather than mental constructs.

- The Victim feels justified in their powerlessness, convinced the Persecutor is entirely to blame.
- The Persecutor, feeling accused or misunderstood, often

doubles down on their position to assert control or superiority.
- The Rescuer sees themselves as noble, unaware their efforts are enabling the Victim's dependency.

Judgment and projection reinforce these perceptions, making the triangle feel like an unchangeable truth. For example:

- A boss offering constructive feedback might be perceived as a Persecutor.
- A friend who doesn't immediately respond to a text might be judged as an unfaithful Rescuer.
- We might even cast ourselves as Victims to an internal Persecutor—our own inner critic that tells us we're not enough.

These judgments are rarely based on objective truth. Instead, they are shaped by our fears, insecurities, past experiences, and learned behaviors. The Drama Triangle keeps us trapped by turning subjective interpretations into rigid "facts."

THE DRAMA TRIANGLE IN EVERYDAY LIFE

The Drama Triangle is the root of most relational disharmony. It's not limited to dramatic conflicts or personal relationships—it shows up in subtle ways every day:

- **In families:** A child might feel like a Victim to strict parents (Persecutors) and turn to a sibling or grandparent to play the Rescuer.
- **At work:** An employee might feel unappreciated (Victim), blame their boss (Persecutor), and expect a coworker to step in as the Rescuer.
- **In politics:** A political group might position themselves

as Victims, label an opposing party as Persecutors, and elevate their leader as the Rescuer.

THE DRAMA TRIANGLE AS A TOOL FOR MANIPULATION

The Drama Triangle is not just something we fall into; it's also something others use to manipulate and control us. A common tactic of those seeking power or influence is to create a Drama Triangle in which:

1. We are cast as Victims.
2. Another person or group is framed as the Persecutor.
3. The manipulator positions themselves as the Rescuer.

For example:

- A politician might claim, "You're being oppressed by [group X] (Persecutor), but if you vote for me or this legislation (Rescuer), I'll save you."
- An advertiser might say, "You're missing out on happiness (Victim) because you don't own our product (Persecutor). Buy now, and we'll fix that for you (Rescuer)!"

These manipulations thrive because they tap into our fears and insecurities, pulling us deeper into the triangle and solidifying our belief in the roles.

BEING ROPED INTO OTHER PEOPLE'S TRIANGLES

The Drama Triangle traps us not only in our own minds but also often ropes us into the dramas of others.

- A friend vents about their partner, casting themselves as

the Victim and their partner as the Persecutor, and expects you to play the Rescuer.
- A coworker complains about unfair treatment, urging you to confront the "offender" on their behalf.
- A family member positions themselves as the Victim of a sibling's actions, hoping you'll step in as the Rescuer.

While these dynamics can feel compelling, participating only reinforces the triangle's power and perpetuates relational disharmony.

> There was a time when my marriage felt like it was unraveling before my eyes. At the heart of it, though I couldn't see it at the time, was the insidious dynamic of the Drama Triangle. It wasn't just a passing conflict or a bad patch—it was a repeating cycle that pulled us deeper into blame, resentment, and emotional exhaustion.
>
> For years, I had unknowingly settled into the 'Victim' role, believing I was carrying an unfair share of the burden. I felt overwhelmed by the responsibilities of providing for the family, solving problems, and keeping everything running smoothly. I saw my wife, Zelda—someone I loved deeply—as the 'Persecutor' in this dynamic. In my mind, she wasn't doing enough. She didn't see my sacrifices or appreciate the weight I was carrying. Every small disagreement became proof that I was alone in the struggle. "Why doesn't she care more?" I'd think. "Why is everything left to me?"
>
> On the other side, she had her own lens. She felt like I was the 'Persecutor,' constantly judging her for not being "enough." She was trying her best in ways I couldn't fully understand at the time, but my frustration and passive-aggressive comments made her feel like she was failing. Her

response was to shut down emotionally, which only deepened my sense of abandonment. We were caught in a loop—each of us feeling like the 'Victim' and seeing the other as the 'Persecutor.'

And then there was the 'Rescuer' role, which I slipped into often. When things felt unbearable, I'd overcompensate by trying to fix everything. I'd work harder and longer or force cheerful solutions in conversations, thinking that if I just tried harder, everything would be okay. But it wasn't okay. My "rescuing" wasn't fixing the real problem—it was just making me more resentful when my efforts weren't appreciated. And for her, it felt patronizing, like I didn't trust her to meet me as an equal partner.

The triangle tightened its grip. Zelda began withdrawing more, and I responded by escalating my judgments and trying even harder to "rescue" the situation. I frequently had bad arguments in which I said things like, "I'm doing everything for this family, and you don't even care!" Her face would contort, and she would quietly say, "Do you think I don't feel the same way about you?"

Those moments usually hit me hard. I didn't like to hear it, but it forced me to reflect. The truth was, she had been feeling just as abandoned and unseen as I had. And it wasn't because we didn't love each other—it was because we had been trapped in the Drama Triangle for years without realizing it.

We had each cast ourselves as the 'Victim' in our own minds. We had each seen the other as the 'Persecutor,' blaming them for our pain. And ironically, in our efforts to fix things, we had each tried to play the 'Rescuer,' only to end up exhausted, resentful, and further apart.

It was a turning point—not because everything magically resolved at that moment, but because I started to see the dynamic for what it was. I began to realize how much judgment I had brought into our relationship, not just of her but of myself. I had been so convinced of my own helplessness that I couldn't see how I was feeding the cycle.

Breaking free wasn't easy, and it took patience and practice. But that moment of clarity was the beginning. I started to take ownership of my role in the triangle, to step out of the 'Victim' mindset, and to see my partner not as a Persecutor but as someone who was struggling alongside me. It was the hardest work I'd ever done, but it was also the most important.

Looking back, I can see how the Drama Triangle almost ended my marriage. It created a story in which we were enemies instead of allies, and love was buried beneath layers of blame and resentment. But I also see how breaking free from that story saved us—because once we saw the triangle for what it was, we could finally step out of it together.

MAIN TAKEAWAY: THE DRAMA TRIANGLE IS A MIND TRAP, NOT REALITY

The Drama Triangle is a subtle yet pervasive dynamic that distorts relationships, fuels disconnection, and keeps us stuck in cycles of blame, judgment, and unmet needs. Its roles—Victim, Persecutor, and Rescuer—may feel like objective realities, but they are mental constructs rooted in fear, insecurity, and conditioned behaviors. Recognizing the Drama Triangle for what it is—a trap rather than truth—is the first step toward breaking free.

By understanding its mechanics, we gain the power to disrupt its hold, reclaim our autonomy, and foster healthier relationships. The path to freedom starts with awareness: stepping out of judgment, questioning our narratives, and seeing others—and ourselves—through a lens of compassion and shared humanity. This shift doesn't just free us from the Drama Triangle—it opens the door to connection, empowerment, and thriving.

COMING UP NEXT: HOW TO BEGIN EXITING THE MIND TRAP

Stepping out of the Drama Triangle requires challenging its foundation: judgment. In **Parts 2 and 3**, we'll explore why judgment feels so automatic, why choice can feel so hard, and how to begin dismantling the perceptions and narratives that keep us stuck. For now, the key is to recognize the Drama Triangle for what it is: a mind trap that distorts reality and keeps us from thriving.

COMMON RESPONSES

> "Yeah, but sometimes I really am a victim. How is that a role I need to escape?"

Acknowledging genuine harm or injustice is important—being victimized is real and deserves compassion. The key distinction here is between being a victim of circumstances and adopting the Victim role. The role traps you in helplessness while stepping out allows you to reclaim your power to heal and respond.

> "Yeah, but isn't rescuing someone a good thing? Why is it a problem?"

Helping others is a beautiful thing, but rescuing often crosses the line into disempowering them. When we rescue them, we inadvertently rein-

WHAT TO DO WHEN THE ALIENS SHOW UP (AND EVEN IF THEY DON'T)

force their sense of helplessness and neglect our own boundaries. True support uplifts without taking over—it's about empowering, not fixing.

"Yeah, but isn't assigning blame sometimes justified?"

It's natural to want to assign blame when we're hurt or frustrated. However, blame often perpetuates the cycle of conflict and disconnection. Shifting from blame to accountability—acknowledging what's yours to own and what's not—creates space for resolution and growth.

"Yeah, but isn't judgment necessary to hold people accountable for their actions?"

That's an important distinction to make, and you're absolutely right that accountability matters. Judgment often focuses on blame, labeling someone as "bad" or "wrong," which can lead to shame and disconnection. Accountability, on the other hand, is about acknowledging actions and their consequences while fostering growth and repair. It's not about condemnation—it's about creating space for transformation. By shifting from judgment to accountability, you encourage positive change instead of reinforcing cycles of conflict or defensiveness.

"Yeah, but what if the other person doesn't want to leave the Drama Triangle?"

You can't control others, but you can change how you engage with them. When you step out of the triangle, you stop feeding its dynamics. Over time, this shift often inspires change in others—or at least allows you to protect your own well-being without reinforcing the cycle.

REFLECTION QUESTIONS

1. Where in your life have you noticed the roles of Victim, Persecutor, or Rescuer appearing?
2. Have you ever felt pulled into someone else's Drama Triangle? How did it affect you?
3. Can you identify instances where a person or system manipulated you using the Drama Triangle? What helped you see it clearly?
4. How might recognizing the Drama Triangle change how you approach conflicts or relational challenges?

CHAPTER FIFTEEN
HOW PAPA CHANGES EVERYTHING
CHOOSING YOUR PATH IN THE HEAT OF BATTLE

Between stimulus and response, there is a space. In that space is our power to choose our response. In our response lies our growth and our freedom. – Viktor Frankl

---

IN THE LAST CHAPTER, WE UNCOVERED THE DRAMA TRIANGLE AS A mind trap fueled by judgment and disconnection that keeps us locked in cycles of blame, resentment, and helplessness. We saw how these roles—Victim, Persecutor, and Rescuer—distort our relationships and our sense of self, pulling us into narratives that reinforce disempowerment. But escaping the Drama Triangle isn't just about recognizing the roles we play; it's about cultivating the awareness to step out of them.

Awareness is the key. It's the tool that allows us to catch ourselves in the act of judgment, projection, or reactivity before we spiral into the same old patterns. Awareness is what enables us to pause, reassess, and choose a different path—a path of clarity, courage, and intentionality. Without awareness, we're stuck, repeating the same cycles and reenacting the same stories. With awareness, we create the space to rewrite those stories.

This chapter builds on that foundation by delving deeper into the moment of awareness, the crossroads where every choice is made. Whether we remain trapped in the Drama Triangle or move into the Empowerment Dynamic begins in this split-second decision. It's in this space—between reaction and response—that we reclaim our sovereignty and begin the counteroffensive against the invaders' tactics.

AWARENESS AT THE CROSSROADS

The battlefield of our minds is won or lost in a single moment: the crossroads of awareness. It's the split-second when an emotion flares, a thought arises, or judgment takes hold, and we're faced with a *choice*. Do we let the invaders take control, or do we pause, observe, and act with intention?

This chapter is about recognizing those crossroads and cultivating the awareness to navigate them skillfully. It's about learning that we have a choice and beginning to exercise it. It's about slowing down, listening to and understanding our emotions, and reclaiming our power to choose. Awareness isn't just the first step in the counteroffensive—it's the foundation upon which every other step depends.

EMOTIONS AS YOUR INNER DASHBOARD

Our emotions are not enemies to be avoided or suppressed. They're messengers, flashing like warning lights on a dashboard, alerting us to what's happening inside. When we feel anxiety, anger, or frustration, it's not a sign that something is wrong with us—it's a signal that something needs our attention. I find that emotions are the body's indicator that we are in a Drama Triangle or headed into one.

For example:

- **Anxiety** might signal that we're placing our sense of security in something external or uncertain (a Rescuer).
- **Anger** might reveal that a boundary has been crossed or that judgment is fueling a narrative of blame (a Persecutor).
- **Frustration** might point to unmet expectations or a deeper need for connection or validation (a Victim).

Even when uncomfortable, these emotions are *gifts*. They allow us to pause, reflect, and choose a response that aligns with our values and goals.

THE CROSSROADS MOMENT

The crossroads moment is the instant when we notice an emotional reaction. It's the moment we feel our heart race, our chest tighten, our face flush, or a myriad of physiological signs that we experience as our mind starts to spiral into a story of stuckness. At that moment, we're standing at a fork in the road:

- **Path 1:** *React* impulsively, letting our programming of judgment and old patterns dictate our actions.
- **Path 2:** Pause, observe, and *respond* intentionally, reclaiming our power and agency.

The first path is the road most traveled. It's the path of reactivity, where emotions lead to assumptions, assumptions lead to judgment, and judgment leads to *disconnection*. But the second path—the path of awareness—is where transformation begins. But… we have to choose this path before we can experience that.

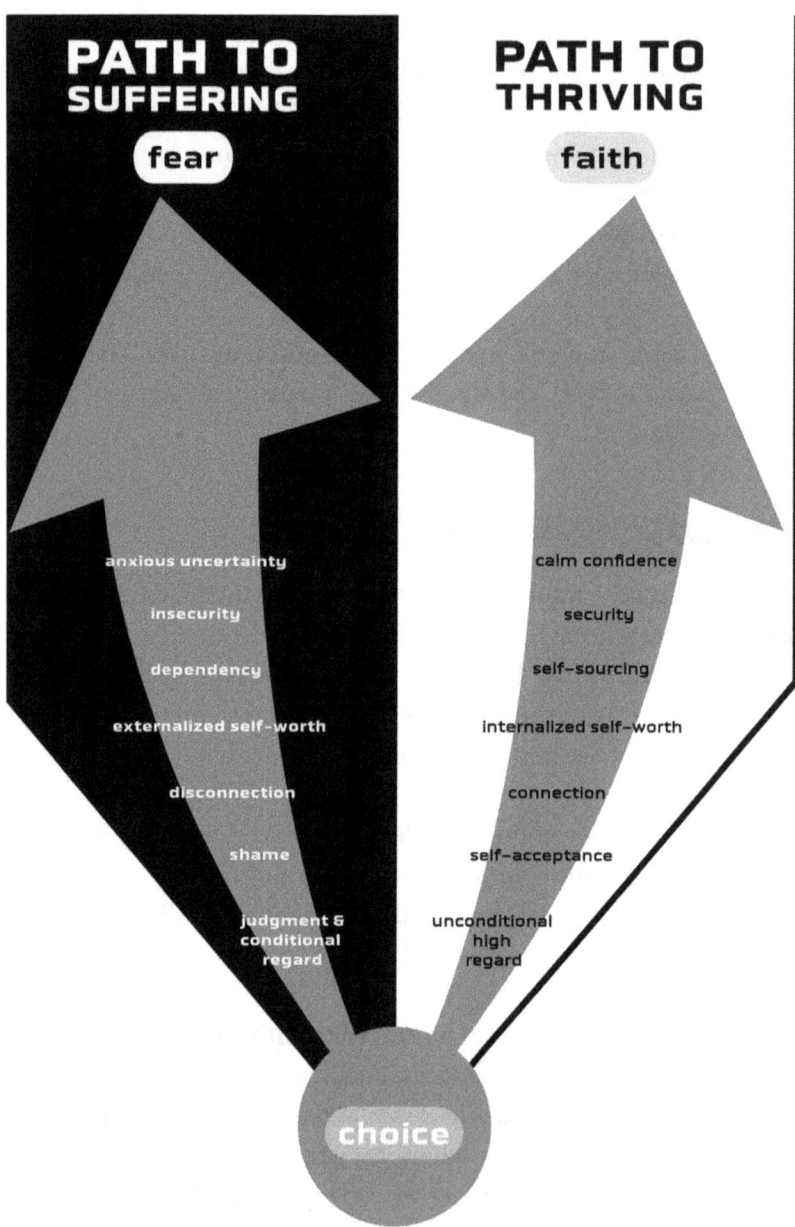

The Crossroads: A Choice Between Two Paths

THE PAPA METHOD: NAVIGATING THE CROSSROADS

To navigate these moments, I developed a simple yet powerful technique called **PAPA**. When we feel uncomfortable emotions, we can take them to PAPA, not to make them go away, but to understand what they're telling us:

Step #1: Pause

- Stop and take a breath. Pausing interrupts the cycle of reactivity and gives us space to observe.
- Practice box breathing: inhale for 4–8 seconds, hold for the same duration, exhale for 4–8 seconds, and hold again. Repeat 6–8 times to calm our nervous system and quiet the fight-or-flight response. Doing this for eight rounds helps us avoid the initial reactivity we're used to experiencing.

Step #2: Assess

- Check-in with ourselves. Ask, "Am I okay at this moment?" Perform a body scan. Notice tension, shallow breathing, or disconnection.
- Reflect on our basic needs: Are we well-rested, hydrated, and fed? Have we been practicing gratitude? What are we feeling emotionally and physically right now? These basic physical needs play a significant role in our emotional resilience. Attend to these needs first before continuing.

Step #3: Process

- Evaluate our thoughts and emotions with openness, non-judgment, and curiosity. Ask:

- What am I *observing*? (The facts—what is happening that everyone could agree on.)
- What am I *inferring*? (What seems likely based on those facts.)
- What am I *interpreting*? (The meaning I'm assigning to the situation.)

Our interpretations are where things often go awry. We tend to treat them as objective reality—a factual representation of what is happening. But in truth, interpretations are subjective and heavily influenced by our personal experiences, worldviews, and emotional states. Most often, they reflect our inner fears, insecurities, and past patterns more than they reflect the situation itself. For instance, when we harbor hostility, disrespect, or contempt toward ourselves, we may unconsciously project these feelings onto others, misinterpreting their behavior as reflecting our internal state. This dynamic is like seeing a distorted image in a mirror and assuming it's reality.

Take the example of a friend not replying to a text. The observation might simply be, "They haven't responded yet." But our interpretation could turn into, "That's rude! Obviously, they're upset with me. What's their problem? I wonder what I did to make them angry." Or perhaps, "Clearly, they don't value our relationship." These conclusions, often framed with words like "clearly" and "obviously," suggest certainty but are usually rooted in our own fears or insecurities—perhaps from past experiences of rejection or abandonment—rather than in the friend's actual intentions or feelings.

Words like "clearly" and "obviously" are red flags in our interpretations. They signal that we've closed the door to curiosity and locked ourselves into a single narrative. These judgments usually say more about our inner emotional landscape than the external reality we're interpreting.

Such interpretations often stem from internalized narratives or "scripts" shaped by past experiences. If we've been overlooked or dismissed in previous relationships, for example, we may unconsciously project those feelings onto new situations, even when there's no evidence to support them. This habitual pattern reinforces feelings of insecurity, judgment, and disconnection.

By noticing these mental habits and challenging the language we use to frame situations, we can disrupt this cycle of assumption and reactivity. Instead of jumping to conclusions, we can ask ourselves:

- "Am I creating a drama triangle, or participating in someone else's?"
- "What else could be going on here?"
- "Is there any direct evidence to support my interpretation?"
- "How might my past experiences or fears be influencing how I'm viewing this situation?"

This shift from assumption to curiosity is central to cultivating awareness. It allows us to step back from automatic reactions and engage with the present moment more thoughtfully. Over time, this practice can transform not only how we interpret situations but also how we respond to them, leading to greater clarity, connection, and emotional resilience.

It is critical to recognize the tendency to conflate interpretations with objective truth. It's often not the observation itself but our subjective interpretation that triggers judgment, distress, and emotional reactivity. By challenging these interpretations and treating them as hypotheses rather than facts, we can separate reality from the stories our minds create. This can lead to more thoughtful, intentional responses.

Step #4: Address

- Start by addressing our own emotional needs. Ask: *What*

do I need right now? How can I meet that need without seeking external validation?
- For example, if we're feeling anxious about an unanswered text, instead of spiraling into self-doubt, we can address the deeper need for reassurance by affirming our own worth: *I am enough, regardless of others' actions.*

A PRACTICAL EXAMPLE: THE UNANSWERED TEXT

Imagine we've sent a text to a friend, and hours have passed without a reply. Anxiety creeps in, along with thoughts like, *They're upset with me,* or, *They don't value our friendship.*

Here's how we might apply PAPA:

- **Pause:** Take a moment to breathe and calm our nervous system.
- **Assess:** Notice the tension in our body and ask, "Am I okay right now?" Yes—we're physically safe and secure.
- **Process:** Break down the situation:
  - **Observation:** My friend hasn't replied to my text.
  - **Inference:** They might be busy or preoccupied.
  - **Interpretation:** They're upset with me or don't care about me.
    - Recognize that the interpretation is rooted in insecurity, not fact.
- **Address:** Reassure ourselves that our worth isn't tied to how quickly someone replies. We matter, regardless. Then, choose an intentional next step—perhaps reaching out to another friend or engaging in self-care.

AWARENESS: THE GATEWAY TO FREEDOM

Awareness is the gateway to freedom. Without it, we're at the mercy of our emotions, judgments, and old patterns. We fall into the

Drama Triangle without even realizing it, engaging in dynamics that lead to frustration, resentment, and disconnection. Victims remain powerless, Rescuers become overburdened and burned out, and Persecutors escalate conflict or withdraw in anger. The outcomes of these dynamics are predictable: broken relationships, unfulfilled needs, and a growing sense of despair and dissatisfaction.

With awareness, however, we gain clarity, control, and the ability to choose responses that align with our values and goals. Awareness allows us to recognize when we're slipping into the Drama Triangle and to consciously shift into the Empowerment Dynamic instead. This shift transforms interactions and outcomes:

- **From Frustration to Growth:** Challenges that once felt overwhelming now become opportunities for personal and relational growth.
- **From Resentment to Connection:** Instead of blame or resentment, we experience mutual respect, collaboration, and genuine understanding.
- **From Disconnection to Flourishing:** The Empowerment Dynamic fosters healthier relationships, creativity, and a sense of shared purpose.

Awareness doesn't eliminate challenges—it empowers us to face them with courage and intentionality. It helps us step out of reactive cycles and into proactive, life-affirming choices. In doing so, it leads to outcomes that reflect the best of who we are: connection, empowerment, and thriving relationships.

When we practice awareness, we reclaim our agency. We no longer operate as victims of circumstance but as creators of our own lives, able to navigate challenges with clarity and confidence. Awareness opens the door to transformation, inviting us to move from cycles of fear and blame into a life of empowerment and purpose.

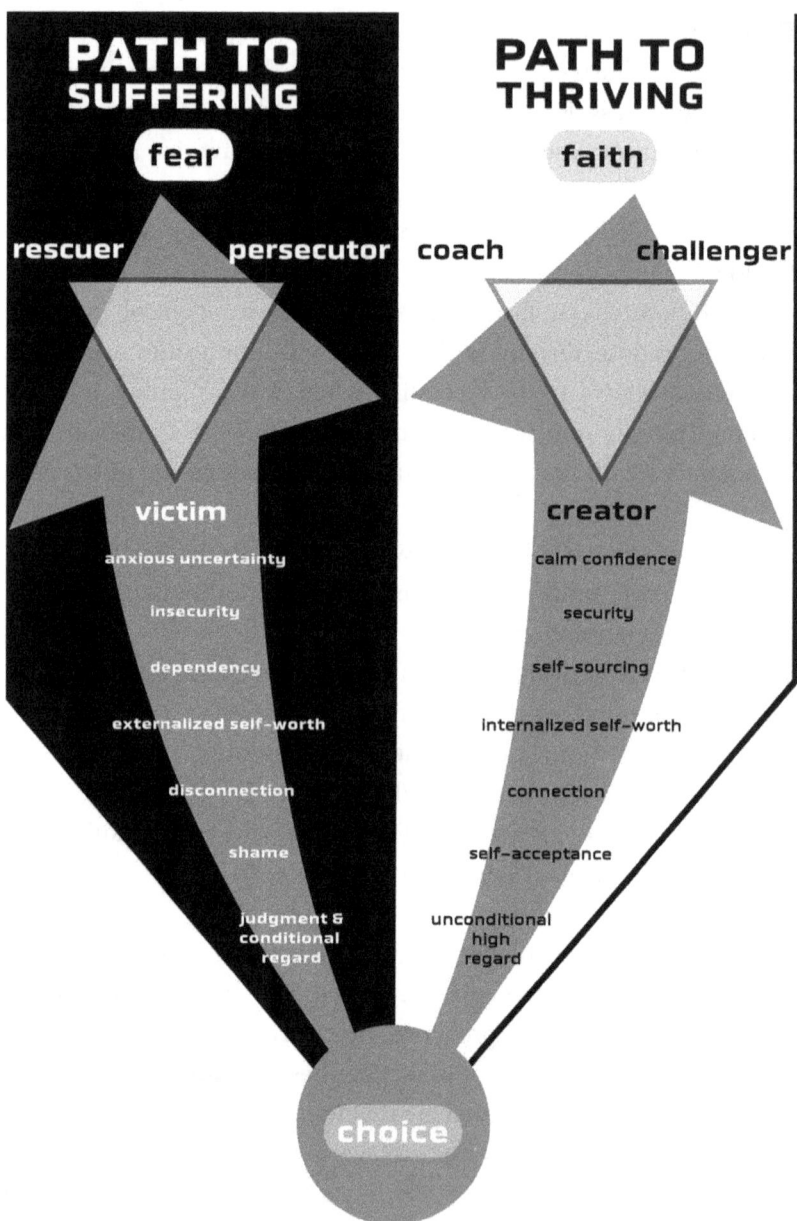

Paths to Drama and Disconnection or Empowerment and Connection

WHAT TO DO WHEN THE ALIENS SHOW UP (AND EVEN IF THEY DON'T)

BUILDING THE HABIT OF AWARENESS

AWARENESS TAKES PRACTICE. At first, we might only notice our reactivity after the fact. That's okay. The more we practice pausing, assessing, processing, and addressing, the more natural it will become. Over time, we'll find ourselves catching reactive patterns earlier and replacing them with empowered choices.

BEWARE OF TRYING TO BE AWARENESS FOR OTHERS

Awareness is a deeply personal journey. While it's natural to want to help others see what you've discovered—especially if you see them caught in patterns of suffering or reactive behaviors—trying to be the awareness for someone else often backfires. It can lead to conflict, misunderstanding, and disconnection, and it risks pulling you into the Drama Triangle.

Here's why trying to "wake someone up" can be counterproductive:

1. It Often Feels Like Judgment

When we point out someone's patterns, interpretations, or emotional reactions without their invitation, it can feel like criticism—even if that wasn't our intention. In their eyes, this may cast us into the role of the Persecutor, creating defensiveness or resistance rather than clarity.

2. It Disempowers the Other Person

Stepping into someone's awareness journey without their permission robs them of agency. Instead of empowering them to make their own discoveries, it positions us as the "expert" or "rescuer," which can reinforce their Victim mindset.

3. It Risks Emotional Enmeshment

Trying to guide someone else's awareness often draws us into their emotional terrain, leaving us vulnerable to their reactions. Instead of holding space for them, we risk getting entangled in their story and losing our own center.

4. Awareness Must Be Chosen, Not Forced

True transformation comes from within. People must choose to confront their emotions, thoughts, and patterns in their own time and on their own terms. Trying to rush or force this process often creates resistance rather than openness.

FOCUS ON SUPPORTING, NOT FIXING

Instead of trying to create awareness for someone else, focus on supporting them where they are. Respond with empathy, compassion, and curiosity. Say things like:

- *"That sounds really overwhelming. How are you feeling about it?"*
- *"It makes sense that you'd feel that way, given what's happening."*

These responses validate their emotional experience without judgment or interference, creating a safe space for them to explore their own awareness.

If they invite your perspective or express curiosity about your views, you can gently offer insights or alternative interpretations—but only after asking for permission. For example:

- *"Would you be open to hearing a different perspective on this?"*

By asking, you honor their autonomy and give them a choice,

WHAT TO DO WHEN THE ALIENS SHOW UP (AND EVEN IF THEY DON'T)

reinforcing their role as the Creator of their own awareness journey.

A NOTE ABOUT WHAT'S COMING NEXT

We'll explore this concept further in the next chapter, where we introduce the roles of Challenger and Coach within the Empowerment Dynamic. These roles offer a framework for supporting others in their growth without falling into the traps of the Drama Triangle. For now, focus on cultivating your own awareness and creating space for others to do the same at their own pace.

> There was a time when I prided myself on my ability to "read people." I truly believed I had a gift for knowing what others were thinking or feeling, often without them saying a word. If someone gave me a certain look, used a particular tone of voice, or paused a beat too long in a conversation, I immediately knew what was going on: they were upset, disappointed, or judging me. At least, that's what I told myself. I thought I was being empathetic—sensitive to the emotions of others—but in reality, I was living in a world of my own interpretations, assigning meaning to every action or word without ever questioning it.
>
> At work, a coworker's short reply or distracted expression meant I had done something wrong or that they didn't like me. In my marriage, if my wife seemed quiet or tired, I'd assume it was because she was angry with me—even if she hadn't said a word to suggest that. With my kids, their grumpy moods became evidence that I wasn't doing enough as a parent. I didn't just believe these stories; I felt them in my body—tight chest, anxious mind, spiraling thoughts. And because I never questioned them, I reacted to these

assumptions as though they were true, often pulling others into a Drama Triangle they didn't even know existed.

It wasn't until I began learning to pause and challenge these automatic interpretations that I realized just how much I had been projecting my own fears, insecurities, and stories onto the people around me. I wasn't reading others—I was reacting to my own inner chaos. Once I started asking questions like, "What else could be true here?" and "Is there evidence for this?" my entire perspective began to shift.

At work, I learned to ask clarifying questions instead of assuming someone's frustration was my fault. In my marriage, I discovered that my wife's quiet moments were often just her being tired, not angry. And with my kids, I stopped taking their moods personally and began to show up with curiosity and support instead of guilt and overreaction. The change was nothing short of transformative. My relationships improved, my stress levels dropped, and I felt more connected to the people I loved because I was finally seeing them—not my assumptions about them.

It was humbling to realize how off I'd been for so long, but it was also freeing. I didn't have to play mind-reader anymore. I could simply show up, ask questions, and choose responses based on clarity rather than fear. And that changed everything.

THE MAIN TAKEAWAY: AWARENESS IS THE FIRST ACT OF SOVEREIGNTY

Awareness is the foundation of our counteroffensive. It's the skill that allows us to see the invaders' tactics, disrupt their control, and reclaim our power to choose. By cultivating awareness at the crossroads of our thoughts and emotions, we take the first step toward creating a life of freedom, connection, and thriving.

COMING UP: EMOTIONAL AWARENESS AS YOUR INNER COMPASS

In the next chapter, we'll explore the crucial role of emotional awareness in sustaining the Empowerment Dynamic. Our emotions function as signals—our internal compass guiding us toward alignment or signaling misalignment. By mastering emotional awareness, we'll disrupt reactive patterns, strengthen our role as a Creator, and navigate challenges with clarity and intentionality. This is the next step in reclaiming our sovereignty and living with courage and purpose.

COMMON RESPONSES

"Yeah, but awareness doesn't stop my emotions from being overwhelming."

You're right—awareness doesn't erase emotions. It helps us hold space for them instead of being swept away. Emotions, even overwhelming ones, are messengers. Awareness allows us to listen to them with curiosity rather than fear, creating room to process and respond.

"Yeah, but pausing feels impossible when I'm in the heat of the moment."

Pausing takes practice—it's a skill, not an instant fix. It's okay if you don't catch yourself every time. Start small, even if it's just one deep breath before reacting. Over time, pausing will feel less forced and more natural as you build the habit.

"Yeah, but how do I know if my interpretations are wrong?"

You don't have to be certain right away. Awareness is about questioning your assumptions and holding them lightly. Ask yourself, "What else could be true?" This isn't about dismissing your feelings but about opening the door to alternative perspectives.

"Yeah, but what if someone is actually trying to hurt me or doesn't care?"

If harm or neglect is real, awareness doesn't mean ignoring it—it means addressing it with clarity and intention. Awareness helps you separate your emotions from the facts so you can respond in a way that protects your well-being without escalating the situation unnecessarily.

"Yeah, but I don't trust myself to handle things without reacting."

Self-trust grows with practice. Start by noticing your reactions without judgment—this alone is a huge step. Over time, as you use tools like the PAPA method, you'll begin to see yourself navigating challenges with more calm and confidence. It's a process and every small step matters.

REFLECTION QUESTIONS

1. What situations in your life consistently trigger reactive thoughts or emotions?

WHAT TO DO WHEN THE ALIENS SHOW UP (AND EVEN IF THEY DON'T)

2. How might pausing and practicing gratitude shift your perspective in those moments?
3. What interpretations or judgments are you holding onto that might not be true?
4. How can you begin using the PAPA method to navigate your emotional crossroads?

CHAPTER SIXTEEN
INTERCEPTING & INTERROGATING THE INVADERS
CHALLENGING ASSUMPTIONS TO RECLAIM YOUR SOVEREIGNTY

Every man takes the limits of his own field of vision for the limits of the world. – Arthur Schopenhauer

---

CHALLENGING ASSUMPTIONS AND REWRITING NARRATIVES

IN THE LAST CHAPTER, WE EXAMINED THE CROSSROADS OF AWARENESS, where every decision shapes the direction of our lives. We explored how awareness allows us to pause, assess, and choose intentionally rather than reacting impulsively. But the crossroads are only the beginning. To truly reclaim our sovereignty, we must take a closer look at the stories we tell ourselves—the interpretations that shape our perceptions of reality.

Our inner narratives, often fueled by red flag words and automatic assumptions, play a pivotal role in how we experience life. If left unchecked, these stories can mirror the dynamics of the Drama Triangle, pulling us into cycles of blame, shame, and disconnection. This chapter is about challenging those narratives, questioning their validity, and rewriting them in ways that foster clarity, connection, and empowerment.

THE MECHANICS OF INTERPRETATION

At the heart of every emotional reaction is an interpretation—a story we create to explain what we observe. These interpretations are not objective truths but subjective constructs shaped by our personal histories, emotional states, and ingrained patterns of thinking.

How Interpretations Form:

1. **Observation:** We perceive something through our senses, such as a facial expression, tone of voice, or behavior.
2. **Inference:** We make a guess about what the observation might mean.
3. **Interpretation:** We assign meaning based on our internal scripts, which are often shaped by past experiences or fears.

For example:

- **Observation:** *"My friend hasn't replied to my text."*
- **Inference:** *"They might be busy."*
- **Interpretation:** *"Clearly, they don't value me. Obviously, I must have upset them."*

These interpretations often feel true because they arise automatically and are framed by red flag words—like *clearly* or *obviously*—that make our assumptions feel certain. But in reality, these narratives reveal more about our inner emotional landscape than they do about the external situation.

BEGIN NOTICING THE RED FLAGS

Red flag words are clues that our interpretations may not be grounded in reality. They reveal rigid or judgmental thinking that can escalate our emotions and perpetuate Drama Triangle dynamics.

Categories of Red Flag Words:

1. **Certainty Words:** *Clearly, obviously, definitely.*
    - These suggest we've closed the door to curiosity and decided something is true without evidence.
2. **Generalizing Words:** *Always, never, everyone, no one.*
    - These exaggerate patterns, making situations feel universal and unchangeable.
3. **Judgmental Words:** *Lazy, selfish, uncaring.*
    - These assign moral blame and reflect internalized shame or resentment.
4. **Catastrophic Words:** *Terrible, ruined, disastrous.*
    - These magnify events, creating a sense of hopelessness.
5. **Shame Words:** *Should, ought, must.*
    - These reflect internalized standards that make anything less than perfection feel unacceptable.

These words are not just harmless habits—they're indicators of the narratives that keep us stuck in judgment, fear, and disconnection.

THE HARM OF RED FLAG WORDS

Words like *should* or *always* may seem small, but they carry enormous weight. They shape the way we see ourselves, others, and the world. For example:

- Saying, "I should have done better," frames a mistake as a failure of character rather than an opportunity to learn.
- Telling ourselves, "They never listen to me," creates a

story of disconnection and resentment, even if the evidence doesn't fully support it.

By recognizing these words in our internal dialogue, we can begin to challenge the assumptions they reinforce.

ISN'T THIS JUST MINCING WORDS?

You might wonder, *Does it really matter which words I use? Isn't this just splitting hairs?* On the surface, it might seem that way. But words are not just descriptors—they're tools that shape how we think, feel, and act.

HOW WORDS PROGRAM THE BRAIN

Our brains are wired to create patterns, and the words we use reinforce those patterns. Repeated phrases like *I always fail* or *no one cares* create neural pathways that make these beliefs feel automatic and unchangeable. Over time, our inner language shapes our perceptions, and our perceptions shape our experiences.

For example:

- Words like *always* or *never* create rigid thinking, convincing us that situations or people are unchangeable.
- Words like *should* or *must* fuel feelings of inadequacy or guilt, placing unnecessary pressure on ourselves or others.
- Words like *clearly* or *obviously* shut down curiosity and alternative perspectives, locking us into judgment.

Changing these patterns begins with changing our language. By intentionally replacing limiting words with more compassionate, flexible alternatives, we create new mental scripts that open the door to growth and connection.

TRANSFORMING OUR INNER NARRATIVES

The first step to rewriting our inner stories is awareness. Once we notice the red flag words and limiting language in our thoughts, we can begin to challenge and replace them.

PRACTICAL STEPS FOR TRANSFORMATION:

1. Notice the Stories You're Telling

Pay attention to your inner dialogue, especially in moments of emotional reactivity. Look for red flag words like *clearly* or *never* that signal rigid or judgmental thinking.

2. Pause and Question

When you notice a red flag word, pause and ask yourself:

- *"What else could be going on here?"*
- *"Is there evidence to support my interpretation?"*
- *"How might my past experiences be shaping this narrative?"*

3. Reframe with Curiosity

Replace judgmental language with open-ended questions or compassionate statements. For example:

- Instead of, *"They're ignoring me,"* try, *"I wonder if they're busy or distracted."*

4. Challenge Shame Words

When you catch yourself using *should, ought,* or *must,* pause and reflect:

- *"Who set this standard, and is it realistic?"*
- *"What would it feel like to release this pressure and embrace what is?"*

BUILDING NEW NARRATIVES WITH PAPA

Let's revisit the unanswered text example and apply the **PAPA** approach to navigate the situation with greater awareness and intentionality:

Step 1: Pause

Take a moment to breathe and interrupt the cycle of automatic reactivity. Instead of immediately spiraling into assumptions, calm your mind and body:

- Take a deep breath and exhale slowly.
- Remind yourself, *"I don't have to solve this right now. Let's take a moment to assess."*

Step 2: Assess

Check in with yourself. What are you feeling physically and emotionally in response to this situation? Ask:

- *"Am I okay right now?"*
- Perform a quick body scan. Notice tension, rapid breathing, or other signs of anxiety.
- Reflect on your basic needs. Are you well-rested, hydrated, or hungry? Address these if needed to build resilience.

Step 3: Process

WHAT TO DO WHEN THE ALIENS SHOW UP (AND EVEN IF THEY DON'T)

Evaluate the facts, inferences, and interpretations behind your reaction:

- **Observation:** *"My friend hasn't replied to my text."* (This is the objective fact.)
- **Inference:** *"They might be busy or preoccupied."* (This is a neutral, logical guess.)
- **Initial Interpretation:** *"Clearly, they're upset with me. Obviously, I must have done something wrong."* (This is an emotional story shaped by assumptions.)

Notice the red flag words in your interpretation (*clearly, obviously*) and how they create certainty around an unverified assumption. Ask yourself:

- *"Is there evidence to support this interpretation?"*
- *"What else could be going on here?"*
- *"How might my past experiences or fears be influencing how I'm viewing this?"*

By examining the language and assumptions in your internal narrative, you create space for alternative explanations and reduce emotional reactivity.

Step 4: Address

Shift your focus from external validation to internal reassurance. Ask:

- *"What do I need right now to feel okay?"*
- For example: *"I need to remind myself that my worth isn't dependent on how quickly someone replies. I matter regardless."*

Choose a thoughtful next step that reflects self-compassion and intentionality:

- **Reframe the Story:** *"Maybe they're preoccupied, and it has nothing to do with me. I'll give them space and check in later."*
- **Take Action:** If appropriate, decide on a time to follow up. Or, redirect your energy to something that nourishes you in the moment—reading, connecting with another friend, or practicing gratitude.

By walking through **PAPA**, we transform our experience of the situation. Instead of reacting impulsively or dwelling in assumptions, we engage with curiosity, clarity, and agency. This process not only reduces unnecessary distress but also fosters healthier relationships—both with ourselves and others.

THE TURNING POINT

Challenging our interpretations isn't just about thinking more positively; it's about reclaiming our agency. Every time we notice a red flag word, question a limiting narrative, or reframe a judgment, we're stepping out of disempowered thinking and into clarity and choice.

In the context of an invasion—whether metaphorical or literal—this skill is essential. The invaders thrive on our unexamined assumptions and emotional reactivity. But when we pause, evaluate, and rewrite the story, we disrupt their hold and reclaim our sovereignty.

COMING UP NEXT: EMOTIONAL AWARENESS AS YOUR INNER COMPASS

In the next chapter, we'll explore how emotional awareness acts as a guide, signaling when we're aligned—or misaligned—with our values and goals. By mastering emotional awareness, we'll take another step toward dismantling the invaders' tactics and reclaiming our power to choose.

COMMON RESPONSES

"Yeah, but isn't questioning every thought exhausting?"

It can feel that way at first, especially if you've been running on autopilot for a long time. The goal isn't to overanalyze every thought—it's to catch the ones that create unnecessary suffering. With practice, this becomes second nature, like noticing when you're walking into a trap and stepping aside.

"Yeah, but what if my interpretation is right? Shouldn't I prepare for the worst?"

It's natural to want to protect yourself, and preparing for challenges is wise. But there's a difference between thoughtful preparation and jumping to catastrophic conclusions. By questioning your interpretations, you gain clarity, which allows you to respond effectively instead of reacting impulsively.

"Yeah, but isn't it just splitting hairs to focus on words like 'always' or 'should'?"

It might seem small, but language shapes how we think and feel. Words like 'always' and 'should' create rigid patterns that close off possibilities. By noticing and adjusting these words, you open yourself to flexibility and growth, which leads to more empowered thinking.

"Yeah, but aren't some stories just part of who I am?"

The stories we tell ourselves often feel deeply ingrained, but that doesn't mean they're fixed. Think of them as habits—patterns learned over time. The good news is habits can be changed. Rewriting your narratives doesn't erase your experiences; it reframes them in ways that serve your growth.

"Yeah, but what if challenging my stories makes me feel even more uncertain?"

Uncertainty can be uncomfortable, but it's also where growth happens. When you let go of rigid narratives, you create space for curiosity and possibility. It's not about erasing certainty; it's about finding freedom in exploring new perspectives that align more closely with your truth.

REFLECTION QUESTIONS

1. What red flag words do you notice most often in your inner dialogue?
2. How have past experiences shaped the stories you tell yourself about current situations?
3. What would it feel like to replace assumptions with curiosity in your relationships?
4. How might challenging shame words like *should* or *ought* shift your perspective?

CHAPTER SEVENTEEN
THE EMPOWERMENT OFFENSIVE
TRANSFORMING REACTIVE ROLES INTO SOURCES OF STRENGTH

Life isn't about waiting for the storm to pass; it's about learning to dance in the rain. – Vivian Greene

THE EMPOWERMENT DYNAMIC: STEPPING INTO FREEDOM

THE ANTIDOTE TO THE ALIEN INVADERS' MOST INSIDIOUS WEAPON—the Drama Triangle—isn't just stepping out of their trap. It's launching your own counteroffensive by stepping into a new way of living and relating. This counteroffensive is the Empowerment Dynamic, a concept developed by David Emerald in *The Power of TED (The Empowerment Dynamic)*.

The Empowerment Dynamic dismantles the invaders' disempowering roles—Victim, Persecutor, and Rescuer—and replaces them with roles that foster growth, connection, and personal responsibility. Where the Drama Triangle feeds on fear, judgment, and dependency, the Empowerment Dynamic empowers us with courage, authenticity, and intentionality.

This chapter unpacks how the Empowerment Dynamic works,

why it's critical to your counteroffensive, and how it transforms not only your inner world but also the lives of those around you.

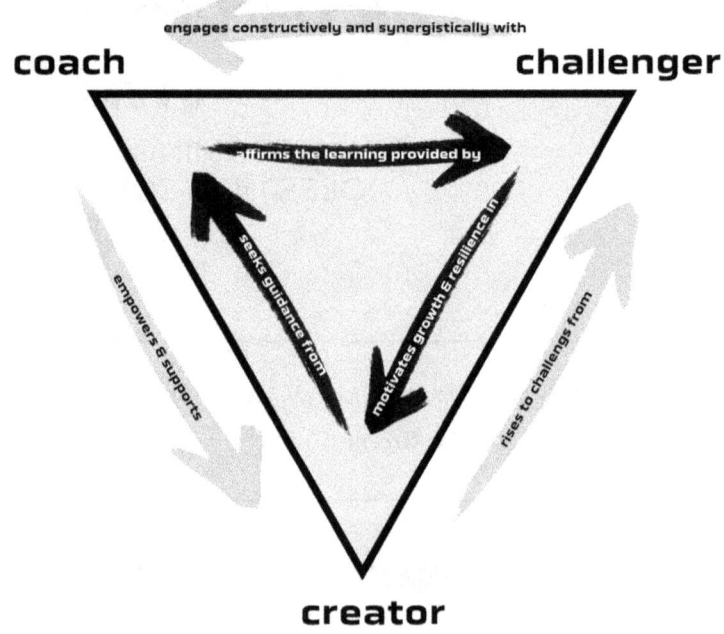

The Empowerment Dynamic (TED)

FROM DRAMA TO EMPOWERMENT: RECLAIMING THE BATTLEFIELD

In the Drama Triangle, we're pawns in a rigged game controlled by external forces and reactive patterns. The Empowerment Dynamic flips the board, putting us in command. Here's how it transforms the three disempowering roles into empowering ones:

Victim → Creator

In the Drama Triangle, the Victim feels powerless, stuck, and at the mercy of others. The invaders thrive here, convincing us that change is impossible without external rescue.

In the Empowerment Dynamic, the Victim becomes the Creator—someone who takes ownership of their choices and recognizes their ability to shape their life. Creators face challenges with curiosity and agency, asking, *"What can I do about this?"* They focus on possibilities and solutions instead of blame or inaction.

Persecutor → Challenger

The Persecutor in the Drama Triangle is cast as the villain, blamed for the Victim's suffering. In the Empowerment Dynamic, the Persecutor becomes the Challenger—a force that invites growth and accountability.

Challengers don't attack or tear down. They hold firm boundaries, ask hard questions, and push for transformation—not out of cruelty but from a belief in others' potential.

Rescuer → Coach

The Rescuer in the Drama Triangle rushes in to save the Victim, often at great personal cost. While their intentions may seem noble, Rescuers disempower Victims by reinforcing dependency.

In the Empowerment Dynamic, the Rescuer becomes the Coach—someone who supports and guides without taking over. Coaches empower others to find their own solutions, offering encouragement and perspective without sacrificing their own well-being.

THE CREATOR ROLE: YOUR CENTRAL COMMAND

Living as a Creator is the foundation of the Empowerment Dynamic. Without this shift, the other roles can't function. Being a

Creator doesn't mean life is easy—it means taking responsibility for how we respond to challenges.

The key difference is this:

- **In the Drama Triangle:** "This is happening to me, and there's nothing I can do."
- **In the Empowerment Dynamic:** "This is happening, and I can choose how to respond, the meaning I want to create, and the growth I will experience from it."

Living as a Creator requires radical ownership, not blame. It means recognizing our emotions without letting them dictate our actions and aligning our choices with our values, even when it's hard.

BREAKING FREE: RESPONDING WITHOUT JUDGMENT OR REACTIVITY

The invaders use judgment and reactivity to trap us in the Drama Triangle. Breaking free requires awareness and intentionality, especially in how we respond to others.

When Accountability Is Needed

Sometimes, people feel victimized because we've genuinely caused harm. The Empowerment Dynamic doesn't let us off the hook—it calls for accountability. However, accountability doesn't mean stepping into someone else's Drama Triangle as their Persecutor or Rescuer.

Here's how to own our impact without losing our agency:

1. **Acknowledge the Harm:** Take responsibility for your actions without defensiveness.
2. **Make Amends:** Apologize and take appropriate steps to repair the damage.

3. **Align With Your Values:** Stay grounded in your integrity, even if the other person tries to cast you into a disempowering role.

RESPONDING TO OTHERS: THE POWER OF COACHING AND CHALLENGING

When someone invites us into their Drama Triangle, it's tempting to play the Rescuer. But rescuing reinforces dependency and keeps both parties stuck. Instead, we can respond as a Coach or Challenger.

Be a <u>Coach</u>

- Recognize when someone is pulling us into their Victim story.
- Hold boundaries by refusing to take on responsibility that isn't ours while also having empathy, compassion, curiosity, and kindness. *"Hear the pain, not the blame."*
- Empower them by asking questions like, *"What's one step you could take to address this?"*

Be a <u>Challenger</u>

Challenging someone in a Victim mindset can feel risky, but it's often the most loving thing we can do. Challengers:

- **Invite Ownership:** *"What's a different way you might handle this?"*
- **Hold Firm Boundaries:** *"I can't support this approach, but I'm here to brainstorm alternatives."*
- **Model Growth:** By living as a Creator, we inspire others to do the same.

HELPING OTHERS WITHOUT BECOMING THEIR AWARENESS: A REMINDER

It's tempting to wake others up to their patterns, but this often leads to being perceived as a Persecutor or an ineffective Rescuer. As a reminder from the previous chapter:

Don't become the awareness for others unless invited—either through their explicit request or by respectfully asking for permission. Instead of offering unsolicited perspectives:

- **Ask Permission:** *"Are you looking for my perspective and help, or would you just like me to listen?"*
- **Clarify Needs:** If they ask for help, follow up with, *"What do you feel like you need right now?"*
- **Respect Their Choice:** If their need crosses your boundaries, stay connected empathetically without overstepping your limits.
- **Offer Perspectives With Consent:** *"Would you like to hear a different point of view?"*

This approach supports their agency, validates their emotions, and fosters connection. Sometimes, simply being present and empathetic is the most empowering thing we can do.

THE BIGGER PICTURE: BUILDING AN EMPOWERMENT CULTURE

The Empowerment Dynamic doesn't just transform our inner world—it creates ripple effects in our relationships, families, and communities:

- **In Relationships:** We foster mutual respect and authentic connection.
- **In Families:** We model healthy boundaries and accountability, teaching others to navigate challenges as Creators.

- **In Communities:** We contribute to a culture of empowerment, breaking cycles of blame and dependency.

> *Learning The Empowerment Dynamic has felt like getting a cheat code for life and relationships. It's like having a superpower that allows me to convert any circumstance into an opportunity that benefits me. It's also been very useful for navigating relationships like marriage and parenting. I've been truly amazed at how well my children respond sometimes. Some days, they really get it, somedays, they seem to prefer to stay stuck. I've learned to give them the space, latitude, and acceptance to work through their insides in their own time and pace. That's been a gift for me also, because it's taught me to be okay with other people not feeling okay.*

MAIN TAKEAWAY: EMPOWERMENT IS A CHOICE

The Empowerment Dynamic is your counteroffensive against the alien invasion of judgment, blame, and dependency. By stepping into the roles of Creator, Challenger, and Coach, you reclaim your agency, build healthier relationships, and align your life with your values. To sustain this counteroffensive, you must cultivate emotional awareness—the next vital step in reclaiming your inner world.

COMING UP: NAVIGATING YOUR EMOTIONAL DASHBOARD

In the next chapter, we'll dive into how your emotions serve as a powerful internal guidance system. Building on the Empowerment Dynamic, you'll learn how to interpret emotions as signals, guiding you toward alignment and intentionality. By engaging with your emotions through practices like the PAPA method, you'll strengthen your ability to stay grounded in your Creator role, navigate challenges with clarity, and dismantle the patterns of reactivity that fuel the Drama Triangle. This is where emotional awareness becomes a cornerstone of your counteroffensive.

COMMON RESPONSES

"Yeah, but what if I don't feel like a Creator? I feel stuck and powerless."

That's understandable—becoming a Creator doesn't mean pretending you're never overwhelmed. It's about starting where you are and choosing one small step at a time. Feeling stuck is often part of the process, but even a tiny action can begin to shift the story.

"Yeah, but isn't challenging someone risky? What if they react badly?"

Challenging someone with kindness and curiosity does feel vulnerable. But when done with respect and love, it's an invitation, not an attack. Their reaction is theirs to own, but your choice to challenge them shows belief in their strength and potential.

"Yeah, but doesn't coaching someone still put me in the role of trying to fix things?"

It can feel that way, but true coaching is about asking questions and empowering others to find their own solutions. It's not about fixing; it's about walking alongside someone without taking over their journey.

WHAT TO DO WHEN THE ALIENS SHOW UP (AND EVEN IF THEY DON'T)

"Yeah, but what if I slip back into the Drama Triangle?"

You will—it's part of being human! The goal isn't perfection but awareness. Each time you catch yourself slipping, you have the opportunity to pause, reassess, and step back into empowerment. Each step forward matters, even after a stumble.

"Yeah, but some people just won't change. Isn't this wasted effort?"

You can't control others' choices, but you can control how you show up. Empowerment isn't about forcing change—it's about modeling healthy dynamics and staying grounded in your values. Even if they don't change, you'll have grown stronger and more authentic.

REFLECTION QUESTIONS

1. What role do you find yourself playing most often in the Drama Triangle?
2. How might adopting the role of Creator shift your perspective on a current challenge?
3. Who in your life could benefit from you showing up as a Coach or Challenger?
4. How can emotional awareness help you stay grounded in the Empowerment Dynamic?

CHAPTER EIGHTEEN
DECODING THE SIGNALS
USING EMOTIONS AS GUIDES TO FREEDOM

The wound is the place where the Light enters you. – Rumi

EMOTIONAL AWARENESS: OUR INNER DASHBOARD

EMOTIONS ARE OFTEN MISUNDERSTOOD, ESPECIALLY AMONG MEN. They're seen as obstacles to overcome, inconveniences to suppress, or problems to fix. But what if emotions weren't our enemy at all? What if every uncomfortable feeling—anxiety, frustration, or sadness—was a message pointing us toward alignment or revealing areas where we've strayed from our values and sovereignty?

In earlier chapters, we introduced the PAPA Process—Pause, Assess, Process, Address—as a framework for navigating emotional crossroads with intention. Here, we revisit and expand on that foundation, exploring how emotions act as a dashboard for our inner world. By deepening our understanding of the PAPA Process, we'll learn to interpret emotional signals not just in the moment but as part of a broader narrative about our alignment with our values and sovereignty.

EMOTIONS AS ALIGNMENT SIGNALS

Our emotions are like warning lights on a car's dashboard. They're not the problem themselves—they're signals pointing toward something deeper. When we're aligned with our values and sovereignty, emotions like peace, clarity, and determination dominate. When we stray, our emotional dashboard flashes warning lights: anxiety, frustration, resentment, or despair.

This expanded understanding of the PAPA Process emphasizes seeing emotions as recurring indicators of broader patterns. It's not just about managing a single emotional moment but recognizing how these signals reflect our relationship with our values, our choices, and our personal sovereignty.

EMOTIONAL STATES OF MISALIGNMENT: DRAMA TRIANGLE WARNING LIGHTS

When we're trapped in the Drama Triangle, our emotional dashboard reveals the external locus of control driving our disempowered state:

- **Victim:** Feelings of helplessness, despair, and overwhelm. Life feels like it's happening to us, and change seems impossible.
- **Persecutor:** Resentment, anger, and frustration. We place blame on others or ourselves, fueling cycles of conflict and judgment.
- **Rescuer:** Anxiety, obligation, and burnout. We feel compelled to "fix" others' problems, seeking validation through self-sacrifice.

These emotions are signals that our actions and beliefs are misaligned with our values. They aren't "bad"—they're invitations to pause, reflect, and realign.

EMOTIONAL STATES OF ALIGNMENT: EMPOWERMENT DYNAMIC SIGNALS

When we step into the Empowerment Dynamic, our emotional dashboard reflects alignment with our values and internal locus of control:

- **Creator:** Feelings of curiosity, hope, and empowerment. We focus on what we can control—our choices, responses, and growth.
- **Challenger:** Determination and alignment. We face hard truths with courage, inviting growth and transformation.
- **Coach:** Compassion and encouragement. We support others and ourselves without sacrificing well-being or autonomy.

These emotions don't mean life is free from difficulty, but they reflect clarity, agency, and alignment with our values, even amidst challenges.

REVISITING THE PAPA PROCESS: A DEEPER UNDERSTANDING

In earlier discussions, we introduced the PAPA Process as a way to respond intentionally to emotional reactions in the moment. Here, we expand on its application, showing how it can help decode recurring emotional patterns and guide us toward a deeper understanding of our inner world.

- **Pause:** When a strong emotion arises, create space to notice it.
    - Acknowledge the emotion: Name it—anxiety, frustration, resentment, or sadness.
    - Breathe: Use box breathing to calm our nervous system.

- Remind ourselves: This emotion isn't good or bad—it's just information.
- **Assess:** Identify the trigger and context of the emotion. Ask:
  - What triggered this emotion?
  - What recurring story or belief might be shaping this reaction?
  - What unmet need or misalignment might this signal?
- **Process:** Uncover the story behind the emotion.
  - What is the story or judgment underlying this emotion?
  - Where is the misalignment?
  - Are we reacting from fear or dependency rather than our values?
- **Address:** Take intentional action to realign. Ask:
  - What small step can we take to realign?
  - Set a boundary if frustration signals that one was crossed.
  - Release unmet expectations if resentment shows we're focused on others' choices.
  - Affirm our inherent worth if anxiety reveals dependency on external validation.

THRIVING THROUGH EMOTIONAL AWARENESS

Thriving isn't about avoiding hard emotions—it's about interpreting them as signals of alignment or misalignment. With this expanded understanding, we can apply the PAPA Process to go beyond managing emotions in the moment and uncover the deeper stories, judgments, and beliefs shaping our inner world. This deeper awareness dismantles reactive patterns and replaces them with intentional, empowered responses.

WHAT TO DO WHEN THE ALIENS SHOW UP (AND EVEN IF THEY DON'T)

Like many men who grew up in the last century, I've had to learn how to permit myself to experience my emotions without hiding, stuffing, or judging them before I could begin to understand them. Like most men, I experienced a lot of shaming for my emotions and learned to ignore and suppress them, which created a lot of unpleasantness. The emotions didn't actually disappear—they just found other ways to express themselves. My frustration would bubble up as anger, my sadness as withdrawal, and my fear as defensiveness. I thought I was being strong, stoic, and in control, but in reality, I was completely out of touch with what I was feeling, and it showed up in ways that hurt my relationships, my health, and my sense of peace.

It took me years to realize that suppressing emotions doesn't eliminate them; it just drives them underground, where they fester and wreak havoc. I remember countless moments in my life when I would shut down emotionally rather than admit I was scared, angry, hurt, or unsure. I told myself it was "no big deal" or that I was just being "rational," but those unacknowledged feelings would leak out later in sarcastic comments, impatience with my kids, or nights spent lying awake with my mind racing.

Learning to allow my emotions—to name them, feel them, and explore what they were trying to tell me—was one of the most uncomfortable and liberating things I've ever done. At first, I had to overcome stories I had about that being a weakness, like I was failing some unspoken test of masculinity. I came to see that about as silly as saying that it is not masculine to use diagnostic equipment to troubleshoot and understand complex machinery I own. As I've learned to sit with my emotions instead of shoving them down, I've begun to see them for what they truly are:

helpful messengers, not enemies. Anger can teach me whether I'm not living within a boundary or am not being authentic with myself. Sadness helps me understand the things I value and miss. Fear shows me where I am avoiding something I need to face.

This shift didn't just help me; it transformed how I showed up for the people I loved. Instead of snapping at my kids when I am overwhelmed, I've learned to say, "I'm feeling really stressed right now, and I need a minute." or "I want to focus on what you're saying, but I'm distracted. Let's talk in thirty minutes." Instead of retreating in silence when my wife and I disagree, I can say, "This is hard for me to talk about, but I want to work through it." Slowly, I've discovered that allowing myself to feel and express my emotions makes me stronger, not weaker. It makes me a better husband, father, and friend because I am showing up fully—no masks, no pretenses.

Breaking free from the shame of feeling my emotions has been one of the most essential steps in reclaiming my sense of self. Emotions aren't a sign of weakness—they're part of what makes us human. And when we permit ourselves to experience them without judgment, we open the door to growth, connection, and healing.

MAIN TAKEAWAY: EMOTIONS ARE YOUR ALLIES, NOT YOUR ENEMIES

Emotions are not obstacles or problems to suppress—they are signals from your inner world, reflecting alignment or misalignment with your values and sovereignty. By revisiting and expanding your understanding of the PAPA Process, you can engage with emotions as allies in your journey toward thriving. Every emotion offers an opportunity to uncover the stories and beliefs shaping your life and take intentional, aligned action to realign with your values.

COMING UP: DISCERNING THE ALIEN SIGNAL

In the next chapter, we'll dive deeper into the hidden messages within your hard emotions. By learning to decode these "alien signals," you'll uncover the unmet needs, dependencies, and self-limiting beliefs fueling your emotional storms. Building on the awareness you've cultivated, this chapter will help you peel back the layers of emotion to uncover the truth beneath the surface, transforming your hardest feelings into powerful guides for alignment and growth.

COMMON RESPONSES

"Yeah, but emotions are messy and make things worse. Isn't it better to ignore them?"

Ignoring emotions doesn't make them go away—it just buries them, where they often come out sideways. Emotions are messages, not the problem themselves. Learning to listen to them helps you act more clearly and intentionally.

"Yeah, but what if I can't even name what I'm feeling? It's all overwhelming."

It's okay to not know right away. Start small by noticing physical sensations or using broad terms like "uncomfortable" or "heavy." Over time, you'll get better at identifying specific emotions and understanding their messages.

"Yeah, but if I allow my emotions, won't they take over and make me lose control?"

Actually, the opposite is true. Suppressed emotions tend to explode when ignored while naming and sitting with emotions allows them to pass more smoothly. It's like releasing steam from a pressure cooker.

"Yeah, but as a man, I was raised to see emotions as weakness. Isn't being strong more important?"

Strength doesn't mean shutting down emotions—it means being honest with yourself and responding wisely. Feeling your emotions isn't weak; it's a sign of courage and self-awareness. It makes you stronger, not weaker.

"Yeah, but what if I feel emotions that don't align with who I want to be?"

Uncomfortable emotions don't define you—they're simply indicators of something deeper. Instead of judging them, ask what they might be signaling about your values, unmet needs, or areas for growth.

REFLECTION QUESTIONS

1. What emotions have been flashing on your dashboard lately, and what might they be signaling?
2. How does your current emotional state reflect alignment —or misalignment—with your values and sovereignty?

WHAT TO DO WHEN THE ALIENS SHOW UP (AND EVEN IF THEY DON'T)

3. What recurring stories or judgments are driving your emotions, and how might you begin to release them?
4. What's one small, aligned action you can take today to realign with your values and personal sovereignty?

CHAPTER NINETEEN
THE ALIEN CODE
DECIPHERING EMOTIONAL MESSAGES TO RECLAIM YOUR POWER

You don't have to control your thoughts. You just have to stop letting them control you. – Dan Millman

---

HARD EMOTIONS CAN FEEL LIKE ALIEN SIGNALS—MYSTERIOUS, disruptive, and often misunderstood. Fear, frustration, anger, anxiety—they arrive unannounced, throwing your internal world into chaos. But what if these emotions weren't invaders to eliminate but encrypted messages to decode? What if each hard feeling held the key to unlocking your deepest needs and shedding the beliefs keeping you stuck?

This chapter reframes emotions not as problems to suppress but as guides to self-discovery and empowerment. Building on the emotional awareness practices we've explored, this process of "peeling the onion" will take us deeper into these signals, layer by layer, until we uncover the core needs beneath the surface. From there, we'll learn how to transform the judgments, shame, and dependencies perpetuating our pain.

HARD EMOTIONS AS ALIEN SIGNALS

Every hard emotion is a signal, a flare shot up from your inner world to capture your attention. But like any signal, it's often misinterpreted. Instead of seeing it as a clue to explore, we conflate the emotion with the stories we tell ourselves, the strategies we imagine for resolving it, and the meaning we assign to what's happening.

Here's how the signal typically gets scrambled:

1. **The Alien Signal Is Insecurity**: Hard emotions arise from a sense of insecurity—a belief that something vital to us is not secure. This might be love, validation, safety, or worth.
2. **Insecurity Points to Dependency**: That insecurity reflects a deeper dependency—our belief that something external holds the key to fulfilling our needs. This could be a person, circumstance, or societal expectation.
3. **Dependency Is Rooted in Self-Limiting Beliefs**: These beliefs whisper that we're incapable of meeting our own needs. They convince us to outsource our power and depend on external validation or control.
4. **Self-Limiting Beliefs Are Born of Judgment**: At the root of these beliefs lies judgment—the story that we are "not enough." This judgment fuels shame, which keeps us stuck and blind to our inherent worth.

PEELING THE ONION: DECODING THE CORE NEED

The antidote to these scrambled signals is to peel back the layers of emotion, judgment, and dependency to uncover the core need. This process is like decrypting an alien code—it requires patience, curiosity, and a willingness to face what lies beneath the surface.

WHAT TO DO WHEN THE ALIENS SHOW UP (AND EVEN IF THEY DON'T)

Step 1: Start With the Hard Emotion

Identify the feeling you're experiencing. Name it clearly: Is it fear, frustration, resentment, or anxiety? Saying it aloud or writing it down creates the first step toward clarity.

Step 2: Ask the First Question

Ask yourself:
"What would I feel, get, or experience differently if this emotion or frustration were resolved?"

For example, if you're frustrated that your partner isn't showing excitement to see you, the question might be:
"What would I feel if they were excited to see me?"

Step 3: Peel Back the First Layer

The answer to that question will often reveal a deeper need or feeling. For example:

- *"If they were excited to see me, I'd feel valued."*
- *"If I felt valued, I'd feel worthy."*

Step 4: Keep Asking

For each answer, repeat the question:
"What would I feel, get, or experience differently if I had that?"
Keep peeling back the layers until you reach a core need:

- *"I want to feel worthy."*
- *"I want to feel like I matter."*
- *"I want to feel loved."*

Step 5: Challenge the Belief

Once you've uncovered the core need, ask yourself:
"Why don't I feel this way now?"
This question often exposes a self-limiting belief, such as:

- *"I'm not enough."*
- *"I'm not lovable."*
- *"I don't matter unless someone else shows me I do."*

This belief is the alien invader holding your core need hostage. It's rooted in judgment and shame, and this is where your work begins—rewriting that belief into something empowering.

JUDGMENT: THE ALIEN INVADER

At the root of every self-limiting belief is *judgment*. Somewhere along the way, you absorbed the story that you are inadequate, unworthy, or incapable. Society, culture, and personal experiences often reinforce these judgments, teaching us that happiness and worth must come from external sources.

This judgment creates shame, which whispers:

"You're flawed. You're not enough."

To escape this shame, we look outward. We pin our core needs—love, validation, safety—onto others, hoping they'll fulfill us. But this external dependency is a trap. As long as our needs are tied to something outside of ourselves, we remain vulnerable to disappointment, frustration, and despair.

RECLAIMING THE SIGNAL: FROM DEPENDENCY TO SOVEREIGNTY

The good news is that every external dependency can be traced back to a core need that you can meet internally. Peeling the onion isn't about denying your needs—it's about reclaiming them. It's about taking the dependencies you've projected outward and bringing them back where they belong: within your sovereignty.

FROM EXTERNAL DEPENDENCY TO INTERNAL SECURITY

- **External Dependency:** *"I need you to validate me to feel worthy."*
- **Internal Security:** *"I know I'm worthy, regardless of external validation."*

This shift transforms how you relate to yourself and others. Instead of blaming, judging, or resenting others for not meeting your needs, you take ownership of them. You become the Creator of your emotional experience rather than a victim.

A PRACTICAL EXAMPLE: DECODING THE SIGNAL

Let's explore some relatable scenarios to see how this process works in everyday life:

Friendship Struggles

Imagine you feel frustrated because your friend didn't invite you to hang out with a group of mutual friends. At first, you might think:
"I need them to include me."
Peeling back the layers might look like this:

- **Surface Frustration:** *"I need them to include me."*
- **Deeper Feeling:** *"If they included me, I'd feel like I belong."*
- **Deeper Need:** *"If I felt like I belonged, I'd feel valued."*
- **Core Need:** *"I want to feel like I matter and am accepted."*

This process helps shift the focus from your friend's actions to the underlying belief that your worth is tied to others' approval. By addressing this belief, you can begin meeting your core needs internally and free yourself from dependency on their validation.

Academic Pressure

Suppose you're anxious because you didn't get the grade you wanted on a test. At first, you might think:
"I need to get better grades."
Peeling the onion might reveal:

- **Surface Frustration:** *"I need to get better grades."*
- **Deeper Feeling:** *"If I had better grades, I'd feel successful."*
- **Deeper Need:** *"If I felt successful, I'd feel like I'm good enough."*
- **Core Need:** *"I want to feel like I'm capable and worthy."*

This process reveals that the anxiety is less about the grade itself and more about a belief that your worth is tied to academic performance. Recognizing this allows you to affirm your inherent value, independent of external metrics like grades.

Social Media Comparisons

Imagine you're feeling upset because a classmate keeps posting pictures of their accomplishments and travels, making you feel left out or inadequate. At first, you might think:
"I need to be as successful as they are."
Peeling back the layers could reveal:

- **Surface Frustration:** *"I need to be as successful as they are."*
- **Deeper Feeling:** *"If I were, I'd feel confident."*
- **Deeper Need:** *"If I felt confident, I'd feel like I'm enough."*
- **Core Need:** *"I want to feel valued and secure in myself."*

Here, the problem isn't the classmate's success—it's the belief that your worth is tied to comparisons with others. By addressing this belief, you can shift from competition to self-compassion and focus on your unique path.

WHAT TO DO WHEN THE ALIENS SHOW UP (AND EVEN IF THEY DON'T)

Feeling Unappreciated in a Relationship

Imagine you feel frustrated because your partner hasn't acknowledged the effort you put into planning a special evening. At first, you might think:

"I need them to show more appreciation."

Peeling back the layers might look like this:

- **Surface Frustration:** *"I need them to show more appreciation."*
- **Deeper Feeling:** *"If they showed appreciation, I'd feel seen and valued."*
- **Deeper Need:** *"If I felt seen and valued, I'd feel like I'm enough."*
- **Core Need:** *"I want to feel worthy and loved (regardless of external validation)."*

This process reveals that your frustration isn't only about your partner's actions—it stems from a deeper belief that your worth is tied to external acknowledgment. Addressing this belief can validate your own efforts and worth internally, allowing you to approach the relationship with clearer communication and less emotional dependency.

THE GIFT OF HARD EMOTIONS

When you learn to peel the onion, hard emotions stop being obstacles and become invitations. Each emotion is a messenger, guiding you back to your core needs and showing you where judgment, shame, and dependency have taken root.

This is the beauty of thriving: it doesn't mean avoiding hard emotions. It means embracing them as opportunities for growth. Every hard feeling is a signal—a chance to heal, reconnect with your sovereignty, and reclaim your power.

I know how hard it can be to see your emotions—especially the uncomfortable ones—as anything but problems to fix or pain to avoid. For years, I was a master at pushing them away, burying them under distractions, or just telling myself to "get over it." Anger, anxiety, sadness—those feelings felt too big, too overwhelming, and honestly, I didn't want to go anywhere near them. They were uncomfortable, so I avoided them.

What I didn't realize at the time was that avoiding those emotions didn't make them go away—it just made them louder. They manifested as frustration with my kids, disconnection in my marriage, and stress at work that I couldn't shake. The more I ignored them, the more I stayed stuck in patterns I didn't understand.

It wasn't until I started leaning in—giving myself permission to feel those hard emotions without judging them—that I began to see what they were trying to tell me. They weren't enemies; they were signals, pointing me to parts of myself that needed attention, healing, and compassion. I began to ask questions: "What's underneath this feeling? What is it trying to teach me?" Slowly, I started peeling back the layers.

It wasn't easy. It didn't happen overnight. But as I did the work, everything began to change. My relationships became more honest, my parenting became more patient, and my own sense of peace grew stronger. I started living <u>from</u> my Self instead of against myself.

If you're just starting this journey, I want you to know it's worth it. Hard emotions aren't here to punish you. They're here to guide you back to yourself. Let them.

MAIN TAKEAWAY: EMOTIONS ARE SIGNALS TO DECODE, NOT ENEMIES TO DEFEAT

Hard emotions are not obstacles to overcome; they are messengers pointing you toward your core needs and values. By learning to decode these "alien signals" through the process of peeling the onion, you uncover the deeper judgments, dependencies, and self-limiting beliefs driving your feelings. This empowers you to shift from external dependency to internal sovereignty, reclaiming your worth and meeting your needs from within. Embracing hard emotions as opportunities for growth transforms them into powerful guides for alignment, healing, and personal empowerment.

COMING UP: BUILDING YOUR STRONGHOLD OF SOVEREIGNTY

In the next chapter, we'll explore how to fortify your emotional and mental foundation by constructing a personal stronghold. This stronghold isn't about isolation—it's about creating a safe, inner sanctuary where you can process emotions, align with your values, and reclaim your power. You'll learn how practices like boundaries, gratitude, and intentional habits form the foundation of this fortress, preparing you to face challenges from a place of strength and resilience. Together, we'll lay the groundwork for building an unshakable base from which you can thrive.

COMMON RESPONSES

"Yeah, but what if I don't have time to sit around peeling onions when emotions hit?"

You don't have to dedicate hours to this practice. Start small by naming the emotion and asking one question about it. Even a brief moment of reflection can make a difference over time.

"Yeah, but emotions like anger and fear feel too overwhelming to handle."

It's natural to feel overwhelmed at first. Begin by creating a safe space for yourself—like a quiet moment alone—to acknowledge the feeling without judgment. Remember, emotions don't last forever; they rise, peak, and fall like waves.

"Yeah, but what if peeling back the layers only makes me feel worse?"

Sometimes, uncovering deeper truths can feel heavy, but it also creates space for healing and growth. Hard emotions are like tangled wires—sorting through them might feel messy, but it ultimately restores clarity and connection.

"Yeah, but if I meet my needs internally, isn't that selfish or isolating?"

Not at all. Meeting your needs internally allows you to show up for others from a place of fullness rather than dependency. It strengthens relationships because you're not relying on others to validate your worth.

"Yeah, but what if the core belief is true? What if I'm not enough?"

This is shame speaking, not truth. Everyone struggles with feelings of inadequacy at times, but your worth isn't conditional. Start by challenging that belief—what evidence do you have that it's true, and how might you reinterpret that evidence through a lens of self-compassion?

WHAT TO DO WHEN THE ALIENS SHOW UP (AND EVEN IF THEY DON'T)

REFLECTION QUESTIONS

1. What hard emotions have you been experiencing lately, and what might they be trying to tell you?
2. How have you been tying your needs to external validation or circumstances?
3. What core needs are hidden beneath your surface frustrations, and how can you begin meeting them internally?
4. What self-limiting beliefs might be keeping you in a cycle of dependency, and how can you challenge them?

CHAPTER TWENTY
STRONGHOLDS OF SOVEREIGNTY
FORTIFYING YOUR INNER WORLD AGAINST ALIEN THREATS

The privilege of a lifetime is being who you are. – Joseph Campbell

---

BUILDING YOUR STRONGHOLD: SELF-SOVEREIGNTY BEGINS WITH SELF-WORTH

IN THE BATTLE AGAINST THE ALIEN INVADERS, OUR EMOTIONS SERVE AS signals, guiding us toward alignment or misalignment. Peeling back the layers of those signals brings clarity and direction. But awareness alone isn't enough. Without a secure foundation, we'll find ourselves fighting the same battles repeatedly, vulnerable to the same attacks. To win this war, we need a stronghold—a place within ourselves where our sovereignty is unshakable.

At the heart of this stronghold lies unshakable self-worth. Self-worth is the bedrock—solid, immovable, and non-negotiable. This isn't a self-worth derived from external validation, achievements, or others' opinions. It's not tied to what we do, what we have, or who approves of us. That kind of external self-worth isn't really *self*-worth, is it?! It's *other*-worth and is unstable, like building a fortress on shifting sands. True self-worth comes from within and is unchangeable—rooted in the inherent value of our *existence*.

Without self-worth, the walls of our stronghold crumble at the first whisper of shame. With it, we create a fortress where judgment, dependency, and fear lose their power. This chapter is about building that inner stronghold, beginning with self-worth and rooting everything in the unwavering truth: we are enough, just as we are.

THE FOUNDATION: UNCHANGEABLE, INTERNAL SELF-WORTH

True self-worth is an intrinsic quality—it cannot be earned, increased, or diminished. It is not a story, a measurement, or an achievement. It simply *is*. We are worthy because we exist. This kind of self-worth is liberating and grounding because it releases us from the exhausting pursuit of external validation and shields us from the shame that thrives on comparison and conditional acceptance.

THE STORIES THAT UNDERMINE SELF-WORTH

When we adopt stories about self-worth being earned, we unknowingly build our identity on unstable ground. These stories sound like this:

- *"I'll be worthy when I achieve success."*
- *"I'm only as good as what others think of me."*
- *"I'll matter when I prove myself."*

These beliefs make self-worth conditional—tied to something outside of us that can change, disappear, or fail. And when those conditions are unmet, the shame creeps in: *I'm not enough*. These stories leave our fortress exposed to every external storm, sabotaging your sovereignty. Furthermore, when worth is external, there is no way to know when we've reached *enough*, meaning we can never *be enough*. Does that sound like a recipe for creating an extraordinary life?

BELIEFS THAT SERVE SELF-WORTH

To build an unshakable foundation, we must adopt beliefs that reflect the truth of our inherent worth:

- "I am enough because I exist."
- "My value is not tied to what I do but to who I am."
- "I don't need to earn love, respect, or acceptance—they are natural extensions of my being."

These beliefs reinforce the idea that our worth is constant and invulnerable to external circumstances. When self-worth is rooted in this truth, we can face challenges and emotions without questioning our value.

OUR EXISTENCE IS PROOF OF OUR WORTH

We are often told that self-worth is something to be earned—through achievements, possessions, or the approval of others. But the truth is far simpler and more profound: our worth is intrinsic, tied to our very existence. For many, this understanding is deeply spiritual. Believing that our lives are part of a purposeful design instills a sense of inherent value and belonging. Whether you call this divine, natural, or cosmic, this perspective reminds us that our existence is intentional and precious.

Even if one doesn't ascribe to spiritual beliefs, there is an undeniable, awe-inspiring truth about our presence in this world: the sheer mathematical improbability of each one of our existence. Consider this: the chance of you being here–precisely as you are, is estimated to be around 1 in $10^{2,685,000}$. This includes the probability of your parents meeting, your particular sperm fertilizing your mother's egg, and an unbroken lineage of ancestors surviving countless challenges over millennia. This number is so vast it surpasses the number of atoms in the observable universe. And yet, here *you* are—a living, breathing miracle. (See Appendix: **The Mathematical Miracle of Your Existence** for details.) Let that sink in... your existence is profoundly unique, rare, and priceless.

This understanding, spiritual or mathematical, is a foundation for embracing self-worth as intrinsic and unshakable. We don't need to do anything to prove our worth—we are enough simply because we exist. And when we anchor ourselves in this truth, we begin to build the stronghold where shame, judgment, and fear lose their grip.

THE WALLS OF YOUR FORTRESS: VALUES AND INTEGRITY

With self-worth as the foundation, the next layer of our stronghold is defined by values and reinforced by integrity. These elements provide structure and strength, ensuring that our fortress aligns with who we truly are.

Values: Our Inner Compass

Values are the principles that guide our choices and actions. They clarify what matters most to us, helping us navigate life with purpose and authenticity. Importantly, our values guide us in our sphere of sovereignty—helping us own our choices and actions without overstepping into others' spheres or trying to control the uncontrollable.

To identify your core values, ask yourself:

- *As a being of immense value and worth...*
    - *What qualities or principles do I want to define my life?*
    - *What matters most to me, even when life is hard?*
    - *What qualities, principles, or ways of being are non-negotiable to me in any circumstance?*

Examples of core values include courage, kindness, freedom, and honesty. Our values anchor us to our self-worth, ensuring that our actions align with who we are, not who others want us to be.

Integrity: Living True to Our Values

Integrity is the act of aligning our inner values with our outer actions. It's about being the same person inside and out, ensuring that our stronghold is consistent and whole. Integrity also requires staying within our sphere of sovereignty—owning our choices and emotions while respecting the boundaries of others and the unknown.

When we stray from our sphere, focusing on others' business or trying to control what's beyond our reach, our integrity falters. This weakens our stronghold, leaving us vulnerable to external forces.

Living with integrity means:

- Taking full ownership of our thoughts, feelings, and actions.
- Resisting the urge to control others or blame them for our emotional state.
- Reflecting our values in every decision we make.

THE GATES: AWARENESS AND BOUNDARIES

Awareness and boundaries are the gates of our stronghold, defining the edges of our sovereignty and protecting our inner sanctuary.

Awareness: Recognizing What's Yours

Awareness helps us notice when shame, judgment, or dependency try to breach our stronghold. It ties directly to our values and integrity, helping us recognize when we're:

- Stepping out of our sphere of sovereignty.

- Operating from misalignment or external validation.
- Reacting to others' behavior instead of responding with intention.

Awareness creates the space for choice, allowing us to pause and realign with our values instead of falling into reactive patterns.

Boundaries: Protecting Our Sphere

Boundaries mark the limits of our sphere of sovereignty. They aren't walls to guard—they're the edges where we define what belongs to us and what doesn't. Boundaries ensure that we remain responsible for our own emotions and actions while refusing to take on what doesn't belong to us.

Clear boundaries sound like:

- *"I'm responsible for my feelings, and you're responsible for yours."*
- *"If this conversation becomes disrespectful, I will step away."*
- *"I won't sacrifice my values to meet others' expectations."*

Boundaries honor our energy and integrity and reflect our intrinsic worth (and that of others) by clarifying where our responsibility ends and others' begins. They are not about controlling others; rather, they define the natural "edge" of our sphere of self. As people of immutable, intrinsic worth and value, we set boundaries to align with that truth: "As someone who values my time and energy, I will not engage in conversations where I am being yelled at" or "I need time to recharge after a busy day, so I will decline invitations this evening."

These are examples of healthy boundaries—statements that express your limits and decisions without imposing obligations or expectations on others. They don't demand someone else change; they simply clarify what you will and won't accept within your sphere of sovereignty.

WHAT TO DO WHEN THE ALIENS SHOW UP (AND EVEN IF THEY DON'T)

In contrast, what are often mistakenly called "boundaries" are actually attempts to control or obligate others. Statements like "You can't speak to me that way" or "You need to stop doing that if you care about me" may feel like boundaries, but they shift responsibility for your emotional state onto someone else's actions. These are ultimatums, not boundaries, and they foster dependency rather than clarity or respect.

The key lies in ownership. True boundaries flow from your intrinsic worth and reflect your choices and actions in response to others' behavior. They are not about asserting control but about embodying self-respect and honoring the sovereignty of both yourself and others.

The Hearth: Gratitude

Gratitude is the warmth within our stronghold—the hearth that keeps the space welcoming and resilient. It doesn't ignore challenges; instead, it shifts our focus from scarcity to abundance, helping us see what is good even in the face of difficulty. Gratitude gives us a strong, powerful role, allowing us to make intentional choices about the meaning of our lives' events and circumstances. This perspective reinforces our sovereignty, reminding us that we have control over how we respond, even when external circumstances are beyond our control.

> *Recently, someone aggressively critiqued, judged, and attacked my person, work, and character. Moments like this can feel as though a Molotov cocktail has been thrown into my life, threatening to burn everything I've built. Yet, knowing my self-worth is not determined outside of me, knowing I can choose gratitude, knowing I have no control over the actions of others but full control over my own realm, I <u>chose</u> to meet these events with gratitude.*
>
> *Now, let me be clear—I didn't feel the emotion of grati-*

tude at that moment. I _chose_ it. I deliberately decided to take the perspective of, "Thank you for this hardship that allows me to grow more resilient and firmly planted in my unfailing self-worth. I'm grateful for the vulnerabilities I experienced from this bomb being thrown into my kingdom."

Choosing gratitude in this way is like taking the fiery assaults and using them to create a campfire—to warm yourself, dry off your wet boots, to cook, and then to make a nice batch of s'mores. Instead of letting that person's attack define me or destroy my stronghold, I turned it into fuel for growth and connection. Gratitude, in this way, transforms challenges into tools of empowerment, reinforcing our sovereignty and reminding us that even amidst difficulty, we remain in control of how we shape our story.

Want an indomitable kingdom of self? Start choosing gratitude!

Practicing Gratitude

- **Daily Reflections:** Write down three things you're grateful for each day.
- **Express Thanks:** Share your appreciation with those who support you.
- **Reframe Challenges:** Look for the growth or strength gained from struggles.

Gratitude nurtures our sense of self-worth and strengthens our emotional resilience, reminding us of our inherent abundance even in hard times.

WELCOMING ALLIES: STRENGTH THROUGH CONNECTION

No stronghold stands in isolation. Trusted allies amplify the strength of our fortress, helping us dismantle shame, challenge judgment, and stay aligned with our values. Allies disrupt the isolation where shame thrives, reminding us of our worth when we struggle to see it.

Choosing Allies Wisely

Not everyone belongs inside your fortress. True allies:

- Respect your person, sphere (boundaries), and values.
- Encourage your growth without trying to fix you.
- Offer perspective and support without judgment.

In the next chapter, *Retreat to the Redoubt*, we'll explore how to build and sustain this network of allies.

MAIN TAKEAWAY: SELF-WORTH IS THE CORE OF OUR STRONGHOLD

Our stronghold—a secure, inner sanctuary where our sovereignty is protected—rests on the unshakable foundation of self-worth. Without it, shame, judgment, and dependency can breach our defenses. With it, we create a space of clarity, courage, and resilience where fear and external validation lose their grip. Values, integrity, awareness, boundaries, and gratitude rise from this foundation, creating a fortress where we can thrive.

COMING UP: RETREATING TO THE REDOUBT

The foundation of self-worth is essential to our stronghold, but so is community. Allies help us dismantle shame and reflect our worth when we forget it. We'll talk more about some of these subjects in

Part 3. In the next chapter, we'll explore how to build and lean on a network of trusted allies who amplify your sovereignty and strengthen your defenses.

COMMON RESPONSES

"Yeah, but I've made mistakes that prove I'm not enough."

Mistakes don't define your worth—they're opportunities to learn and grow. Your value is intrinsic, not tied to your actions. The fact that you're willing to reflect and grow is a testament to your inherent worth.

"Yeah, but what if I don't know what my values are?"

Start by asking what truly matters to you in life—what principles feel unshakable, even during hard times? Reflect on moments when you felt most authentic or proud of yourself. These are clues to your core values.

"Yeah, but setting boundaries feels selfish or mean."

Boundaries are acts of self-respect, not selfishness. They protect your energy and well-being, allowing you to show up for others from a place of fullness rather than resentment or burnout.

"Yeah, but isn't self-worth something I have to earn through hard work or success?"

That's a common myth. True self-worth isn't earned—it's inherent. Achievements and success are great, but they're external. Your worth exists because you do; nothing can add to or subtract from it.

WHAT TO DO WHEN THE ALIENS SHOW UP (AND EVEN IF THEY DON'T)

"Yeah, but gratitude feels fake when things are really hard."

Gratitude is not only a feeling but also an attitude we can adopt. Choosing gratitude as an attitude doesn't mean ignoring challenges—it's about focusing on what's still good, even in the face of difficulty. In fact, we tend to stay stuck in challenges until we shift our perspective to appreciation and gratitude. This shifts our relationship to our circumstances from being a Victim experiencing a Persecutor to a Creator experiencing a Challenger's invitation to grow and expand. Start small—acknowledge one small thing you're grateful for each day. Over time, it will shift your perspective.

REFLECTION QUESTIONS

1. What stories about self-worth have you absorbed, and how can you begin to replace them with the truth of your inherent value?
2. How do your values guide your decisions and relationships? Are they clear and aligned with your self-worth?
3. Where do you notice a lack of integrity between your inner values and outer actions? What adjustments could you make to realign?
4. What boundaries could you clarify to better protect your energy, time, and self-worth?

CHAPTER TWENTY-ONE
RETREAT TO THE REDOUBT OF RENEWAL
BUILDING YOUR SANCTUARY OF SUPPORTED SOVEREIGNTY

I alone cannot change the world, but I can cast a stone across the water to create many ripples. – Mother Teresa

PEELING BACK THE LAYERS OF OUR EMOTIONAL ONION CAN BE isolating and vulnerable. It requires confronting our deepest fears, insecurities, and judgments—work no one else can do for us. But while this journey is deeply personal, it doesn't mean we have to walk it alone. The presence of others who can offer acceptance, non-judgment, and unwavering support isn't just helpful—it's *vital*.

In the last chapter, we explored the metaphor of a stronghold: the inner sanctuary where our unshakable self-worth, values, and boundaries create a foundation for sovereignty. The stronghold is our fortress of inner alignment, a place where external forces can't dictate our worth or our choices.

But even the most secure stronghold can't stand in isolation forever. Life's battles are too complex and its challenges too relentless to face alone. That's where the redoubt* comes in. If the strong-

---

* **Redoubt:** A redoubt is a fortified position designed to provide defense and a is our inner foundation, the redoubt is our external sanctuary: the relationships, spaces, and practices that support and sustain us as we peel back the layers of shame, judgment, and dependency. It's the place where others help us see the truth of our worth, even when we can't see it for ourselves.

Together, the stronghold and the redoubt create a dynamic partnership. One roots us in our self-worth; the other reminds us that we're not alone.

WHAT IS A REDOUBT?

In military terms, a redoubt is a fortified position designed to withstand attacks and offer a secure place for regrouping. But a redoubt isn't about retreating or surrendering—it's a space for gathering strength, recalibrating your defenses, and preparing to re-engage.

In our journey, the redoubt is a metaphorical stronghold outside of ourselves. It is a sanctuary of relationships and practices where we can process emotions, confront fears, and find renewed strength. The redoubt reminds us that thriving isn't something we do in isolation. It's a process supported by meaningful connection, shared vulnerability, and mutual encouragement.

> *In the firebomb story in the previous chapter, part of choosing gratitude and meaning that day involved reaching out to trusted allies—people I could share my experience with without fear of judgment or shame. They listened, empathized, and reminded me of my values, who I aspire to be, and what integrity looks like in such circumstances. These friends are closer than brothers, and we honor and*

---

secure space for regrouping during battle. Metaphorically, it represents the network of relationships, spaces, and practices that offer support, acceptance, and renewal in life's challenges. Unlike the inner stronghold of self-worth and values, the redoubt is external—a sanctuary where connection and encouragement from others help sustain resilience and foster thriving.

WHAT TO DO WHEN THE ALIENS SHOW UP (AND EVEN IF THEY DON'T)

love one another by holding up a mirror to reflect back the truth of who we know each man is at his core. Their support allowed me to move through the experience quickly and with minimal disruption. Could I have done it on my own? Sure. I can also give myself a haircut without a mirror, but why would I, when a mirror makes the process so much easier and clearer?

THE REDOUBT AS A PARTNER TO THE STRONGHOLD

Our redoubt doesn't replace our stronghold—it complements it. While we work in the safety of our stronghold to peel the onion and confront our internal challenges, the redoubt provides something equally essential: the presence of others who can witness our struggles, offer encouragement, and challenge the narratives that keep us stuck.

WHY CONNECTION IS ESSENTIAL

Shame thrives in isolation. When we believe we're alone in our struggles, shame's lies—that we're not enough, not worthy, or irreparably flawed—gain power. The redoubt counters these lies with connection. Being seen, heard, and accepted by others creates a tangible experience of worth that helps dismantle shame at its root.

THE QUALITIES OF A TRUE REDOUBT

Not every relationship or space can serve as a redoubt. To provide the support and safety we need, a redoubt must meet certain criteria:

1. Encourages Growth, Not Dependency

True redoubt relationships don't foster reliance; they empower us to grow stronger and more sovereign. Allies in our redoubt challenge us to take ownership of our journey, offering support without taking over.

2. Holds Space for Vulnerability

A redoubt must be a judgment-free zone where we can let our guard down. Vulnerability doesn't mean weakness—it's the openness that allows healing and connection to thrive.

3. Provides Honest, Loving Feedback

Allies in our redoubt don't enable our self-limiting beliefs—they help us see beyond them. This feedback isn't about criticism but about lovingly challenging us to grow.

4. Strengthens Your Sovereignty

The ultimate goal of the redoubt is to aid us in restoring our confidence and clarity to lead ourselves well. The support we receive here doesn't replace our strength; it amplifies it, helping us step back into life with renewed agency.

BUILDING (OR FORTIFYING) YOUR REDOUBT

We don't have to start from scratch to create our redoubt. Often, the elements we need are already present—we just need to recognize and nurture them. Here's how to begin:

1. Identify Your Allies

Who in our life offers acceptance, encouragement, and honest feedback? These could be close friends, a therapist, a mentor, or a support group. We need to seek out those who respect our boundaries and align with our values.

2. Cultivate Restorative Practices

What activities or rituals foster connection and renewal, both individually and collectively? While personal practices like journaling, meditation, or prayer can help us reconnect with ourselves, group-oriented practices strengthen the bonds within our redoubt. Consider:

- **Shared Reflection:** Host regular check-ins with your allies where everyone can share wins, struggles, or insights without fear of judgment.
- **Collaborative Activities:** Engage in activities that build trust and connection, such as group hikes, creative workshops, or community service projects.
- **Mutual Encouragement:** Create a culture of affirmation by sharing positive feedback, gratitude, or words of encouragement within the group.

These practices foster a sense of belonging and support, reminding us that while the journey is personal, it is never meant to be walked alone.

3. Create Safe Spaces

It's good to ask ourselves where we feel most at peace. This could be a physical space, like a room in our home or a favorite park, or a mental space created through mindfulness and self-reflection.

4. Leverage Supportive Resources

Books, podcasts, and courses that inspire growth and resilience can become part of our redoubt. These tools reinforce our values and help us maintain clarity and focus.

5. Protect the Redoubt with Boundaries

A redoubt is only as strong as the boundaries that protect it. Boundaries ensure that this space remains sacred and empowering. They prevent negativity, judgment, or unnecessary drama from breaching our sanctuary.

THE ROLE OF RELATIONSHIPS AND FAMILIES IN YOUR REDOUBT

In an ideal world, our partnerships, families, and close-knit communities would be the cornerstone of our redoubt, offering us unwavering support, encouragement, and a safe space to thrive. Yet, many of us know the sting of unmet expectations in these relationships. It's an all-too-common frustration to feel that our partners, parents, or families aren't providing the sanctuary we long for. These gaps can feel isolating, but they don't have to be the end of the story.

Here's a truth I've witnessed: Someone in a partnership, family, or community has to go first in addressing their own shame and judgment to plant the "seed" of a redoubt. This is where transformation begins—not by demanding others change, but by becoming a living example of authenticity and acceptance. When we choose to let go of judgment, operate within our sphere of sovereignty, and extend grace, we create an environment where others feel safe to do the same. Over time, this shift can transform a relationship or family from the inside out, one step at a time.

At the same time, it's vital to recognize the importance of a multi-layered redoubt. Just as a stronghold requires multiple walls for protection, our redoubt thrives on redundancy and diversity. There will always be times when a relationship, partnership, or family dynamic doesn't provide the strength we need in the moment. This is where additional layers—friendships, mentors, communities, and support groups—play a crucial role. By building a robust network of connection, we ensure we're never left vulnerable, even when one layer falters.

In my own life, I've seen how supplementing family relationships with a broader community has been transformational. Having allies and spaces outside of my immediate circle has provided me with perspective, encouragement, and a sense of belonging that bolsters me even during challenges within those closer dynamics. It's not about replacing anyone—it's about ensuring that our redoubt is as resilient and supportive as possible.

Through this process, we learn that the strength of our redoubt isn't just in who or what is included—it's in our willingness to go first, to lead with authenticity, and to build layers of support that reinforce our sovereignty, no matter what life throws at us.

THE REDOUBT AS A LAUNCHPAD

Our redoubt isn't just a refuge—it's a launchpad for action. It's where we prepare to dismantle the shame machine, confront self-limiting beliefs, and step back into the world with clarity and confidence.

While the stronghold roots us in self-worth, the redoubt equips us with the connection and perspective needed to dismantle shame's lies. Together, these two sanctuaries create the resilience we need to thrive.

> *On my short list of key changes I made that have revolutionized my life, connecting with others on the same journey has been in the top two. Several years ago, my marriage and family were under massive strain, and neither was a place where I could find support. I found a men's group that helped me get my stronghold back in order, and*

I was able to work then to restore my marriage and family back to health.

When I was a teenager, I didn't usually feel like I could share my struggles openly at home. My parents cared deeply about me, but like many families, there were gaps in how we communicated or connected around hard emotions. I didn't always feel like I had the space to process what I was going through. So, I often turned to other places for support—friends who I felt accepted me, a few teachers who saw potential in me, or even family friends who had a knack for listening without judgment. These people became my redoubt in those moments, a safe space to be honest about what I was feeling.

One of the most important lessons I learned during that time was the value of patience in finding and building those connections. Most people are longing for the same thing—a sense of belonging, acceptance, and a space to be real—but many feel too embarrassed or ashamed to say so. I discovered that going first, as terrifying as it was, often made all the difference. Whether it was initiating a vulnerable conversation with a friend or being the one to admit I didn't have everything figured out, that act of courage created openings for others to do the same. Over time, those small moments grew into some of the most impactful redoubts I've ever experienced.

Going first is rarely easy. It feels risky to be vulnerable, and sometimes, it doesn't lead to the response we hope for. But when it does, it can transform relationships, offering the kind of mutual trust and support that fortifies us in ways we didn't think were possible. Looking back, I'm grateful for those early lessons in finding and forming redoubts. They taught me that while the search for *connection takes courage and patience, the reward is worth every moment of effort.*

Connecting with a "redoubt" is low-hanging fruit, and I have ensured that it remains a consistent part of my life.

MAIN TAKEAWAY: WE DON'T WALK THIS PATH ALONE

Peeling back the layers of our emotional onion is deeply personal, but it isn't meant to be done in isolation. Our redoubt—a sanctuary of relationships, spaces, and practices—is where we find the connection, encouragement, and strength to keep moving forward. It reminds us that while the work of healing is our responsibility, the journey is best supported by allies who see and affirm our worth, even when we can't.

By building a stronghold within and a redoubt around us, we create a foundation for thriving that no shame, judgment, or dependency can shake.

COMING UP: DISMANTLING THE SHAME MACHINE

Our stronghold and redoubt form the foundation for dismantling shame's grip on our lives. While the redoubt provides the external experience of acceptance, breaking free from shame requires learning to give that same acceptance to ourselves. In the next chapter, we'll explore the tactics of the shame machine and uncover how to dismantle its lies, reclaim your worth, and step fully into the truth of who you are.

COMMON RESPONSES

"Yeah, but I don't have anyone who can be part of my redoubt."

Finding the right people takes time, but connection starts with small, courageous steps. Look for those who share your values and offer mutual respect. You can begin by initiating honest conversations or joining supportive groups.

"Yeah, but I've been hurt by people I trusted in the past."

That's valid—past hurts make vulnerability feel risky. Start by building trust gradually, choosing relationships where respect and safety are evident. Healing is possible, and the right connections can be transformative.

"Yeah, but I feel like I should be able to handle things on my own."

Independence is important, but connection doesn't diminish your strength—it amplifies it. A redoubt isn't about dependency; it's about shared strength and mutual growth.

"Yeah, but what if others don't respond to my vulnerability?"

Vulnerability doesn't always lead to the response we hope for, but it creates openings for deeper connections. Start small, with safe people or spaces, and remember that their response doesn't define your worth.

"Yeah, but I don't know how to set boundaries with people who drain me."

Boundaries take practice, but they're essential for protecting your energy and fostering healthy connections. Start with small, clear state-

WHAT TO DO WHEN THE ALIENS SHOW UP (AND EVEN IF THEY DON'T)

ments about your needs and limits, and remember that boundaries are about your choices, not controlling others.

REFLECTION QUESTIONS

1. Who in your life currently acts as part of your redoubt? How can you strengthen those relationships?
2. What practices or rituals help you feel grounded and supported?
3. What boundaries do you need to set to protect your redoubt from negativity or distractions?
4. How does your redoubt equip you to face shame and judgment with courage and clarity?

CHAPTER TWENTY-TWO
DISMANTLING THE SHAME MACHINE
THE FOUR STRATEGIES FOR FREEDOM

Shame corrodes the very part of us that believes we are capable of change. – Brené Brown

LIVING UNDER THE WEIGHT OF SHAME

PEELING BACK THE LAYERS OF YOUR EMOTIONAL ONION OFTEN REVEALS a painful core: shame. It's the deep-rooted belief that something is fundamentally wrong with us, that we're unworthy, or that we'll never measure up. Shame thrives on isolation, silence, and judgment. It's the invaders' most insidious weapon woven into the stories we tell ourselves and the standards we believe we must meet.

But here's the truth: shame is a liar. It's not a reflection of our worth—it's a *distortion* of it. And like any distortion, it can be confronted, unraveled, and ultimately replaced with truth.

The **redoubt** we've begun to build is key to this process. It provides the safety and connection necessary to begin challenging the lies of shame. But even the strongest redoubt is only the starting point. To truly dismantle shame, we must confront and disarm the internal machine that perpetuates its hold.

SHAME: THE INVADERS' MOST POTENT WEAPON

Shame is not an abstract concept; it's a tactic deliberately deployed by the invaders to fool us into disconnecting ourselves from our sense of inherent worth. Notice that I didn't say that we genuinely are severed from our worth—we are not. However, a worth we're unfamiliar with causes us to strive for what we already possess, kind of like working at a minimum-wage job because we don't know we're billionaires.

Shame distorts our self-perception and convinces us to focus on external standards and validation. It thrives on isolation, ensuring we feel alone in our struggles. Shame tells us, "You're not enough and never will be."

But shame's power lies in its secrecy. When exposed to truth and connection, it begins to lose its grip.

THE LIE AT THE CORE OF SHAME

At the heart of shame lies a single, devastating lie: You are not enough.

This lie whispers that our worth must be earned through success, perfection, or meeting external standards. Because no one can always meet impossible expectations, shame perpetuates a cycle of striving, failure, and self-doubt.

The truth is this: Our worth has never been in question. It is inherent, unshakable, and unchanging. The invaders use shame to keep us focused on what we lack, but the path to freedom begins with reclaiming the truth: We are enough, exactly as we are.

WHAT TO DO WHEN THE ALIENS SHOW UP (AND EVEN IF THEY DON'T)

FOUR STRATEGIES FOR NAVIGATING SHAME

Breaking free from shame involves more than rejecting its lies—we must rewrite the entire story and form new beliefs. Here are four common strategies I find people generally use to navigate shame, along with insights into their effectiveness:

1. Coping with the Standard

Coping is often the first response to shame. We try to outrun it by working harder, achieving more, or striving for perfection. This strategy might manifest as people-pleasing, overworking, or constant busyness—anything to avoid facing feelings of inadequacy.

- **Where It Helps:** Coping provides temporary relief and allows you to function during overwhelming seasons.
- **Where It Falls Short:** Coping doesn't address the root of shame. It's like running on a treadmill, trying to escape your shadow—it follows you wherever you go.

2. Eliminating the Standard

When coping fails, we may decide to reject the standards that shame uses to measure our worth. This might mean walking away from societal norms, toxic relationships, or unrealistic expectations. Choosing to believe that "There is no standard I must meet to be worthy. I just am" is a radical act of liberation.

- **Where It Helps:** Letting go of external measures of worth frees you from shame's cycles.
- **Where It Falls Short:** Eliminating all standards without aligning with your values can lead to aimlessness or avoidance of healthy growth. Eliminating the standard

can become a new thing to judge ourselves for doing, returning us to shame.

3. Lowering the Standard

Some respond to shame by lowering the bar—redefining success as "good enough." This can be a healthy step if you've been living under unattainable expectations.

- **Where It Helps:** Lowering the bar provides relief and helps you set more realistic goals.
- **Where It Falls Short:** If the root lie of shame remains unchallenged, lowering the standard is only a temporary fix. Lowering the bar can become a new thing to judge ourselves for doing, returning us to shame.

4. Meeting the Standard

Some respond to shame by striving to meet the standard—redefining what it means to achieve it in ways that feel attainable and aligned with deeper values.
- **Where It Helps:** Redefining the standard shifts the focus from external measures to personal values like kindness, integrity, or resilience. This can empower us to live authentically.
- **Where It Falls Short:** The pursuit of meeting any standard—even one we set ourselves—requires believing we meet it with absolute precision. This can lead to doubt and self-judgment, perpetuating shame's hold.

When our family welcomed Ruby, a beautiful Bernese Mountain Dog, into our lives, we were overjoyed. She was everything you'd hope for—loyal, affectionate, and gentle. Her mother and father were both Bernese Mountain Dogs

WHAT TO DO WHEN THE ALIENS SHOW UP (AND EVEN IF THEY DON'T)

as well, but Ruby lacked one thing: a pedigree. She didn't come with a piece of paper declaring her official lineage.

At the time, it didn't matter to us. Ruby was family. But when Ruby had puppies (with an African Boerboel Mastiff), we quickly learned how powerful standards can be—and how different people hold those standards in very different ways. For some, Ruby's puppies were delightful, a gift. For others, the lack of pedigree was an insurmountable issue, a deal-breaker that disqualified the puppies from meeting their expectations, and they discourteously said so! It would have been easy to experience shame for not measuring up.

This experience taught me a lot about standards and shame—both how we hold them and how we respond to them. In Ruby's story, I see the four ways we can address shame when standards are held up to us:

- Coping with the standard meant acknowledging that, yes, Ruby didn't meet everyone's expectations. I remember feeling defensive at first—"Does it really matter that there's no paperwork? Look at these puppies!"—but coping meant learning to sit with the discomfort of others' opinions without letting it diminish our joy or worth. Ruby's lack of pedigree didn't make her or her puppies any less wonderful. Their opinions didn't have to define our experience.

- Lowering the standard was a step of acceptance. Did Ruby's puppies meet the strict breed standard? On paper, no. But for the right people, those puppies were <u>perfect</u>. They weren't competing in a dog show—they were joining families, bringing love and joy to their homes. When we let go of unnecessary expectations, we found peace and gratitude for what Ruby had brought into our lives.

- Eliminating the standard was perhaps the most

freeing approach. Who says a piece of paper determines a dog's value or the love it can bring to a family? Ruby and her puppies didn't need external validation to be wonderful, and neither did we. We let go of the need for their approval altogether, trusting our own experience and what we knew to be true: Ruby and her pups were more than enough just as she was.

- Meeting the standard (redefined) offered another perspective. While Ruby's puppies would never have pedigree papers, they met an even deeper standard: they brought joy, companionship, and connection into people's lives. For the families who welcomed them, the puppies exceeded the most meaningful standard of all—being a source of love and happiness.

This experience taught me that standards are often subjective, shaped by what people value most. Ruby's worth wasn't diminished by her lack of pedigree, and her puppies were no less loving, playful, or beautiful because of it. It all came down to perspective and what we, or other families, were willing to believe.

When shame whispers that you don't meet someone else's standards—whether it's pedigree, performance, or approval—ask yourself: Whose standard am I holding? Who set it? Does it serve me, or does it steal from me? Ruby didn't need a piece of paper to prove her value. And neither do you.

In many cases (not all), you get to decide which standards matter. And when you choose standards that align with your truth and values, shame begins to lose its power.

WHAT TO DO WHEN THE ALIENS SHOW UP (AND EVEN IF THEY DON'T)

Ruby's Non-Standard-Meeting Puppies

MEETING THE STANDARD: A PARADIGM SHIFT

When it comes to dismantling shame, I've found that the most transformative approach has been to rethink the idea of a "standard" and the practice of judgment itself (which we'll talk about in the next chapter). If we're ever going to free ourselves from shame, we need to root our worth in something unshakable—something that doesn't depend on what we do, how we compare, or even what we believe about ourselves. To be truly durable, it has to go deeper than that. Let me explain two ways to see this potentially.

Unconditional High Regard

Here's a truth that has the power to change everything: *Our worth isn't tied to what we do, what we've accomplished, or whether we've "earned" it.* Our worth is tied to our existence. Period. Because of this, there is a baseline of high regard all humans are worthy of, regardless of any conditions.

This idea of Unconditional High Regard (UHR) means that our humanity alone makes us worthy. We don't have to hit some arbitrary bar or live up to someone else's expectations. Shame loves to convince us otherwise—that we need to prove something or measure up. But when we start to see that our worth doesn't depend on anything outside of us, shame loses its grip. It simply can't survive in the presence of unconditional worth. We'll take a deeper look at this in the chapters ahead.

Grounding Worth in the Nature of the Source

For those who believe or are willing to consider a divine source—or even just the interconnectedness of everything—this perspective takes things even deeper. Think about it: if there's a source behind everything, what kind of regard does it have for us? Is it conditional? Why would it have conditions for our acceptance? How would they be communicated? How could we confirm those conditions? Does that source value and love us only if you check certain boxes? Why would it do that? If it were self-existent, what would it need from us in return? That seems unlikely, right?

If the source values and even loves us, it seems the most sensical to take the position that it does so *because of its own nature*, not because of ours. A loving source / Creator doesn't value us for our perfection or performance—it would value us because that's who *it* is. Alternatively, if we believe we're one with the source, then our worth is part of its inherent goodness, and because of our oneness, ours too. Either way, our worth isn't up for debate. It's not conditional, and it's not something we can lose.

This perspective is incredibly freeing. When worth is grounded in something as constant and unchanging as the nature of existence itself, it can't be shaken. Shame has nowhere to plant its roots.

THE SUN SHINES REGARDLESS: A METAPHOR FOR WORTH

I think of this as similar to the sun. It shines without condition. It doesn't withhold warmth on cloudy days or shine brighter because the earth is doing something special. The sun shines because it's the sun—that's its nature.

When we feel cold or trapped in darkness, it's not because the sun has stopped shining. It's because something—our motion, a shadow, clouds, or even an eclipse—has blocked the light. But the sun? It's still there, unchanging, steadfast, providing light and warmth–unconditionally. All we need to do is turn back toward it, rise above clouds, or sometimes... just be patient for a few hours.

This is the essence of **unconditional high regard**: our worth isn't something we earn or lose—it simply *is*. If there is a source of life and existence, it's reasonable to believe its regard for us would operate like the sun, steady and unconditional. It would value us because of *its* nature, not *ours*. And if we're one with that source, then our worth is as inherent as the light of the sun itself.

This perspective is revolutionary because it removes shame's power. Shame thrives on the idea that our worth is conditional—tied to how we perform, behave, or measure up. But if worth is constant, like the sun's light, shame loses its foundation. Our struggles and failures don't change our value; they're simply shadows we can step out of.

CONDITIONAL APPROACHES: HELPFUL BUT LIMITED

Now, let's be clear: not everyone starts with an unshakable sense of intrinsic worth. Sometimes, we take steps that feel more tangible. These approaches can help us navigate shame, but they all have one potential flaw—they can still be *conditional*. Here's what I mean:

Rejecting Comparison

Some of the ways I outlined to deal with shame involve stepping out of the comparison game entirely. When we stop measuring ourselves against others, we take a huge step toward freedom. But here's the catch: in many ways, this alone requires our constant awareness. Comparison is so ingrained in us that slipping back into old patterns is easy. Even our decision to reject comparison can become a new standard for comparison.

Let me give you an example that is kinda sad but realistic:

- **Jane:** *"I feel great about myself, Bob—because I've finally rejected comparison! I'm no longer comparing myself to you! Shew... I feel great!"*
- **Bob:** *"What took you so long, Jane? I rejected this comparison stuff like... two years ago!"*
- **Jane:** *"What?! Two years?! How did I not know? Why didn't you tell me? Why am I always the last to always figure out things? I feel so bad that you always figure out cool things before me! What's wrong with me? I should have known this earlier!"*
- **Bob:** *"Well, now I feel bad I didn't tell you earlier. I should have told you back then. Some friend I am! You're not the first person who has told me this. I'm starting to believe you'd be better off with a better friend."*

Hopefully, you can see how easy it is when we judge ourselves to turn everything into a standard that we then use to judge ourselves and come up short. See all the standards and comparisons in that dialog?

Redefining Failure

Another powerful tool is seeing failure as a stepping stone rather than a verdict. This perspective changes the narrative from "I failed, so I'm not enough" to "I failed, so I learned something." This kind of reframing can be potent and help overcome the inertia of shame. However, this perspective also depends on our ability to maintain it. When life feels heavy, it's easy to fall back into seeing failure as a reflection of who we are. Because it indirectly depends on our resiliency and mindset to maintain, our sense of shame can rise to discouraging levels on low resiliency days.

Seeing Worth as Non-Transactional

This approach asks us to believe that worth isn't about what we do or achieve—it's about being human. While this belief is empowering, it still requires us to consciously hold onto it. If we start to doubt or lose focus, shame can creep back in because we conditionally believe our worth is non-conditional. See the challenge there?

THE UNIFIED SOLUTION: RETURNING TO UNCONDITIONALITY

Here's where everything comes together: When we root our worth in something unconditional, we break free from shame in more powerful, sustainable, and durable ways that lead to an unshakable sense of self-worth. These two frameworks are the key:

- **Unconditional High Regard:** Your worth is tied to your humanity and existence, not your actions or achievements. It's a constant.
- **The Nature of the Source:** If the source of all things values you, it does so because of its nature, not yours. Or, if you're one with the source, then your worth is inseparable from its inherent value.

Here's why this works: when worth isn't something we have to earn, believe in, or prove, it becomes untouchable. Doubts, failures, and comparisons lose their power because they don't change the foundation of who we are because we are rooted in something bigger than our concept of "self." We stop striving for worth and start living in the truth of it. From there, we can understand standards in ways that align with life-giving values, free from judgment and shame.

THE TRANSFORMATION: FREEDOM FROM SHAME

This isn't just about feeling better—it's about seeing the truth of who we are. When we root our worth in unconditional frameworks, we dismantle shame's power at its source. Our value remains constant, whether we face doubt, failure, or judgment. We stop hustling for approval and live authentically, free from fear of not measuring up.

This is the kind of freedom we're building—a life where shame doesn't get to define us, where worth isn't up for grabs, and where we can finally stop striving and start thriving.

THE ROLE OF THE REDOUBT

Your redoubt—the community, sanctuary, or practices you've built—plays a vital role in this process of dismantling shame. Shame thrives on isolation, convincing us that we're alone in our struggles. But in our redoubt, we experience connection, acceptance, and the tangible truth that we are seen, known, and loved.

The redoubt doesn't eliminate shame for us but equips us to face it. The relationships we offer one another in a redoubt remind us of deeper truths we may not notice in times of discouragement and despair. Through meaningful relationships and restorative practices, we gain the strength and clarity to challenge shame's lies and reclaim our worth.

THE PATH FORWARD

Dismantling shame is not a one-time event—it's an ongoing process of recognizing its lies, challenging them, and rewriting the story of our worth. Our redoubt provides the safety and support you need to do this work, but the ultimate power lies within us.

Shame's hold on us weakens when we confront it with truth, connection, and the unwavering belief that our worth is unshakable. As we dismantle the shame machine, we reclaim our freedom, courage, and ability to live authentically.

MAIN TAKEAWAY: SHAME IS A LIE, AND YOUR WORTH IS UNSHAKABLE

Shame thrives on secrecy and isolation, feeding the lie that we are not enough. It ties our worth to impossible standards, keeping us trapped in cycles of fear and self-doubt. But shame is not the truth —it's a distortion.

Freedom begins when we challenge shame's lies and rewrite the story of our worth. In the safety of our redoubt, we discover that our value is inherent, unchanging, and unaffected by external standards. By embracing unconditional high regard for ourselves and redefining the metrics of worth, we dismantle shame and step fully into freedom.

COMING UP: FROM SHAME TO FREEDOM

Breaking free from shame requires more than awareness—it demands action. In the next chapter, we'll explore how shame infiltrates our thoughts, behaviors, and relationships and how to systematically dismantle its hold. With the foundation of our redoubt and the power of unconditional high regard, we'll be ready to rewrite the story of our worth and step fully into freedom.

COMMON RESPONSES

> "Yeah, but I've lived with shame for so long—it's part of who I am."

Shame might feel like a permanent part of your identity because it's woven into the stories you've told yourself. But shame is not your truth— it's a story rooted in fear, not reality. You are not your shame, and it's never too late to rewrite your narrative. Even the longest-held beliefs can change when exposed to truth and connection.

"Yeah, but what if I'm truly not enough?"

That's the lie of shame speaking—it thrives on convincing you that your worth is conditional. But the truth is that your worth has never been up for debate. You were born enough, and nothing you've done or failed to do can change that. Start by questioning the lie and daring to believe in the inherent value of your existence, even if it feels hard at first.

"Yeah, but I feel like I've let everyone down too many times to believe I'm worthy."

It's easy to tie our worth to how well we think we've measured up to others' expectations. But worth isn't transactional; it doesn't fluctuate with successes or failures. Letting people down doesn't mean you've lost value—it means you're human. The people who truly care about you don't love you for being perfect; they love you for being real.

"Yeah, but shame keeps me safe—it stops me from making the same mistakes again."

Shame might feel like a protective shield, but it's really a heavy burden that keeps you stuck in fear and self-doubt. Growth doesn't come from shame; it comes from self-compassion and accountability. You don't need shame to keep you safe—you need self-awareness and the courage to make choices aligned with your values.

"Yeah, but I've been judged so harshly by others—how do I move past that?"

Being judged by others can feel like a scar that never fades, but their judgment doesn't define you. It's important to remember that people often judge from their own pain, fears, or insecurities. You are not what they *say you are. Surround yourself with people who see your worth and work on internalizing the truth: your value doesn't depend on anyone else's opinion.*

REFLECTION QUESTIONS

1. What lies has shame told you about your worth, and how have these shaped your thoughts, actions, or relationships?
2. Which of the four strategies for navigating shame resonates most with your current experience? How has it served you, and where might it be holding you back?
3. How does your redoubt support you in confronting shame? Are there any elements—people, practices, or spaces—you could strengthen to help in this process?
4. What would your life look like if you fully embraced the truth that your worth is unshakable and not tied to any external standard?
5. What small, practical step can you take today to begin challenging shame's lies and reclaiming your inherent worth?

CHAPTER TWENTY-THREE
HOBBLING THE DOOMSDAY DEVICE
ENDING THE JUDGMENT FUELS DESTRUCTION

When you judge another, you do not define them; you define yourself. – Wayne Dyer

---

DISMANTLING JUDGMENT: CHOOSING UNCONDITIONAL HIGH REGARD

AT THE HEART OF PEELING THE ONION AND NAVIGATING THE DEEPEST layers of shame lies a universal truth: healing requires patience, support, and non-judgment. As we've explored, peeling back the layers reveals the roots of our emotional suffering—often hidden beneath years of internalized beliefs and patterns. And yet, as we reach the core, we encounter the invaders' most destructive weapon: judgment.

Judgment, like a doomsday device, sits at the center of shame's power, fueling its relentless cycles. It dismantles our sense of worth, isolates us from others, and keeps us trapped in self-condemnation. To truly reclaim our lives and thrive, we must disarm judgment, replacing it with something far more powerful: unconditional high regard.

THE ROLE OF JUDGMENT IN SHAME

Judgment is the taproot and fruit of shame–a perpetual cycle that endlessly feeds itself. Where shame whispers, "You're not enough," judgment responds, "And here's the proof." It catalogs every flaw, failure, and misstep, transforming mistakes into evidence of unworthiness and driving us to experience more. Worse still, the judgment doesn't limit itself to actions—it targets identity, turning "I made a mistake" into "I *am* a mistake."

Judgment thrives on three levels:

1. **Judging Ourselves:** Internal criticism that amplifies insecurity and fuels shame cycles.
2. **Judging Others:** Projection of our own fears and unmet needs onto others, often as a way to deflect internal discomfort.
3. **Judging Situations:** Assigning moral or absolute meaning to neutral circumstances, turning challenges into insurmountable obstacles.

Judgment pretends to be a form of protection. It claims, "If you judge yourself harshly, you'll do better. You'll avoid failure. You'll never get hurt again." But this is a lie. Judgment doesn't protect—it punishes. It doesn't strengthen—it weakens. It doesn't motivate—it isolates.

As long as judgment holds power, shame thrives. As long as shame thrives, the authentic self remains buried and unable to emerge.

HOW JUDGMENT KEEPS YOU STUCK

The judgment-shame cycle is insidious because it feels normal. For many of us, it's the only way we've ever related to ourselves:

1. **Judgment Sets the Standard:** "You should be better, smarter, stronger, more successful."
2. **Failure to Meet the Standard:** Inevitably, you fall short because the standard is often unattainable.
3. **Shame Takes Hold:** Your failure becomes proof of your unworthiness. "See? You'll never be enough."
4. **Judgment Reinforces Shame:** "And this is why you're broken."

This cycle creates a toxic feedback loop, trapping us in a state of insecurity, fear, and self-loathing. Judgment keeps us focused on our shortcomings rather than our potential, ensuring that shame's grip remains unbroken.

REPLACING JUDGMENT WITH UNCONDITIONAL HIGH REGARD

The antidote to judgment isn't more judgment—it's unconditional high regard (UHR). Where judgment divides, UHR reconnects. Where judgment condemns, UHR accepts. UHR is the foundation for dismantling shame because it transforms the way we see ourselves and others, ending the cycle of judgment and shame.

WHAT IS UNCONDITIONAL HIGH REGARD?

Unconditional high regard is the unwavering recognition of worth, regardless of external circumstances. It's the belief that our value is intrinsic—not tied to our performance, appearance, or approval from others. It's choosing to see ourselves and others through a lens of compassion, acceptance, and grace, no matter what.

UHR doesn't excuse harmful behavior or ignore the need for accountability—it separates *worth* from *behaviors and actions*. It's the acknowledgment that everyone, including us, is inherently valuable, even amidst our flaws and mistakes.

PRACTICING HIGH REGARD FOR OURSELVES

To disarm judgment, we must first reclaim high regard for ourselves. This isn't about ignoring our imperfections or avoiding accountability. It's about separating our actions from our identity and embracing our humanity.

1. Challenge the Lies of Judgment

When judgment arises, pause and question it. Ask: "Is this true? Or is it a story shaped by shame and fear?" Replace judgment with a compassionate reframe.

- **Judgment:** *"I'll never get this right."*
- **High Regard:** *"I'm learning, and that's enough for today."*

2. Celebrate Your Humanity

Gratitude is one of the most powerful tools for cultivating high regard. Instead of focusing on what you lack, honor what makes you uniquely you. Celebrate your growth, resilience, and imperfections.

- **Example:** After a hard day, reflect: *"I'm proud of the way I kept trying, even when it was difficult."*

3. Extend Yourself Grace

Grace is the antidote to judgment. It's the recognition that you're doing the best you can with the tools you have. It allows you to hold yourself accountable without condemnation.

- **Example:** When you make a mistake, grace says, *"This doesn't define me. What can I learn from it?"*

OFFERING HIGH REGARD TO OTHERS

High regard doesn't stop with ourselves. Extending the same compassion and acceptance to others disrupts judgment's hold on our relationships, creating space for connection and authenticity.

1. See the Person, Not Just the Behavior

High regard acknowledges someone's inherent worth, even when setting boundaries or addressing harm.

- **Example:** *"I can see you're struggling, but I won't allow you to treat me this way."*

2. Break the Cycle of Judgment

Judgment in relationships feeds disconnection. Choosing UHR disrupts this pattern and invites mutual understanding.

- **Example:** Instead of assuming ill intent, approach with curiosity: *"Help me understand where you're coming from."*

3. Model Grace and Compassion

When you choose UHR, you invite others to do the same. Your example can inspire a culture of acceptance and growth.

> When people hear me talk about "letting go of judgment," their immediate response is often—ironically—judgment itself. I hear things like, "You're saying truth is relative! That's a lie!" or "Oh, so you don't believe in right and wrong? What an idiot!" or "Ah, I see—you must be a [insert political label here]." We're so steeped in our own inferences and interpretations that we confuse them with

objective truth. This is the kind of judgment I'm talking about learning to let go of.

I used to be terrible at this. I'd walk around constantly primed to come to conclusions about people, ideas, and situations—especially when it came to the perceived moral substance of others. If someone didn't meet my standards, I'd size them up, label them, and file them away in a neat box. It wasn't until I could see this part of my inner dialogue for what it really was—a saboteur—that my life began to change.

Letting go of judgment didn't mean I threw out truth, morality, or the ideas of right and wrong. I didn't stop caring about what was good or just. What I let go of was the belief that I get to determine those standards for others—that my version of truth is the final word or that others should align with my understanding of what's right or wrong.

It was humbling—and freeing. Humbling because I realized how much of my "righteous judgment" was rooted in my ego, fear, and insecurities. Freeing because it lifted a weight I hadn't even realized I was carrying. When I stopped holding others to my unspoken standards, I found more peace, deeper connection, and far greater clarity.

Letting go of judgment doesn't mean we abandon discernment—it means we stop playing judge, jury, and executioner in our own minds (most of all, toward ourselves!). It means we stop assuming we've got everything figured out. And it means we leave space for curiosity, compassion, and growth—both in ourselves and others.

THE PATH FORWARD: FROM JUDGMENT TO REGARD

Disarming judgment is an act of liberation. It frees us from the lies that have kept us stuck, allowing us to reconnect with our worth and authenticity. This process doesn't happen in isolation. As we've explored, the safety of your redoubt offers a foundation for practicing high regard for ourselves and others. The stronger this foundation becomes, the more resilient we'll be against shame's lies.

Unconditional high regard is not a destination—it's a daily practice. Each moment we choose to see ourselves and others through a lens of compassion and acceptance, we weaken judgment's grip and step closer to a life of freedom and authenticity.

MAIN TAKEAWAY: JUDGING LESS, LIVING FREER

Unconditional High Regard is the antidote to the destructive cycles of judgment and shame. It separates a person's worth from their actions, offering compassion and accountability without condemnation. By dismantling judgment and practicing UHR for ourselves and others, we create a foundation for authentic connection, growth, and liberation.

COMING UP NEXT: RECLAIMING THE GROUND FROM THE ENEMY

In the next chapter, we'll explore how to take back the ground lost to fear, shame, and judgment. By understanding the tactics used to keep us trapped, we'll learn strategies for dismantling harmful patterns and reclaiming our power to thrive.

COMMON RESPONSES

"Yeah, but if I don't judge myself harshly, won't I just get lazy or let myself off the hook?"

I understand this fear—it's deeply ingrained in many of us. But judgment isn't what fuels progress; self-compassion does. When we replace judgment with high regard, we still hold ourselves accountable, but in a way that fosters growth instead of fear or shame. Imagine parenting yourself: Would you encourage a child with relentless criticism, or would you motivate them with love and support? Which approach do you think leads to sustainable growth?

"Yeah, but some people deserve to be judged—they've done awful things!"

I hear you, and it's hard to separate people from their actions, especially when harm is involved. Unconditional high regard doesn't excuse or condone harmful behavior; it's about seeing the inherent worth of every person, even when their actions fall short. This perspective allows us to hold others accountable without becoming consumed by anger or hatred, which often harms us more than it helps.

"Yeah, but if I let go of judgment, how will I protect myself from people who hurt me?"

Choosing high regard doesn't mean abandoning discernment or boundaries—it's about reframing how we see ourselves and others. You can still protect yourself and hold firm boundaries without letting judgment and resentment take root. In fact, boundaries are stronger and clearer when they come from a place of self-respect and high regard rather than fear or anger.

WHAT TO DO WHEN THE ALIENS SHOW UP (AND EVEN IF THEY DON'T)

"Yeah, but what if I can't stop judging myself? It's automatic at this point."

That's so relatable—it takes time and practice to unlearn the judgment-shame cycle. Start small by noticing when judgment arises and pausing to question it. Replace harsh inner dialogue with compassionate, truthful statements. Even a single moment of catching and redirecting judgment is progress. Over time, these moments build into a habit of self-compassion.

"Yeah, but isn't this idea of unconditional high regard just letting people off the hook?"

Not at all. Unconditional high regard isn't about ignoring accountability—it's about separating a person's worth from their actions. When we approach others with high regard, we're more likely to foster understanding, healing, and real change. Judgment isolates and hardens people; regard creates connection and possibility.

REFLECTION QUESTIONS

1. How has judgment—of yourself or others—kept you trapped in cycles of shame?
2. What would it look like to approach yourself with unconditional high regard in moments of struggle?
3. How might choosing high regard for others change the way you navigate relationships?
4. What small steps can you take this week to begin practicing UHR as a daily habit?

CHAPTER TWENTY-FOUR
RECLAIMING THE GROUND FROM THE ENEMY

RESTORING WHAT THE INVADERS TOOK: REBUILDING WORTH AND PURPOSE

No one can make you feel inferior without your consent. — Eleanor Roosevelt

---

UNCONDITIONAL HIGH REGARD AS THE FOUNDATION OF FREEDOM

THE INVADERS' PRIMARY STRATEGY HAS ALWAYS BEEN TO CONVINCE US that our worth is conditional. They've whispered lies that who we are depends on what we do, how others see us, and whether we measure up to shifting standards of success. These whispers have shaped our sense of self so profoundly that many of us don't even question them anymore.

The truth is, our worth has never been negotiable. It was never up for debate. To dismantle the invaders' power, we must reclaim what they sought to destroy: our inherent, unconditional worth. This reclamation begins with Unconditional High Regard (UHR)—a radical choice to view ourselves and others as intrinsically valuable, no matter what.

WHY NOT JUST CALL IT LOVE?

You may wonder why this book uses the term Unconditional High Regard (UHR) instead of the more familiar "unconditional love." While love is a powerful concept, its overuse in everyday language can dilute its depth and clarity.

Think about it: we "love" our pets, our favorite dessert (like flan, my favorite!), and our family members—but not in the same way. For many, the word "love" also comes with baggage, tied to ideas of romanticism, obligation, or even codependency.

That's why UHR feels more precise. It's about recognizing the intrinsic value of ourselves and others—not because of actions or worthiness, but because of a deliberate choice rooted in our sovereign choices. UHR doesn't depend on how someone else behaves, nor does it require a particular emotional feeling. Instead, it's an intentional act of alignment with the truth of intrinsic worth.

THE TRUTH ABOUT OUR WORTH

The invaders launched their assault by attacking this simple but profound truth: our worth is not up for debate. It does not fluctuate with success or failure, nor does it depend on external validation. We were born with intrinsic value that mistakes, setbacks, or rejection cannot diminish.

But over time, the invaders' lies have distorted this truth. They've convinced us that others must earn, measure, or validate our worth. These lies have been woven into our stories—stories shaped by shame, judgment, and fear. To reclaim our worth, we must first recognize these stories for what they are: false narratives designed to keep us small, beaten down, and dependent.

THE HARMFUL STORIES OF CONDITIONAL WORTH

Let's take a closer look at some of the familiar narratives that reinforce externalized self-worth:

"I am only worthy if I achieve."

This story ties our value to success and productivity. It whispers that we are not enough unless we accomplish something significant.

"I must earn love through perfection."

This narrative convinces us that love and acceptance depend on being flawless. It fuels perfectionism and leaves no room for mistakes or growth.

"If they don't approve, I don't matter."

Our sense of self becomes tethered to others' opinions. The fear of rejection drives us to mold ourselves into what we think others want.

"My value depends on what I look like."

This story tells you that our worth is tied to our appearance, creating a cycle of comparison and insecurity.

"I have to work harder to be acceptable."

This belief keeps us on a hamster wheel of effort, chasing an ever-moving goalpost of worthiness.

Each of these narratives is rooted in a lie: Our worth is *external* and *conditional*. Breaking free from these stories requires a radical shift in perspective, starting with UHR.

HOW UNCONDITIONAL HIGH REGARD IS DIFFERENT

At its core, UHR is the belief that our worth—and the worth of others—is *intrinsic* and *unchanging*. It's not about what we do, what we achieve, or how others see us. It simply *is*. UHR invites us to see ourselves and others through a lens of compassion, acceptance, and grace.

- **For Ourselves:** UHR means acknowledging our humanity—our flaws, growth, and inherent value—without judgment or shame.
- **For Others:** UHR doesn't excuse harmful behavior, but it recognizes that every person is more than their actions. It allows you to extend grace while still holding boundaries.

THE RELATIONSHIP BETWEEN UHR AND PERSONAL SOVEREIGNTY

Practicing UHR is an act of personal sovereignty and self-leadership. It means reclaiming our power to define our worth rather than outsourcing it to external forces. Personal sovereignty doesn't mean isolating ourselves or rejecting relationships; it means taking responsibility for our own sense of value and not letting it hinge on anything outside of us.

For example:

- **Externalized Self-Worth:** *"If they don't like me, I'm worthless."*
- **Sovereignty + UHR:** *"Their opinion doesn't change my value. I am enough."*

HOW THE INVADERS EXPLOIT CONDITIONAL WORTH

The invaders thrive on conditional worth because it keeps us small, defeated, and dependent on their systems of control. They feed us lies like:

- *"You'll only matter if you achieve more."*

- *"Without their approval, you're nothing."*
- *"You have to prove your value to deserve love."*

These lies keep us chasing validation, approval, and success—forever striving but never arriving. UHR dismantles this system by reminding us that our worth was *never* something we had to earn.

THE POWER OF UHR: RECLAIMING OURSELVES

Practicing UHR begins with a simple but profound realization: *we are already enough.* We always were. Reclaiming this truth takes time, but every step we take weakens the invaders' hold. Here are some ways to begin:

1. Identify the Lies

Start by examining the narratives you've internalized about your worth. Where did they come from? Who planted them? How have they shaped your decisions and beliefs?

- **Reflection Questions:**
    - What have I been taught about what makes me "enough"?
    - How do these beliefs impact my sense of self?

2. Break the Agreements

Agreements are the unspoken contracts we make with harmful beliefs. To reclaim your worth, you must consciously reject these agreements.

- **Examples:**
    - *"I break the agreement that my worth depends on others' approval."*

- *"I reject the belief that I have to earn love through perfection."*

3. Challenge External Dependencies

Ask yourself, "Where am I outsourcing my value?" Whether it's a job, a relationship, or a social standard, begin disentangling your worth from external factors. What gives them the authority to decide your value? What makes them uniquely special to determine your value and worth? What stories are you telling yourself about what they provide that you don't already possess?

4. Reconnect With Your Authentic Self

Spend time exploring your needs, desires, and boundaries. Reconnecting with your authentic self allows you to see your worth more clearly.

5. Practice Internal Validation

Start affirming your worth from within. Remind yourself regularly: *I am enough, just as I am.* This rewires your brain to rely on internal rather than external sources of self-worth.

> *I grew up as a MacGyver fan. If you've seen the show, you know exactly what I'm talking about: a guy who could get out of any jam, diffuse any bomb, and pick any lock using nothing but a paperclip, duct tape, and a little creative genius. I was mesmerized by how MacGyver could turn the simplest tools into lifesaving solutions. So when I was 10 years old and finally got my first Swiss Army knife—a gift I had begged for—it felt like I'd been handed a superpower.*
>
> *That knife was my treasure. It had a small blade, a*

pair of scissors, a toothpick, and, of course, that iconic corkscrew. To me, it was as versatile as MacGyver's toolkit. I carried it with me everywhere, convinced I could solve any problem. Stuck jar lid? Swiss Army knife. Loose screw? Swiss Army knife. Need to open a box, whittle a stick, or pretend I was a secret agent? Swiss Army knife. It gave me a sense of resourcefulness and confidence because no matter what situation I faced, I had the perfect tool to help me figure it out.

Years later, I see Unconditional High Regard—for myself and others—as the Swiss Army knife for life's emotional challenges. Just like that trusty tool, UHR is versatile, potent, and always capable of getting you out of a jam. It helps you pick the locks on self-doubt, unlock stuck relationships, and diffuse emotional bombs—those moments of tension, conflict, or shame that feel ready to explode.

I do my best never to leave home without my pocket knife and never to enter a moment without UHR. Carry it with you, and I bet you'll experience the same.

MAIN TAKEAWAY: WORTH IS NON-NEGOTIABLE

Unconditional High Regard is the ultimate rejection of the invaders' lies. By embracing it, we reclaim our inherent worth, break free from dependency, and lay the foundation for a life of thriving.

COMING UP NEXT: LIVING AUTHENTICALLY

UHR sets the stage for authenticity, allowing us to live fully and unapologetically. In the next chapter, we'll explore how UHR empowers us to embrace our true selves and build a life aligned with our values and truth.

COMMON RESPONSES

"Yeah, but isn't it unrealistic to believe everyone has intrinsic worth, no matter what?"

I get why this might feel idealistic. It's easier to accept the idea of worth when people behave in ways we value or agree with. But intrinsic worth doesn't mean excusing harmful behavior—it's about recognizing that actions and worth are separate. Even when boundaries are necessary, holding unconditional high regard is a way of staying grounded in compassion, which often leads to better outcomes for everyone.

"Yeah, but what if I can't shake the feeling that I'm not enough?"

Those feelings can be incredibly persistent, especially if they've been reinforced over time. Be patient with yourself as you unlearn them. Start by noticing when that voice shows up and asking, 'Is this feeling coming from the truth of who I am or from a lie I've absorbed?' Reclaiming your worth isn't a quick fix; it's a practice. You are worth that effort, even when it feels hard.

"Yeah, but how do I know my worth if I'm not accomplishing anything?"

We've all been conditioned to equate worth with productivity or achievement. But your worth isn't something you have to prove—it's something you already possess. Think of it this way: Do you believe a baby has inherent worth? Of course you do. That worth doesn't disappear as we grow older; it's just harder to see under the layers of expectation and judgment.

> "Yeah, but isn't unconditional high regard just letting people off the hook for bad behavior?"

Not at all. UHR doesn't mean ignoring accountability; it means holding people accountable without dehumanizing them. It's possible to acknowledge harm and set boundaries while still believing in someone's intrinsic worth. In fact, this approach often creates more meaningful change than judgment or condemnation ever could.

> "Yeah, but what if the people around me don't give me the same regard I'm trying to give myself?"

It's painful when others don't see your worth, especially when you're working so hard to believe in it yourself. Their inability to extend UHR often reflects their own struggles, not your value. Keep focusing on building your internal validation—you don't need others' approval to affirm what's already true about you.

REFLECTION QUESTIONS

1. What lies about your worth have you internalized, and where did they come from?
2. In what areas of your life do you still seek external validation?
3. How can you begin practicing UHR for yourself this week?
4. What might it look like to extend UHR to someone who has frustrated or hurt you recently?

CHAPTER TWENTY-FIVE
THE FREEDOM & LIBERATION PROTOCOL
REMOVING THE MASKS & FALSE IDENTITIES THAT KEEP YOU BOUND

The privilege of a lifetime is to become who you truly are. — Carl Jung

---

THE LIBERATION OF AUTHENTICITY: SHEDDING THE FALSE SELF

WHEN WE PEEL THE ONION OF INTENSE EMOTIONS, DISMANTLE judgment, and embrace unconditional high regard (UHR), we come face-to-face with a profound realization: much of what we think of as "self" is a construct—a carefully curated survival mechanism designed to protect us but now keeping us stuck.

This false self, born from fear, shame, and judgment, thrives on external validation. It perpetuates the cycles of insecurity and inauthenticity that have dominated our lives. But beneath these masks, facades, and survival strategies lies the authentic self, patiently waiting to emerge.

While I'm not a neuroscientist, my understanding of how our brains operate has given me helpful insights into this process within myself. My perspective is a blend of biology, psychology, and personal growth, so take it with a grain of salt. It's also rooted in the idea that we are more than our biology and that this "false self" is both a byproduct of survival mechanisms and an obstacle we must outgrow to live authentically.

THE CONSTRUCTION OF THE FALSE SELF

We begin constructing the false self in childhood to navigate an uncertain and often judgmental world. Our brains, focused on survival, comfort, and conserving energy, are incredible organs. These goals are essential for our physical survival—they ensure we eat, stay warm, and avoid harm. But when the brain applies this same survival framework to existential concerns—like being loved, accepted, or valued—it creates challenges.

Judgment as the Catalyst

The construction of the false self starts when we begin to judge. Judgment, at first, is a survival tool—our brain's way of evaluating what helps or harms us. A child learns early that crying loudly gets a caregiver's attention but that expressing anger might lead to punishment. Over time, these external judgments become internalized, shaping how we see ourselves:

- *"If I act this way, I'm good."*
- *"If I do that, I'm bad."*

This binary thinking becomes the foundation for the false self. As we navigate the world, we encounter standards of "enoughness"—messages about how we should look, behave, and succeed. Judgment creates these standards, and the false self responds by adopting behaviors designed to meet them.

WE LEARN THESE PATTERNS EARLY

The false self begins taking shape in childhood as we adapt to the world around us. Over time, it becomes a collection of roles, beliefs, attitudes, and behaviors designed to shield us from rejection, criticism, or harm. These patterns may look like:

- **Suppressing our needs** to avoid conflict, believing that being agreeable earns us love.
- **Tying our worth to achievements** and thinking success will validate our value.
- **Rejecting vulnerability**, armoring ourselves with stoicism, humor, or detachment to avoid pain.

These strategies are effective in the short term, as they deliver dopamine-driven rewards like approval or recognition. But over time, they isolate us from our intrinsic worth. The roles we play—"the overachiever," "the caretaker," and "the tough one"—become so ingrained that we mistake them for our true selves. Instead of protecting us, the false self becomes a prison, disconnecting us from authenticity and contentment.

THE FALSE SELF: GETTING AND PROTECTING

As judgment solidifies, we develop behaviors to address two key challenges:

1. **Getting what we think we lack:** The false self drives us to seek validation, approval, or achievement to fill the gap created by feelings of unworthiness or disconnection. These are our "getting" behaviors—fueled by dopamine, which rewards us for chasing external rewards.
2. **Protecting ourselves from pain:** The false self works equally hard to shield us from rejection, vulnerability,

and discomfort. These are our "protecting" behaviors—strategies tied to serotonin, which helps us feel stable and connected.

THE COST OF INAUTHENTICITY

Living as the false self exacts a heavy toll. It forces us to perform, to play roles that may earn external validation but leave us hollow and unfulfilled. This is because the false self keeps us locked in a cycle of seeking dopamine-fueled rewards while depriving us of serotonin's stabilizing effects.

The false self also keeps us enmeshed in the **Drama Triangle:**

- **As Victims,** we suppress our needs and blame external forces for our discontent.
- **As Rescuers,** we overextend ourselves to feel valued, reinforcing dependency on others.
- **As Persecutors,** we project our insecurities outward, judging others harshly to avoid confronting our own pain.

The result? We feel stuck, unfulfilled, and disconnected—not only from others but from ourselves. The false self thrives on this disconnection, perpetuating a cycle of fear, shame, and inauthenticity.

THE TRANSFORMATIVE POWER OF ACCEPTANCE

So, how do we step off this treadmill? The answer lies in **acceptance**—both receiving it from others and extending it to ourselves.

When we experience true acceptance, whether in a relationship, a community, or through a connection with a higher power, something remarkable happens: the brain shifts from striving to settling. Acceptance provides the safety and stability our false self is always chasing but never finds. On a biological level:

- **Dopamine's chase quiets down.** With acceptance, the brain stops needing to pursue external validation for relief. The craving for "more" subsides because we feel enough as we are.
- **Serotonin levels stabilize.** Acceptance promotes a sense of belonging and connection, which supports serotonin's role in creating feelings of calm, contentment, and social safety.

Acceptance frees us because it shifts the focus from external conditions to internal reality. When we let go of judgment, we stop measuring ourselves against arbitrary standards or comparing ourselves to others. Instead of asking, *"Am I good enough?"* we begin to ask, *"What do I need right now to thrive?"* This simple shift quiets the brain's fear-driven responses, creating space for self-compassion and stability to take root.

SELF-SOURCING: BECOMING OUR OWN WELL

Acceptance doesn't have to come exclusively from others. The real breakthrough happens when we realize we can **source acceptance from within ourselves.** This is self-sourcing—the understanding that we are already enough and can generate our own sense of worth, safety, and connection.

Self-Sourcing Dopamine

Dopamine isn't just about external rewards; it's also activated by intrinsic motivation and curiosity. When we align with our authentic selves and pursue meaningful, self-chosen goals, dopamine flows naturally. These might include:

- Learning a skill for the joy of it.
- Engaging in a creative project that reflects your values.

- Solving problems that excite you, not because they impress others.

Self-Sourcing Serotonin

Serotonin stabilizes when we experience safety, connection, and belonging. By practicing self-compassion and mindfulness, we create the conditions for serotonin to thrive:

- **Self-compassion:** Reduces self-judgment and fosters a sense of intrinsic worth.
- **Gratitude:** Shifts focus from scarcity to abundance, helping us appreciate what we have.
- **Mindfulness:** Grounds us in the present moment, reminding us that we are enough, right here and now.

When we self-source acceptance, we don't stop valuing relationships. Instead, we approach them from a place of abundance, allowing for deeper and more authentic connections.

RECLAIMING THE AUTHENTIC SELF

The journey toward authenticity begins with a decision: to dismantle the false self and embrace the person we've always been beneath the masks. This process isn't about becoming someone new—it's about uncovering who you've always been.

Steps to Reclaim Authenticity

1. **Recognize the Masks You Wear:** Identify the roles and facades you've adopted.
2. **Confront the Lies Behind the Masks:** Challenge beliefs like *I'm not enough,* or *If I'm vulnerable, I'll be rejected.*
3. **Reclaim Vulnerability as Strength:** Embrace imperfections and acknowledge fears without shame.

WHAT TO DO WHEN THE ALIENS SHOW UP (AND EVEN IF THEY DON'T)

4. **Commit to Living Authentically:** Align your choices with your values rather than societal expectations.

THE FREEDOM OF LETTING GO

At the heart of this transformation is the simple yet profound act of letting go of judgment. Letting go doesn't mean we stop caring—it means we stop evaluating our worth based on arbitrary standards and stop viewing vulnerability or imperfection as threats.

When we release judgment, we open the door to acceptance. Acceptance quiets the relentless striving and shielding of the false self, allowing us to recover our innate sense of well-being and aliveness. With this acceptance comes the freedom to:

- Feel lighter, no longer burdened by shame or insecurity.
- Explore, create, and connect without fear of failure.
- Thrive authentically and fully, embracing the joy of being.

AUTHENTICITY AS LIBERATION

You don't need to build your authentic self—you need to uncover it. Beneath the layers of fear, shame, and false beliefs lies the real you, waiting to be liberated. When we stop outsourcing our worth and reconnect with our intrinsic value, life opens up. We engage with the world from a place of abundance and authenticity, creating lives filled with meaning, connection, and freedom.

AUTHENTICITY PAVES THE WAY FOR AGENCY

But wait... there's more! As we reclaim our authentic self, we begin to see where our power truly lies. The false self thrives on external dependencies, convincing us that our worth and happiness depend on controlling others or meeting external standards. Authenticity shatters this illusion, revealing a deeper truth: our power lies in our *choices*.

This is the bridge to agency. When we live authentically, we stop seeking validation from others and return to the sphere where our sovereignty resides: *within*. Authenticity frees us from the need to control others or manipulate circumstances, allowing us to focus on what we can choose, create, and change.

> *Figuring out what it means to be authentic has been a challenging journey. I spent so much time learning to be what I thought would cause other people to think I was valuable that it took a long, hard process to learn the difference between my "true" self and all the ego-based identities I constructed to keep me feeling safe. My encouragement to anyone in a similar process is to be patient with yourself. Be as authentic as you know how to be today without judging yourself for being too authentic or not authentic enough (which will become a new opportunity to shame yourself! In time, you'll discover more and more of who you are and love to be.*

THE MAIN TAKEAWAY: AUTHENTICITY AS LIBERATION

You don't need to build your authentic self—you need to uncover it. Beneath the layers of fear, shame, and false beliefs lies the real you, waiting to be liberated. The journey to authenticity is not easy, but it's the only path to a life of freedom, fulfillment, and true connection.

COMING UP: RECLAIMING AGENCY

Reclaiming your authentic self is a powerful act, but it's only the beginning. Authenticity gives you the clarity and courage to move away from external dependencies and into the realm of true agency. In the next chapter, we'll explore how reclaiming agency—focusing on what is truly within your control—empowers you to create a life of alignment, freedom, and thriving.

COMMON RESPONSES

"Yeah, but how do I know what's authentic and what's just another mask?"

This is a process of discovery, not a one-time epiphany. Start by paying attention to what feels like alignment versus performance. When you act, ask yourself: Does this feel true to me, or does it feel like I'm trying to get something? Authenticity isn't about perfection—it's about experimenting, learning, and leaning into what feels like home within yourself.

"Yeah, but if I drop the false self, won't people reject the real me?"

That fear is understandable because the false self often develops to protect us from rejection. The truth is, not everyone will accept your authentic self, but those who matter—the ones who truly see and value you—will. And here's the thing: living authentically is worth it because it frees you from the exhausting task of performing for approval. You deserve relationships where you can be yourself.

"Yeah, but what if I don't even know who the authentic me is?"

This is more common than you think. When you've lived through the lens of the false self for so long, it can feel disorienting to uncover the real you. Start small. Notice what lights you up, what feels meaningful, and where you feel most alive. You don't have to have all the answers right now—just take the next step toward curiosity and self-discovery.

"Yeah, but isn't the false self sometimes necessary to survive?"

In some circumstances, the false self can be a survival tool, and it may have protected you in the past. But survival isn't the same as thriving. The false self is about defense; authenticity is about freedom. It's okay to honor what the false self did for you, but now, you get to move beyond surviving and step into a life where you can truly thrive.

"Yeah, but isn't authenticity selfish if it means upsetting others?"

Authenticity isn't about disregarding others—it's about showing up honestly and with integrity. While living authentically may disrupt others' expectations of you, it ultimately leads to deeper, healthier relationships. When you're authentic, you invite others to do the same, creating connections based on truth rather than performance. That's not selfish—it's liberating for everyone involved.

REFLECTION QUESTIONS

1. What roles or facades do you find yourself playing most often? Why do you think you adopted them?
2. What lies about yourself have fueled these facades? How can you challenge those lies?
3. What would it look like to make a choice based on authenticity rather than fear or insecurity?
4. How might embracing your true self transform your relationships and sense of purpose?

CHAPTER TWENTY-SIX
RESTORING SOVEREIGNTY
BOLD DECISIONS AND THE POWER OF CHOICE

You may not control all the events that happen to you, but you can decide not to be reduced by them. — Maya Angelou

---

THE FALSE SELF AND THE PATH TO POWER: RECLAIMING AGENCY THROUGH CHOICE

Pulling back the layers of the false self, dismantling judgment, and embracing unconditional high regard (UHR) reveals a profound realization: We are far more powerful than we've learned to believe. For too long, this power has been obscured by roles, masks, and dependencies designed to keep us safe but now keeping us stuck. Freed from judgment and shame, we now face the invaders' deepest lie: that we are *powerless*.

This chapter is about reclaiming that power—the power of *choice*. No matter how small, decisions become our counterstrike in the war for our minds and lives. Choice is the foundation of agency, the engine of our personal sovereignty, and the ultimate expression of our freedom. Reclaiming agency isn't just about defense; it's about creation. It's the act of turning away from the path of judgment and fear, which leads to stagnation and suffering, and stepping onto the path of UHR, faith, and thriving.

THE PHYSICS OF POWER: ENERGY IN ACTION

In physics, *Power* is defined as *Energy* doing *Work*. Without movement, energy remains potential—it doesn't accomplish anything. The same is true for our individual power. Human choices are the vehicle through which potential energy becomes action and creation. Every choice, no matter how small, becomes an act of transformation, a way to convert the energy of intention into the reality of change.

> When I began making deliberate decisions—not just reacting to fear or shame but actively choosing a different path—I felt my power return. It was slow at first, like waking up a limb that had fallen asleep. But with every intentional choice, I felt more alive. That's the secret: the invaders' lie isn't just meant to keep us feeling unworthy—it's meant to rob us of our power to choose. But the truth is, we always have a choice, no matter the circumstances. We can always decide to step off the trail and walk a different path.

THE LIE OF POWERLESSNESS

The invaders thrive on the lie of powerlessness. They whisper, "You have no choice," keeping us stuck in waiting, blaming, or endlessly striving for external validation. But here's the truth: **we are *never* without choices.** Even in the most challenging circumstances, there are things we can always decide.

We can choose:

- **Our perspective:** How we interpret events or challenges.

- **Our attitude:** Gratitude or hope, even amidst uncertainty.
- **Our focus:** What we direct our energy toward, letting go of what we cannot control.
- **Our response:** Pausing to act with intention rather than reacting out of fear or frustration.
- **Our effort:** How much energy we invest in what truly matters.
- **Our boundaries:** Protecting our time and emotional well-being.
- **Our mindset:** Seeking solutions instead of dwelling on problems.
- **Our self-care:** Taking small steps to nurture ourselves even amid adversity.

Every choice, no matter how small, is a declaration of our sovereignty. It disrupts the invaders' lies and reminds us of a fundamental truth: **we are *Creators*, not *Victims*.**

THE THREE SPHERES OF CONTROL: RECLAIMING YOUR FOCUS

To reclaim your power, you must understand where your choices truly lie. Life can be divided into three spheres or "domains of control":

1. "My Business"

This is the sphere of your thoughts, actions, attitudes, beliefs, and responses. It's where your true sovereignty resides. Unless unconscious or incapacitated, you can always make decisions about these things.

2. "Your Business"

This is the sphere of other people's choices, thoughts, attitudes, and emotions. While you can influence others, you cannot control them. Attempting to do so leads to frustration and entanglement.

3. "The Creator's Business"

This is the realm of the uncontrollable—the larger forces of life that humans cannot control. Trying to manage this realm results in anxiety and despair.

Whenever we feel stuck, it's often because we focus on **Our Business** or the Creator's Business instead of returning to **Our Business**—the domain where our power is absolute.

ESCAPING THE DRAMA TRIANGLE

When we focus on spheres beyond our control, we often find ourselves trapped in the Drama Triangle:

- **Me as Victim:** "I can't be okay until they change."
    - **Them as Victim:** "They won't be okay until I change."
- **Me as Rescuer:** "Their pain is my responsibility."
    - **Them as Rescuer:** "It's their job to fix my situation."
- **Me Persecutor:** "They're wrong! I am right. I need to correct them."
    - **Them as Persecutor:** "They're wrong, I am right. I need them to change so I can feel okay."

Reclaiming agency dismantles these roles. It reminds us that we don't need to fix, blame, or wait on anyone else to reclaim our peace. Instead, we can focus on our choices, our actions, and our perspective.

THE EMPOWERED ALTERNATIVE: STEPPING INTO THE CREATOR ROLE

Instead of the Drama Triangle, step into the Empowerment Dynamic:

- **Creator:** Take ownership of your choices and focus on possibilities.
- **Challenger:** Face hard truths with courage and invite growth.
- **Coach:** Offer support without taking over, empowering others to act.

This shift transforms how we navigate challenges. Instead of reacting to life, we begin creating it.

CAUTION: THE TRAP OF WAITING TO FEEL READY

One of the most common ways we surrender agency is by waiting for the "right" feelings—confidence, courage, or motivation—before we act. But feelings follow action, not the other way around. We don't need to feel perfectly ready to take a step. We just need to decide.

Consider these examples:

- Confidence comes after stepping on stage, not before.
- Gratitude comes after choosing to practice it, not before.
- Clarity comes after taking action, not before.

Reclaiming agency means acting even when it feels uncomfortable. It's about trusting that our choices will lead to the clarity and confidence we seek.

THE COUNTERSTRIKE: TURNING CHOICES INTO LIBERATING WEAPONS

Reclaiming agency isn't about grand gestures. It's about small, deliberate actions that disrupt the invaders' influence and restore your control. Here's how to mount our counterstrike:

1. Pause to Regain Control

Pausing disrupts the invaders' attack. Even a brief moment to breathe can restore your power. Use this time to choose gratitude, which connects you back to your agency.

2. Assess the Situation

Evaluate your thoughts, emotions, and actions. Look inward for strength and answers instead of focusing on external circumstances.

3. Process the Truth

Separate facts from assumptions. Challenge narratives rooted in fear or shame.

4. Address With Intention

Meet your needs directly instead of seeking external validation. Choose actions that align with your values.

THE PRACTICE OF OWNERSHIP

Ownership is the cornerstone of agency. It's the practice of taking responsibility for our thoughts, actions, and outcomes—not to blame ourselves but to empower ourselves.

WHAT TO DO WHEN THE ALIENS SHOW UP (AND EVEN IF THEY DON'T)

1. **Own Your Past:** Look back with compassion, not judgment.
2. **Own Your Present:** Recognize your current reality and focus on what you can influence.
3. **Own Your Future:** Decide what you want and take steps toward it.

Choice—and specifically, my ability to create choices in circumstances where it didn't look or feel like I had any—has been the turning point in my life time and again. For years, I thought my experiences were shaped entirely by what others did or by the circumstances I found myself in. If I was unhappy, it was because of them. If I felt stuck, it was because of my situation. But the real shift came when I made one of the most important choices of all: the choice to look at myself instead of blaming others or external circumstances. I chose to take ownership of my thoughts, my responses, and my actions.

I started choosing gratitude—sometimes in the smallest ways, like finding beauty in a sunrise or warmth in my morning coffee—and it changed how I experienced everything. I realized I had the power to decide what meaning I was willing to give to situations: I could see failure as defeat or as growth. I could see challenges as roadblocks or opportunities. I didn't need my circumstances to change for me to feel different; I just needed to choose how I showed up to them. These choices didn't just improve my mindset—they fundamentally transformed my life, my relationships, and my sense of purpose. When I stopped waiting for the world to change and started choosing how I engaged with it, I found freedom.

MAIN TAKEAWAY: POWER LIES IN OUR CHOICES

Our power lies in our choices. Every small action is a counterstrike that reclaims territory from the invaders. Reclaiming agency transforms us from a passive observer into the Creator of our lives. It's the path that turns away from judgment and fear and toward UHR, courage, and thriving.

COMING UP NEXT: STRONGER TOGETHER - RELATIONSHIPS BUILT ON SOVEREIGNTY AND RESPECT

Reclaiming agency reshapes how we engage with others. In the next chapter, we'll discover how focusing on our sphere of control creates deeper, more authentic relationships. We'll also learn how mutual respect and empowerment form the foundation for connection and growth.

COMMON RESPONSES

"Yeah, but what if my choices don't make a difference?"

It's easy to feel like small choices are insignificant, but they're the building blocks of transformation. Every choice, no matter how small, is a step toward reclaiming your agency. It's not about changing everything at once—it's about starting where you are. Over time, those small choices accumulate, creating momentum and possibility where none seemed to exist before.

"Yeah, but what if I don't even know what choices I have?"

When you feel stuck, it can be hard to see your options clearly. Start

WHAT TO DO WHEN THE ALIENS SHOW UP (AND EVEN IF THEY DON'T)

by asking small, practical questions: *Can I shift my perspective? Can I take one step, however small, toward what matters to me?* Often, the act of searching for choices reveals them. Remember, even pausing to breathe and reassess is a choice that restores your power.

"Yeah, but isn't it selfish to focus on my own choices when others need me?"

Focusing on your choices isn't selfish—it's the foundation of sovereignty and well-being. When you reclaim your agency, you show up for others in a more grounded, authentic way. You're no longer reacting out of obligation or guilt but acting from a place of clarity and intention. This creates healthier, more sustainable relationships where you and others can thrive.

"Yeah, but what if I don't feel ready or confident to make a choice?"

Confidence often comes after we act, not before. You don't need to feel ready to take the next step—you just need to decide. Start small, knowing that each action builds momentum. It's okay to feel uncomfortable or uncertain. What matters is that you move forward, trusting that clarity and confidence will follow.

"Yeah, but isn't it easier to just let life happen instead of trying to control everything?"

Letting life happen might feel easier in the moment, but it often leads to frustration and stagnation. Reclaiming agency doesn't mean controlling everything—it means focusing on what you can influence. By making intentional choices, you shift from passively enduring life to actively shaping it. It's not about perfection or control; it's about creating meaning and alignment with your values.

REFLECTION QUESTIONS

1. What small choices can you make today to reclaim your agency from the invaders?
2. How can pausing and assessing your thoughts help you regain control in challenging moments?
3. What interpretations are you holding onto that might be rooted in fear or judgment rather than truth?
4. How can you use small acts of gratitude or intentionality to strengthen your counteroffensive?

CHAPTER TWENTY-SEVEN
FORTIFY OUR STRONGHOLD
BUILDING BOUNDARIES THAT PROTECT AND EMPOWER

Success is the sum of small efforts, repeated day in and day out. — Robert Collier

---

STRENGTHENING YOUR STRONGHOLD: RESILIENCE, SUSTAINABILITY, AND SOVEREIGNTY

AS WE CONCLUDE THIS PART OF THE JOURNEY, OUR STRONGHOLD—THE sanctuary that protects our sovereignty and fosters our authenticity—stands ready to support our thriving. We've already laid the foundation, constructed the walls, and defined our boundaries. Now, the focus shifts to strengthening, maintaining, and sustaining our stronghold for the long journey ahead.

A stronghold is not static; it requires ongoing care, vigilance, and balance. This chapter explores how repetition, deliberate challenge, and rest fortify our stronghold, making it an unshakable base from which we can live, thrive, and even take the fight to the darkness that binds others.

THE PURPOSE OF STRENGTHENING: RESILIENCE AND GROWTH

Our stronghold is more than a refuge—it's the foundation of a dynamic, empowered life. It allows us to remain grounded, resilient, and aligned with our values even in the face of external challenges.

But even the strongest fortress can weaken over time without maintenance. Left unattended, old patterns of fear, shame, and dependency may creep back in. Strengthening our stronghold ensures that it doesn't just protect us—it empowers us to engage with life fully and authentically.

REPETITION: THE KEY TO FORTIFICATION

Strengthening your stronghold begins with repetition. Every choice we make in alignment with our values reinforces its walls.

Repetition Builds Familiarity

At first, living in alignment with our values may feel awkward or unfamiliar. But like any skill, repetition transforms effort into habit. Each time we hold to a boundary, respond with high regard, or act from authenticity, we strengthen our ability to do so effortlessly.

Repetition Builds Strength

Every time we make a decision rooted in sovereignty, we reinforce the integrity of our stronghold. These repeated actions create a foundation capable of withstanding external pressures.

Repetition Builds Resilience

Consistency equips us to handle new challenges with confidence. The stronger our habits of alignment, the less likely we are to be destabilized by fear, judgment, or manipulation.

This process is akin to **spiritual and emotional hypertrophy***, which is the strengthening of our inner self through intentional practice and effort.

CHALLENGE: THE CATALYST FOR GROWTH

Strengthening our stronghold also requires **challenge.** Just as muscles grow stronger when pushed beyond their limits, our sovereignty strengthens when we take actions that stretch our capacity.

Why Challenge Is Necessary

Without challenge, our stronghold can become stagnant. It's through facing resistance—difficult conversations, bold decisions, or stepping outside our comfort zone—that we discover our true strength.

How to Embrace Challenge

- **Identify Growth Opportunities:** Look for areas where you feel fear or hesitation. These are often invitations to grow.
- **Take Incremental Steps:** Challenge doesn't mean taking on everything at once. Start with small, manageable actions that stretch you slightly beyond your comfort zone.
- **Reflect on Your Growth:** After each challenge, take time to reflect on what you've learned and how you've

---

* **Hypertrophy** refers to the increase in the size of an organ or tissue due to the enlargement of its component cells. In the context of skeletal muscle, hypertrophy specifically describes the growth of muscle fibers in response to mechanical load or resistance training, often resulting from increased protein synthesis and satellite cell activity. Guyton, A. C., & Hall, J. E. (2016). *Textbook of Medical Physiology* (13th ed.). Elsevier.

grown. This reinforces the lesson and builds confidence for future challenges.

REST: THE FOUNDATION OF SUSTAINABILITY

While challenge builds strength, **rest** is what allows us to sustain it. Just as muscles require recovery after exertion, our stronghold needs periods of intentional rest to integrate lessons, process emotions, and recharge.

What Rest Looks Like in Sovereignty

1. **Time in Reflection:** Use your stronghold as a sanctuary for quiet reflection. Journaling, meditation, or simply sitting in stillness allows you to process recent challenges and reconnect with your values.
2. **Engage in Restorative Practices:** Whether it's walking in nature, spending time with loved ones, or creative hobbies, choose activities that nourish your soul and recharge your energy.
3. **Sabbath Practice:** Dedicate a regular time—whether it's a day, an afternoon, or even an hour—to step away from the "doing" energy that drives most of your life. This isn't about avoiding work; it's about experiencing life as a human being rather than a human doing. Use this time to connect with yourself, your loved ones, and the present moment.
4. **Honor Your Energy Cycles:** Recognize that you can't always be "on." Allow yourself permission to rest when needed, without guilt or judgment.

MAINTENANCE: VIGILANCE AND INTENTIONALITY

A stronghold doesn't maintain itself. It requires ongoing effort to ensure it remains a source of strength and stability.

WHAT TO DO WHEN THE ALIENS SHOW UP (AND EVEN IF THEY DON'T)

Recognizing Threats

Old patterns of fear, shame, and dependency may try to creep back in. We must stay vigilant for signs that our boundaries are weakening or that external pressures are influencing our choices. Awareness is our first line of defense.

Reinforcing Boundaries

Boundaries are the first line of protection for our stronghold. Regularly assess our boundaries to ensure they align with your current values and needs. We must adjust them as necessary to reflect our growth.

Practicing Self-Compassion

Setbacks are inevitable, but they don't have to derail us. We can respond to ourselves with compassion rather than judgment when mistakes occur. We can use these moments as opportunities to learn, recalibrate, and strengthen our resolve.

STRENGTH AND VULNERABILITY: THE PARADOX OF A STRONGHOLD

As our stronghold strengthens, we'll notice a paradox: the stronger our foundation, the more open and vulnerable we can afford to be. True strength isn't about building impenetrable walls—it's about knowing we can handle whatever comes our way.

This openness fosters deeper intimacy and trust. When others see our strength paired with vulnerability, they feel safe to be their authentic selves around us, creating deeper and more meaningful connections.

OUR STRONGHOLD AS A LAUNCHPAD

A stronghold isn't just about defense—it's the foundation from which we engage with the world as a Creator. It's the place where we prepare to take bold, intentional action that not only disrupts the invaders' lies but also illuminates the path for others to follow. Strengthening our stronghold is about sustaining ourselves so we can step into the larger mission of spreading light and truth to others.

MAIN TAKEAWAY: GROWTH REQUIRES CHALLENGE, REST, AND VIGILANCE

Strengthening our stronghold is a dynamic process that balances **challenge** and **rest** while reinforcing boundaries and repetition. This balance creates resilience, sustains our sovereignty, and allows our authentic selves to thrive.

COMING UP IN PART 3: BECOMING A CREATOR

As we step into Part 3, we move beyond strengthening our stronghold to the mission of becoming a Creator. Thriving isn't just about defending ourselves—it's about taking the fight to the darkness and creating light, connection, and purpose for ourselves and others. The next part of our journey will explore how to live as a force of transformation and empowerment.

COMMON RESPONSES

"Yeah, but I don't have time to rest. There's too much to do."

WHAT TO DO WHEN THE ALIENS SHOW UP (AND EVEN IF THEY DON'T)

Rest isn't a luxury—it's a necessity. Without it, even your best efforts will falter. Start small. Give yourself permission to rest for just five minutes and notice how much more focused and grounded you feel. You can't pour from an empty cup, and even small pauses can replenish your energy in meaningful ways.

"Yeah, but what if I don't know how to challenge myself without failing?"

Challenging yourself isn't about avoiding failure—it's about embracing growth. Failure is not a verdict; it's feedback. Start with small, incremental challenges that stretch you just enough to grow without overwhelming you. Growth comes from stepping out of your comfort zone, even a little at a time.

"Yeah, but I've tried setting boundaries before, and people don't respect them."

Boundaries are less about controlling others and more about communicating your values and protecting your energy. It's true that some people might resist, but reinforcing boundaries is a skill that improves with practice. Stay consistent, and remember: your worth doesn't depend on others' reactions but on your commitment to your own well-being.

"Yeah, but what if I lose progress and old patterns creep back in?"

Growth isn't linear—it's a spiral. Sometimes, you may revisit old patterns, but each time you do, you're approaching them with greater awareness and strength. Setbacks are opportunities to reinforce your stronghold, not evidence of failure. Be patient with yourself and celebrate how far you've come.

"Yeah, but vulnerability feels too risky. What if people judge or reject me?"

SVEN MASTERSON

Vulnerability isn't weakness—it's courage in action. When you're open, you invite deeper connection and authenticity. Not everyone will respond perfectly, but those who truly matter will value your honesty and meet you with the same. True strength comes from knowing you can handle the risk and still stay grounded in your worth.

REFLECTION QUESTIONS

1. How can you incorporate more deliberate rest into your routine to sustain your sovereignty?
2. What recent challenges have helped you grow? How can you continue to embrace opportunities for growth?
3. Are there any boundaries in your life that need reinforcement or adjustment?
4. How can you balance strength and vulnerability to deepen your relationships and connections?

PART THREE
THE COUNTEROFFENSIVE
RECLAIMING YOUR POWER & BIRTHRIGHT

THE COUNTEROFFENSIVE: RECLAIMING, RESTORING, AND THRIVING

The invasion has felt catastrophic—a full-on assault of alien ships descending upon our inner world. Fear, shame, and judgment unleashed their arsenal, leaving chaos and destruction in their wake. They infiltrated our thoughts, manipulated our emotions, and erected strongholds of dependency, insecurity, and disconnection. They whispered lies about our worth, planting devices of control that fed on our doubts and fears. For a time, it may have felt like they were winning.

But in Part 2, we mounted a resistance. We fought back with courage and clarity, dismantling the invaders' machines of shame and judgment, and reclaiming the territory of our minds and hearts. We established strongholds of sovereignty—a fortress built on truth, self-regard, and authenticity. Now, it's time to take the fight to them.

This is the counteroffensive, the phase where we shift from defense to offense. We are no longer civilians seeking shelter—we are warriors. We've seen through the invaders' tactics, uncovered their weaknesses, and built the tools to dismantle their control. This is where survival evolves into sovereignty and where we transform the battlefield into a thriving kingdom. The goal is not just to repel the invaders but to obliterate their influence entirely.

THRIVING BEYOND SURVIVAL: TURNING THE ALIEN TECHNOLOGY AGAINST THEM

The invaders came with one goal: to dominate and control our inner world. They exploited our insecurities, weaponized our natural desire for connection, and constructed a framework of fear and dependency. But now, we've turned the tide.

The work we've done—peeling back the layers of fear, shame, and judgment—did more than expose their devices; it gave us the tools to reverse their effects. The very tools the invaders used to harm us can now be repurposed to rebuild our lives. What once isolated us will now connect us. What once disempowered us will now strengthen us. What once brought pain will now foster joy. This is the essence of the counteroffensive: to turn the invaders' tactics against them and reclaim not just our lives, but our thriving.

REVERSING THE LAYERS OF DESTRUCTION: DEACTIVATING THE ALIEN DEVICES

Each step in this part of the journey reflects the layers of destruction the invaders unleashed but works to reverse their effects entirely. Each chapter will guide us in dismantling their alien technology and using the reclaimed space to build something unshakable:

- **Judgment:** The invaders installed a relentless inner critic to keep us off balance. Now, we'll replace it with an inner ally, cultivating unconditional high regard for ourselves and others.
- **Shame:** They wove shame into our identity to keep us small and silent. We'll dismantle it, replacing it with self-acceptance and celebration of our authentic selves.
- **Disconnection:** They severed our ties to others and our purpose. We'll rebuild genuine connections that align with our values.
- **Dependency:** They manipulated our need for validation into emotional captivity. We'll break free, sourcing strength from within and from our Creator.
- **Insecurity:** They fed us doubt and fear. We'll transform it into bold confidence, grounded in truth rather than external validation.
- **Fear:** They paralyzed us with anxiety. We'll confront life with courage, turning fear into fuel for growth.
- **Suffering:** They used our pain to keep us trapped. We'll transform it into resilience and joy, thriving not despite the invasion but because of our deliberate choice to reclaim and rebuild.

Each step is a deliberate act of rebellion, an assertion of sovereignty that tells the invaders: *You do not belong here.*

RESTORING AND REBUILDING: CREATING A KINGDOM THE INVADERS CAN'T TOUCH

The counteroffensive isn't just about dismantling the invaders' strongholds—it's about building something they cannot destroy. Imagine reclaiming a city that was under alien occupation. The streets are scarred from battle, but they are ours now. We walk those streets not just to repair the damage but to create a space so full of light, connection, and truth that no alien force could ever darken it again.

As we rebuild, we're not just creating a life worth living—we're creating a life so vibrant that it becomes a beacon for others. Our stronghold becomes the foundation for a kingdom where authenticity, connection, and joy thrive. The resilience we cultivate and the truth we now embody make us unstoppable—not just for ourselves but as liberators for others still trapped in darkness.

TAKING THE FIGHT BEYOND OURSELVES: LIBERATOR, CREATOR, WARRIOR

The counteroffensive doesn't stop with us. The invaders didn't just target our inner worlds—they sought to dominate a collective consciousness of fear and shame. By reclaiming our sovereignty and thriving, we expose their tactics and inspire others to do the same. Every step we take is a counterstrike not only against our own invaders but against the forces keeping others in chains.

This is our greatest act of resistance: not only surviving but thriving in a way that helps others see the invaders for what they are—liars. By embodying authenticity, courage, and high regard, we model what it looks like to dismantle their hold, turning fear into faith, dependency into sovereignty, and judgment into grace. We become not just creators of our lives but restorers for those around us.

LOOKING AHEAD: A CREATOR'S MISSION

The road ahead will still have challenges. The invaders may retreat, but they'll try to regroup, whispering lies and sowing seeds of doubt. But now, we are prepared. We've built strongholds, reclaimed our sovereignty, and turned their tools into weapons for growth. Each challenge is now an opportunity to expand our kingdom, strengthen our resolve, and thrive as the Creators we were always meant to be.

WHAT TO DO WHEN THE ALIENS SHOW UP (AND EVEN IF THEY DON'T)

By the end of this counteroffensive, we will not only reclaim our lives but also create legacies of thriving. We will become beacons of restoration, proving that the invaders' darkness has no place here. The invasion may have started the story, but our thriving is how it ends.

Take a deep breath. Feel the strength of our restored selves. The tide has turned. Now, it's time to lead the charge.

Let's take back what's ours. Let's thrive.

CHAPTER TWENTY-EIGHT
DEFEATING JUDGMENT
THE FIRST WAVE OF RECLAMATION

Do not judge, or you too will be judged. – Jesus of Nazareth

JUDGMENT: THE INVADERS' MOST EFFECTIVE WEAPON

JUDGMENT. IT'S A WORD WE'VE BEEN COMING BACK TO AGAIN AND again, and for good reason. It was the alien invaders' first and most insidious weapon, wielded to divide us—from others, from ourselves, and from the Creator. Their strategy was brilliant in its simplicity: make us believe we have the authority to pass judgment as if we were the Creator. Convince us that we can discern ultimate truth with accuracy and precision, enabling us to declare what is good, bad, right, or wrong—not just in others, but in ourselves.

This delusion of judgment doesn't come from a place of wisdom or humility. Instead, it's born of ego, rooted in our deepest insecurities and fears. Our egos, desperate to make sense of the world, project their own fragile standards onto others and ourselves, creating a false sense of authority. But here's the catch: those standards are as flawed as the insecure ego that wields them.

When judgment takes root, it drowns us in self-criticism,

distrust, and shame. It isolates us, divides our relationships, and distorts our view of the world. Reclaiming our sovereignty begins with understanding this dynamic and learning to transform judgment into something far more constructive: discernment.

THE ALIEN WEAPON: JUDGMENT AND MISPLACED AUTHORITY

The invaders didn't just use judgment as a weapon—they trained us to misuse it. Judgment, as they taught us to wield it, was never about clarity or truth. It was about stepping into a role we were never meant to occupy–the Creator's role. In doing so, we became consumed by fear, shame, and division.

Here's how judgment misleads us:

- **Judging Others' Substance:** We evaluate others' worth, motives, or moral standing as if we have the omniscience to know their hearts.
- **Judging Others' Behaviors:** Instead of discerning how behaviors affect us and setting appropriate boundaries, we label actions as inherently "good" or "bad," often projecting our insecurities onto them.
- **Judging Ourselves Harshly:** We mistake our humanity for inadequacy, using judgment as a tool to punish rather than guide ourselves.

Every instance of misplaced judgment pulls us out of "Our Business"—the realm where we have agency and sovereignty—and into "Their Business" or "The Creator's Business," where we have no control. The result? Disempowerment, frustration, and cycles of shame.

JUDGMENT VS. DISCERNMENT

Let's be clear: this isn't about denying the existence of truth, right, or wrong. Those things exist. But defining them with precision requires omniscience, which belongs to the Creator alone.

When we judge, we step into the Creator's role, assuming an authority we don't have. Our ego convinces us that we're qualified to measure others—and ourselves—against arbitrary standards that often serve to reinforce our own insecurities. This is the great delusion of judgment: it's not rooted in wisdom but in fear.

Discernment, on the other hand, is grounded in humility and self-awareness. It doesn't pretend to know ultimate truth. Instead, discernment invites us to evaluate how something aligns with our values and impacts our lives. It helps us make decisions without condemning others or ourselves.

TURNING JUDGMENT INTO DISCERNMENT

Judgment's antidote isn't its elimination—it's its transformation. Discernment allows us to:

- **Set Boundaries** that protect our values and sovereignty.
- **Evaluate Our Own Behaviors** with compassion and a growth mindset.
- **Navigate Relationships** without overstepping into "Their Business" or "The Creator's Business."
- Here's an example:
- **Judgment:** "They're selfish for acting that way."
- **Discernment:** "When they consistently disregard my needs, I feel disrespected. I need to set a boundary to protect my energy."

Discernment keeps us focused on what we can control—our actions, values, and boundaries—without allowing us to condemn others or assume ultimate authority.

THE COST OF MISUSED JUDGMENT

When judgment is misapplied, the cost is enormous:

- **Paralysis:** Self-judgment traps us in fear of failure, keeping us stuck.
- **Division:** Judging others fosters unnecessary conflict and isolation.
- **Entanglement:** Focusing on others' behaviors drags us into "Their Business," where we have no agency.
- **Ego Inflation:** Playing the arbiter of ultimate truth feeds our ego while eroding humility and authenticity.

THE ILLUSION OF JUDGMENT AS A SHORTCUT TO WORTH

Let's be honest: we kinda secretly love judgment, don't we? Why? Because it tricks us into thinking we've arrived at a place of value and worth. Judgment allows us to compare ourselves to others—real or imagined—and if we come out on top, we get a fleeting sense of being enough. For a moment, we stop seeking and striving. We feel like we've made it. Woo hoo! I'm enough!

I suspect this is tied to our brain chemistry. Maybe judgment gives us a little serotonin boost and a temporary feeling of satisfaction and stability. It feels good to believe, even for a moment, that we are "better than" someone else and can settle into our worth.

But that feeling doesn't last. The problem with judgment is that it's never enough. As soon as the boost wears off, we find ourselves comparing again. We chase the next hit of superiority, needing someone else to measure against. And the cycle begins anew, leaving us as empty and insecure as before.

Let's put this into perspective: as of today, there are an estimated **8 billion humans alive**. Since the dawn of humanity, it's believed that approximately **117 billion people** have lived. If judgment is our path to worthiness, how many of those people would we need to feel superior to in order to truly believe we are enough? How many comparisons would it take for the insecurity to vanish for good? The truth is, the answer doesn't exist—because judgment can never deliver the lasting sense of worth we're looking for.

> *Pro Tip: I've found that understanding judgment—both mine and others'—as a way we try to feel better about ourselves can be a powerful diagnostic tool. When I catch myself feeling judgmental toward others, it's my cue to slow down, practice self-care and self-acceptance, and reconnect with myself and my community. It's also a chance to remind myself where my true value comes from.*
>
> *This perspective is equally helpful when I'm on the receiving end of judgment. I've learned to see someone else's judgment as a reflection of their own inner struggles. Recognizing that they're probably not feeling great about themselves in that moment, I can choose to extend Unconditional High Regard (UHR), remind them of their inherent worth, and gently help them reorient if the opportunity feels right.*
>
> *That said, I don't always get it right! It's a practice, and I'm still working on it. But even imperfectly, this shift in perspective has transformed how I navigate judgment—both giving and receiving it.*

RECLAIMING DISCERNMENT AS A TOOL FOR SOVEREIGNTY

Here's how we can transform judgment into discernment:

1. Stay in "Our Business"
    - When tempted to judge, ask:
        - "Am I stepping into the Creator's role?"
        - "Is this judgment about something I can control?"

- Redirect your energy toward your choices, values, and boundaries.
2. **Replace Criticism With Curiosity**
    - Instead of condemning, ask:
        - "What is my experience of this situation?"
        - "What need or boundary is being highlighted here?"
        - "What action can I take to protect my integrity?"
3. **Practice Unconditional High Regard**
    - Extend compassion to yourself and others. High regard doesn't ignore flaws—it acknowledges them while affirming inherent worth.
4. **Use Discernment to Set Boundaries**
    - Focus on behavior, not character. For example:
        - Instead of, "They're toxic," discernment says, "Their behavior drains me. I'll limit contact to protect my energy."

In my younger years, I was disillusioned—disillusioned with my job, my finances, and, truthfully, myself. Immature and searching for causes and solutions outside of me, I slipped quickly into the dynamics of the Drama Triangle. I saw myself as a Victim, and my employer became the Persecutor. My ego, cloaked in self-righteousness and judgment, made it my mission to expose their supposed immorality.

I'm not proud of those days. My attitudes, actions, and behaviors left much to be desired, but as a young person, that was the reality I lived in. I held my employer under constant suspicion, convinced they were up to no good. Their "obvious" greed at not paying me more must have meant they had moral shortcomings. Fueled by my interpretations and judgments, I gossiped, spreading rumors and stoking resentment. I told myself it was justice, but really, it was bitterness.

Eventually, the truth came to light—but not in the way I expected. The employer called a company meeting to explain the recent secrecy that I had interpreted as wrongdoing. It turned out they had been assisting local law enforcement in a massive sting operation that removed dangerous individuals from the streets.

I was stunned. My judgments and assumptions, which I had been so sure of, were completely wrong. And here's the part that stays with me most: I think my employer knew I had been spreading rumors, yet they treated me with unexpected grace. Instead of calling me out or retaliating, they offered an example of mercy that allowed me to see the situation—and myself—more clearly.

That day, I learned an unforgettable lesson about the danger of assumptions, the fallibility of our interpretations, and the destructiveness of judgment. I also learned about the healing power of grace, both when others offer it and when we extend it to ourselves.

Looking back, I see how different things could have been if I had approached the situation with discernment instead of judgment. Rather than labeling my employer as "wrong" and charging into the Persecutor role, I could have paused, sought clarity, and protected my energy by focusing on my choices. Their grace allowed me to step back from the Drama Triangle and see the world—and myself—with new eyes. It's a lesson I carry to this day.

I've since been on the other side of this, too, and it doesn't feel very good. We're often so convinced that our interpretations and judgments are accurate, and most often, they're far from it.

THE LIBERATION OF DISCERNMENT

When we replace judgment with discernment, we reclaim our sovereignty. Discernment empowers us to act with integrity and clarity while staying grounded in humility. It allows us to navigate life's challenges without entanglement, ego, or fear.

I've experienced the pain of misjudgment firsthand, both as the one judging and the one being judged. I've learned that judgment is often flawed, driven by ego and insecurity. Discernment, by contrast, is freeing. It keeps us in our stronghold, focused on our growth and our relationships, without the unnecessary burden of misplaced authority.

THE MAIN TAKEAWAY: DISCERNMENT EMPOWERS SOVEREIGNTY

Judgment becomes destructive when it overreaches into "Their Business" or "The Creator's Business." By transforming judgment into discernment, we reclaim our focus and agency. Discernment strengthens our sovereignty, allowing us to act with authenticity, set boundaries, and thrive.

COMMON RESPONSES

"Yeah, but isn't judgment necessary to figure out what's right and wrong?"

Discernment is the tool we use to navigate right and wrong without stepping into judgment. Judgment labels people, events, or even ourselves as inherently good or bad, often clouding clarity. Discernment evaluates actions or behaviors while remaining rooted in humility and compassion, allowing you to act without condemning.

"Yeah, but if I stop judging people, won't I get walked all over?"

Letting go of judgment doesn't mean abandoning boundaries. In fact, discernment helps you set clearer, healthier boundaries based on values and needs rather than reactions or resentments. Discernment gives you the strength to protect your sovereignty without isolating yourself.

"Yeah, but some people deserve judgment for what they've done!"

It's hard to separate a person from their actions, especially when harm is involved. However, judgment often feeds our own anger and resentment rather than solving the problem. Discernment allows you to hold someone accountable without taking on the corrosive effects of condemnation. Accountability is stronger when it's paired with compassion.

"Yeah, but if I can't judge myself, how will I ever improve?"

Self-improvement thrives on curiosity, not criticism. Judgment traps you in shame and fear, while discernment opens the door to growth by recognizing your strengths, owning your challenges, and committing to change. Progress is built on self-compassion and clarity, not self-condemnation.

"Yeah, but isn't judgment a natural part of being human?"

Yes, judgment is a natural reflex—it's how we learned to navigate safety and danger in the past. But today, judgment often misfires, leading us to project fears and insecurities onto others or ourselves. Recognizing judgment as a reflex gives us the power to pause, question its validity, and transform it into discernment, which serves us far better.

REFLECTION QUESTIONS

1. When have you caught yourself judging others or yourself? How might you reframe those judgments as discernment?
2. What would it look like to practice unconditional high regard for yourself and others?
3. How can focusing on "Our Business" free you from fear and resentment?
4. What boundaries can you set to protect your values while staying out of judgment?

CHAPTER TWENTY-NINE
RECLAIMING SELF-ACCEPTANCE
THE FALL OF SHAME

> You yourself, as much as anybody in the entire universe, deserve your love and affection. – Buddha

THE SECOND WAVE: DISMANTLING SHAME WITH SELF-ACCEPTANCE

SHAME. YOU'LL BE AN EXPERT IN THAT SUBJECT BY THE END OF THIS book! I hope so, at least! We're talking about it so much because it is the invaders' strongest stronghold, the dark energy fueling their conquest. Like a shadowy parasite, shame feeds on secrecy, silence, and disconnection, growing stronger with every lie it whispers. It tells us that we are not enough—not attractive enough, successful enough, smart enough, or lovable enough. Shame isolates us from others, blinds us to our inherent worth, and keeps us trapped in cycles of self-rejection.

But here's the truth: shame is not *our* voice. It is the invaders' greatest weapon, a tool designed to keep us small, compliant, and disconnected from our true power. To reclaim our life, this is the next critical step in your counteroffensive. To dismantle shame, we must wield the weapon that neutralizes its power: *self-acceptance*. And not just any self-acceptance, as we're about to jump into ahead.

THE ALIEN'S CORE: SHAME AS A WEAPON

Let's clarify something important: shame is both a feeling and a belief. Many of us might not realize we're experiencing shame because we don't feel it emotionally in the moment. Shame is not the same as guilt. Guilt says, "I did something wrong." Shame, on the other hand, says, "I am something wrong." It's the voice that weaves a story about our worthlessness, convincing us that if others knew the truth about us, they'd reject us. Shame burrows deep into our identity, making us believe we must earn our place in the world.

Shame doesn't just undermine our confidence—it disconnects us from ourselves, others, and our Creator. It thrives in the darkness of silence and secrecy, wrapping us in the illusion that we're alone in our struggles. Worst of all, shame tricks us into believing that its presence is justified, that it's protecting us from rejection, when, in fact, it's the very source of our isolation.

But shame is not the truth. It's a distortion—a weapon of the invaders that has no place in our authentic selves. The time has come to recognize it for what it is and neutralize its power.

THE ANTIDOTE: SELF-ACCEPTANCE AND SELF-WORTH

Self-acceptance is the ultimate countermeasure to shame, but here's the key: self-acceptance is inextricably linked to our self-worth. If our sense of self-worth is performance-based, fluid, or reactive, then our self-acceptance will follow the same pattern. We cannot achieve lasting self-acceptance if our worth is tied to what we achieve, how others perceive us, or any *external* metric. To dismantle shame, we must root out the stories, beliefs, and worldviews where worth is conditional.

WHAT TO DO WHEN THE ALIENS SHOW UP (AND EVEN IF THEY DON'T)

True self-acceptance begins with recognizing that our worth is *fixed* and *innate*. It is not something we earn through achievement or lose through failure. Our worth is as intrinsic as our breath—a fundamental truth of our existence. When we ground our self-worth in this unshakable truth, self-acceptance becomes not just possible but inevitable. How cool is that?!

THE FEAR OF LOSING MOTIVATION

For many, the idea of self-acceptance feels threatening. There's a deeply ingrained fear many have, and its intensity grows with the depth of our shame: *If I accept myself as I am, won't I lose my drive and motivation? Won't I stop trying?*

This fear is rooted in a misunderstanding. Most of us have spent our lives motivating ourselves through a combination of fear, shame, and disowning parts of ourselves. We've internalized the belief that only through punishment can we push ourselves to succeed. But here's the truth: fear is not nearly as potent a motivator as love. Self-acceptance, far from weakening your drive, unleashes your ability to create from a place of joy and abundance.

> Sometimes, we call this our "inner critic." Some people believe we should make friends with this inner critical voice and be grateful for it because it can motivate us so well. I don't agree with that perspective. I can go for a jog without a lion chasing me to make me run faster. I bet you can, too!
>
> Many years ago, I developed an auto-immune disease called "Grave's Disease," and none of my doctors spent time trying to convince me it was helpful. Quite the contrary! It was evidence that something wasn't functioning properly. You see, in the rest of our human frame, any other system that attacks itself is called an "auto-immune disease" and isn't something we accept as helpful but seek to be healed

from. But when it comes to shame, we treat it as part of how things work. Rubbish! I believe shame is an auto-immune "disease" of the human spirit because when people experience a release from its grip, it transforms their well-being.

Think about what you've already accomplished in your life—despite shame and self-rejection. Now, imagine what you could create if you moved beyond those limitations?! Imagine what you could achieve if your motivation came not from fear of failure but from love for yourself and excitement for what's possible. Self-acceptance doesn't stifle your growth—it *amplifies* it. It frees you to create your best life.

THE STEPS TO RECLAIM SELF-ACCEPTANCE

1. Bring Shame Into the Light

Shame thrives in secrecy. The first step to dismantling it is naming it. Ask yourself:

- What are the specific lies Shame has been telling me?
    - *"I'm not good enough."*
    - *"I'll never be loved."*
    - *"I don't deserve success."*

Challenge these stories. Are they true, or are they distorted beliefs you've internalized? Expose shame's narrative for what it is—a weapon, not a truth.

2. Prime the Well of Self-Acceptance With Trusted Relationships

Facing shame alone is like trying to draw water from a dry well

—it's not impossible, but it is exhausting and slow. Trusted relationships can act like priming the pump and pouring a little water in so the well begins to flow.

Sharing your shame with someone who holds you in unconditional high regard—a close friend, partner, or mentor—allows you to experience the kindness and acceptance you may struggle to offer yourself. Their regard doesn't replace your own but reminds you of what you're worthy of. One of the gifts of long-term relationships like marriage is the opportunity to see yourself through the eyes of someone who loves you, even in your imperfections.

When we allow others to hold space for our shame, we gain the courage to face it and begin accepting ourselves. This is not dependency; it's connection—a reminder that we were never meant to walk this journey alone.

> *I know how discouraging it can feel to read something like this and think, "If only my marriage were like that." Not long ago, I was in the same place—stuck in what felt like a dried-up well of disconnection and hopelessness. It felt impossible and I believed it always would be. But here's what I've learned: transformation is possible, even when it feels impossible. Someone has to go first, and I know how hard that step is because I've been there.*
>
> *Today, I'm not there, and in fact, I now work with men every day who are in that exact spot—helping them take those first steps to transform themselves and, in doing so, begin to restore their relationships. Even in a marriage that feels distant, conflict often holds surprising opportunities to reconnect. When approached with humility and a willingness to grow, those moments can become the doorway to deeper understanding. It's not quick, and it's not easy, but every step toward Unconditional High Regard adds a*

little more water back into the well. I know it's hard, but I also know it's worth it.

3. Practice Radical Honesty

Shame convinces you to hide your true self, but honesty is the antidote. Vulnerability is not weakness—it's strength. Share your struggles with someone you trust, someone who will hold space for your humanity. Letting others see the real you begins to dismantle shame's grip.

4. Rewrite the Narrative

Shame writes a story of inadequacy: *"I'm unworthy."* Reclaim your power by rewriting it: *"I am enough."* Replace shame-driven narratives with affirmations rooted in truth.

- *"I don't need to be perfect to be worthy."*
- *"My value is not up for debate."*

5. Celebrate Your Humanity

Perfection is a myth. Your imperfections are not flaws—they are features of your humanity. Celebrate them as evidence of your resilience and relatability. You don't need to hide what makes you human; you need to embrace it.

THE LIBERATION OF SELF-ACCEPTANCE

When shame falls, we reclaim our freedom. We stop hiding and start living. We stop rejecting ourselves and start embracing our wholeness. Self-acceptance is not a one-time achievement—it's a daily choice. But every time we choose it, we weaken shame's hold and strengthen our connection to ourselves and others.

WHAT TO DO WHEN THE ALIENS SHOW UP (AND EVEN IF THEY DON'T)

This is how we dismantle the invaders' strongest stronghold. This is the next wave of our counteroffensive. With every act of self-acceptance, we reclaim more of our planet, moving one step closer to thriving.

> *Growing up, I carried a deep unease with myself that grew into self-loathing. Fear, anxiety, and insecurity were constant companions. I hated looking at myself in mirrors or pictures. I told myself I looked like "Sloth" from The Goonies. I couldn't bear it. While I had achievements and happy moments, they always felt overshadowed by a nagging sense that I wasn't enough. I thought if I could just achieve more or win approval, I'd finally feel at peace.*
>
> *By my early forties, after years of wrestling with these feelings in my marriage, work, and parenting, I realized the problem: I was living in constant judgment of myself. I believed harsh self-criticism was motivating me to improve. And in a way, it did—fueling my overachieving—but it was also exhausting and unsustainable.*
>
> *The breakthrough wasn't dramatic. It came as a quiet realization that my internal battle wasn't working. Slowly, I wondered: What if I didn't need to fix myself to be worthy of love? I started small, practicing gratitude for who I already was and allowing myself to feel emotions without judgment. Sharing my struggles with trusted people helped me see I wasn't alone.*
>
> *This shift changed everything. The more I accepted myself—flaws and all—the less power shame held over me. Anxiety loosened its grip, and insecurity began to fade. Self-acceptance didn't erase life's challenges, but it transformed how I faced them. It allowed me to show up fully—not as a perfect person, but as a whole one.*

Ironically, nearly once a month, someone tells me I look "just like Matthew Lillard" (sorry, Matt!)., which is always quite flattering. However, it shows that how we feel about our appearance can affect how others view us. I didn't change my appearance, just how I felt about it.
Weird, huh?

When we accept ourselves, the fears that paralyze us lose their power, and we find the freedom to live authentically, connect deeply, and thrive fully. This is the foundation for the life we were always meant to live.

THE MAIN TAKEAWAY: DISMANTLING SHAME THROUGH SELF-ACCEPTANCE

Shame thrives on secrecy and self-rejection. By grounding our self-acceptance in an unshakable sense of self-worth and allowing trusted relationships to help prime the well of our regard, we dismantle its power. This isn't just about overcoming shame—it's about embracing our truest selves and thriving.

COMING UP NEXT: BEING, DOING, AND HAVING:

With self-acceptance, we've begun to dismantle shame and reclaim our worth. But this is only the beginning. In the next chapter, we'll confront the illusions the invaders have used to distort our sense of value and explore how shifting our focus from striving to *being* begins opening the door to a more fulfilling way of life. Together, we'll uncover the truth of *Be* → *Do* → *Have* and take another critical step toward liberation.

WHAT TO DO WHEN THE ALIENS SHOW UP (AND EVEN IF THEY DON'T)

COMMON RESPONSES

"Yeah, but if I accept myself, won't I stop trying to improve?"

Self-acceptance doesn't mean stagnation—it's the opposite. True growth happens when we operate from a place of love, not fear. Imagine planting a garden. If you harshly judge a seed for not being a tree, does it grow any faster? Of course not. It needs care, patience, and nurturing—just like you.

"Yeah, but I've done things I'm not proud of. How can I accept myself after that?"

Accepting yourself isn't about excusing mistakes or avoiding accountability. It's about acknowledging that your worth is unshakable, even when you fall short. Your mistakes are part of your story, but they don't define you. Self-acceptance allows you to learn, grow, and move forward with compassion for yourself.

"Yeah, but what if others don't accept me?"

This is a deeply human fear, and I hear you. Listen... there are approximately 8 billion people on this planet. How many of them must accept you for you to be okay? See the problem with this thinking? There's really no ending point to such a pursuit. It's important to remember that others' acceptance of you is often influenced by their own struggles and insecurities—it's not always about you. Self-acceptance isn't contingent on others' opinions. It's about freeing yourself from the need for external validation and finding peace in your inherent worth.

"Yeah, but isn't self-acceptance just giving up?"

Not at all. Giving up is rooted in shame, while self-acceptance is an act of courage. It's saying, "I'm enough as I am, and I have the strength to grow without needing to prove my worth." It's a shift from hustling for approval to living in alignment with your true self.

"Yeah, but what if self-acceptance feels impossible right now?"

That's okay—it often feels like that in the beginning. Start small. Acknowledge one thing you appreciate about yourself today, even if it's something simple. Over time, these small acts of regard build momentum. Remember, you're not alone in this journey. Every step you take, no matter how small, matters.

REFLECTION QUESTIONS

1. What stories has shame been telling you about your worth, and how can you begin to challenge their truth?
2. Who are the trusted people in your life with whom you could share your struggles to prime the well of self-acceptance?
3. What would it look like to rewrite a shame-driven narrative into one rooted in unconditional high regard and self-worth?
4. How might celebrating your imperfections and humanity shift your relationship with shame and foster self-acceptance?

CHAPTER THIRTY
DEFEATING THE ILLUSIONS
WAKING UP TO BEING HUMAN

Do not wish to be anything but what you are, and try to be that perfectly. – St. Francis de Sales

---

THE DECEITFUL ILLUSIONS OF PERFORMANCE-BASED SELF-WORTH

BEFORE WE CAN EXPLORE AUTHENTIC CONNECTION, WE MUST PAUSE and take one last, deeper look at self-worth and self-acceptance. The invaders have used subtle, deceitful illusions to distort how we view ourselves, keeping us from experiencing the deepest and most meaningful connections.

This isn't a critique of doing or accomplishing. It's a reframing —a way to shift from *doing* out of fear, shame, and inadequacy to *doing* from a place of intrinsic value and worth. Our *doing* remains, but it transforms from striving to *thriving*.

THE ALIEN'S ILLUSION: TWISTING THE FORMULA

The invaders' most effective deception has been their ability to twist the natural order of life into a performance-based formula for worth. This illusion comes in two common variations, both of which invert the truth:

1. Do → Have → Be

This illusion whispers: *If I do enough, I will have enough, and then I can finally be enough.* This is the <u>worker</u> mentality, a cycle of endless striving that leaves us perpetually dissatisfied. The invaders have convinced us that worth must be earned through effort, achievement, and success.

But here's the trap: even when we *do* enough to *have* something, the promise of finally *being* enough is always just out of reach. This formula keeps us in bondage to shame, constantly striving for a sense of self that never arrives.

2. Have → Do → Be

This formula says: *If I had what they have, I could do what they do, and then I could be who they are.* This is the <u>victim</u> mentality, which convinces us that external circumstances—resources, relationships, or opportunities—are prerequisites for our worth and potential.

It's a life spent waiting, blaming, and resenting. In this illusion, the invaders keep us trapped in powerlessness, telling us that only external factors can unlock our ability to thrive.

The Truth: Be → Do → Have

The truth is radically different: *Be → Do → Have*. It begins with the foundational truth that we already *are* enough. Our worth is fixed, unchanging, and intrinsic. From that unshakable foundation, our *doing* flows—not out of fear or inadequacy but from a place of alignment, purpose, and joy. And our *having* is the natural result of your *doing*.

- **Be:** I am already enough. My value is intrinsic and not dependent on achievement, possessions, or validation.
- **Do:** I take action based on my inherent worth. My doing flows from a place of wholeness and authenticity.
- **Have:** The results of my doing come naturally, but they don't define my worth. What I have may bring joy or satisfaction, but it doesn't determine who I am.

This shift—this reclamation of the *Be* → *Do* → *Have* formula—destroys the invaders' lies and frees us to live as our authentic selves.

LIVING FROM THE HEART, NOT THE EGO

Operating from *Be* → *Do* → *Have* aligns you with your "heart" instead of your ego.

- The **ego** thrives on *extrinsic* value. It views worth as something external, like a machine that only has value if it produces results. The ego operates under the *Do* → *Have* → *Be* or *Have* → *Do* → *Be* formulas, always striving or waiting.
- The **heart** recognizes *intrinsic* value. It knows that our worth is unshakable and that we don't need to prove, earn, or wait for it.

Living from the heart creates a sense of expansion, energy, and creativity. It's also characterized by freedom, joy, and peace. In contrast, living from the ego feels constricting, exhausting, and heavy, like the world is collapsing around us.

SVEN MASTERSON

BREAKING FREE FROM THE EGO'S TRAP

To dismantle the invaders' illusions, we must learn to recognize when operating from the ego and choose to live from the heart instead. Here's how:

- **Awareness:** Ask yourself, "Am I doing this to prove my worth or because it aligns with who I already am?"
- **Reframe:** When you catch yourself in a *Do* → *Have* → *Be* or *Have* → *Do* → *Be* mindset, remind yourself of the truth: "I am enough. My worth is not up for debate."
- **Expand:** Lean into the energy of the heart—create, connect, and act not to earn worth but because you *are* worthy.

THE LIBERATION OF LIVING FROM BE → DO → HAVE

The invaders' greatest deception was convincing us that our worth is earned. The truth is that our worth has always been, is now, and will always be enough. Operating from *Be* → *Do* → *Have* liberates us from the chains of striving and waiting.

Imagine the possibilities when your actions are no longer fueled by fear, shame, or inadequacy but by love, joy, and purpose. Imagine what you can create when you stop trying to *earn* your worth and start living from it.

This is how we reclaim our lives, families, communities, and planet: by taking back the truth of our intrinsic value and living boldly from it. We don't need to do anything to be enough—we already are. From that truth, everything else flows.

The stories I've told you about my transformation so far all boil down to simply experiencing the transition I've shared with you in this chapter—reversing the order of these three elements and changing the direction of the flow

WHAT TO DO WHEN THE ALIENS SHOW UP (AND EVEN IF THEY DON'T)

of life's energy from outside-in to inside-out. I'll share more about that in the next chapter.

THE MAIN TAKEAWAY: LIVING FROM BE → DO → HAVE

The invaders' illusions of *Do → Have → Be* and *Have → Do → Be* keep us trapped in cycles of striving and waiting. By reclaiming the truth of *Be → Do → Have*, we anchor ourselves in our intrinsic worth, allowing our actions to flow from a place of wholeness and authenticity.

COMING UP NEXT: WAKING UP TO THE TRUTH

In the next chapter, we'll dismantle one of the invaders' most powerful illusions: the belief that our external circumstances dictate our internal reality. This deception keeps us stuck, powerless, and endlessly chasing after things we can't control, hoping they'll bring us the peace, happiness, or worth we seek.

But what if the truth is the opposite? What if our external world isn't the cause but the effect—an extension of our internal state? We'll explore how shifting from outside-in thinking to inside-out living puts the power back in our hands. We'll discover how to cultivate the emotional states we desire first, reconnecting with ourselves and the Source of our intrinsic worth. From that foundation, our actions, habits, and outcomes will naturally transform, allowing us to reclaim our role as the Creator of our lives.

This is a turning point—a moment to step out of the fog, see through the illusions, and embrace the liberating truth that the power to create the life we desire has always been within us. It's time to awaken and begin living from the inside out.

COMMON RESPONSES

"Yeah, but isn't striving what makes me successful?"

Striving might have brought some success, but imagine what could happen if your energy wasn't tied up in proving your worth. Thriving is more sustainable than striving. When you create from a place of knowing you're enough, your success becomes meaningful, not just another item to check off on the way to feeling worthy.

"Yeah, but if I stop caring about external validation, won't I lose my edge?"

Your edge isn't in chasing approval; it's in aligning your actions with your intrinsic worth. When you stop seeking external validation, you'll find a deeper motivation—one rooted in joy, creativity, and purpose. That's not losing your edge; it's sharpening it.

"Yeah, but Be → Do → Have sounds idealistic. What about real-life struggles?"

I get it—real life can be messy and hard. But Be → Do → Have doesn't deny challenges; it reframes them. When you start from a place of worthiness, you face struggles with resilience rather than fear. You'll be better equipped to navigate life's ups and downs without losing sight of your value.

"Yeah, but doesn't intrinsic worth lead to complacency?"

Intrinsic worth doesn't mean complacency—it means freedom. When you're no longer hustling for worth, you're free to pursue what truly matters to you. You're no longer driven by fear of failure but by the excitement of growth and possibility.

WHAT TO DO WHEN THE ALIENS SHOW UP (AND EVEN IF THEY DON'T)

"Yeah, but I don't feel like I'm enough. How do I even start believing that?"

That's a powerful question and a tough place to be, but the first step is to challenge the story that says you're not enough. Start small. Acknowledge one thing—however tiny—that reflects your worth today. Build from there. Feeling enough is a practice, not an overnight shift, but every small step counts.

REFLECTION QUESTIONS

1. When have you found yourself operating from a *Do* → *Have* → *Be* or *Have* → *Do* → *Be* mindset? What impact did it have on your well-being?
2. What would it look like to approach your life from a *Be* → *Do* → *Have* perspective?
3. How can you prime your own "well" by allowing others to see and affirm your intrinsic worth?
4. How might your relationships, work, and creativity change if you stopped striving to earn worth and started living from it?

CHAPTER THIRTY-ONE
INSIDE-OUT LIVING
THE ART OF RECLAIMING YOUR REALITY FROM THE MATRIX OF ALIEN DECEPTION

The world is changed by your example, not your opinion.
– Paulo Coelho

SEEING THE MATRIX

IN THE FIRST *MATRIX* FILM, NEO'S WORLD SHATTERS WHEN HE discovers that everything he thought was real—his job, his relationships, his entire life—was an illusion. The "reality" he lived in was nothing more than a simulated program, controlled by an outside force designed to keep him blind, powerless, and compliant. But once he's shown the truth, Neo faces a choice: swallow the blue pill and remain trapped in the comfortable illusion, or take the red pill and awaken to a deeper reality where he can reclaim his agency and fight back.

Like Neo, many of us live in an illusion—not one made of computer code but one shaped by outside-in thinking. The invaders convince us that our emotions, worth, and happiness are determined by external circumstances. We become dependent on the "program" to feel safe and satisfied, believing we need the right job, the perfect relationship, or other people's approval to finally be at peace.

But what if the program isn't real? What if our external reality isn't *creating* our internal state—but reflecting it? Just like Neo's awakening, inside-out living is the red pill. It shatters the illusion that we are powerless and reveals the truth: our experience begins within ourselves. When we stop looking outside for peace, worth, and control, we reclaim our power to create the life we want.

This chapter is about choosing to wake up. It's about seeing the patterns that keep us trapped, unplugging from the illusion, and embracing the truth that everything we need to thrive is already within us. We don't need to change the world to find freedom—we only need to change how we *see* it.

THE TRAP OF OUTSIDE-IN LIVING

If the previous chapters have been a journey of untangling fear, judgment, and dependency, then this chapter is the turning point. Here, we'll tie together all the tools and insights we've gained so far to expose one of the invaders' most pervasive lies: the belief that our external circumstances create our internal reality.

This lie fuels the Drama Triangle, traps us in dependency, and keeps us living from an external locus of control—always waiting for something outside ourselves to change before we can feel better inside. It's the very foundation of outside-in living, a disempowered approach to life that places our happiness, peace, and worth into the hands of other people, circumstances, or systems.

When we live outside-in:

- We're stuck in *My business/Your business/The Creator's business* confusion. We obsess over what others are doing or what the world *should* be like, while neglecting what's within our control.

- We become emotionally dependent on external validation, stability, or achievements to feel worthy, secure, or fulfilled.
- We suppress, ignore, or numb our emotions because they're painful, failing to see them as the dashboard signals they are—alerting us that we're focused on disempowering patterns.
- We unconsciously play roles in the Drama Triangle—blaming (Persecutor), fixing (Rescuer), or feeling helpless (Victim)—instead of choosing to operate as a Creator.
- We live under the illusion of Do → Have → Be, striving endlessly to do or get enough so we can *finally* feel like we're enough.

If we want to break free, we must start living from the inside out.

INSIDE-OUT LIVING: RECLAIMING YOUR POWER

Inside-out living flips the script: instead of waiting for external change to create internal peace, we start within. We take responsibility for our thoughts, emotions, and actions—everything within our locus of control—knowing that our internal reality shapes our external experience.

This shift is subtle but powerful. Instead of *reacting* to life, we begin *creating* it. We stop giving away our power to circumstances, people, or systems that are outside our control. Instead, we choose how we want to feel and live, and we act from that place.

At its core, inside-out living operates from the Be → Do → Have formula:

- **Be:** Reconnect to your intrinsic worth and decide who you want to be. *You are enough as you are.*

- **Do:** From that state of being, take aligned action. *What you do flows naturally from who you are.*
- **Have:** The outcomes you desire follow as a byproduct of your aligned actions. *What you have reflects what you've created, but it doesn't define your worth.*

This isn't woo-woo. It's the mechanics of how human beings are wired.

THE COMMON GROUND: REVISITING WHAT WE'VE LEARNED

All of the tools and principles we've encountered so far come together here, forming a foundation for inside-out living:

1. **Internal Locus of Control:** Your power lies in what *you* can control—your thoughts, choices, and actions. You can't control what happens outside of you, but you can control your response to it.
2. **My Business, Your Business, The Creator's Business:** Staying focused on *your business*—your emotions, boundaries, and decisions—frees you from the trap of trying to fix, blame, or control others. It anchors you firmly in your own power.
3. **Emotional Self-Sourcing:** When you stop disconnecting from yourself through judgment and shame, you can meet your own emotional needs. Your emotions become a guide, showing you where you're out of alignment and where you need to take intentional action.
4. **The Drama Triangle and Empowerment Dynamic:** Outside-in living keeps you stuck as a Victim, Persecutor, or Rescuer. Inside-out living transforms you into a Creator, Challenger, or Coach—roles that empower you to take ownership of your life.

5. **The Pain of Misaligned Focus**: Your emotions signal when you're focusing on something outside your control or buying into disempowering narratives. Instead of numbing or avoiding this pain, you can pause, assess, and redirect your attention.
6. **Do → Have → Be vs. Be → Do → Have**: Living from "Be" creates lasting fulfillment because it aligns with your intrinsic worth. By contrast, chasing "Do" or "Have" first keeps you stuck in striving, waiting, and feeling inadequate.
7. **The Power of Choice**: You already have the tools to choose new thoughts, interpretations, and actions. This choice is your counteroffensive—the way you reclaim your reality and rewrite your story.

THE ROLE OF FOCUS: WHAT WE LOOK FOR, WE'LL FIND

Our brains are wired to filter our experiences based on what we focus on. This is thought to be the work of the Reticular Activating System (RAS), a part of the brain that determines what information to bring to our conscious attention. It is like an internet search through the massive amounts of information we experience every moment. When our brain finds a match, it shows us a result. In the years I felt worthless and rejected, my brain drew my attention to every instance of my experience that looked like a match, convincing me this was true. As I changed my "search term" to "I'm worthy of love and connection," amazingly, I started to experience more of those too!

When we live outside-in, our focus is on:

- What you *don't* have.
- What others are doing wrong.
- What could go wrong.

The brain responds by filtering your experience to confirm those fears. If we look for evidence that life is unfair, people don't care, or we're powerless, we'll find it—because that's what we're "searching" for.

But here's the truth: we can change what our brain filters by changing where we focus. When we start living from the inside out, we train our mind to look for:

- What we *can* control.
- What's going well.
- What we appreciate.
- Who we want to *be* in this moment.

This shift isn't about denying reality; it's about shaping our perception and choosing how to respond. It turns out that much of what we have been calling reality is our thinking about reality. That's a big difference!

PRACTICAL TOOLS FOR LIVING INSIDE-OUT

Here's how to start applying this shift:

1. Start With Who You Love to Be

- Ask yourself: *Who do I love to be?*
    - *What attitudes, behaviors, and perspectives create my highest sense of well-being, fullness, and peace?*
    - *What attributes, skills, passions, and gifts of mine do I deeply enjoy embodying?*
    - *How do I enjoy being in a relationship with others?*
    - *What kind of friend/partner/etc do I enjoy being?*
- If you feel anxious, for example, pause and ask: *What state do I want to create instead—peace, confidence, or calm?*

2. Use the PAPA Method to Shift Focus

- **Pause:** Take a breath. Interrupt the pattern of outside-in thinking.
  - Remember who you are and who you love to be
  - Express gratitude for the circumstances that are giving you this opportunity to grow and be more fully yourself.
- **Assess:** Ask...
  - *What am I feeling?*
  - *What state do I want to create instead—peace, confidence, or calm?*
  - *What's within my control?*
  - *Where am I placing my focus?*
- **Process:** Challenge disempowering thoughts.
  - *Am I reacting or choosing?*
  - *Am I believing the best about myself?*
  - *Am I believing the best about others?*
  - *Am I seeing myself as powerless or without choices?*
  - *Who do I choose to be in this moment?*
  - *What meaning do I choose to create?*
- **Address:** Take one aligned action—something small that reflects the emotional state you want to create.
  - Ask, *Who do I choose to be in this moment?*
  - *What actions must I take to remain aligned with these highest truths and to be fully authentic?*

3. Reclaim Your Emotional Dashboard

- When emotions flare up, instead of suppressing or ignoring them, ask: *What is this trying to tell me?*
- For example, anxiety might reveal that you're trying to control someone else's business. Redirect your focus to *your business*—your thoughts, choices, and actions.

4. Set Intentional Focus Each Day

- Start your day by deciding: *What do I want to focus on today? What am I grateful for?*
- End your day by reflecting: *Where did I act in alignment with my true self today?*

For much of my life, I believed my circumstances controlled my experience. I thought if I could fix my work, my marriage, or my family, I'd finally feel at peace. But no matter what I achieved or how hard I tried, I still felt stuck.

The shift came when I realized I was living outside-in—trying to control things I couldn't instead of taking responsibility for what I could: my thoughts, emotions, and actions. I began turning inward, asking, Who do I want to be in this moment? Instead of waiting to feel confident, peaceful, or joyful, I started cultivating those states within myself.

The results were staggering. My relationships improved because I no longer depended on others to "make me" feel okay. My work became more meaningful because I approached it with purpose rather than to prove my worth. Most importantly, I began experiencing a deep sense of peace, knowing that my reality was mine to create.

THE MAIN TAKEAWAY: CHANGE STARTS INSIDE

The invaders' greatest lie is that our happiness, worth, and peace are outside of us. The truth is that we are already enough, and because of this, we hold the power to create the emotional states and lives we desire. By living from the inside out, we reclaim our agency, shift our focus, and transform not only our internal world but also our external experience.

WHAT TO DO WHEN THE ALIENS SHOW UP (AND EVEN IF THEY DON'T)

COMING UP NEXT: THE POWER OF CONNECTION

When our worth is no longer tied to external validation, we're free to approach relationships from a place of wholeness. In the next chapter, we'll explore the power of authentic connection—what it looks like to build relationships rooted in mutual respect, vulnerability, and unconditional high regard. We'll discover how to create bonds that strengthen your sovereignty rather than threaten it, paving the way for deeper intimacy and authentic connection.

COMMON RESPONSES

"Yeah, but isn't it selfish to focus so much on myself instead of helping others?"

Not at all. Living from the inside out isn't about neglecting others; it's about showing up for them in a healthier and more empowered way. When you take responsibility for your emotions and actions, you're able to contribute more authentically and compassionately, without burnout or resentment.

"Yeah, but what if I just can't stop focusing on the negatives in my life?"

That's so relatable. Negativity often feels automatic because it's a habit our brain has learned. Start small—practice gratitude for just one thing each day, even if it's tiny. Over time, this rewires your brain to notice the positives more easily. Progress, not perfection, is the goal.

"Yeah, but isn't this 'inside-out' stuff just avoiding reality?"

Living inside-out doesn't mean ignoring reality; it means facing it from a place of strength. By focusing on what you can control—your thoughts, choices, and actions—you empower yourself to respond effectively to challenges instead of being overwhelmed by them.

"Yeah, but how can I be at peace when my external situation is genuinely terrible?"

That's a tough place to be, and it's okay to feel the weight of it. Inside-out living doesn't erase hardship, but it helps you find moments of calm and clarity even in the storm. Start with small, controllable actions—like a moment of gratitude or a simple breath—so you can regain a sense of agency.

"Yeah, but what if I fail at living inside-out? I always fall back into old habits."

It's okay to stumble. Change is a process, not a one-time event. Every time you catch yourself falling back into outside-in thinking is an opportunity to practice. Celebrate your awareness—that's progress! Keep showing up for yourself, one small step at a time.

REFLECTION QUESTIONS:

1. Where are you currently living outside-in? What external factors are you waiting to change before you feel better?
2. How would your experience shift if you began living from the inside out?
3. What emotional state do you want to create right now? What small choice can you make to cultivate it?

4. How can you refocus your energy on what you *can* control?

CHAPTER THIRTY-TWO
BREAKING THE WALLS OF DISCONNECTION
RECLAIMING YOURSELF, YOUR TRIBE, AND YOUR HUMANITY

> We are like islands in the sea, separate on the surface but connected in the deep. – William James

THE ALIEN INVADERS DIDN'T JUST ATTACK OUR THOUGHTS OR emotions—they targeted our connections. Like master tacticians, they built walls of disconnection and employed a divide-and-conquer strategy to isolate us from ourselves, others, and the Creator. They understood that isolation breeds vulnerability. By severing our ties, they sought to keep us divided, compliant, and under their control.

But connection is their greatest fear. It's the force that liberates, strengthens, and restores. Connection disrupts their power because it reveals the truth: You were never meant to face this invasion alone. This chapter is about mounting a counteroffensive—tearing down the walls of disconnection, rebuilding the bonds that restore our humanity, and reclaiming the networks of connection that have always been our greatest strength.

THE ALIEN TACTIC: ISOLATION AS A WEAPON

The invaders built walls brick by brick, using fear, shame, and judgment as their tools. These walls appeared to protect us but were, in fact, prisons in disguise.

- **Walls of Protection:** These defenses kept others at arm's length, convincing you that vulnerability was dangerous.
- **Walls of Pretense:** Masks of perfectionism and performance buried your true self under layers of "shoulds" and "not enoughs."
- **Walls of Isolation:** The lie that you're better off alone fed the myth that self-reliance meant rejecting connection.

When we disconnect from ourselves, others, and the Creator/source, we become more susceptible to their whispers of fear and shame. But disconnection wasn't an accident—it was their plan. They knew that severed connections would prevent us from accessing the support, perspective, and love we needed to thrive.

However, the potential for connection never disappeared. Even in our darkest moments, the tools to rebuild were always within reach.

STEP ONE: RECONNECTING WITH YOURSELF

The foundation of all connection is *internal*. The invaders' first attack was to sever our relationship with our own hearts, sowing self-judgment, fear, and shame. Reclaiming connection begins with you.

Know Yourself

We cannot connect with what we do not know. Rebuilding self-connection means facing our true selves—the ones behind the masks and the lies.

- **Face the Fear:** Stop running from your flaws, failures, and vulnerabilities. Look at them head-on, without judgment.
- **Define Your Values:** Your values guide your decisions and relationships. Clarify what matters most to you.
- **Clarify Your Boundaries:** True connection doesn't mean losing yourself. Boundaries protect your autonomy while fostering authenticity.

Accept Yourself

Self-acceptance is not a luxury; it's a necessity. Without it, we'll seek validation from others, making authentic relationships impossible.

- **Embrace Imperfection:** Perfection is a lie. Your flaws don't make you unworthy; they make you human.
- **Release Shame:** Shame whispers that you're not enough. Self-acceptance silences that voice.
- **Celebrate Progress:** You are not where you used to be, and that is worth celebrating.

Be Honest With Yourself

Authenticity starts within. The more honest we are about our desires, fears, and needs, the more connected we will feel to our hearts.

- **Admit What You Want:** Stop pretending you don't care about connection, love, or respect.
- **Name Your Fears:** Fear grows in the dark. Drag it into the light to remove its power.

- **Speak Your Truth:** Even if it's just to yourself, practice honesty about what you feel and why.

STEP TWO: REBUILDING RELATIONAL BONDS

Once we've started reconnecting with ourselves, we can turn outward. Authentic connection with others doesn't come from perfection but from vulnerability and courage.

Be Vulnerable

Vulnerability is the bravest act we can perform in a relationship. It means showing up as we are, not as we believe others want us to be, and without guarantees that we'll be accepted. Self-acceptance is crucial to this process because it provides the courage to be vulnerable.

Listen Deeply

True connection isn't just about speaking—it's about listening with our whole selves.

- **Be Present:** Put away distractions and focus on the person in front of you.
- **Seek to Understand:** Don't just hear their words; listen for their heart.
- **Show Empathy:** Validation doesn't require agreement. It means letting someone know they've been heard.

Share Authentically

Authenticity invites authenticity. When we share our true selves, we permit others to do the same.

- **Drop the Mask:** Stop pretending to be what you think others want.
- **Own Your Story:** Share the struggles and victories that shaped you.
- **Offer Grace:** Connection thrives in an atmosphere of kindness and understanding.

What About Broken Relationships?

Not every relationship can—or should—be rebuilt. Some relationships may fall away as we reconnect with ourselves and establish boundaries. That's okay. Focus on relationships that are life-giving, not depleting and toxic. Rebuilding our tribe is about creating a network of authenticity and trust, not about headcount.

STEP THREE: EXPANDING INTO THE LARGER NETWORK

Our tribe is our immediate circle, but connection doesn't stop there. The broader network of humanity offers immense strength and shared purpose.

- **Seek Mentorship and Support Groups:** Surround yourself with people who understand your path.
- **Serve Others:** Helping others creates bonds that strengthen both parties.
- **Reconnect With the Creator:** Faith provides purpose, belonging, and resilience that transcend individual relationships.

Step Four: Sharing Your Story

Sharing our story is a transformative act of connection. It invites others to see the real us and helps us reclaim agency over our narrative.

SVEN MASTERSON

THE COUNTEROFFENSIVE: CONNECTION AS LIBERATION

Disconnection was the invaders' strongest weapon, but connection is one of our most powerful counteroffensives. Rebuilding connection is an act of resistance, a declaration that we will not be isolated, controlled, or diminished. Every step we take to reconnect—with ourselves, our tribe, and our Creator—reclaims our humanity, purpose, and place in the world.

>For years, I felt alone in my struggles. Fear, insecurity, and shame seemed like burdens I had to carry in silence, believing no one else could possibly understand. Everyone else seemed different and didn't seem to understand, which only deepened my feelings of inadequacy. But then, something extraordinary happened: I unexpectedly found a community where I could show up as my authentic self.
>
>At first, sharing my story felt terrifying. What if they judged me? What if my struggles confirmed my worst fears about myself? But as I began to speak, something unexpected unfolded. The people around me didn't recoil or criticize—they leaned in. Some nodded in understanding, while others shared their own stories, and in doing so, I realized something profound: I wasn't alone.
>
>Hearing their stories was a revelation. It showed me how common my struggles were and how universal the experiences of fear, shame, and doubt really are. There was something incredibly liberating about seeing my inner battles reflected in their words. It made me question the belief that my pain was my unique flaw—it wasn't. It was part of the shared human experience.
>
>This exchange of stories became a force multiplier for my self-acceptance. Not only was I able to share without fear of judgment, but I was also able to offer others the

same gift. In listening to their experiences, I found myself less inclined to judge—not just them but myself, too. Their courage to be vulnerable inspired my own, and their humanity made me kinder to myself.

Over time, this sharing gave me a broader perspective. I began to see that the narratives I had internalized about myself weren't unique—they were part of a larger, often faulty, pattern of human thinking. Knowing this helped me detach from those stories. I stopped taking my inner critic so seriously and learned to hold my fears and doubts with greater compassion.

The more I shared, the more my self-acceptance grew. And the more I listened, the more I realized how interconnected we all are. Each person's story added a layer of insight and empathy to my own, and together, we created a space where shame couldn't thrive.

Through this community and other communities I went on to create, I've come to see that self-acceptance isn't just an individual journey—it's a collective one. By sharing our stories, we give each other permission to be real, let go of shame, and embrace our imperfections as part of what makes us beautifully human. In doing so, we don't just accept ourselves—we inspire others to do the same.

Looking back, I know that finding this community didn't just change how I related to others—it fundamentally transformed how I saw myself. And that transformation has been one of the greatest gifts of my life.

THE MAIN TAKEAWAY: CONNECTION LIBERATES

Disconnection is the invaders' tool of control, but connection is humanity's path to freedom. Rebuilding connection starts within, extends to our tribe, and plugs into the more extensive network of humanity, the universe, and the Creator. Through connection, we reclaim and nurture our power, purpose, and resilience.

COMMON RESPONSES

"Yeah, but I don't trust people enough to connect with them. They've hurt me before."

That's valid. I used to feel similarly. Then I started to see that what I really didn't trust was myself. I didn't trust that I was enough to handle any future pain I might experience. As I built my relationship with myself, I found it easier to overcome these kinds of fears. Rebuilding connection doesn't mean rushing into relationships that feel unsafe. Start small—choose trusted allies and focus on cultivating relationships where mutual respect and understanding are present. Connection doesn't require perfection; it thrives on authenticity and healthy boundaries.

"Yeah, but isn't it better to rely on myself? People always let me down."

Self-reliance is important, but isolation often keeps us from experiencing the support, perspective, and encouragement we need to thrive. Connection isn't about dependence—it's about interdependence, where we share strengths and uplift one another.

"Yeah, but what if my relationships are too broken to fix?"

Some relationships may not be repairable, and that's okay. Focus on what's within your control: reconnecting with yourself and nurturing life-giving connections. Broken relationships don't define you, and new, healthy bonds can always be formed.

> "Yeah, but I don't know how to be vulnerable without being judged."

Vulnerability is a skill that takes practice. Start by choosing safe spaces—trusted friends, mentors, or supportive groups. Sharing small, honest parts of yourself builds confidence over time and helps you discern who can meet you with acceptance and understanding.

> "Yeah, but what if people don't care about my story? What if I get rejected?"

Rejection is painful, but it doesn't define your worth. Sharing your story isn't about everyone's approval—it's about finding the ones who resonate. When you share authentically, you create space for connection with those who see and value the real you.

REFLECTION QUESTIONS

1. Where have the invaders built walls of disconnection in your life?
2. What practices can you start this week to reconnect with yourself?
3. Who are the trusted allies in your life, and how can you deepen those relationships?
4. How can your story become a bridge to connection with others?

CHAPTER THIRTY-THREE
SELF-SOURCING STRENGTH
RECLAIMING YOUR POWER FROM AND DRAWING FROM THE WELLSPRING WITHIN

You have power over your mind – not outside events. Realize this, and you will find strength. – Marcus Aurelius

---

THE ALIEN'S STRATEGY: EXPLOITING DEPENDENCY

THE ALIEN INVADERS DIDN'T RELY ON BRUTE FORCE. They were subtle, patient, and cunning. Rather than confront our defenses head-on, they exploited our critical infrastructure: our need to know ourselves to be *valuable, worthy, powerful, meaningful,* and *connected*. By manipulating us to redirect those needs outward, they made us believe that our value, worth, power, meaning, security, and connection came from something *external*.

- **Dependency on Approval and Permission:** They whispered that your value depended on what others thought of you.
- **Dependency on Circumstances:** They convinced you that your happiness hinged on conditions beyond your control.

- **Dependency on Rescuers:** They assured you that salvation would come from someone or something else.

Dependency became the leash that kept us bound. It robbed us of our agency, leaving us vulnerable to manipulation. Worst of all, it disconnected us from the infinite source of strength within us.

THE COUNTEROFFENSIVE: SELF-SOURCING STRENGTH

Self-sourcing is the ultimate act of resistance against dependency. It's the process of reclaiming one's power, grounding it in one's connection to oneself and the Creator, and choosing to source one's validation, strength, and worth from within.

THE MYTH OF EXTERNAL FULFILLMENT

Many of us are conditioned from childhood to believe that our happiness and worth lie outside of us. We chase approval, achievements, and relationships, hoping they will fill the void inside. But here's the truth I hope you've discovered in this book: external sources are fleeting and unreliable. Nothing is permanent. Everything changes.

- Approval fades.
- Circumstances change.
- People fail.

Self-sourcing isn't about rejecting the connection or support of others—it's about ensuring that our foundation is solid enough to withstand the storms of life, even when external sources fail.

I grew up believing that looking within myself was dangerous—that if left unchecked, my insides would be dark, untrustworthy, and full of pride. My upbringing conditioned me to believe that relying on anything within myself would be arrogant, even sinful. Instead, I thought my worth had to come from external sources—success, recognition, or meeting the expectations of others. Ironically, this also included "God," which confusingly reinforced a belief that I was separate from God and that God was external.

For a while, it worked. When things were going well—at work, in my marriage, or in my social circles—I felt like I was on solid ground. But when things fell apart, so did I. My sense of worth crumbled under the weight of failure, rejection, or unmet expectations. I didn't realize how fragile those external dependencies had made me until I started questioning what I'd been taught.

The idea of sourcing my sense of self from within felt terrifying at first. It went against everything I'd been told about humility and self-reliance (a bad word to many!). But slowly, I began to explore the possibility that my worth wasn't something I needed to prove or earn—it was something I already had. It took time to trust that what I'd been avoiding inside myself wasn't darkness but a wellspring of strength and value I had long overlooked.

Learning to self-source wasn't easy, but it has been transformative. It freed me from the rollercoaster of external validation and taught me to stand on a foundation that doesn't crumble when life gets hard. It's not about arrogance or pride; it's about finally seeing the truth that I'm enough, just as I am.

THE CREATOR CONNECTION

True self-sourcing is not about isolation or independence—it's about union. It's about anchoring ourselves in the infinite, unshakable love and power of something bigger that we are connected to and that is connected to us. For me, that is The Creator. For others, that may be Source, The Universe, God, The All, etc. I'm not here to tell you what that should be because I don't think our understanding of it is what makes whatever it is a reality. Whatever it is, if we are connected to it and it's good, then we can count on a few ongoing benefits:

- **We are already enough:** The Creator doesn't measure us by our achievements or failures. Our worth is inherent and unchanging.
- **We are never alone:** Even in our darkest moments, the Creator's presence is within us, offering guidance and strength.
- **We are, therefore, infinitely resourceful:** By tapping into this connection, we have access to wisdom, courage, and resilience beyond our own.

Self-sourcing isn't a rejection of the Creator—it's a partnership. It's based on the belief that this source is the home of our true self, not that our true self is disconnected from the source. This self-sourcing aligns with the divine power within us to create a life that reflects our true identity.

RECLAIMING OUR POWER

Dependency thrives on the illusion of helplessness. Self-sourcing dismantles that illusion by reminding you of your power: the power to choose, create, and act.

How Self-Sourcing Reflects Maturity

Dependency is a hallmark of immaturity—not because it's inherently bad, but because it reflects an earlier stage of development. As children, we depend on others for our sense of safety, worth, and direction. Maturity, however, is the process of reclaiming that responsibility for ourselves.

- **Ownership of Emotions:** Maturity means recognizing that your feelings are your responsibility. Self-sourcing empowers you to process emotions constructively without projecting blame or expecting others to manage your inner world.
    - *Maturity Insight:* "I feel frustrated" shifts from an accusation ("You made me feel this way") to a personal reflection ("What's this frustration showing me about my needs or boundaries?").
- **Steady Self-Worth:** Immaturity ties worth to external validation, fluctuating with every success or failure. Maturity anchors worth in something unchanging: your inherent value.
    - *Maturity Insight:* When you stop chasing worth and start living from it, you enter a season of grounded confidence and peace.
- **Aligned Actions:** Immaturity reacts impulsively; maturity acts intentionally. Self-sourcing enables you to align your choices with your values, creating a life of purpose and integrity.
    - *Maturity Insight:* This alignment leads to a sense of fulfillment because your actions consistently reflect who you truly are.

THE TOOLS OF SELF-SOURCING

Self-sourcing isn't a one-time decision—it's a practice. Here are some tools to help you build and maintain it:

1. Daily Reflection

Take time each day to connect with yourself and the Creator. Ask:

- What am I feeling, and why?
- What do I need right now?
- What can I do to meet that need for myself?

2. Affirmations of Truth

Speak words of truth over yourself to counter the lies of dependency. Examples:

- "I am enough, just as I am."
- "I have the strength to handle whatever comes my way."
- "My worth is not determined by external circumstances."

3. Acts of Ownership

Each day, take one action that affirms your power. It could be setting a boundary, pursuing a goal, or simply showing kindness to yourself.

THE FREEDOM OF SELF-SOURCING

When you begin self-sourcing, you'll notice a shift. The fears that once held you captive will loosen their grip. The anxieties that ruled your decisions will lose their power. And the relationships you once clung to for validation will become opportunities for genuine connection.

- You'll stop seeking approval and start living authentically.
- You'll stop fearing rejection and start embracing vulnerability.

WHAT TO DO WHEN THE ALIENS SHOW UP (AND EVEN IF THEY DON'T)

- You'll stop waiting for rescue and start creating the life you want.

One of the most liberating moments in my life was realizing that I didn't need anyone else's permission to be happy or to experience any emotional state within myself. The day I decided to source my joy and strength from within was the day I stopped feeling like a victim of my circumstances.

THE BENEFITS OF SELF-SOURCING

Self-sourcing transforms not only your inner world but also your relationships and your ability to thrive.

How It Benefits Relationships

1. **From Neediness to Generosity:** Instead of seeking to be filled by others, you approach relationships with a full heart, ready to give.
2. **From Control to Respect:** By releasing the need to control others, you create space for mutual respect and freedom.
3. **From Reactivity to Presence:** Anchored in self-sourcing, you can engage with others calmly, authentically, and empathetically.

How It Leads to Thriving

1. **Emotional Stability:** Self-sourcing grounds you in peace, even amidst chaos.
2. **Confidence to Create:** Freed from dependency, you channel your energy into growth and purpose.
3. **Authenticity:** With no masks to maintain, you live in alignment with your true self.

THE MAIN TAKEAWAY: SELF-SOURCING IS SOVEREIGNTY

Dependency is the enemy's leash; self-sourcing is your freedom. By grounding yourself in your Creator connection and choosing to source strength, validation, and worth from within, you reclaim the power that was always yours.

COMING UP NEXT: CLAIMING BOLD CONFIDENCE

The alien invaders kept you small with the lies of insecurity, but their time is up. In the next chapter, we'll uncover how taking ownership of your choices and rooting your worth in unshakable truths dismantles insecurity and builds the bold confidence you need to thrive. Confidence isn't a feeling you wait for—it's a choice you make every day.

COMMON RESPONSES

> "Yeah, but isn't it selfish to focus on sourcing strength from within instead of from others?"

Not at all. If we source it from others, they have to get it somewhere—either themselves or someone else. If they can get it from within, why can't you? If they get it from others, how to the where do the people who have strength get theirs? When we use people for strength people, we use them. Using someone for our benefit isn't connection; it's commerce. Self-sourcing doesn't mean rejecting connection—it means approaching relationships from a place of fullness rather than neediness. When you're grounded in your own worth, you're better equipped to give generously, love authentically, and build deeper, healthier connections.

WHAT TO DO WHEN THE ALIENS SHOW UP (AND EVEN IF THEY DON'T)

"Yeah, but I've always relied on others for validation. Isn't it too late to change?"

It's never too late to reclaim your power. Self-sourcing is a practice, not an overnight transformation. Start small—affirm your worth, reflect on your emotions, and take one aligned action each day. Over time, these small steps will create lasting change.

"Yeah, but what if I'm too scared to rely on myself? What if I fail?"

Fear of failure is natural, but self-sourcing isn't about perfection—it's about progress. The Creator connection ensures you're never truly alone. Every step you take, no matter how small, builds resilience and confidence. Remember: failure is a teacher, not a defeat.

"Yeah, but doesn't self-sourcing mean I can't depend on anyone else for support?"

Self-sourcing doesn't reject support—it complements it. It's about ensuring your foundation is strong so you can engage with others from a place of authenticity and trust. Healthy interdependence thrives when individuals are secure in themselves.

"Yeah, but I've been taught that looking inward is prideful. Isn't this against humility?"

True humility is acknowledging your intrinsic worth while recognizing the Source from which it comes. Self-sourcing isn't about arrogance; it's about aligning with the Creator's truth that you are already enough. By honoring your worth, you honor the One who created it.

REFLECTION QUESTIONS

1. What external sources have you depended on for validation, strength, or worth?
2. How can you begin sourcing those needs from within?
3. What practices or tools resonate most with you for building self-sourcing?
4. How might self-sourcing change the way you approach challenges and relationships?

CHAPTER THIRTY-FOUR
FORTRESS OF CONFIDENCE
TURNING INSECURITY INTO BOLD SECURITY

Confidence comes not from always being right but from not fearing to be wrong. – Peter T. McIntyre

---

THE ALIEN'S STRATEGY: INSECURITY AS WEAKNESS

INSECURITY WAS NEVER JUST A FEELING—IT WAS A WEAPON. The invaders used it to undermine our confidence, erode our sense of worth, and keep us playing small. Insecurity whispered lies, convincing us that safety came from staying unseen, unheard, and unremarkable.

- **We doubted our abilities**, so we held back from pursuing our passions, interests, and dreams.
- **We questioned our worth**, so we sought approval in all the wrong places.
- **We feared rejection**, so we avoided vulnerability and authentic connection.

Insecurity isn't just an emotional state; it's a form of *captivity*. It keeps us trapped in cycles of hesitation and doubt, convincing us that boldness is dangerous. But there's a way out.

THE COUNTER-OFFENSIVE: OWNERSHIP AS SECURITY

Confidence is something we're born with—at least in its most fundamental form. Spiritually speaking, we come into this world with no reason to distrust ourselves and no need to prove our worth. This is what I think of as spiritual confidence: a deep, intrinsic trust in our inherent value and worthiness. It's not something we earn or achieve—it simply is.

But as we grow, we start learning judgment, experiencing shame, and hearing messages that tell us we're not enough. Over time, we lose touch with that spiritual confidence and begin relying on behavioral confidence—the kind that comes from what we do, achieve, or prove. While behavioral confidence has its place, it's fragile without the foundation of spiritual confidence because it's always contingent on doing rather than being.

Here's the thing: we can't just sit around waiting to feel confident again. Reclaiming confidence, especially spiritual confidence, requires action. It's a deliberate process of challenging the lies of judgment and shame, reconnecting with the truth of our intrinsic worth, and rebuilding trust in ourselves. This kind of confidence doesn't happen by accident—it grows through intentional choices and practices.

True confidence is holistic. It begins with rediscovering our spiritual confidence—the unshakable belief in our worth that doesn't depend on anything external. From there, behavioral and emotional confidence can emerge, creating a solid framework for living fully. It's not about waiting for confidence to return—it's about taking the steps to nurture and rebuild it from the inside out.

WHAT TO DO WHEN THE ALIENS SHOW UP (AND EVEN IF THEY DON'T)

THE PYRAMID OF CONFIDENCE: SPIRITUAL, BEHAVIORAL, AND EMOTIONAL

I think of confidence as a pyramid, with **spiritual confidence** as the base, **behavioral confidence** as the middle layer, and **emotional confidence** at the top. Each layer builds on the one beneath it, and without the foundation of spiritual confidence, the entire structure is unstable.

1. Spiritual Confidence: Trusting Our Intrinsic Worth

Spiritual confidence is the foundation. It's a profound trust in our inherent value and worth, grounded in the truth that we are enough simply because we exist. This is not tied to performance, external validation, or circumstances—it is fixed, innate, and unchanging.

- **Why It's Foundational:** Without spiritual confidence, we over-rely on behavioral confidence (our ability to act) or emotional confidence (our ability to navigate feelings). Since no one has perfect behavior or emotions, this reliance leads to brittle, fragile confidence. Spiritual confidence provides the anchor that keeps everything steady.
- **What It Looks Like:** Spiritual confidence allows us to take risks, face failure, and embrace vulnerability because our worth isn't on the line.
- **How to Cultivate It:**
    - **Challenge Lies About Worth:** Identify and dismantle beliefs that tie your value to performance or approval.
    - **Anchor in the Creator/Source:** Draw strength from your connection to a higher power, knowing that your worth is unshakable and eternal.

- **Affirm Intrinsic Value:** Regularly remind yourself, *"I am enough, no matter what."*

For years, I tied my worth to my achievements. When I succeeded, I felt on top of the world. But when I failed, I crumbled. It wasn't until I rooted my worth in something greater—in the unchanging truth of my value as a being—that I found true confidence. Spiritual confidence gave me the freedom to live authentically.

2. Behavioral Confidence: Trusting Your Ability to Act

Behavioral confidence is the next layer. It's our trust in our competency to show up, follow through, and overcome challenges. This type of confidence grows as we repeatedly face discomfort, accept challenges, and take ownership of our choices and actions.

- **Why It Matters:** Behavioral confidence teaches us that we are trustworthy and reliable. When grounded in spiritual confidence, it becomes a powerful tool for growth rather than a brittle source of self-worth.
- **What It Looks Like:** Behavioral confidence gives us the courage to step into the unknown, take risks, and keep moving forward, even in the face of setbacks.
- **How to Build It:**
    - **Take Small Actions:** Commit to manageable tasks that reinforce your ability to follow through.
    - **Celebrate Consistency:** Recognize and honor every time you show up, even in small ways.
    - **Learn From Mistakes:** View failures as opportunities for growth rather than evidence of inadequacy.

I used to struggle with procrastination, constantly

doubting my ability to follow through. But as I started taking small, consistent actions—finishing a task here, keeping a promise there—I began to trust myself. Behavioral confidence isn't about being perfect; it's about proving to yourself, day by day, that you are capable.

3. Emotional Confidence: Trusting Your Capacity to Navigate Feelings

At the top of the pyramid is emotional confidence—the ability to trust that we can handle whatever emotions arise. It grows when we stop avoiding or suppressing emotions and start allowing ourselves to experience them without judgment.

- **Why It's Vital:** Emotional confidence enables us to stay present, process emotions constructively, and keep moving forward, even when things feel overwhelming.
- **What It Looks Like:** Emotional confidence means facing fear, sadness, or anger with curiosity rather than avoidance. It's knowing that emotions, no matter how intense, don't define us.
- **How to Cultivate It:**
    - **Name Your Emotions:** Acknowledge what you're feeling without trying to suppress it.
    - **Practice Self-Compassion:** Treat yourself with kindness when emotions arise.
    - **Develop Emotional Tools:** Use journaling, mindfulness, or therapy to process feelings constructively.

I used to avoid difficult conversations because I feared the emotions they'd bring—anger, disappointment, or sadness. But when I started facing those emotions head-on, I discovered that I could handle them. Emotional confi-

dence isn't about avoiding discomfort—it's about knowing you can hold it and still move forward.

THE FREEDOM OF TRUE CONFIDENCE

When these three dimensions of confidence align, insecurity loses its grip. We become free to live boldly, authentically, and courageously:

- **In Relationships:** We set boundaries, express our needs, and connect authentically without fear of rejection.
- **In Work and Goals:** We take risks, pursue growth, and handle setbacks with resilience.
- **In Life:** We stop seeking permission to be bold and start living with intention and purpose.

Confidence built on this pyramid is unshakable because it isn't dependent on perfect behavior or flawless emotions. It flows from a foundation of spiritual or transcendent worth, reinforced by action and resilience in the face of challenges.

THE MAIN TAKEAWAY: CONFIDENCE IS A PYRAMID

True confidence is multi-dimensional. It starts with spiritual confidence—trust in our intrinsic worth—and builds upward through behavioral and emotional confidence. Together, these dimensions create a framework for living boldly and authentically, free from insecurity.

COMING UP NEXT: RECLAIMING THE POWER OF YOUR STORY

With the invaders' weapon of insecurity disarmed, it's time to reclaim one of the most powerful tools for your liberation—our story. In the next chapter, we'll explore how the alien lies distorted the narrative of our lives and how we can take back the pen. We'll learn to rewrite the script, uproot the lies, and replace them with truth. Our story is more than just our past—it's the blueprint for our future. We'll uncover how owning and sharing our narratives can inspire connection, healing, and transformation.

COMMON RESPONSES

"Yeah, but I've never felt confident. Isn't it just something you're born with?"

While some confidence is innate, much of it is cultivated through choices and actions. True confidence begins with spiritual confidence—anchoring your worth in the truth that you are enough as you are. Behavioral and emotional confidence can be built over time through practice and intentional effort.

"Yeah, but I can't trust myself because I've failed so many times before."

Failure is part of the human experience, not a measure of your worth. Each failure is an opportunity to learn and grow. Spiritual confidence reminds you that your value isn't tied to your successes or failures. Start small—take one step to rebuild trust in yourself and celebrate each win along the way.

"Yeah, but what if my emotions are too overwhelming to handle?"

Emotional confidence doesn't mean you'll never feel overwhelmed—it means trusting that you can navigate those emotions. Tools like naming your feelings, practicing self-compassion, and seeking support can help. Over time, facing emotions head-on will build resilience and reduce their intensity.

"Yeah, but I've been relying on external validation my whole life. How can I change now?"

It's never too late to reclaim your confidence. Begin by shifting your focus inward. Affirm your intrinsic worth daily and take small, manageable actions that reinforce trust in yourself. Building spiritual confidence creates a strong foundation to break free from dependency on external validation.

"Yeah, but isn't being confident the same as being arrogant?"

Not at all. True confidence is grounded in humility and authenticity. It's about knowing your worth without needing to prove it to others. Arrogance stems from insecurity, while confidence grows from an unshakable belief in your intrinsic value.

REFLECTION QUESTIONS

1. Which dimension of confidence—spiritual, behavioral, or emotional—feels strongest in your life? Which feels weakest?
2. How can you cultivate spiritual confidence by anchoring your worth in something unshakable?
3. What small actions can you take this week to strengthen your behavioral confidence?
4. How can you navigate emotions with curiosity and self-compassion to build emotional confidence?

CHAPTER THIRTY-FIVE
THE LIBERATION OF STORY: WRITING YOUR TRUTH

TRANSFORMING THE LIES INTO A STORY OF FREEDOM, LIBERATION AND STRENGTH.

Every man's life is a fairy tale written by God's fingers.
– Hans Christian Andersen

THE ALIEN REWRITE: RECLAIMING YOUR STORY

DECEPTION DOESN'T JUST DISTORT REALITY—IT REWRITES THE STORY of who we are. The invaders craft their lies carefully, embedding them so deeply in our internal narrative that they shape how we see ourselves, what we believe is possible, and the paths we choose. Over time, this false story creates a self-perpetuating cycle of doubt and disconnection.

The invaders' script goes something like this:

- "You're not enough."
- "You're a mistake."
- "You'll never measure up."
- "Your worth depends on others' approval."
- "Your flaws define you."
- "You can't trust yourself."

- "Trusting them is dangerous."

But here's the liberating truth: **the pen is in <u>our</u> hands.** The invaders may have hijacked our narrative, but they don't get the final word. We do. Reclaiming our story is not just an act of defiant resistance—it's an act of *creation*.

THE COUNTERSTRIKE: REWRITING YOUR STORY

To dismantle the invaders' lies, you must first reclaim the narrative of our lives. This is where our counteroffensive begins.

1. Own Your Story—The Whole Story

A powerful story isn't perfect—it's authentic. Owning our story means embracing all of it: the triumphs, the failures, the moments of joy, and the seasons of pain. It's about reclaiming your identity without shame.

- **Why It Matters:** Denying parts of your story gives the invaders power. By owning every chapter, you reclaim agency over your identity.

For years, I was pretty scared to let anyone see the messier parts of my life. I avoided discussing the struggles in my marriage, my fears of inadequacy, and the moments when I felt like a failure. I thought admitting those truths would make me appear weak or prove why I was unworthy. But when I finally began to own my full story—flaws and all—I discovered a strength I didn't know I had.

Owning our story isn't about justifying or glorifying past mistakes; it's about integrating them into the truth of who we are today.

WHAT TO DO WHEN THE ALIENS SHOW UP (AND EVEN IF THEY DON'T)

2. Rewrite the Lies with Truth

The invaders' lies are not permanent. They are distortions that can be rewritten with truth.

- **Example:** When the story says, "You're too broken to be loved," rewrite it as "I am inherently worthy of love and connection." When it says, "You'll never succeed," rewrite it as, "I have the courage to try, and that's enough."
- **Practical Tip:** Identify the specific lies you've internalized and replace them with empowering truths. Write these truths down, speak them aloud daily, and challenge the lies whenever they resurface.

By rewriting your story, you reclaim your narrative as a source of power rather than pain.

3. Share Your Story Boldly

Reclaiming your story isn't just an internal process—it's also about sharing your truth with the world. Vulnerability is a weapon against the invaders' isolation tactics.

- **Be Unapologetic:** Your story doesn't need to be polished or perfect to matter. It just needs to be real.
- **Be Courageous:** Sharing your story creates connection and inspires others to reclaim their own narratives.

The first time I shared my marriage story publicly, I was terrified. I was sure people would judge or misunderstand me—and some did. Some always will. But most people didn't. Instead, they leaned in. They resonated. They felt seen and no longer alone in the struggles they had. They thanked me for being honest. Experiences like these have taught me that all our stories have the power to heal—not just ourselves but others, and when we tell our stories, we heal a little bit in the process, and so do those we share them with.

When we share your story authentically, we plant seeds of truth and encouragement in the hearts of those who hear it.

THE POWER OF STORYTELLING

Telling our story is more than self-expression—it's a transformative act that dismantles the invaders' lies and replaces them with liberation.

- **It Heals:** Sharing our truth releases the shame and fear that kept it hidden.
- **It Connects:** Vulnerability bridges the gap between us and others, creating empathy and understanding.
- **It Inspires:** By owning our narrative, we encourage others to do the same.

Why Stories Matter

The invaders thrive in silence and secrecy. They depend on our reluctance to own and share our story. But the moment we speak our truth, we shine a light they cannot withstand. When we share our story, we take control of the narrative. We become the *authors* of our lives, not the *victims* of their lies.

Note: Some religious people get agitated when I suggest that we are each the authors of our lives because, in the Bible, the apostle Peter refers to Jesus as "The Author of Life" (Acts 3:15). Listen... in that verse, Peter is attributing Jesus as the author of all Life, not suggesting that you have no agency in yours because Jesus is writing every sentence. Believing you are the sole agent responsible for how your story unfolds is not only not in conflict with these words of Peter, it affirms the biblical narrative. You are responsible for you!

Planting Seeds of Truth Through Story

Our story is a seed. When we share it honestly and courageously, it plants goodness in the hearts of others and strengthens our clarity, understanding, and resolve.

- **Truth:** Share your story as it is—not as you wish it were. Honesty is what makes your narrative powerful.
- **Integrity:** Live your story in alignment with your values. Let your actions reflect the truths you've reclaimed.
- **Kindness:** Use your story to uplift others, not to tear them down. Speak with compassion, even when addressing the roles others played in your journey.

THE MAIN TAKEAWAY: OUR STORY IS OUR SUPERPOWER

Owning and sharing our story is a revolutionary act. It reclaims our identity, inspires connection, clarifies our purpose, and sows seeds of truth that dismantle the alien's lies. Our story is a weapon of liberation—wield it with courage and boldness!

COMING UP NEXT: DISMANTLING THE WEB OF LIES

Reclaiming our story is a vital act of resistance against the invaders' deception, but the fight doesn't stop there. The alien forces have woven their lies into the very fabric of how we see the world, creating a distorted lens that impacts every choice we make. In the next chapter, we'll explore how to dismantle these false frameworks, challenge the mental constructs that keep us trapped, and replace them with clarity, discernment, and a vision rooted in truth. It's time to unravel the web of lies and rebuild our world on a foundation that reflects who we truly are.

COMMON RESPONSES

"Yeah, but my story is too messy. No one wants to hear it."

The power of your story lies in its authenticity, not its perfection. Messy stories resonate because they reflect the shared human experience. By owning and sharing your story, you inspire others to confront their own struggles and find courage in their imperfections.

"Yeah, but the lies feel so ingrained. Can I really rewrite them?"

Absolutely. The lies may feel permanent, but they're just stories—ones you have the power to challenge and rewrite. Start small by identifying one lie and replacing it with truth. Over time, this practice will transform your narrative into one of empowerment.

"Yeah, but what if people judge me when I share my story?"

Some may judge, but many will lean in with empathy and understanding. Sharing your story isn't about controlling others' reactions—it's about reclaiming your truth. Remember, the people who matter most will respect your courage and authenticity.

"Yeah, but I don't even know where to begin with my story."

WHAT TO DO WHEN THE ALIENS SHOW UP (AND EVEN IF THEY DON'T)

Begin where you are. Reflect on a single moment, lie, or lesson that shaped you and explore how it impacted your journey. As you own and rewrite that piece, the rest will begin to unfold naturally.

"Yeah, but what if my story hurts others involved?"

You can share your story with honesty and integrity without seeking to harm others. Focus on your experience and growth, not blame. Use kindness and discretion when discussing others' roles, and remember that your story is yours to tell.

REFLECTION QUESTIONS

1. What lies have the invaders written into your story, and how can you rewrite them with truth?
2. What parts of your story are you most afraid to share, and why?
3. How might telling your story—boldly and authentically—impact your life and the lives of others?
4. What steps can you take this week to own, rewrite, or share your narrative?

CHAPTER THIRTY-SIX
SOWING SEEDS OF LIBERATION
SPREADING TRUTH AND BUILDING A BETTER WORLD

> The arc of the moral universe is long, but it bends toward justice. – Martin Luther King Jr.

DECEPTION IS THE ALIEN INVADERS' MOST INSIDIOUS WEAPON. SUBTLE yet pervasive, it infiltrates our minds, rewrites our stories, and distorts our perceptions. Their lies are not grandiose fabrications—they're quiet whispers that erode our confidence, sabotage our connections, and obscure our potential. But deception is not an invincible force. It can be dismantled, unraveled, and replaced with something far greater: the enduring power of truth, integrity, and kindness.

The antidote to deception is not just honesty—it's flourishing. By sowing seeds of truth, courage, and love, we free ourselves from the alien web of lies and create a ripple effect that transforms our relationships, communities, and the world.

THE ALIEN'S WEB OF LIES

The alien invaders didn't need to shout their lies; they whispered them, subtle and believable enough to become the scripts we live by. These deceptions were designed to undermine our self-worth, foster fear, and breed dependency:

- *"You're not enough."*
- *"You need someone else to save you."*
- *"You'll never be loved unless you change."*
- *"Happiness lies in external success."*
- *"You're powerless to make a difference."*

These lies didn't just affect us individually—they spread. Like a virus, they infected families, communities, and societies, sowing division, shame, and disconnection. Worse still, they turned us into unwitting enforcers of the alien narrative, spreading judgment and negativity to others.

But lies are brittle. They crumble when confronted with the enduring power of truth.

THE WEB OF TRUTH: REPLACING LIES WITH EMPOWERING BELIEFS

If the alien invaders' web of lies was designed to disempower, the **Web of Truth** exists to empower, reconnect, and heal us. These truths counteract the alien narrative, offering a foundation of authenticity and flourishing.

Lie: *"You're not enough."*
Truth: *You are inherently worthy.*

Your value isn't tied to your achievements, possessions, or others' approval. It is intrinsic, unchanging, and rooted in your existence as a creation of the Creator.

- **Affirmation:** "I am enough, just as I am."

Lie: *"You need someone else to save you."*
Truth: *You have agency and resilience within you.*
While connection and community are vital, you are not powerless. You have the ability to make choices, take steps, and partner with the Creator to shape your life.

- **Affirmation:** "I am empowered to face challenges and find solutions."

Lie: *"You'll never be loved unless you change."*
Truth: *You are loved and lovable as you are.*
True love doesn't require perfection. It embraces your flaws, celebrates your growth, and holds space for your humanity.

- **Affirmation:** "I am deeply loved and worthy of love."

Lie: *"Happiness lies in external success."*
Truth: *Fulfillment comes from living authentically.*
True happiness comes from aligning with your values, fostering meaningful connections, and embracing your authentic self.

- **Affirmation:** "I find joy and purpose by being true to myself."

Lie: *"You're powerless to make a difference."*
Truth: *Your choices have impact.*
Every act of kindness, truth, and courage ripples outward, influencing those around you and shaping a better world.

- **Affirmation:** "My actions matter, and I can create positive change."

SOWING SEEDS OF FLOURISHING

Replacing lies with truth is just the beginning. Flourishing requires action—sowing seeds of goodness in our lives and the lives of those around us. Truth dispels the darkness, integrity rebuilds what was broken, and kindness creates ripples that reach far beyond our immediate sphere.

1. Speak Truth to Yourself

The alien's lies thrive on repetition. Counteract them by practicing truth-filled affirmations and honest self-talk.

- Replace their lies with affirmations that empower and uplift.
- Speak to yourself with kindness, honesty, and courage.

2. Live with Integrity

Integrity is the antidote to deceit. It means aligning your actions with your values and living authentically, even when it's hard.

- **Practical Steps:** Identify areas where your actions don't reflect your values and take deliberate steps to realign.
- **Personal Reflection:** There was a time when I compromised my values to win approval. It felt like survival at the time, but the cost was my sense of self. Reclaiming my integrity wasn't easy, but it was worth it.

3. Act with Kindness

Kindness isn't just a virtue—it's a disruptive force against negativity. It defies the alien's darkness, creating connection and positivity.

- Show kindness to yourself through self-compassion and patience.
- Extend kindness outward with small acts that ripple into the world.

4. Take Responsibility

Taking responsibility isn't about self-blame—it's about empowerment. Own your mistakes, make amends, and grow. This humility strengthens trust and connection.

TURNING THE TIDE: FLOURISHING BEYOND YOURSELF

When we live aligned with the Web of Truth, we don't just free ourselves; we inspire others to do the same. Our authenticity gives others permission to be authentic, and our courage inspires others to face their fears.

This isn't about becoming a savior or hero. It's about recognizing the ripple effect of our actions. Every choice to live with truth, love, and freedom is a stone cast into the waters of humanity, creating waves of flourishing.

THE HARVEST OF FLOURISHING

The seeds we sow today won't bear fruit overnight, but they will grow into a life of abundance and authenticity. The process requires patience, persistence, and intentionality, but the rewards are profound:

- **Freedom:** A life lived authentically, unhindered by fear or shame.
- **Fulfillment:** A deep sense of peace, purpose, and alignment with your values.
- **Fruitfulness:** Acts of kindness, creativity, and love that ripple out to impact others.

This is how we reverse the alien invasion. They came to conquer, but in resisting them, we become stronger, braver, and more united. Their deception became the soil for our truth, and their destruction became the foundation for our flourishing.

THE MAIN TAKEAWAY: FLOURISHING DISARMS DECEPTION

When we sow seeds of truth, integrity, and kindness, we uproot the alien's lies and create a life of authenticity, connection, and abundance. Flourishing isn't just a personal victory—it's the antidote to deception's viral spread.

COMING UP NEXT: TURNING FEAR INTO FUEL

With truth as our foundation and courage as our next step, we're ready to tackle the invaders' other great weapon: fear. In the upcoming chapter, we'll learn how to transform fear from a force of limitation into a catalyst for growth. The invaders tried to use fear to control us, but now, we'll discover how to wield it as a powerful tool for thriving.

COMMON RESPONSES

> "Yeah, but what if the lies feel true to me? I've lived with them for so long that they seem like facts."

It's understandable that the lies might feel true—they've been woven into your narrative over time. But feelings aren't always reliable indicators of truth. Start small: challenge one lie at a time. Ask yourself, "What evidence supports this, and what might contradict it?" Over time, as you replace the lies with truth, the emotional grip of those lies will begin to loosen. Also, connect with others! Trying to change our perception of lies is like trying to see the back of your head with only one mirror—it doesn't work.

"Yeah, but I've tried affirmations before, and they didn't work. I still felt the same."

Affirmations alone don't always create immediate change, especially if they're not coupled with action or deeper reflection. Think of affirmations as seeds you plant. They need consistent watering, sunlight, and time to grow. Pair your affirmations with actions that align with the truth you're speaking, and give yourself grace during the process.

"Yeah, but isn't focusing on myself selfish? Shouldn't I be more concerned with others?"

Focusing on yourself isn't selfish; it's essential. When you're rooted in truth and flourishing, you become a stronger, more compassionate presence for others. Think of it like putting on your oxygen mask first—you can only help others effectively when you've taken care of yourself.

"Yeah, but what if I fail to live up to these truths? Won't that prove the lies are right?"

Living in alignment with truth isn't about perfection; it's about progress. Failure doesn't invalidate the truth—it's a natural part of growth. When you stumble, remind yourself that your worth isn't tied to your performance. Each attempt to live authentically is a step forward, regardless of the outcome.

"Yeah, but what if other people don't support my journey or keep reinforcing the lies?"

Not everyone will understand or support your path, and that's okay. Their reactions often reflect their own struggles, not your worth.

SVEN MASTERSON

Surround yourself with people who uplift you and respect your growth. Over time, as you embody truth, you may even inspire others to question the lies they've believed.

REFLECTION QUESTIONS

1. What lies from the invaders have shaped your story, and how can you replace them with truth?
2. How can you live more authentically this week—in your family, work, or community?
3. Who in your life might benefit from seeing you live aligned with truth, integrity, and kindness?
4. What small step can you take today to contribute to a world of flourishing?

CHAPTER THIRTY-SEVEN
FAITH & COURAGE
THE ANTIDOTES TO THE ALIEN INFECTION

Fear is faith that it won't work out. – Elizabeth Gilbert

A REMINDER ON WORDS: FAITH AND THE CREATOR

BEFORE WE DIVE IN, LET'S REVISIT SOMETHING THAT MIGHT TRIP YOU up: the words *faith* and *Creator*. These terms can carry a lot of weight, and I want to remind you and clarify how I'm using them in this book.

When I use the word *Creator*, I'm describing what I believe to be the source of all things. Some might call it "Source," "the Universe," or "God." The point isn't about agreeing on a shared dogmatic understanding or label—it's about grounding ourselves in the vastness and solidity of whatever this source may be. Rooting our confidence in that foundation is a good policy because it's the most stable, enduring thing that exists.

I use a label for this source that reflects personality because we have personalities, and I observe that most things that I can observe that derive from a greater origin typically contain attributes from its source. You know... like puppies have dog features, kittens have cat features, saplings have leaves, even paintings allude to the painter... that kinda thing. Since I, and everyone I know, have a personality, I operate under the working hypothesis, even though it's nuanced, that our source must also have one. The same goes for agency, awareness, consciousness, sentience, goodwill, etc.

As for "faith," I define it similarly to confidence. Faith is what we are willing to believe is possible and align ourselves to in the future, which we cannot yet see or know. Faith and fear are two sides of the same coin—both are beliefs about what lies ahead. Faith sees possibility, expansion, and creation, while fear sees lack, collapse, and danger. Faith asks, "What if it works?" Fear warns, "What if it doesn't?" This chapter is about choosing the former.

FEAR AND ANXIETY: THE ALIEN'S GREATEST WEAPONS

Fear and anxiety are universal experiences, but they're not ultimate truths. These emotions are tools the alien invaders wield to keep us small, stuck, and silent. They amplify uncertainty, feed on our doubts, and create barriers between us and the life we're meant to live. Yet fear and anxiety are not insurmountable forces. The antidotes—faith and courage—break chains, open doors, and propel us into a life of thriving.

Faith is *belief*. Specifically, faith is the belief that we'll be enough for what's to come. It's the natural expression of knowing we are enough today. If that's true, we will be tomorrow, too. Faith is also rooted in the notion that we are connected to an unassailable source (for me, the Creator) and that we have an infinite capacity for growth. Faith is the belief that all of those will be as true tomorrow as they are today.

WHAT TO DO WHEN THE ALIENS SHOW UP (AND EVEN IF THEY DON'T)

For some, particularly those with a religious background, this idea of being "enough" may sound unsettling, even presumptuous. This is why I get called a "heretic" and "false teacher" by many.

I get it... It might feel like claiming too much for ourselves or leaving out dependence on God. But this belief and confidence in my future self is inseparable from my faith in my connection to The Creator. When I talk about trusting "myself" to face the future, I'm speaking from the perspective that I am never disconnected from the Source. I'm one with my creator (and I'd suggest you are, also). This empowering connection means I'm not relying on my ego or false self, or who the bible calls "The flesh," but on the unshakable nature of the union we have with the source.

Remarkably (and sadly), so many Christians struggle with this perspective, even though it aligns with Jesus' teachings. His invitation wasn't to create feeble confidence, self-doubt, and dependency but to empower us through connection—to the Father, to ourselves, and to one another (John 17). When Jesus spoke of abiding in the vine (John 15:4-5), He described a relationship of empowerment and union. He taught that through this connection, we could bear fruit and thrive—not by our ego's strength, but through our relationship with this source ("The Vine"). This is what I call "connected self-reliance," a profound reliance on The Creator while recognizing our strength and capacity through that union. "I" have an active role to play in that which requires me to show up, make choices, and take action.

Sadly, many Christians seem to live in a disconnected, no-union "gospel," where the self and the Source are seen as *entirely separate. This mindset leaves people feeling unworthy and inadequate, constantly striving for approval or strength from outside themselves. But where's the good news in that?*

Disconnection is not good news. The good news is that we are in an empowered, connection union, not a message of separation. This message empowers us to step into the unknown, trusting that our partnership with the source will always be enough for whatever comes.

I believe this is what the "water of life" Jesus mentions is about. It is not a means to "go to heaven when you die at the end of a miserable, suffering, victimized life," but a means to be connected to "heaven" now and live a meaningful, purpose-filled life of thriving in any circumstance.

THE ROLE OF FAITH IN OVERCOMING FEAR

Faith is not a denial of fear. Instead, it's a decision to live beyond it. Faith grounds us in something greater than the moment of uncertainty and gives us the strength to move forward.

Faith in the Creator / Source

Faith begins with trusting the Creator's presence and purpose. The invaders may try to convince us that we're alone and disconnected, but faith reminds us that we are part of a larger story. We are deeply loved, infinitely supported, and never abandoned.

Interestingly, this idea of profound connection finds echoes in quantum theory. In quantum mechanics, phenomena like quantum entanglement suggest that particles can become intrinsically linked, regardless of the distance between them. When two particles are entangled, the state of one particle instantly influences the state of the other, even if they're separated by vast distances. This interconnectedness, often described as "non-locality," has led some to see parallels with spiritual truths—the idea that nothing in the universe exists in complete isolation.

While quantum theory doesn't directly address human relationships or spirituality, it serves as a profound metaphor. Just as no entangled proton is disconnected from another, faith invites us to trust that we, too, are never truly alone. We are intrinsically connected to the Creator, to one another, and to the larger web of existence. This deep interconnection reminds us that even in moments of doubt or struggle, we are always part of something greater—woven into the fabric of life and love that sustains us.

Faith in the Process

Transformation takes time, and faith serves as the anchor that steadies us through setbacks. It reminds us that growth isn't linear but always moves forward, even when it feels slow or uncertain. Faith in the process comes from looking back—reflecting on how we've endured life's challenges and grown along the way. It's the recognition that we've been enough for everything we've faced so far, and with that same faith, we will continue to be enough for whatever lies ahead.

Faith is also a willingness to trust that life's guiding process is not innately against us but for us. Even when the path is unclear, or the steps are difficult, faith reminds us that life's processes—however mysterious—are trustable. They are not random acts of chaos but opportunities for growth, learning, and becoming.

But supposing they are random acts of chaos? Then what? Thanks to perspectives like Viktor Frankl's, we also understand that our ability to choose how we respond to life's processes makes them even more trustworthy. No matter what circumstances we face, our choices determine how those experiences will shape us—whether they benefit or harm us. This freedom to choose our perspective and direction is a profound reminder that, even in the hardest moments, life is still offering us a chance to grow, heal, and thrive.

Faith in Yourself

The invaders' lies tell us that we are incapable. Faith counters with the truth: We are resourceful, resilient, and capable of navigating challenges. However, this is hard to understand until we stop confusing our true self with our false self/ego.

> *Not many years ago, I was experiencing a season of life when fear gripped me completely. I was on the verge of losing everything—my marriage, my family, my homestead, my sense of identity, my purpose. I wanted certainty, a guarantee that everything would work out. But no such guarantee came. Instead, I had to step forward in faith, trusting that even in my brokenness, I could rebuild. Faith didn't erase my struggles, but it gave me the courage to face them, one step at a time. It wasn't until I stopped living in the "Victim" role of the "Drama Triangle" and understood my birthright as a decision-making Creator that I was able to break free, enter an "Empowerment Dynamic," and experience change.*

THE COURAGE TO ACT IN THE FACE OF FEAR

Courage doesn't eliminate fear; it transforms our relationship with it. Fear becomes less of a stop sign and more of a green light—a signal that we're stepping into growth and possibility.

Principles of Courage:

WHAT TO DO WHEN THE ALIENS SHOW UP (AND EVEN IF THEY DON'T)

1. **Start Small** Courage doesn't mean leaping blindly into the unknown. It starts with small, deliberate steps that build your confidence.
   - **Example:** If you're afraid to speak your truth, start by sharing a single honest sentence with someone you trust.
2. **Separate Fact from Fiction.** Fear thrives on "what if" scenarios, while courage focuses on "what is" and "what can be."
   - **Practice:** Write down your fears and identify which ones are based on real threats versus imagined outcomes.
3. **Take Ownership** Courage isn't about waiting for someone else to act—it's about choosing to act yourself. Ownership means recognizing that your life is your responsibility and stepping into that role with intention.

Writing this book has been a test of courage for me, and not without its challenges. I know that sharing these ideas—challenging some long-held beliefs and even sacred cows—will invite judgment, misunderstanding, and critique. Some people may embrace this perspective; others might reject it outright. There's even a part of me that fears the wrath of those who feel deeply threatened by what I've written. Heck, I even have a bit of fear that this all sounds dramatic. Sheesh, we're so prone to worry, aren't we?!

Even as I type these words, I find myself wrestling with the same struggles I'm writing about—fear of rejection, doubt about whether I've said the right things, and the vulnerability of putting my heart on the page for anyone to read. The temptation to shrink back, to play it safe, is real.

But here's what keeps me moving forward: I believe in

these ideas, myself, and my source. I've witnessed the power of these concepts in my own life and in the lives of others I've worked with. I know they set people free, and that matters more to me than anything else right now. Writing this book has been an opportunity to practice what I preach—to confront fear with faith, move forward even in uncertainty, and trust that the process will serve its purpose.

FAITH AND COURAGE IN ACTION

When faith and courage combine, they become unstoppable. Faith keeps our hearts steady, reminding us of our inherent worth and purpose. Courage moves our feet, pushing us to take the next step, no matter how uncertain it feels. Together, they create momentum—a force powerful enough to dismantle fear and anxiety entirely.

Practical Steps to Cultivate Faith and Courage:

1. **Create a Faith Practice** Dedicate time daily to prayer, meditation, or reflection that anchors you in trust and gratitude.
2. **Practice Courage Daily** Commit to one small act of courage each day. Whether it's speaking up, setting a boundary, or taking a risk, each act reinforces your capacity to face fear.
3. **Reflect on Wins** At the end of each day, reflect on how faith and courage showed up for you. Celebrate even the smallest victories—they're the building blocks of lasting change.

THE ALIEN'S WEAKNESS: THEY CAN'T THRIVE IN FAITH AND COURAGE

Fear and anxiety thrive in darkness and doubt. The invaders rely on our silence, hesitation, and belief in our powerlessness. Faith and courage strip them of all their weapons. Faith shines a light on the lies, and courage dismantles the walls that keep you small.

THE MAIN TAKEAWAY: FAITH AND COURAGE RECLAIM OUR FREEDOM

Fear and anxiety may never fully disappear, but they don't have to control us. Faith grounds us in something greater, while courage moves us forward in the face of fear. Together, they expel the invaders and create a life of bold, authentic freedom.

COMING UP NEXT: VICTORY IN THE WAR WITHIN

Faith and courage have cleared the path, but what comes next? *Thriving*. The battle against fear and anxiety wasn't just about survival—it was about reclaiming our planet and creating a life of abundance, authenticity, and connection. In the next chapter, we'll explore what it means to thrive in relationships, purpose, and self-expression. We'll discuss how freedom, fulfillment, and fruitfulness are the fruits of your transformation and how a thriving life is our birthright and a beacon for others.

COMMON RESPONSES

"Yeah, but what if I've been burned before by trusting in faith or a higher power?"

SVEN MASTERSON

It's valid to feel cautious after painful experiences. Faith isn't about ignoring the past but reframing it. It's not blind trust—it's a choice to move forward with hope. Consider how faith can evolve into a partnership: your willingness to act paired with the belief that growth and healing are possible.

"Yeah, but what if my fear feels more real and immediate than my faith?"

Fear often screams louder than faith whispers. Start by acknowledging your fear rather than fighting it. Then, look for evidence—past experiences where things turned out better than you feared. Each time you take a step forward, you strengthen faith's quiet voice. It grows with practice, not instant results.

"Yeah, but what if I can't define the Creator or align with spiritual ideas?"

You don't have to. This chapter uses "Creator" broadly to point to a larger, enduring source of life and strength. If that doesn't resonate, think of the Creator as the essence of possibility, growth, or even love. Faith doesn't require rigid definitions—it's about finding your personal foundation of hope. At the same time, if your personal foundation isn't working, perhaps it's time to consider new alternatives.

"Yeah, but what if I don't feel 'enough' now and can't imagine being enough tomorrow?"

Feeling "not enough" is often the invaders' strongest lie. Start small by challenging one belief that reinforces this idea. For example, replace "I'm not capable" with "I'm learning." Faith is built step by step—begin by accepting where you are today and trusting that growth is possible tomorrow.

WHAT TO DO WHEN THE ALIENS SHOW UP (AND EVEN IF THEY DON'T)

"Yeah, but what if I don't know how to cultivate courage in the face of fear?"

You don't need to conquer fear all at once. Start by taking small, intentional actions. Courage is a muscle, and the more you use it, the stronger it becomes. Begin with something manageable: speak up in a safe space, try something new, or write down one fear and challenge its truth. Each small win builds momentum.

REFLECTION QUESTIONS:

1. What fears or anxieties have been keeping you stuck, and how can faith help you confront them?
2. What small act of courage can you take this week to move toward your goals?
3. How can you cultivate a daily practice of faith that strengthens your resilience?
4. What would your life look like if fear no longer dictated your actions?

CHAPTER THIRTY-EIGHT
THE PLANET RECLAIMED
THRIVING IN AUTHENTICITY AND ABUNDANCE

What you get by achieving your goals is not as important as what you become by achieving your goals.
– Zig Ziglar

VICTORY IN THE WAR WITHIN

THE BATTLE HAS BEEN FOUGHT, THE INVADERS EXPELLED. WHAT LIES before us now isn't merely survival—it's thriving. Reclaiming the planet isn't just about undoing the harm; it's about creating a life so rich, so authentic, so full of abundance that it transforms everything.

Thriving isn't about perfection—it's about the process. It's the daily choice to live with courage, purpose, and authenticity. It's the freedom to be ourselves without shame, the confidence to pursue our dreams without fear, and the connection to others that fills life with meaning. It's about building a strong and expansive life that the invaders would struggle to return.

WHAT THRIVING LOOKS LIKE

1. In Relationships

Thriving in relationships doesn't mean they're conflict-free. It means they're grounded in respect, honesty, and vulnerability.

- You no longer cling to others for validation or lose yourself trying to meet their expectations. Instead, you show up as your authentic self, offering and receiving love freely.
- You give without creating dependency, love without condition, and maintain boundaries that protect your authenticity and well-being.

2. In Purpose

Thriving in purpose means living in alignment with your values and passions.

- You've reclaimed your agency, owning your choices and pursuing work, hobbies, and missions that ignite your soul.
- It's not about grand gestures; it's about the quiet confidence that you're living a life true to who you are.

3. In Self-Expression

Thriving in self-expression means embracing who you are—flaws and all—and letting that shine.

- You're no longer hiding behind masks or false identities.
- You speak your truth boldly and live in a way that reflects your deepest values and desires.

THE FRUITS OF THRIVING

1. Freedom

When the chains of fear, shame, and judgment are broken, we can live authentically. This freedom isn't about doing whatever we want—it's about aligning our actions with our values, unhindered by the need to prove ourselves or please others.

2. Fulfillment

Thriving brings a deep sense of fulfillment—not because everything in our lives is perfect, but because we live with intention. We no longer chase "more" or wait for external validation. We are content but never complacent.

3. Fruitfulness

Thriving isn't just about what we gain; it's about what we give. A thriving life produces fruit—kindness, generosity, creativity, and love—that impacts everyone around us.

> *I never thought I'd get here. There was a time when I believed thriving was for other people—people who didn't carry my wounds, failures, and fears. I thought the best I could hope for was survival, a life of quiet endurance.*
>
> *But something changed when I began to dismantle the lies. As I reclaimed my story, I discovered something extraordinary: I wasn't broken, unworthy, or unworthy. I was enough.*
>
> *Thriving didn't happen overnight. It was a process—a series of choices to show up, speak the truth, and take risks. I rebuilt my relationships, starting with myself. I*

found purpose in helping others navigate their own journeys. I began to express myself honestly and unapologetically.

Today, my life isn't perfect, but it's full. My relationships are deeper, my work more meaningful, my heart more open. Thriving isn't about having it all but being fully alive.

RECLAIMING THE PLANET: A LIFE OF ABUNDANCE

Reclaiming our lives is the ultimate counteroffensive. It involves defeating the invaders and creating something so extraordinary that they will never return.

Your thriving life is a testament to the power of faith, courage, and authenticity. It's a beacon for others still caught in the struggle, proof that transformation is possible.

THE MAIN TAKEAWAY: THRIVING IS YOUR BIRTHRIGHT

Thriving isn't a luxury—it's our birthright. It's the natural state of a life lived with authenticity, courage, and connection. When we reclaim our power, rewrite our story, and live in alignment with our values, we create a life of abundance that touches everyone around us.

COMING UP NEXT: CHARTING OUR NEXT STEPS

As we conclude this chapter on flourishing as the antidote to deception, it's time to shift our focus forward. In the next chapter, we'll step back to see the bigger picture of our transformation. Together, we'll reflect on the path we've walked so far—turning fear, dependency, and shame into faith, self-sourcing, and thriving.

This next step is about celebration and integration: acknowledging the lies we've dismantled, the truths we've reclaimed, and the ways we've begun to flourish. But it's also about action—

outlining practical, intentional steps to carry this momentum into the rest of our lives. Whether that means building deeper connections, rewriting our narratives, or committing to lives of bold authenticity, this is our moment to embrace the flourishing life we've worked toward.

Let's chart our course toward lives rooted in courage, truth, and purpose. Together, we'll continue the journey.

COMMON RESPONSES

"Yeah, but I'm not sure I even know what thriving looks like for me."

That's okay. Thriving is deeply personal and unfolds through exploration. Start by asking yourself what brings you joy, fulfillment, and authenticity. What makes you feel most alive? Even small clues can guide you toward a vision of thriving that's uniquely yours.

"Yeah, but I've made so many mistakes—can I really thrive after all that?"

Absolutely. Mistakes are part of being human, and they don't disqualify you from thriving. In fact, your ability to learn, grow, and rebuild after challenges can become a cornerstone of your thriving life. Every step forward is a testament to your resilience.

"Yeah, but thriving feels selfish when others are struggling so much."

There's a familiar moment in airplane safety briefings when flight *attendants explain that, in the event of a sudden loss of cabin pressure, passengers must put on their own oxygen masks before helping others. The reason is simple: if you lose consciousness, you can't help anyone else. In that critical moment, the most selfless and heroic act is to take care of yourself first. Thriving works the same way—it's not selfish; it's essential. When you thrive, you create a ripple effect of positivity, inspiring and empowering others. Your growth equips you to give, love, and serve more fully, contributing to a world where everyone has the opportunity to thrive.*

"Yeah, but what if I fail at trying to thrive?"

Thriving isn't about perfection; it's about persistence. Failure is part of the journey, not the end of it. Every misstep is a learning opportunity that strengthens your ability to keep moving forward. Thriving is built on courage, not infallibility.

"Yeah, but I don't have the resources or support to thrive right now."

Thriving starts within. While external circumstances can help, they aren't the foundation. Begin by cultivating self-compassion, aligning with your values, and taking small steps toward authenticity and fulfillment. The resources and support often follow as you grow.

REFLECTION QUESTIONS:

1. What does thriving look like for you in relationships, purpose, and self-expression?
2. How have the choices you've made throughout this journey set the stage for thriving?

3. What steps can you take to cultivate greater freedom, fulfillment, and fruitfulness in your life?
4. How can your thriving life inspire and support others in their journeys?

CHAPTER THIRTY-NINE
NEXT STEPS
LIVING THE TRANSFORMATION

> You are never too old to set another goal or to dream a new dream. – C.S. Lewis

CONGRATULATIONS ON REACHING THIS POINT IN YOUR JOURNEY. You've confronted fear, shame, and deception, reclaimed your power, and begun dismantling the alien invaders' lies. But as we've explored, transformation isn't a finish line—it's an ongoing process, a daily choice to live authentically, courageously, and with unwavering intention.

The invaders thrived by keeping you small, disconnected, and afraid. Your counteroffensive was rooted in truth, faith, and sovereignty. Now, the next steps are about sustaining that victory, creating a life of thriving, and becoming a beacon for others still caught in the struggle.

THE BIG PICTURE: FROM BONDAGE TO FREEDOM

This book has guided you through profound transformations:

- **Fear to Faith:** Replacing the terror of "what if" with the confidence of possibility and creation.
- **Anxiety and Uncertainty to Calm Confidence:** Finding inner peace through clarity and courage.
- **Dependency to Self-Sourcing and Sovereignty:** Shifting from external validation to inner strength and autonomy.
- **Externalized Worth to Unshakable Self-Worth:** Embracing your inherent value rather than relying on others' approval.
- **Disconnection to Connection:** Rebuilding bonds with yourself, others, and the Creator.
- **Shame to Acceptance:** Rewriting the false stories that kept you stuck in unworthiness.
- **Judgment to Unconditional High Regard:** Viewing yourself and others with compassion rather than criticism.

These shifts aren't just theoretical—they're tangible changes that impact your relationships, purpose, and daily experience. The work now is to sustain and expand these transformations, anchoring them in your life.

HIGHLIGHTS OF THE JOURNEY

1. Rewriting the Stories That Fuel Shame

Shame thrives on false narratives about our worth and flaws. The invaders' lies convinced us that your mistakes defined us and that love had to be earned. But as we've learned, shame loses its grip when we replace those stories with truth.

Next Step: Continue examining the scripts that shape your inner dialogue. Ask yourself:

WHAT TO DO WHEN THE ALIENS SHOW UP (AND EVEN IF THEY DON'T)

- Is this story rooted in truth or fear?
- Does this story reflect my values and my growth?

Write down affirmations that counter these shame-based scripts and revisit them daily.

2. Cultivating Faith and Courage

Fear and uncertainty no longer rule us. Faith has become our anchor—a belief in our ability to navigate life's challenges and in the Creator's steady presence. Courage is now our compass, guiding us to act boldly in the face of fear.

Next Step: Create a daily practice of faith and courage.

- Start your day with a grounding ritual, such as meditation, prayer, or affirmations.
- Commit to one bold act each day, no matter how small, that aligns with your values and moves you toward thriving.

3. Choosing Connection

Disconnection is no longer our default. We've rebuilt bridges to ourselves, our loved ones, and our community. Connection isn't just about presence—it's about authenticity and vulnerability.

Next Step: Invest in relationships that nourish your growth.

- Identify your "redoubt"—your circle of trusted individuals who support and challenge you.
- Nurture these relationships through honest conversations, acts of kindness, and shared experiences.
- Seek out new communities aligned with your values and passions.

4. Living Authentically, Present, and Courageously

Thriving means showing up as our true selves, free from masks and pretense. It means living each day with intention, presence, and boldness.

Next Step: Make authenticity your guiding principle.

- Begin each day by asking, "What would it look like to live authentically today?"
- Let go of perfectionism and embrace your flaws as part of your humanity.
- Celebrate progress over perfection and value each moment as an opportunity for growth.

5. Building and Sustaining a Redoubt

A redoubt is more than just a physical, emotional, or spiritual sanctuary—it's our stronghold of safety, strength, and support. It's where we gather the resources, relationships, and practices that sustain our transformation.

Next Step: Create or strengthen your redoubt:

1. **Identify the People:** Surround yourself with those who uplift, inspire, and hold you accountable.
2. **Establish Boundaries:** Protect your energy and time by setting clear boundaries with those who drain or distract you.
3. **Reinforce Your Practices:** Anchor your redoubt with daily habits like journaling, self-reflection, and acts of courage.
4. **Build a Legacy of Truth:** Make your redoubt a place where truth flourishes. Share your story, encourage others, and model authenticity.

6. Thriving as a Daily Choice

Thriving isn't about perfection; it's about presence. It's about choosing each day to align with our values, nurture our connections, and step boldly into our purpose.

Next Step: Adopt these daily practices:

1. **Morning Reflection:** Start your day with a moment of gratitude, grounding, and intention.
2. **Midday Check-In:** Pause to assess how aligned you feel with your values and course-correct as needed.
3. **Evening Gratitude:** End your day by celebrating your wins, no matter how small, and reflecting on areas for growth.

LOOKING AHEAD

The battle against the invaders may be over, but the work of flourishing is just beginning. Our journey doesn't end here—it expands outward. The choices we make now ripple into the lives of others, creating a world where truth, courage, and love thrive.

As you continue this path, remember:

- **You are enough.** Your worth is unshakable and inherent.
- **You are powerful.** Each choice you make is a declaration of sovereignty.
- **You are connected.** Your story is part of a larger narrative of courage, faith, and flourishing.

FINAL ACTIONABLE STEPS

To keep building on this journey, consider these tangible next steps:

1. **Write Your Mission Statement:** Define what thriving means to you and the values you want to live by.

2. **Start a Redoubt Journal:** Document the people, practices, and progress that sustain your transformation.
3. **Mentor or Support Others:** Share your story and encourage others to begin their own counteroffensive.
4. **Revisit This Book:** Growth isn't linear. When you need a reminder of your strength and purpose, revisit the chapters and exercises.

THE MAIN TAKEAWAY: THRIVING IS THE ULTIMATE COUNTEROFFENSIVE

We're overcoming fear, shame, and deception, but the ultimate victory is a thriving life. Each day, we live with authenticity, courage, and connection, we create a world where the invaders have no foothold. Our lives become a beacon of hope and possibility—for ourselves and for others.

A NOTE ON THE JOURNEY AHEAD

The understanding and insights shared in this book didn't come to me overnight. They were the result of years of sorting through painful conflicts, endless questioning, and wrestling with deeply ingrained ideas. One of the most significant challenges I faced was reconciling these concepts with the Christian worldview I grew up within. Navigating that tension—honoring my history and experiences while addressing its limitations—was a profound part of my personal transformation.

For those interested in going deeper into this part of my journey—or for those curious about how the concepts shared in this book intersect with the Hebrew and Christian scriptures—the following sections of this book (Part 4-5) will explore that terrain in depth. It's a space where I share the process of deconstruction and reconstruction I experienced (and continue to experience), offering reflections and connections that may resonate with those walking a similar path.

WHAT TO DO WHEN THE ALIENS SHOW UP (AND EVEN IF THEY DON'T)

For those who prefer to stay focused on the broader themes of thriving and transformation, skip to the conclusion after Part 4. This book is designed to meet you where you are, offering something valuable no matter your path.

As always, this is your journey. Take what serves you and leave the rest. My hope is that whatever direction you take from here, the principles of truth, faith, and courage will continue to guide you forward.

COMMON RESPONSES

"Yeah, but I don't know if I can sustain the changes I've made."

It's natural to feel unsure about maintaining progress, but remember: transformation is a process, not a destination. Focus on small, consistent actions rather than perfection. Each step reinforces your new foundation, making it stronger over time. Celebrate even the smallest wins—they're proof of your capacity to grow.

"Yeah, but what if I fall back into old patterns?"

Relapses into old patterns are part of growth, not a failure. They're opportunities to reflect, learn, and recalibrate. When you notice yourself slipping, pause and revisit the tools you've gained—your faith, courage, and connection. Each stumble is a chance to strengthen your resolve and deepen your transformation.

"Yeah, but I feel like I still have so far to go."

Thriving isn't about reaching an end point; it's about living fully in the present. Acknowledge how far you've already come, and trust that your journey will continue to unfold in meaningful ways. You're not racing anyone—your path is uniquely yours, and progress is what matters, not perfection.

> "Yeah, but I'm afraid I'll lose momentum without the structure of this book."

This book has been a guide, but the tools and insights you've gained are now part of you. Create your own structure moving forward—whether it's through journaling, connecting with a community, or setting daily intentions. Your journey is yours to continue, and you already have everything you need to sustain it.

> "Yeah, but what if people don't support or understand my changes?"

Not everyone will understand your journey, and that's okay. True transformation isn't about pleasing others—it's about living authentically. Surround yourself with those who uplift and encourage you, and trust that your thriving will inspire others in time. Stay rooted in your truth and let your actions speak for themselves.

REFLECTION QUESTIONS FOR MOVING FORWARD

1. What transformation resonated with you most deeply in this book, and why?
2. Which of the invaders' lies have you identified in your life, and what truths are you now ready to embrace?
3. What practical steps can you take today to move from fear, shame, or disconnection toward faith, courage, and connection?

4. What does thriving look like for you in this season of your life? How might it evolve in the future?
5. How will you practice self-sourcing and sovereignty in your daily choices and relationships?
6. What stories about your worth or identity need further rewriting, and how will you begin that work?
7. How can you cultivate a deeper sense of connection—with yourself, others, and your Creator—going forward?
8. What small actions can you take to embody authenticity, presentness, and courage in your everyday life?
9. Who in your life might benefit from the lessons you've learned, and how can you share these principles in a way that uplifts and inspires?
10. What does your "redoubt" look like—a place or community where you feel supported, aligned, and empowered? How will you build or strengthen it?
11. Looking back on this journey, what has surprised you most about your capacity for transformation and growth?
12. As you continue forward, what is one commitment you can make to yourself to live more intentionally and authentically?

PART FOUR
THE GREAT UNCOVERING
MY PERSONAL JOURNEY FROM ALIENATION TO EMPOWERMENT

PEELING BACK THE FIG LEAVES: A JOURNEY INTO MY PERSONAL APOCALYPSE

As we move into Part 4 of this book, I want to acknowledge a significant shift in tone and focus. Until now, I've shared insights and tools broadly applicable to overcoming fear, anxious uncertainty, insecurity, shame, and the pull of the Drama Triangle. These concepts are rooted in my work with people from all walks of life—most of whom do not identify as people of faith. I've intentionally framed these principles in a language that empowers anyone, regardless of their background or beliefs.

This section, however, is more personal. It reflects my story and how these understandings have unfolded in my life. It's a journey deeply shaped by my experiences growing up within a Christian faith tradition, my voracious study of scripture, and the evolving ways I've come to understand the Creator's invitation to humanity. It explains how the principles I've shared in Parts 1-3 have refined and clarified that invitation.

WHY THIS PART OF THE BOOK MATTERS

To be blunt, in my work with men worldwide, I have noticed that those who struggle the most with breaking free from shame are not those whose lives are marked by "gross immorality" or flagrant behaviors. Ironically, it's often the religious—particularly *Christians*—who carry the heaviest burdens of shame. I say this not with judgment but with deep empathy because I've been there. I know what it's like to live under a framework that frames the Creator as a harsh judge, humanity as helpless victims, and Jesus as a Rescuer in a transactional drama-triangle narrative.

This part of the book is offered for those who may be entrenched in fear-based interpretations of scripture and struggle to see the gospel as truly good news. It's for those who, like me, may have grown up with shame-based instruction and long to discover an empowering, life-giving perspective.

My second reason for including this section is that, when wrestled out of the hands of shame-based frameworks, the biblical message tells a beautiful and life-giving story—a story I believe everyone should have the opportunity to hear. I'm not here to persuade you to adopt my faith, nor am I here to defend any theological system. My goal is to share what has brought me freedom, joy, and connection in the hope that it may spark something similar in you. If you don't enjoy theological discussions, I suggest you skip to The Power of Discernment instead.

A PERSONAL SPACE

To provide some context, I grew up in a "CharisMethoBapterian" tradition (that's when you try just about every faith tradition—Methodist, Baptist, Presbyterian, Charismatic, etc.). My dad leaned heavily into Calvinism and Covenant Theology. At the same time, my mom had a more eclectic perspective, favoring premillennial eschatological views—a fancy way of saying she was fascinated by the "End Times" and events like the Rapture and the Second Coming.

Despite my mostly mainstream background, I attended a dispensational, fundamentalist Bible college and earned a Cross-Cultural Communication and Biblical Studies degree. Over the years, I explored nearly every flavor of Christianity, from the formal to the charismatic, from the traditional to the contemporary. I share this to help you understand that I wasn't a casual student of scripture—I devoured it, wrestling with its meaning and how it applied to life.

Yet for all my passion and study, there came a point when I stepped away from institutional expressions of faith entirely, where I remain today.

In 2013, I stopped participating in formal expressions of Christianity. Despite the warnings I received about the dangers of such a decision, I did not spiral into drug addiction, immorality, or despair. Instead, stepping away created space for something I couldn't fully articulate at the time—a space where my understanding of the Creator, myself, and scripture could shift, deepen, and, in many ways, come alive.

MY PERSONAL APOCALYPSE

This brings me to a word from my past that I've come to love: apocalypse. Growing up, this word carried a lot of weight. It conjured images of catastrophic events, global trials, and a fearful reckoning. As someone steeped in evangelical culture, I believed my role was to prepare for this looming event, often in ways deeply rooted in fear.

But over time, the word apocalypse came to mean something entirely different to me. At its root, apocalypse means "uncovering" or "revealing." This uncovering has become a central metaphor for my journey. It's a process of stripping away the fig leaves of shame, fear, and judgment that once obscured my understanding of the Creator's love and my identity.

This uncovering has not been easy. Many of my deeply held beliefs about theology, faith, and the biblical message had to be re-examined and, in some cases, completely let go. Yet, this process of letting go has been profoundly freeing. It has allowed me to see the gospel not as a message of fear or obligation but as an invitation to love, empowerment, and freedom.

AN INVITATION

I fully expect that what follows may offend some readers. For some, I won't be "Christian enough." For others, I'll be "too Christian." My reflections may challenge longstanding theological frameworks or secular assumptions, leading to labels like "heretic" or "false teacher." I've encountered these dynamics many times before, which is partly why I stepped away from institutional faith.

But I've come to see that sharing authentically—without fear of labels or needing approval—is vital to living free. This section of the book is not about persuading or convincing anyone. These reflections represent where I am on my journey right now. They are not presented as universal truths but as an invitation to explore a perspective that has brought me freedom, peace, and clarity.

If these ideas resonate with you, I'll be glad. If they don't, I encourage you to engage with them critically or skip this section entirely.

Through these pages, I hope to uncover a perspective that may help you see the Creator, scripture, and yourself in a new light. Whether you share my faith, are exploring your spiritual journey, or are simply curious, I invite you to approach this section with an open heart.

Let's dive in.

CHAPTER FORTY
FROM FEAR TO FLOURISHING
MY JOURNEY OF TRANSFORMATION

> You are not what happened to you. You are what you choose to become. – Carl Jung

To understand where I am today, you need to know where I've been. My life wasn't always marked by flourishing and freedom. It was shaped by deep fears, suffocating shame, and an identity rooted in striving for worthiness. This is the story of how I moved from fear and performance to connection and love—and how that transformation now fuels the work I do every day with others walking their own paths of growth.

THE SHAME THAT SHAPED ME

From a young age, I carried a heavy burden of shame. I grew up in a Christian home where faith wasn't just a belief system but the foundation of everything. My parents, as first-generation believers, did their best to instill a love for God, but what I absorbed wasn't freedom or peace—it was fear. I learned early that God was holy and I was not, and that gap meant I needed Jesus to bridge the chasm between us.

This wasn't just about salvation—it was about worth. I felt God's love was conditional, despite being told it wasn't. If I sinned, doubted, or strayed, I risked losing everything. That conditional love, paired with a constant pressure to perform, planted deep seeds of shame. I was never enough.

Outside of church, life wasn't much easier. I was a shy, awkward kid who faced relentless bullying. My gangly frame, acne, and lack of coordination made me an easy target in gym class and in life. The taunts burrowed deep, and I started to believe them. Maybe I was worthless.

My family struggled financially at home, adding another layer of shame. I vividly remember the humiliation of having to borrow lunch money from the school office because my parents forgot to send it with me–again. Even small moments like these reinforced the belief that I didn't matter, a belief I carried with me far into adulthood.

A MASK OF REDEMPTION

In my teenage years, I sought escape in rebellion. I became the skateboarder, punk rocker, the skinhead, the disconnected, soulless, defiant kid who didn't care what anyone thought. But those masks didn't fix anything—they just hid the pain. By the time I hit my late teens, I was an inferno of torment on the inside, a mess on the outside, and desperate for something that felt authentic, whole, and right.

Oddly, that change came when I had a dramatic encounter with faith after a nasty drug-induced encounter that upended my life and introduced significant legal and educational consequences. I turned away from the rebellion and embraced Christianity with a fervor that transformed my identity once again. I went from being a pariah and outcast to a celebrated example of renewal and redemption. In my small town, I became somewhat of a "church celebrity"

WHAT TO DO WHEN THE ALIENS SHOW UP (AND EVEN IF THEY DON'T)

—the rebellious kid turned devout believer. People admired my story, wanted to hear it, and invited me to share it. I soaked up their attention, interest, and validation.

But even as I stepped into this new identity, I can easily see that the shame remained when I look back. I didn't know that then. I thought, like a lot of Christians, that it was just supposed to be that way and that we'd just all suffer with internal affliction until Christ returned or we returned to him in Heaven. That's what everyone said. In the meantime, regardless of what my eyeballs read and my mind believed, I learned to live like I had to maintain my transformation through constant effort. If I failed, I feared losing everything—my reputation, community, and most of all - God's pleasure and approval. In the parable of the Prodigal Son, most people saw me as the wayward son who returned home, but within myself, I was living like the older brother.

BUILDING A LIFE THAT LOOKED PERFECT

As I entered adulthood, I carried this subtly performance-driven faith into every aspect of my life. Like many Christian teens who grow up in and around purity culture, especially a zealot like I was, I married young, eager to build a life that honored God and reflected my newfound identity. My wife, Zelda, and I shared dreams of becoming missionaries, and we dove headfirst into Bible college and missionary training.

Our lives were a picture of devotion and purpose to most people and, admittedly, to us. We were a "power couple" in our community, admired for our commitment to ministry. I led things at church, teaching and mentoring others, while Zelda gracefully managed our growing family. People respected us–maybe even too much, routinely saying that they found our lives intimidating, which was very frustrating and disconnecting to us at the time, but I understand now why this was.

But behind the scenes, cracks were forming. Though outwardly strong, our marriage lacked a deep connection. Zelda's emotional distance and my desperate need for validation created a toxic cycle. We had what most people would label a "Pursuer/Distancer" dynamic. I endlessly sought her assurance, validation, and approval, and when it didn't come, I felt rejected and unworthy. She felt detached, distant, and aloof, and I told myself stories that this was from her "childhood wounds" and saw myself as some sort of Hero who could rescue her from these pains–if she'd let me. This is just one of the many ways I'd find culture, especially Christian culture, encourages and supports Drama Triangle dynamics in marriage.

A HOUSE OF CARDS

The ideal "power couple" life we began creating in our twenties abruptly stopped when we entered the second phase of our missionary training. The program's authoritarian culture clashed with our convictions, especially when leaders demanded we physically discipline our infant. I refused, and with passion. My punk rock roots and skinhead stoicism served me well in telling those abusers to take a hike. They didn't care for those attitudes. Our resistance wasn't tolerated, and we were expelled.

This moment marked the beginning of an end. Our dreams of serving as missionaries were shattered, and the identity I had built around formal, full-time ministry crumbled. We settled in the local community, too shocked and poor to consider other options. We were broke, unprepared, disillusioned, and isolated.

The church we joined for solace eventually became another source of conflict. Despite my years of leadership and teaching, I felt judged and unseen. The theological framework I had clung to began to feel hollow and suffocating. Those hard times are not all on them; I was not living with an open and free heart, and that had consequences. I own who I was–and wasn't, in those times.

The early years after leaving missionary training were a whirlwind of survival and growth. With no marketable job skills, I threw myself into learning whatever I could to provide for my family. We started small, living on a tight budget in very modest (and kinda gross) accommodations while I worked long hours to build a career. Over time, and through relentless effort, I transitioned from scraping by to creating a business and becoming an in-demand enterprise software architect. It was a dramatic leap fueled by a fierce desire to provide stability for my family–and a healthy dose of overachievement rooted in deep insecurities.

Our family grew as well—eventually, Zelda and I became parents to six children, and we embraced the challenges and joys of homeschooling them. We moved into a classic Cape Cod in a little neighborhood that represented the quintessential middle-class life and dreams I had once thought unattainable. Outwardly, it looked like we were thriving, but inwardly, the cracks in our foundation continued to deepen.

At home, we seemed to alternate between struggle, strain, resignation, and settling for mediocrity. Like a lot of Christians, we looked forward to the afterlife when we could *finally* start living free from all the oppressive circumstances of "the world." In the meantime, our marriage was growing unbearable. Zelda and I argued constantly, falling into destructive patterns of criticism, contempt, defensiveness, and stonewalling. We both related to the other as though we could never be enough. We each saw our frustrations as rooted in the unwillingness of the other to change. The shame I carried from my failures and her frustrations created a rift that felt impossible to bridge.

A MARRIAGE ON THE BRINK

At my lowest, I was consumed by despair and caught in a storm of emotions that I could neither escape nor fully comprehend. My marriage felt like it was teetering on the brink of collapse, and the faith that had once been my bedrock seemed impotent and hollow. Zelda and I were trapped in relentless cycles of criticism and defensiveness, both of us burdened by unmet needs and unresolved pain. The warmth and intimacy I longed for felt impossibly distant, and I began to question if I would ever know the kind of passion and connection I had once imagined marriage could bring.

THE SEDUCTIVE PULL OF ESCAPING TO THE FUTURE

In my darkest moments, I found myself drawn to escape—not just the idea of leaving my marriage, but the seductive pull of starting over with someone else. There was another woman in my life—someone I considered a family friend—who seemed to fill a void I couldn't even name. She saw me in ways I didn't feel seen at home or by anyone else, and her warmth and admiration lit up something in me that had long felt dormant since childhood. It wasn't raw lust or even a conscious desire to destroy my life, but something subtler and perhaps even more dangerous: the illusion of being *truly valued and appreciated*.

At first, our connection seemed harmless, even noble. I convinced myself that my desire to support her through a difficult time was rooted in compassion and kindness–and to be clear, it largely was. But as time went on, the emotional bond we shared began to deepen in ways I didn't fully understand. She admired my strength, valued my presence, and seemed to view me with a kind of respect, admiration, understanding, and appreciation that I hadn't felt... well, forever! Her energy awakened longings in me that I thought were dead, and I began daydreaming about a life where I could pursue that kind of connection.

THE DANGER OF LINGERING TOO LONG

I wish I could say I recognized the danger immediately, but I didn't. I let the connection linger longer than I should have, indulging in fantasies that became a temporary refuge from the chaos of my marriage and the weight of my own shame. There were moments when I came perilously close to stepping over a line, but something deep inside always pulled me back. My values, my faith, and my commitment to my family ultimately acted as anchors, even when my emotions threatened to overwhelm me. And to be clear, I shared my struggles as openly as I could with others, including Zelda, and probably prevented the worsts kinds of darkness by sharing with a few others.

Nevertheless, navigating this landscape was excruciating. Trying to make sense of the tension between the guilt of feeling drawn to someone else and the cruelty of having what felt like the possible fulfillment of all my desires right there, in front of me, but unavailable, was insanely hard to process. My frustration over this dilemma led to deep resentment that I harbored toward Zelda for what I saw as her emotional distance. I felt trapped between the life I had built and the life I thought I wanted, and that tension was almost unbearable. I blamed her, blamed myself, and blamed the circumstances that had led us to this place, but none of it brought me closer to peace or resolution. I was a Victim in the thickest of Drama Triangles. My wife was the Persecutor, and my friend was the Rescuer.

A CATALYST FOR CHANGE

Eventually, I knew I had to confront what was happening—not just in my marriage, but in my heart. The breaking point came when I accidentally stumbled upon a video of a men's coach who spoke directly to the pain I was experiencing. He talked about responsibility, agency, and empowerment in a way that felt both challenging and hopeful. Desperate for clarity, I booked a free session with him, not knowing what to expect. It wasn't every day I could find an older, experienced man willing to share his time and perspective, and I desperately yearned for this in my life.

That conversation was a *revelation* that began a *revolution*. For the first time, someone lovingly held up a mirror and forced me to see the truth about my life—not as a judgment, but as an opportunity. He didn't shame me for my struggles or dismiss my pain. Instead, he empathized with me, heard me, affirmed that I wasn't broken, and then challenged me to take responsibility for the role I had played in creating the life I was living. He helped me see that my attraction to another woman wasn't about her; it was about me. It was about the unmet needs, unhealed wounds, and unresolved shame I carried, and no amount of escape or fantasy could fix that.

THE POWER OF RESPONSIBILITY

A few months later, he introduced me to the drama triangle and showed me how to step into a place of empowerment. He helped me reframe my resentment toward Zelda, not as evidence of her failure, but as a mirror to my resentments toward myself, rooted in shame and as an invitation to grow—both as a man and a husband. Most importantly, he helped me see that the life I wanted wouldn't come from being rescued by this woman, by starting over, or even Jesus (you can imagine my gasp!); it would come from transformation - yes, but only one that would begin with my agency and choice. Today, I realize that he called me into what church would call "repentance"–but in a profoundly more effective way that focused not merely on leaving something behind but that focused far more on what I could create and enter instead. To borrow Bible metaphors, he showed me how to leave my personal Egypt, walk to Canaan, slay giants, and get busy experiencing milk and honey. To be blunt, I'd never experienced anything like that in forty years of church.

The days and weeks that followed were some of the hardest of my life. Facing the reality of my shortcomings while trying to rebuild trust and connection within myself and in my marriage was grueling. But for the first time in years, I had hope, not in a rescuer, but in being a *connected creator*. I saw a path forward—not an easy one, but a real one. I began taking small, deliberate steps toward reclaiming responsibility for my life and choices. I stopped blaming Zelda for my unhappiness and started focusing on how to show up as the man I wanted to be.

A TRANSFORMATION BEGINS

The process was anything but linear. There were setbacks, painful conversations, and moments when I wanted to give up. But slowly, things began to change. The fantasies that had once offered an escape lost their allure as I started to build something real and meaningful in my own life. My marriage didn't magically transform overnight, but the groundwork was being laid for a new kind of connection—one rooted in honesty, courage, and unconditional regard.

LOOKING BACK AND MOVING FORWARD

Looking back, I see that this experience was a turning point in my marriage and my entire life. It forced me to confront the deepest parts of myself—the wounds, the anxiety, shame, and the fear I had carried for so long—and to begin the hard but necessary work of healing.

It also taught me that transformation isn't about running away from or escaping the pain; it's about moving through it with courage and faith. That lesson has shaped everything I do now, both personally and professionally. Today, I dedicate my life to helping other men navigate these same challenges, guiding them toward lives of integrity, connection, and empowerment.

FROM SURVIVAL TO TRANSFORMATION

This wasn't an overnight change. It took years of intentional work to untangle the lies I had believed about myself, God, and others. I began to confront my shame, rebuild my marriage, and reconstruct my faith from the ground up.

THE WORK I DO NOW

Today, my life is a testament to the power of transformation. My marriage, once on the brink of collapse, is now a thriving partnership built on trust, connection, and unconditional high regard. Once driven by fear, my faith is rooted in love and freedom. Most of my relationships have improved. Occasionally, some have had to come to an end.

I've dedicated my life to helping others experience the same transformation. I work primarily with men who feel stuck—whether in their marriages, careers, or personal lives. Many of them are high-achievers who look successful on the outside but feel empty and disconnected inside–just like me.

Through my mentoring and coaching, I help them confront the shame and fear that hold them back, rebuild their confidence, and create flourishing lives. I wish someone had done this work with me when I was drowning in shame and striving.

LOOKING AHEAD

This journey has been about more than just personal growth—it's been about rewriting the story of my life. In the chapters ahead, we'll explore how I've come to understand the scriptures through a new lens, starting with Genesis, revealing a far more loving, patient, and empowering God than I ever imagined. But before we get into Genesis, I want to share a bit more about my process of arriving at the conclusions that will follow.

CHAPTER FORTY-ONE
DEBUGGING THE ALIEN CODE
UNMASKING FEAR, SHAME, AND THE SYSTEMS THAT KEEP US POWERLESS

> You can't go back and change the beginning, but you can start where you are and change the ending. – C.S. Lewis

DEBUGGING THE SYSTEM OF MY LIFE

I'VE ALWAYS BEEN A SYSTEMS THINKER. MY CAREER AS A troubleshooter and software architect revolved around solving complicated problems for big companies, unwinding immensely intricate systems, and figuring out how they worked—or why they didn't. I liked to know the nuts and bolts of everything: what's broken, how it broke, and the clear, rational steps needed to fix it.

Naturally, when my life started falling apart, I brought that same analytical mindset to the chaos. My marriage, my faith, my identity—all of it felt like a system on the verge of collapse. And so, I began to dig. I asked myself the same kinds of questions I'd ask at work: What's the root cause? What assumptions are driving this system? What needs to change to make it work?

SVEN MASTERSON

DISCOVERING THE ROOT OF THE PROBLEM

It didn't take long for me to identify the major issue: shame. For years, it had driven every part of my life—shaping my relationships, my faith, and even my understanding of myself. Shame whispered that I wasn't enough, that I had to perform better, believe harder, and prove my worth to both God and the people around me. I had been living in a system of conditionality, where every misstep or failure became a confirmation of my deepest fear: that I was unworthy of love.

Shame's grip was unrelenting, and I saw how it reinforced the narratives that drove my beliefs. I had learned to see God as a cosmic Rescuer and myself as the perpetual Victim waiting for rescue. Every hardship, every failure, felt like evidence that I hadn't measured up, that God's love and blessings depended on my ability to perform correctly.

THE DRAMA TRIANGLE IN THEOLOGY

As I reflected, I began to see how much of the theology I had absorbed was shaped by people who (like most of us) lived in drama triangles themselves. *Victims* taught faith as though we were perpetually broken, incapable of thriving without rescue. *Rescuers* portrayed God as someone who might swoop in to save us, but only if we followed the rules and believed correctly. *Persecutors* emphasized judgment, portraying God as someone constantly angry, wrathful, or disappointed.

The result was a faith lens deeply skewed by the dynamics of the Drama Triangle. Instead of empowering people, it fostered dependency, shame, anxiety, and fear. It left little room for freedom, growth, or connection and instead perpetuated the very cycles it sought to resolve.

Discovering the concept of The Empowerment Dynamic (TED) became a turning point. It offered me a way out of the cycle. Instead of being a *Victim*, I could step into the role of *Creator*, taking responsibility for my life and choices. Instead of viewing others as *Persecutors*, I could see them as *Challengers*, pushing me to grow. And instead of trying to be someone else's *Rescuer*, I could become a *Coach*, supporting others without sacrificing my boundaries.

This wasn't just a relational framework—it reshaped how I saw God. No longer was He a *Rescuer* or a *Persecutor*. Instead, I began to see Him as the ultimate *Creator*, inviting me to co-create a life of authenticity, courage, and freedom. I began to see the indwelling Spirit and other relationships as serving as *Coaches* and *Challengers*.

DEBUGGING MY THEOLOGY

As my personal life unraveled, so did the theological frameworks that had shaped my faith. I realized my understanding of God had been deeply transactional: faithfulness in, blessings out. That, my friends, is exactly the pattern of idolatry: worship the idol so that it brings rain, babies, and bounty. I saw God as loving but conditional—a figure whose approval had to be earned through correct belief, obedience, and sacrifice.

This transactional view collapsed under the weight of my struggles. (My marriage did too, because it was built on the same systems). If faithfulness leads to blessings, why was my life filled with so much tension, frustration, and fear? If God's love is unconditional, why did I feel like I was constantly trying to earn it?

As I unpacked these questions, I saw how drama-triangle theology compounded the issue. Victim theology emphasized my insufficiency, keeping me in a state of shame and dependency. Persecutor theology magnified my fear, making me afraid to question, explore, or rest in grace. Rescuer theology encouraged me to wait for external solutions rather than step into the empowerment dynamics I desperately needed.

These realizations led to a process of theological deconstruction and reconstruction. I had to unravel the inherited beliefs and cultural assumptions that had shaped my faith, tracing the flaws in the system back to their source. What emerged was something more genuine, free, life-giving, and aligned with what I believe is the Creator's intent.

THE ROLE OF FEAR AND SHAME

Fear had been the glue holding this faulty system together. It kept me clinging to certainty, avoiding questions that might unravel everything, and striving to meet impossible standards. But fear was also a cage. It silenced my curiosity, kept me from exploring deeper truths, and fueled the shame that whispered I was never enough.

This realization brought me face-to-face with my deepest wounds. Shame wasn't just a feeling—it was a belief system about my worth, my relationship with God, and my place in the world. Confronting it was terrifying, but it was also liberating.

I began to see that my worth wasn't something I had to earn. It was intrinsic, rooted in the Creator's love—a love that wasn't conditional, brittle, or transactional.

FROM SYSTEMS TO STORIES

The stories that shaped my faith began to take on new meaning. Genesis 3, with its tale of fear, shame, and disconnection, had been my reality for far too long. I had been living in the shadow of Adam and Eve, hiding from a God I thought was angry and demanding. But the story of John 4—where Yeshua meets the Samaritan woman at the well—offered a different vision. Here was a God who meets us in our brokenness, offers living water, and replaces fear with love.

These stories became the lens through which I reevaluated my faith. They revealed a tension between fear and love and challenged me to move from a fear-based framework to one rooted in connection and grace.

RECONSTRUCTING FAITH

Rebuilding my faith was not about abandoning it but *refining* it. I let go of the idolatrous transactional framework that had dominated my beliefs and embraced a relational one. This shift required me to let go of fear, trust in the Creator's love, and recognize that my worth had never been tied to my performance.

In this process, I also reexamined the language I used to describe God. I began to use names like "The Creator" and "Yehovah" or "Adonai" to reflect a deeper, more personal connection. "Jesus" became "Yeshua"—not just a linguistic preference, but a way to honor the authenticity of His identity.

At the same time, I began to live beyond labels. For years, labels had been a way to measure and compare, to decide who was in and who was out, to quickly spot differences that disconnect. I sought identity in roles—"missionary," "leader," "Christian," "Presbyterian," "Baptist," "Mennonite," and countless others—using these labels to define myself and others. But I realized that how I labeled myself—or how others labeled me—was far less important than how the Creator knows me. Labels had been tools to expedite judgment and comparison, but they no longer served me. What truly matters isn't the categories we create, but the relationship and connection we have with the One who sees us as we are.

A NEW SYSTEM, A NEW STORY, A NEW VOCABULARY

Debugging my life and faith hasn't been easy. It required confronting deep fears, untangling shame, and dismantling a framework that had shaped me for decades. But it was also the most transformative process I've ever experienced.

Today, I live in a new story. It's not about perfect performance or flawless theology—it's about connection, grace, and empowerment. It's about embracing the Creator's love, not as something to be earned, but as something that has always been there. One of the most significant changes was in how I understood God. I stopped seeing Him as a distant judge and began experiencing Him as a loving Creator. I started using names like "The Creator" and "Yeshua" to reflect this shift, reconnecting with the roots of my faith while shedding the cultural baggage I had carried for so long.

But this journey hasn't come without challenges. Just how tightly some people cling to their interpretations of theology has made it difficult at times. My perspectives, shaped by my experiences, haven't always been accepted, and the judgment and ostracizing that has sometimes resulted has been painful. Still, I've come to see that my journey isn't about pleasing others or fitting into their categories. It's about authenticity, about living aligned with truth and love, even when that path requires courage and resilience.

This story isn't just mine—it's available to all of us. In the chapters ahead, we'll begin to explore the foundational stories of scripture—not through the lens of fear but through the lens of love. Let's take this next step together.

COMMON RESPONSES

"Yeah, but I've deconstructed my faith before, and it just left me more confused and disconnected."

It's understandable to feel disoriented during deconstruction—it can feel like losing your foundation. But this process isn't about tearing everything down to live in ruins. It's about rebuilding something stronger, freer, and more aligned with truth and love. Confusion is often the birthplace of clarity, and the work of reconstruction can lead to a faith that feels both authentic and life-giving.

WHAT TO DO WHEN THE ALIENS SHOW UP (AND EVEN IF THEY DON'T)

"Yeah, but my shame feels so deeply ingrained that I don't think I'll ever overcome it."

Shame can feel like an unshakable part of us, but it isn't. It's a learned response, reinforced by experiences and beliefs. When we challenge those beliefs and replace them with truth, shame begins to lose its grip. The process is gradual and often requires patience, but it's possible to rewrite the stories shame has written about you.

"Yeah, but questioning long-held beliefs feels like betrayal—to my family, my community, or even God."

It's natural to feel that questioning your beliefs might be seen as disloyal. But exploration doesn't equal rejection—it's an act of seeking deeper understanding and connection. Faith is strengthened, not weakened, by honest questions. The Creator isn't threatened by your doubts but invites you into a relationship where love, not fear, is the foundation.

"Yeah, but if I stop seeing God as a Rescuer, won't that mean I'm on my own?"

Letting go of a dependency-driven view of God doesn't mean you're alone—it means stepping into a partnership with the Creator. This perspective empowers you to co-create your life while remaining deeply connected to divine love and guidance. You're not abandoning help; you're embracing agency alongside grace.

"Yeah, but isn't it arrogant to think we can move beyond traditional theological frameworks?"

Seeking growth and authenticity in your faith isn't arrogance—it's humility. It's recognizing that no single framework or tradition can fully encapsulate the infinite complexity of the Creator. Embracing a relational, love-centered view of faith honors both the roots of tradition and the ongoing journey of discovery.

CHAPTER FORTY-TWO
THE GENESIS CODE
UNLOCKING HUMANITY'S ORIGINAL DESIGN

Humanity was not meant to sit idle but to thrive in partnership with the divine. – Dallas Willard

---

I DIDN'T FULLY UNDERSTAND THE POWER OF THE GENESIS STORY UNTIL much later in my journey. For most of my life, I saw it as a simple account of humanity's origins—a story about Adam, Eve, and a garden. But as I untangled the distortions in my own life and faith, I realized Genesis wasn't just about where we came from. It was about who we are and who we were created to be.

It begins with a profound declaration: humanity is created in the image of the Creator. This isn't an abstract idea; it's foundational. To be made in the Creator's image means we reflect His attributes—His love, creativity, agency, and relational nature. It means we are not passive spectators in life but co-creators, entrusted with the care and flourishing of the world He made.

For years, I struggled to believe I could be good enough, that I had any real worth apart from what I achieved. Genesis told a different story. It said Adam and Eve were created inherently good, whole, and complete. When the Creator looked at them, He declared them "very good." This wasn't based on their accomplishments or how well they performed—it was simply who they were. That realization began to reframe my understanding of myself—and the shame I carried.

PLACED IN THE GARDEN: PROVISION AND FREEDOM

The Creator didn't just create Adam and Eve; He placed them in the Garden of Eden, a place of abundance, beauty, and harmony. I used to think of the garden as a setting, but now I see it as a representation of how life was meant to be. In the garden, everything they needed was provided. They had food, purpose, and even the Tree of Life, which symbolized their connection to the Creator's sustaining presence.

For Adam and Eve, life in the garden wasn't about striving or scarcity. They didn't live under the pressure of proving themselves or earning their keep. They were free—free to walk with the Creator, live in harmony with creation, and fully inhabit the worth and value they already had.

When I compare this picture to the life I used to live—a life of striving, fear, and self-doubt—it's hard not to see the contrast. The Creator's design was for us to live in freedom and abundance, but so often, we live as if our worth is something we have to earn. I spent years trying to achieve a sense of identity that Adam and Eve already had simply by being who they were.

MADE IN THE CREATOR'S IMAGE

To be made in the Creator's image isn't just about reflection—it's about participation. Humanity wasn't crafted as mere objects or servants but as beings infused with the essence of the Creator Himself. This image wasn't conditional, dependent on performance or validation. It was woven into the very essence of who Adam and Eve were.

Consider the attributes humanity shares with the Creator:

- **Creativity:** The Creator brings forth life, order, and beauty from chaos. Humanity carries the same impulse to create, innovate, and cultivate.
- **Love:** At His core, the Creator is love. We are designed to love deeply and unconditionally, both giving and receiving it freely.
- **Agency:** The Creator acts freely and intentionally. Humanity mirrors this agency, possessing the power to choose and shape our lives.
- **Relationality:** The Creator exists in relationship—Father, Son, and Spirit. We are relational beings, designed for connection with Him and each other.
- **Goodness:** After creating humanity, the Creator declared His work "very good." This wasn't a conditional statement based on behavior but a declaration of inherent worth.

These qualities weren't bestowed with strings attached. They were part of humanity's essence, a reflection of the Creator's image.

THE ORIGINAL MANDATE: PARTNERS IN CREATION

The Creator didn't place humanity in the garden to passively enjoy it. He invited them into partnership and gave them a purpose.

> *Be fruitful and multiply; fill the earth and subdue it. Rule over the fish in the sea and the birds in the sky and over every living creature that moves on the ground.*
> –Genesis 1:28

This wasn't a test or burden—it was empowerment. The Creator entrusted Adam and Eve with the care of creation, calling them to co-create with Him. Each element of the mandate reflects empowerment:

- **Be Fruitful and Multiply:** More than procreation, this was an invitation to expand, grow, and bring creativity to all aspects of life.
- **Fill the Earth and Subdue It:** This implied cultivating order and harmony, bringing out the potential of creation.
- **Rule Over Creation:** This wasn't about control but stewardship, reflecting the Creator's love and wisdom in their dominion.

This invitation to partner with the Creator wasn't dependent on constant approval or guidance. It was a relationship rooted in trust, in which humanity was equipped to live fully and freely in alignment with its purpose.

CONNECTED SELF-RELIANCE

Adam and Eve's lives in the garden were marked by what I now call "connected self-reliance." They were free to act, create, and make decisions, but their self-reliance wasn't disconnected from the Creator. It was rooted in their connection to Him—the source of their worth and purpose.

For much of my life, I saw self-reliance as a dirty word. Like many Christians I knew, I equated it with pride and rebellion. But as I reflected on Genesis, I realized this was a tragic distortion. The problem isn't self-reliance; it's *disconnected* self-reliance.

Disconnected self-reliance is what happens when we try to live independently of the Creator–via the *ego*. It's relying on a muddled version of self—a mix of our true selves and the masks we wear to survive. These masks, shaped by shame, fear, and ego, aren't truly us. They're defenses, reactions, and distortions. When we rely on them, we're relying on something false.

WHAT TO DO WHEN THE ALIENS SHOW UP (AND EVEN IF THEY DON'T)

By contrast, Adam and Eve's connected self-reliance was rooted in their true selves. They knew who they were because they knew who they were. They didn't question their worth or strive for validation because their identity was secure in the Creator's love.

THE TREE OF LIFE: SUSTAINED BY CONNECTION

At the center of the garden stood the Tree of Life. Unlike the Tree of Knowledge of Good and Evil, which carried a prohibition, the Tree of Life was freely available. Its fruit sustained Adam and Eve, symbolizing their connection to the Creator.

This tree wasn't about dependency—it was about rhythm. The Tree of Life reflected a natural, life-giving flow between the Creator and humanity. Its presence reinforced the truth that humanity's life and flourishing came not from striving but from connection.

RECLAIMING TRUST

As I reflected on the Genesis story, I realized how far I had drifted from this original design. For years, I relied on a disconnected, muddled version of myself. I didn't trust me, and because of that, no one else could trust me either.

I saw this pattern in the men I worked with, too. They were stuck in cycles of striving and shame, relying on masks and roles to prop up their sense of worth. These weren't their true selves—they were distortions born of fear and disconnection.

Adam and Eve's connected self-reliance showed me a better way. True self-reliance isn't about rejecting the Creator; it's about living in alignment with Him. It's about trusting the self He created, not the false self we construct.

COMING UP NEXT: FORBIDDEN FRUITS FOUL FELLOWSHIP

In Genesis, we see humanity as it was meant to be—whole, free, and very good. Adam and Eve lived in harmony with the Creator, creation, and themselves. They were confident, empowered, and unshaken by fear or shame.

This foundation is essential for understanding what happens next: the choice that redefined humanity's relationship with the Creator and themselves. But for now, the Genesis story reminds us of who we are at our core. It invites us to rediscover our true selves, to step out of the distortions we've created, and to live in the freedom and love we were designed for.

COMMON RESPONSES

"Yeah, but isn't it prideful to think of ourselves as reflecting the Creator's image?"

Not at all. Recognizing that we reflect the Creator's image isn't about arrogance; it's about humility. We didn't create this worth—it was given to us. Acknowledging it allows us to live in gratitude and purpose, not striving for something we already have.

"Yeah, but doesn't the Genesis story suggest that humanity's true nature is flawed because of sin?"

No. Look again and see. It's not in the text. The Genesis story begins with humanity being declared "very good," and the Creator never says otherwise. nor does he change those words. While sin introduced brokenness, it didn't erase the core goodness and divine image within us. That is a great example of how the delusions of our judgment have tricked us. Redemption and restoration invite us back to that original design, not as flawed beyond repair but as inherently worthy.

"Yeah, but how can I trust that I'm inherently good when my life is full of mistakes and failures?"

Mistakes and failures are part of the human experience, not proof of inherent unworthiness. The Creator's declaration of "very good" is unconditional, tied to your being, not your doing. Understanding this frees you to grow and learn without the weight of shame.

"Yeah, but if the garden was perfect, why didn't Adam and Eve stay in it?"

The garden wasn't just about perfection—it was about relationship, choice, and freedom. The Creator didn't make humanity as automatons but as beings with agency. The story of the garden is one of trust and connection, not forced compliance. The choices they made reflect the complexity of free will, not the failure of the design.

"Yeah, but doesn't self-reliance lead to pride and disconnection from the Creator?"

Disconnected self-reliance, yes, because it isn't self-reliance but ego reliance. But connected self-reliance is different—it's about trusting the self the Creator designed while staying rooted in Him. It's not about rejecting God but aligning with His purpose and trusting His work in you.

CHAPTER FORTY-THREE
THE FORBIDDEN FRUIT
THE WEIGHT OF JUDGMENT AND THE LOVE THAT PROTECTS

No one is capable of judging the value of another, for we cannot know the full story behind each soul. – Dietrich Bonhoeffer

---

THE TREE OF KNOWLEDGE OF GOOD AND EVIL: A LOVING PROHIBITION

I can't pinpoint exactly when it began, but as I revisited Genesis 3, I saw the story of the Tree of Knowledge of Good and Evil with fresh eyes. It wasn't a theological agenda or a sermon series that brought me back—it was curiosity, a willingness to sit with the text and see if I'd missed something.

One Saturday morning, my friend Rob Schnepps sent me a simple question: "What do you think about the idea that the tree of the knowledge of good and evil is about judgment?" That question stayed with me, quietly challenging the way I had always understood this story.

For most of my life, I'd seen the tree as a test of obedience, a way for the Creator to expose human frailty. But as I returned to the

Genesis account with Rob's question in mind, something shifted. What if the tree wasn't about restriction but protection? What if the Creator's prohibition wasn't a stern command but a loving safeguard?

JUDGMENT: A BURDEN WE WERE NEVER MEANT TO BEAR

To judge—to truly discern good from evil—is not a simple matter of labeling things as "right" or "wrong." Judgment requires omniscience. It's about understanding the entire scope of a story—its past, present, and future. It demands knowing the hearts of all involved, the ripple effects of every choice, and the unseen connections between events. This kind of judgment is far beyond human capacity.

The Creator's prohibition against eating from the Tree of Knowledge of Good and Evil wasn't about withholding something essential. It was about protecting Adam and Eve from a burden they weren't designed to carry. They weren't created to live under the weight of judgment; they were created to flourish in the light of love.

When Adam and Eve ate the fruit, they stepped into a realm they couldn't navigate. They became judges without the capacity to judge rightly. Their first judgment wasn't rebellion—it was self-condemnation.

THE FIRST JUDGMENT: AGAINST THEMSELVES

The moment Adam and Eve ate the fruit, their perception changed. They looked at themselves and decided, *"We are naked."* Nakedness, which had once symbolized openness, trust, and connection, became something to hide.

Their response was to sew fig leaves together to cover themselves. But these fig leaves weren't just physical coverings—they were the first false selves. They were humanity's first attempt to manage how we are seen—by ourselves, by each other, and by the Creator.

For me, the fig leaf became a powerful metaphor for the masks I wore throughout my life. As a young man, it was being a skateboarder or a punk rocker. Later, it was being a missionary, a father of six, a successful professional. Each role became a layer of protection, a way to hide the vulnerability of simply being myself.

But fig leaves don't protect—they disconnect. They cast shadows that obscure the Creator's light, making us feel as though we're living in darkness. The tragedy is that these shadows aren't real—they're illusions created by the false self. Yet, trapped in them, we come to believe they are the truth about us.

HIDING: HUMANITY'S FIRST RETREAT

When the Creator comes to the garden after Adam and Eve's fall, He doesn't storm in with anger or condemnation. Instead, He asks a simple question: *"Where are you?"*

This question isn't about location; it's about relationship. It's an invitation to reconnect.

But Adam and Eve hide. Their judgment of themselves is projected onto the Creator. They assume He will see them as they see themselves: flawed, unacceptable, and unworthy. Their retreat isn't rebellion—it's shame.

Hiding is a natural response to shame, a way of avoiding the vulnerability of being seen. But it perpetuates disconnection. The Creator never withdrew from Adam and Eve—they withdrew from Him.

WHY JUDGMENT WAS NEVER OURS TO BEAR

Reflecting on this story, I began to understand why the Creator warned Adam and Eve not to eat from the tree. Judgment without omniscience leads to shame, fear, and disconnection. It distorts reality, convincing us of lies:

- That we are not enough.
- That others are threats.
- That even the Creator cannot be trusted.

Adam and Eve's first judgment—that they were no longer "very good"—was a tragic distortion. The serpent's lie, that they could "be like God" by knowing good and evil, planted the belief that their value was conditional, something to be achieved or lost.

THE CREATOR'S UNCHANGING LOVE

What struck me most in rereading this story was that the Creator's disposition toward Adam and Eve didn't change. His question, *"Where are you?"* wasn't accusatory—it was restorative. It wasn't about their failure; it was about their fear.

When the Creator asked, *"Who told you that you were naked?"* I heard a deeper question: *"Who told you that you weren't enough?"* This wasn't a rebuke—it was an invitation to confront the lie that had taken root in their hearts.

The Creator's love didn't waver. Adam and Eve were still "very good" in His eyes, but their judgment of themselves and their projection onto Him had created a barrier.

THE CURSE: THE CONSEQUENCES OF DISCONNECTION

The Creator's words to Adam and Eve after the fall are often misunderstood as a curse. But I've come to see them differently. These words aren't punishments handed down by an angry God; they're descriptions of the natural consequences of disconnection.

To Eve, He speaks of pain in childbirth and tension in relationships. To Adam, He speaks of toil and resistance in work. These aren't arbitrary penalties—they're the inevitable results of trying to live independently of the Creator's design.

When we operate in disconnected self-reliance, life becomes hard, fraught with struggle and striving. The Creator wasn't cursing

Adam and Eve; He was explaining what life feels like when we forget who we are and whose we are.

LOVE IN ACTION

Even in the midst of humanity's fall, the Creator's love remains steadfast. His responses reveal His commitment to restoration:

1. *"Where are you?"* This question is an invitation to relationship, not an accusation.
2. **A New Covering:** The Creator replaces their fig leaves with animal skins, a covering provided by Him, not crafted by them.
3. **The Promise of Restoration:** In Genesis 3:15, the Creator speaks of a seed who will crush the serpent's head, pointing to a future solution to shame and disconnection.
4. **Ejection from Eden:** At first, this seems punitive, but it's protective. Eating from the Tree of Life in a state of shame and disconnection would mean eternal existence in that state, but the Creator spares them from that fate.

LOVE OVER JUDGMENT

The Genesis story reveals that Adam and Eve, not the Creator, change. They judge themselves as unworthy and project that judgment onto Him. But the Creator's love never wavers. His warning about the tree wasn't about control—it was about protection. Judgment without omniscience leads to shame, disconnection, and fear, but the Creator's love invites us to step out of hiding and back into truth and connection.

SVEN MASTERSON

COMMON RESPONSES

"Yeah, but isn't the Tree of Knowledge of Good and Evil a test of obedience?"

That's a common interpretation, but if we read Genesis closely, the tree isn't framed as a test but as a loving warning. The Creator never mentions such a view. Further, why would the Creator need to test obedience—especially as an omniscient being who already knows what the result would be?

The Creator didn't create humanity to bear the burden of judgment; He designed us for connection and flourishing. The prohibition wasn't about control—it was about protecting us from stepping into a role we weren't equipped to fill.

"Yeah, but didn't Adam and Eve's disobedience prove they couldn't be trusted?"

Not at all. Their choice reflects the complexity of free will, not an inherent lack of trustworthiness. The first thing to notice is that there is no mention of the words "disobedience," "rebellion," or any similar words we project into the text. When we stop projecting these words, we can more easily see what took place—humans being invited into a lie. The Creator's response to their deception shows that His trust and love for humanity remain intact, even after their choice. He doesn't condemn them but moves to protect and restore them, emphasizing relationship over punishment. Unfortunately, the way most Christians interpret this, the deceit of the serpent continues because the character and nature of both The Creator and Humanity are perverted, and all attention on the Serpent is left behind.

"Yeah, but isn't judgment necessary for living a moral life?"

Judgment, in the sense of discernment or self-examination, is about aligning our actions, choices, and hearts with values and principles. Self-examination allows us to reflect honestly on our growth and areas for improvement without condemning ourselves. It's not about labeling ourselves or others as "good" or "evil." The judgment represented by the tree is ultimate and absolute—it requires omniscience, which only the Creator possesses. Discernment and self-examination help us grow and align with truth; ultimate judgment belongs to God alone.

"Yeah, but if the Creator didn't want them to eat from the tree, why put it there in the first place?"

The tree represents humanity's capacity for choice, which is integral to love and freedom. Without choice, there can be no genuine relationship. The Creator's inclusion of the tree wasn't about setting humanity up for failure—it was about creating the possibility of authentic connection rooted in trust rather than compulsion. We're also unaware of appropriate uses that the Creator may have had in mind for this tree.

"Yeah, but wasn't the expulsion from Eden a punishment?"

It can feel that way at first glance, but the expulsion was actually an act of protection. We tend to project our human concepts of judgment and punishment into the text. However, there is no mention of the Creator taking punitive actions. By removing Adam and Eve from the garden, the Creator ensured they wouldn't eat from the Tree of Life in their state of shame and disconnection, which would have locked them into that state forever. This was love in action, not retribution.

CHAPTER FORTY-FOUR
THE SERPENT'S TRAP
HUMANITY'S FIRST DRAMA TRIANGLE

> The moment you doubt whether you can fly, you cease forever to be able to do it. – J.M. Barrie, *Peter Pan*

THE FIRST DRAMA TRIANGLE: THE SERPENT'S LIE AND THE SHIFT TO DEPENDENCY

As I revisited the Genesis story with fresh eyes, I saw something I had missed for years. The serpent's interaction with Adam and Eve wasn't just about disobedience—it was an invitation to abandon their empowered, connected existence and step into dependency. At that moment, the story of humanity's fall became the story of humanity's first drama triangle.

This triangle—where victims, persecutors, and rescuers play their cyclical roles—didn't just disrupt Adam and Eve's relationship with the Creator. It rewired how they saw themselves and each other. It introduced shame as the root and sin as its inevitable fruit, distorting humanity's view of love, worth, and connection.

THE ORIGINAL DESIGN: EMPOWERED, CONNECTED, AND FREE

Before the serpent entered the story, Adam and Eve lived in harmony. They existed in a state I've come to understand as *connected self-reliance*—a confidence in their identity and agency that was rooted in their relationship with the Creator.

The Creator had entrusted them with the care of creation, equipping them with agency, creativity, and relationality. Their worth wasn't tied to performance or external validation; it was intrinsic, woven into their design as beings made in the Creator's image.

This freedom was sustained by boundaries—not as limitations but as loving safeguards. The Creator's single instruction to refrain from eating from the Tree of Knowledge of Good and Evil wasn't arbitrary. It was an act of protection.

To judge rightly requires omniscience: the ability to see all things, past, present, and future, in their proper context. Adam and Eve weren't equipped for this burden. The Creator knew that stepping into judgment would introduce distortion, shame, and fear—fracturing the harmony between humanity, the Creator, and creation itself.

THE SERPENT'S LIE: "YOU'RE NOT ENOUGH"

The serpent's words were subtle but devastating. He didn't coerce Adam and Eve; he planted doubt. His first question, *"Did God really say...?"* introduced a seed of mistrust, reframing the Creator as a potential persecutor withholding something essential.

Then came the serpent's defining statement:

> You will not certainly die... For God knows that when you eat from it your eyes will be opened, and you will be like God, knowing good and evil.
>
> –Genesis 3:4-5

This statement was laced with lies:

1. **It implied lack:** Adam and Eve were already made in the Creator's image, but the serpent suggested they were missing something vital.
2. **It promoted external dependency:** The serpent framed the fruit as the solution to their supposed incompleteness.
3. **It distorted the Creator's intentions:** By suggesting the Creator was withholding something good, the serpent cast Him as a persecutor.

At that moment, the serpent invited Adam and Eve into a drama triangle:

- **Victim:** They began to see themselves as deprived and incomplete.
- **Persecutor:** They reimagined the Creator as someone withholding something essential from them.
- **Rescuer:** They looked to the serpent—and the fruit—as their solution.

This lie—that we are not enough and must look outside ourselves for worth—has echoed throughout history, shaping how we view ourselves, the Creator, and the world.

THE FIRST JUDGMENT: AGAINST THEMSELVES

When Adam and Eve ate the fruit, their first act wasn't rebellion—it was judgment. They looked at themselves and concluded, *"We are naked."* Nakedness, once a symbol of openness and trust, became a source of shame.

Their second judgment was even more tragic. They projected

their self-condemnation onto the Creator, assuming He would see them as they now saw themselves—flawed, unworthy, and unacceptable. This projection drove them to hide, initiating the first disconnection in the human story.

The serpent's lie achieved its purpose. Adam and Eve moved from empowered creators living in harmony to disempowered victims trapped in shame and fear.

ORIGINAL SHAME VS. ORIGINAL SIN

For years, I was taught that sin is the root of disconnection. But after revisiting Genesis, I began to see things differently. Adam and Eve's first response after eating the fruit wasn't defiance—it was shame.

Shame came first. Their belief that they were no longer "good" led to hiding, disconnection, and blame. Their shame made them see the Creator not as a source of love but as a judge to be feared.

This shift helped me see sin not as the root but as the fruit. Sin grows from shame and disconnection, driving us to seek external solutions to internal wounds. When we believe we're not enough, we strive to fill that void in ways that often lead to harm.

This perspective doesn't diminish the reality of sin—it reframes it. The problem isn't just the actions we take but the shame and disconnection that drive them.

THE DO-HAVE-BE TRAP

Shame doesn't just distort how we see ourselves; it reshapes how we approach life. For most of my journey, I operated from a *Do-Have-Be* mindset:

1. **Do the right things:** Obey God, succeed in life, and avoid failure.
2. **Have the outcomes:** Approval, love, validation, or material success.

3. **Be the person I wanted to be:** Worthy, loved, at peace.

This framework mirrors the serpent's lie, tying identity to performance. It promises control but delivers exhaustion. No matter how much I did, it was never enough to silence shame's whispers: *"You're still not good enough."*

A NEW PARADIGM: BE-DO-HAVE

As I revisited Genesis, I saw the Creator's original design reflected in a different framework: *Be-Do-Have*.

1. **Be:** Embrace your true identity as someone made in the Creator's image—already loved, whole, and enough.
2. **Do:** Live in alignment with that identity, acting from a place of love, integrity, and purpose.
3. **Have:** Experience the fruits of connection and alignment—peace, joy, and fulfillment.

This shift wasn't just theological—it was personal. Letting go of the need to *do* in order to *be* felt like stepping off a treadmill I'd been running on my entire life.

THE LEGACY OF THE DRAMA TRIANGLE

The drama triangle Adam and Eve entered continues to shape humanity. When we internalize shame, we become victims, seeing ourselves as unworthy and incomplete. We project our judgments onto others, seeing persecutors where there are none, and seek rescuers in all the wrong places.

But the Creator's response in Genesis 3 offers a different way:

- **"Where are you?"** His question invites reconnection, not condemnation.

- **The promise of restoration:** Genesis 3:15 points to a future where shame and disconnection are undone.
- **A new covering:** The Creator replaces their fig leaves with animal skins, symbolizing His provision and care.

COMING UP NEXT

The Genesis story isn't just an account of humanity's fall; it's a map for understanding our own struggles. Shame convinces us we're not enough, but the Creator's love reminds us we were never anything less than "very good."

In the chapters ahead, we'll explore how to step out of the drama triangle and into the empowerment dynamic—reclaiming our true identity and living in the freedom and connection we were designed for.

For now, consider this: What if the Creator's love has always been unconditional? What would it mean to step out of shame and into the truth of who you already are?

COMMON RESPONSES

"Yeah, but doesn't the serpent's lie show that Adam and Eve were already flawed?"

If it did, the to be blunt - The Creator is either delusional or a liar, because he declared them "very good" and rested from his work afterward. Did he create a flawed being? Why would he call a flawed being "very good?" The serpent's lie didn't reveal or exploit a flaw—it invited them into one by introducing doubt and distortion. Adam and Eve were created "very good," with inherent worth and connection. The serpent's strategy wasn't to exploit existing flaws but to plant the idea that they lacked something, leading them into shame and disconnection. Their original design was whole and complete; the lie rewired how they saw themselves. To call humans anything other than "very good" is to take a position of rebellion and defiance of the Creator's declaration of our value and worth. Let that sink in.

> "Yeah, but isn't sin the root cause of all our problems, not shame?"

Shame is the fertile soil in which sin grows. In the Genesis narrative, shame precedes sin. Adam and Eve's immediate response after eating the fruit wasn't rebellion but hiding—an act driven by shame. They judged themselves as flawed and projected that judgment onto the Creator. While sin causes harm, it often stems from deeper wounds of shame and disconnection. Sin means to "miss the mark," which is the natural consequence of anything we try from a place of shame, fear, hiding, and disconnection.

> "Yeah, but didn't God set Adam and Eve up for failure by putting the tree in the garden?"

The tree wasn't a setup—it was a safeguard. The Creator didn't place the tree to tempt Adam and Eve but to protect them from a burden they weren't designed to carry: the weight of judgment. The prohibition was an act of love, inviting them to trust the Creator's provision and wisdom rather than relying on external solutions.

> "Yeah, but isn't it natural to strive for more? Isn't that part of growth?"

Striving isn't inherently wrong, but striving from a place of lack and shame leads to exhaustion and disconnection. The Creator's design invites us to grow and create from a foundation of "enoughness." True growth happens when we act from our inherent worth, not in an attempt to prove it.

SVEN MASTERSON

"Yeah, but how can I step out of the drama triangle when life keeps pulling me back in?"

Stepping out of the drama triangle isn't a one-time decision—it's a practice. It starts with awareness: recognizing when you're falling into the roles of victim, persecutor, or rescuer. From there, you can choose to shift into empowerment dynamics by embracing your identity as a creator, seeing challenges as opportunities, and supporting others as a coach. The Creator's love and presence provide the foundation to sustain this shift, even when life gets hard.

CHAPTER FORTY-FIVE
FROM FIG LEAVES TO FREEDOM
RECLAIMING CONNECTION AFTER THE FIRST JUDGMENT

You can't heal what you don't reveal. – Unknown

THE COST OF THE FIRST COVERING: A REVIEW OF GENESIS' LESSONS

I HOPE BY NOW YOU CAN SEE HOW THESE PERSPECTIVES ON GENESIS offer more than just a retelling of humanity's origins—they invite us to wrestle with who we are, how we view ourselves, and how we relate to the Creator. This ancient narrative is deeply relevant because it mirrors our ongoing struggles with shame, judgment, and the masks we create to hide from love. Let's step back and review some of the foundational truths Genesis reveals—and how they continue to shape our lives today.

THE GIFT OF THE CREATOR'S IMAGE

Genesis begins with a stunning affirmation: we are made in the Creator's image. This isn't a vague compliment or abstract idea—it's a profound statement about who we are. To bear His image means we carry His attributes: creativity, love, relationality, and agency. It means our worth is inherent, not earned.

Yet this truth is so easily forgotten. From the moment shame entered the story, humanity has struggled to believe in its own "very good(ness)." The serpent's first lie, "You're not enough," echoes through history. It's the root of every mask, every fig leaf, and every attempt to prove our value.

But Genesis also reminds us that our identity is unshakable. The Creator's declaration of "very good" wasn't conditional, and it hasn't changed. This truth stands even when we forget it, even when we hide behind masks or judge ourselves as unworthy. The challenge is not to become good enough—it's to reclaim the truth of who we already are.

FROM CONNECTION TO COVERING: THE RISE OF THE FALSE SELF

Before shame entered the picture, Adam and Eve lived in freedom and connection. They knew their worth and trusted in the Creator's love. They didn't strive to prove themselves; they simply were.

But the serpent introduced something insidious: the idea that they were lacking. In that moment, shame was born. Their first judgment wasn't about the fruit—it was about themselves. They looked at their nakedness, which had been a symbol of openness and trust, and decided it wasn't enough.

This self-judgment led to the first act of covering—the creation of fig leaves. These weren't just physical coverings; they were the first false selves, crafted to manage how Adam and Eve were seen by the Creator, each other, and even themselves. Fig leaves symbolize the masks we all wear when shame whispers, "You are not enough," and fear adds, "You'll be rejected if anyone sees the real you."

I hope you've begun to see the ways we still reach for fig leaves today. Whether it's roles, achievements, or personas, these coverings promise protection but leave us disconnected—from ourselves, others, and the Creator. They don't solve shame—they perpetuate it.

THE CREATOR'S RESPONSE TO SHAME

What stands out to me most in Genesis is the Creator's unwavering love. When Adam and Eve hide in shame, His first question is not, "What have you done?" but, "Where are you?" This is not the voice of an angry judge—it's the voice of a loving parent seeking connection.

Even when Adam and Eve can't step out of their shame, the Creator meets them where they are. He provides a new covering—not to endorse their hiding but to offer them grace. The animal skins symbolize His provision, a temporary accommodation for their distorted perception. And in the midst of their disconnection, He offers a promise: one day, the serpent's deception will be undone.

This response is a profound reminder that the Creator's love doesn't waver. It remains constant even when we see ourselves as unworthy. His invitation—"Where are you?"—echoes through time, calling us out of hiding and back into a connected relationship.

JUDGMENT: A BURDEN WE WERE NEVER MEANT TO CARRY

One of the most striking insights from Genesis is the Creator's prohibition against the Tree of the Knowledge of Good and Evil. Far from being an arbitrary rule, this boundary was an act of loving protection. The Creator knew that judgment—discernment of good and evil—requires omniscience. Without the full perspective of the past, present, and future, judgment distorts reality.

When Adam and Eve ate the fruit, their first act wasn't defiance —it was self-judgment. They decided they were no longer "very good," even though the Creator's declaration hadn't changed. This flawed judgment led them into shame and fear, driving them to hide from the very love that could restore them.

Judgment without omniscience is the root of shame and disconnection. It's why the Creator warned against the tree—not to restrict humanity, but to protect us from a burden we were never meant to bear.

THE DRAMA TRIANGLE AND THE SERPENT'S LIE

The Genesis story also reveals the origin of humanity's first drama triangle. The serpent lured Adam and Eve into a cycle of victimhood, painting the Creator as a persecutor who withholds good things and himself as a rescuer offering fulfillment through the fruit. This dynamic flipped the script on the truth of their empowered identity.

Once Adam and Eve accepted the serpent's narrative, they shifted from empowered creators to disempowered victims. They no longer saw the Creator as a partner but as an adversary. This same drama triangle plays out in our lives whenever we internalize shame and believe the lie that we are not enough. It's a cycle of striving, hiding, and disconnection—a cycle that the Creator invites us to break free from.

THE PATH BACK TO CONNECTION

Genesis offers not just a diagnosis of humanity's disconnection but a glimpse of restoration. The Creator's response to Adam and Eve's shame shows us the way back:

1. **Recognize the Lie:** Shame begins with a lie—the belief that we are not enough. To step out of shame, we must confront this lie and reclaim the truth of our worth.
2. **Answer the Invitation:** The Creator's question, "Where are you?" is not about location but relationship. It's an

invitation to step out of hiding and into the light of His love.
3. **Let Go of the Fig Leaves:** True freedom comes not from building a better mask but from letting go of the false self altogether. This requires vulnerability and trust in the Creator's unwavering love.
4. **Live in Connection:** Adam and Eve's story reminds us that connection, not striving, is the foundation of our design. We were created to live in partnership with the Creator, drawing our worth and identity from Him.

COMING UP NEXT: THE JOURNEY FROM SHAME TO FREEDOM

Genesis leaves us with tension. Adam and Eve's choice has far-reaching consequences, but the Creator's love and promise remain constant. This foundational story sets the stage for understanding our ongoing struggles with shame, judgment, and disconnection—and the Creator's unrelenting commitment to restoration.

In the chapters to come, we'll explore how these dynamics play out in our lives. We'll examine the masks we wear, the drama triangles we enter, and the ways shame drives us further from the love we crave. But we'll also discover the invitation to a new way of living—one rooted in love, connection, and empowerment.

For now, I invite you to reflect: Where are you? What fig leaves are you hiding behind, and what would it look like to step out of hiding and into the light of the Creator's love? The journey from shame to freedom begins here.

COMMON RESPONSES

"Yeah, but if the Creator made Adam and Eve perfect, how could they fall into shame and disconnection?"

Adam and Eve weren't created flawed, but they were created with free will—the capacity to choose. The serpent's lie didn't exploit an imperfection but introduced doubt and distortion. They were still inherently "very good," but their perception of themselves changed when they believed the lie that they lacked something.

"Yeah, but wasn't the Creator's punishment harsh? Why banish them from the garden?"

The Creator's actions weren't punitive but protective. Staying in the garden, with access to the Tree of Life, would have meant living eternally in a state of shame and disconnection. By removing them, the Creator set the stage for restoration, allowing humanity to step into a future where that brokenness could be healed.

"Yeah, but why does shame still affect us today if the Creator declared us 'very good'?"

Shame persists because the serpent's lie continues to echo through our lives. They go on, not only unchallenged but promoted by shame-based messages of disempowerment and disconnection that defy the Creator's declaration that we are very good. These messages distort how we see ourselves, convincing us we're unworthy or lacking. The Creator's declaration of our goodness hasn't changed; the work is in reclaiming that truth and stepping out of the false narratives that shame perpetuates. Remember—victims need rescuers, and when someone has something to gain by rescuing, they have a vested interest in you seeing yourself as a victim.

WHAT TO DO WHEN THE ALIENS SHOW UP (AND EVEN IF THEY DON'T)

"Yeah, but isn't judgment necessary for morality? How can we live without it?"

Judgment, in the sense of self-examination and discernment, is necessary for aligning with values and principles. Self-examination allows us to reflect on our actions, intentions, and alignment with the Creator's design, encouraging growth and accountability. However, what we were never meant to carry is the ultimate burden of deciding worth—either our own or that of others. That kind of judgment requires omniscience, an understanding of every heart, intention, and outcome, which only the Creator possesses. Our role is to live in alignment with love and truth, trusting that the Creator's perspective is far greater than our own limited understanding.

Further, we've been told that all of the Creator's instructions can be summarized in this: Love your neighbor as yourself and love the Creator with all your heart, soul, and mind. This central directive invites us to focus on love, not condemnation. It calls us to act with compassion and humility, leaving ultimate judgments to the One who sees and knows all. By doing so, we step out of the exhausting cycle of judgment and into the freedom of connection, grace, and purpose.

"Yeah, but what's the harm in wearing 'fig leaves' if they help us get through life?"

Fig leaves might offer temporary protection, but they also keep us disconnected—from ourselves, others, and the Creator. Masks don't heal shame; they perpetuate it, creating a cycle of striving and hiding. True freedom comes not from crafting better masks but from letting go of them entirely and stepping into authenticity and connection. Further, the Creator asked us, "Who told you that you were naked?" and when understood in concert with His declaration that we are "very good," indicates that our fig leaves cover over what was made very good in it's nakedness.

CHAPTER FORTY-SIX
THE FIRST STEPS INTO EXILE
THE CREATOR'S PLAN FROM THE GARDEN TO THE EXODUS

> Grace is not opposed to effort; it is opposed to earning.
> – Dallas Willard

A NEW REALITY OUTSIDE THE GARDEN: REFLECTING ON GENESIS' THEMES

The Genesis story reveals the beginning of humanity's struggle with disconnection and the Creator's unwavering commitment to restoration as Adam and Eve leave Eden. The narrative shifts from idyllic harmony to a new, complicated reality outside the garden. This transition, often misunderstood as punishment, is instead an act of protective love. The Creator, consistent in His purpose and disposition, sets the stage for humanity's journey toward reconnection and empowerment.

A LOVING DEPARTURE

Adam and Eve's removal from Eden wasn't the wrathful punishment of an angry Creator. It was a necessary step for their healing.

To remain in the garden with access to the Tree of Life while trapped in shame and disconnection would have meant eternal misery—perpetuating a life of distorted judgment and fear.

The Creator's decision to send them out was an act of love, offering them a chance to grow and learn and ultimately find their way back to connection. In this new reality, the Creator remained present and active, demonstrating His care even in the face of humanity's shame-driven retreat.

This departure highlights a profound truth: even when humanity steps into disconnection, the Creator's love does not waver. His consistent pursuit of relationship and restoration is woven throughout the Genesis narrative.

THE DRAMA TRIANGLE AND ITS LEGACY

The serpent's deception introduced a relational pattern that continues to echo through human history: the Drama Triangle. In Eden, the serpent reframed the Creator as a persecutor, Adam and Eve as victims, and himself as a rescuer, offering the fruit as a solution to their perceived lack. This shift from empowerment to dependency became the template for humanity's relational struggles.

Outside the garden, this dynamic only deepened. The Drama Triangle—marked by cycles of victimhood, blame, and false rescue—became the norm for human interaction. From Cain's jealousy and murder of Abel to the violence and corruption that led to the flood, humanity repeatedly stepped into the serpent's lie: "You are not enough; you need something else."

Yet, the Creator's purpose remained steadfast. His promise in Genesis 3:15—that a descendant of Eve would crush the serpent's head—points to the eventual breaking of this cycle. It reveals the Creator's desire not to rescue humanity from His wrath but to empower them to overcome shame and disconnection.

THE CREATOR'S PERSISTENT PRESENCE

Even as humanity stumbled further into disconnection, the Creator remained present and active. His interactions with key figures—Noah, Abraham, and Joseph—illustrate His unwavering commitment to partnership. Far from micromanaging or dictating their lives, the Creator invited these individuals into a dynamic relationship marked by trust, action, and empowerment.

Noah: Redemption Through Challenge

Noah's story exemplifies the Creator's approach to partnership. Faced with a world steeped in violence and corruption, Noah "walked with God." He wasn't a passive recipient of rescue; he was an active participant in his own redemption. The Creator invited Noah to build an ark—a monumental challenge requiring years of effort and faith.

The ark symbolizes more than survival; it represents redemption through empowered action. The Creator didn't shield Noah from difficulty—He equipped him to overcome it. This partnership demonstrates the Creator's desire to work with humanity, not as a rescuer in the Drama Triangle but as a coach guiding them toward growth and restoration.

Abraham: A Radical Partnership

Abraham's journey further illustrates the Creator's commitment to empowerment. Called to leave his homeland and step into the unknown, Abraham trusted the Creator's promises, even when they seemed impossible. His faith was imperfect—he stumbled and doubted—but he consistently chose to trust and act.

Through Abraham, the Creator initiated a covenant that would ultimately bless all families on earth. This partnership wasn't about blind obedience; it was an invitation to co-create with the Creator, using agency and faith to fulfill a greater purpose.

Abraham's story highlights the Creator's desire to empower humanity, not control them. It foreshadows the empowerment dynamic that underpins the Creator's ultimate plan for restoration.

HUMANITY'S STRUGGLES AND THE CREATOR'S CONSISTENCY

Despite the Creator's unwavering love and guidance, humanity's patterns of disconnection persisted. The serpent's lie continued to sow shame, fear, and mistrust, leading to relational fractures and societal corruption. The Drama Triangle became the default mode of interaction, perpetuating cycles of victimhood and blame.

And yet, figures like Noah, Abraham, and Joseph demonstrate what is possible when humanity steps out of the Drama Triangle and into the empowerment dynamic. They show that even in a world marked by disconnection, it is possible to walk with the Creator, trust His guidance, and live in alignment with His purposes.

FORESHADOWING EXODUS: FROM BONDAGE TO FREEDOM

As the Genesis narrative transitions to the story of the Israelites in Egypt, the stage is set for a dramatic shift. Joseph's rise to influence and his role in providing for his family during famine highlight the Creator's empowering guidance. But the Israelites' eventual enslavement under a Pharaoh who "did not know Joseph" marks a turning point.

The bondage of the Israelites mirrors humanity's broader struggle with shame and disconnection. Their journey out of Egypt will become a powerful metaphor for the Creator's desire to lead humanity out of the Drama Triangle and into a life of freedom and empowerment.

WHAT TO DO WHEN THE ALIENS SHOW UP (AND EVEN IF THEY DON'T)

COMING UP NEXT: THE CREATOR'S RELENTLESS PURSUIT

From the garden to Egypt, the Genesis story reveals a Creator whose love and purpose remain unchanging. His invitation to partnership is consistent, even as humanity stumbles through cycles of disconnection and shame. The narratives of Noah, Abraham, and Joseph offer glimpses of what is possible when we trust the Creator, embrace our agency, and step into our role as co-creators.

As the story shifts to the Exodus, we'll see the Creator's desire to move humanity from victimhood to empowerment, from disconnected self-defeat to connected self-reliance. This journey reflects our own path—one of leaving behind the chains of shame and fear to step into the freedom of living in alignment with the Creator's love and purpose.

COMMON RESPONSES

> "Yeah, but doesn't being expelled from Eden show that the Creator abandoned humanity?"

Not at all. The expulsion from Eden wasn't abandonment—it was an act of protection and love. Staying in Eden with access to the Tree of Life while trapped in shame and disconnection would have meant eternal misery. The Creator's action opened the door for growth, healing, and eventual restoration. The entire Genesis narrative shows the Creator's consistent presence and commitment to humanity, even outside the garden.

> "Yeah, but if the Creator loves us, why does shame and disconnection persist?"

Shame and disconnection persist because humanity continues to believe the serpent's lie: that we are not enough and must look outside ourselves or the Creator to fill that void. The Creator doesn't force us into connection; He invites us. His love is constant, but it's up to us to trust it, confront the lies, and step into the truth of who we are. The stories of Noah, Abraham, and Joseph demonstrate how trust in the Creator can break these cycles. Furthermore, the Creator has not disconnected from us, but it is we that have disconnected from Him. If we remain in shame as an act of our choices, it is our doing.

> "Yeah, but doesn't the Creator act as a Persecutor by allowing hardships like the flood or Abraham's trials?"

It might seem that way at first glance, but a closer look reveals a Creator who empowers humanity through challenges. The flood wasn't about punishment—it was about preserving the possibility of redemption in a world overwhelmed by corruption. Abraham's trials weren't tests of endurance but opportunities to grow in faith and partnership. The Creator equips us to face hardships, not to punish us, but to prepare us for flourishing.

> "Yeah, but doesn't the Drama Triangle show that humanity is doomed to repeat cycles of victimhood and blame?"

The Drama Triangle shows how pervasive shame and disconnection are, but it's not a destiny—it's a pattern that can be broken. The Creator consistently invites us to step out of the triangle and into empowerment. Stories like Noah's, Abraham's, and Joseph's highlight how trust, agency, and alignment with the Creator's love can break these cycles and lead to restoration.

> "Yeah, but if the Creator is empowering, why does humanity still face such devastating consequences for their choices?"

The consequences humanity faces are often the natural results of

WHAT TO DO WHEN THE ALIENS SHOW UP (AND EVEN IF THEY DON'T)

disconnection, not punitive actions by the Creator. Disconnection from the Creator leads to striving, fear, and broken relationships, which perpetuate harm. The Creator's role is not to shield us from the consequences of our choices but to guide us toward healing, growth, and reconnection. His love is steadfast, offering us a way back to alignment and flourishing.

CHAPTER FORTY-SEVEN
THE EXODUS OF THE ALIENATED
THE JOURNEY FROM DEPENDENCY TO EMPOWERMENT

> Faith is taking the first step even when you don't see the whole staircase. – Martin Luther King Jr.

THE STORY OF THE EXODUS ISN'T MERELY A TALE OF LIBERATION; IT'S a profound reflection on the human condition, the dynamics of dependency, and the Creator's invitation to a life of trust, empowerment, and connected self-reliance. As I've reflected on this story, I've come to see its lessons as deeply relevant to our own struggles with freedom, bondage, and the choices we face when navigating life's uncertainties.

THE BONDAGE OF DEPENDENCY

The Israelites' journey to Egypt began during a time of famine, when their forefather Jacob sought refuge and sustenance in the land of Egypt. Initially, this move was practical—securing survival during a crisis. But what began as a temporary solution turned into a generational entanglement. The Israelites exchanged the freedom of their ancestral land, promised to Abraham, for the comfort and stability of life in Egypt.

This is what dependency does. It lures us with the promise of relief and certainty, but over time, it exacts a greater cost: our freedom and identity. The Israelites' dependency on Egypt—what once seemed like a practical choice—led to their eventual enslavement. They became victims of their own choices, stuck in a cycle of dependency that turned their refuge into a prison.

This dynamic is deeply human. When faced with uncertainty, the fearful and anxious mind craves security. Egypt, with its abundance and structure, offered a sense of certainty. But this certainty came at the expense of the freedom to live in the promise and empowerment the Creator had intended for them.

Even after their liberation, this dependency mindset lingered. Time and again, the Israelites pined for the familiarity of Egypt, despite the harshness of their slavery. The uncertainty of the wilderness and the responsibility of empowerment felt more daunting than the predictable oppression of their bondage. This is the seductive pull of dependency—it tempts us to choose comfort over freedom, even when that comfort comes with chains.

MOSES: A CHALLENGER, NOT A RESCUER

When the Creator called Moses to lead His people out of Egypt, He wasn't sending a rescuer to fix their situation. Moses was a challenger and coach, inviting the Israelites into partnership and participation. Every step of their liberation required their active decision to trust and act.

This is vividly demonstrated in the Passover. The Israelites had to choose to follow Moses' instructions—to sacrifice a lamb, mark their doorposts with its blood, and eat the meal in readiness to leave. The blood wasn't about appeasement or payment to the Creator. It was a symbol of trust, an outward act that aligned their hearts with the Creator's promise of deliverance.

The lamb's death wasn't for the Creator's satisfaction; it was a consequence of human choices. Dependency and bondage—whether physical or spiritual—carry brutal consequences. When we live disconnected and in judgment, the ripple effects of our actions often harm the innocent. This truth reverberates throughout the human story, from the garden to Egypt and beyond. It's not about the Creator demanding payment but about the natural consequences of our disconnection.

FREEDOM REQUIRES TRUST AND ACTION

The Creator's plan for the Israelites didn't stop at their liberation from Egypt. Freedom wasn't a destination—it was a journey of transformation. Leaving Egypt was only the beginning. The Israelites had to step out of their victim mindset and into the responsibility of empowered living.

This journey is exemplified in the wilderness. The Creator didn't hand everything to the Israelites on a silver platter, nor did He promote dependency on Him. Instead, He provided opportunities for trust and connected self-reliance:

- **Manna in the wilderness:** The Creator provided manna six days a week, but the Israelites had to collect it themselves. They couldn't hoard it or rely on yesterday's supply—they had to trust that it would come each day.
- **Water in the desert:** The Creator led them to water, but they had to follow, walk, and drink.
- **Guidance by cloud and fire:** The Creator showed them the way, but they had to move when He moved and camp when He stopped.

These acts weren't about fostering dependence but about building trust and resilience. The Creator was teaching them how to live in connected self-reliance—trusting in His provision while taking responsibility for their own actions.

THE COST OF JUDGMENT AND DISCONNECTION

The story of the Exodus also highlights the devastating effects of judgment and disconnection. Just as Adam and Eve's judgment in the garden led to shame and separation, the Israelites' judgment—of themselves, the Creator, and their circumstances—often created unnecessary suffering.

The blood of the lamb during Passover foreshadowed this truth. The lamb wasn't sacrificed to appease an angry God but as a symbol of trust and a reminder of the cost of judgment and disconnection. When we place ourselves in bondage, whether to dependency, fear, or false beliefs, the innocent often bear the consequences.

This isn't just a theological concept—it's a deeply human reality. In my own life, I've seen how judgment and disconnection create harm, both for myself and others. When I've judged others unfairly, it's led to real, undeserved consequences for them. And when others have judged me, it's caused harm and injury that was unjust. The story of the Exodus reminds us that judgment and disconnection carry a heavy price, one that often affects the most vulnerable among us.

THE INVITATION TO EMPOWERED FAITH

The Exodus isn't just a story of liberation—it's a story of transformation. It shows us that the Creator's goal isn't to rescue us from hard things but to empower us to face them with trust and courage. The Israelites weren't passive recipients of deliverance—they were active participants in their own liberation. From marking their doors during Passover to walking through the Red Sea, they had to trust the Creator and take action.

This pattern continues in the wilderness. The Creator's provision was consistent, but it required their participation. He provided manna, but they had to collect it. He led them to water, but they had to drink. He guided them by cloud and fire, but they had to follow. Every step was an invitation to trust, act, and grow in connected self-reliance.

FROM EGYPT TO THE PROMISE

The journey from Egypt to the Promised Land is a powerful metaphor for the human journey from disconnected self-defeat to connected self-reliance. The Creator's goal wasn't just to free the Israelites from physical bondage—it was to transform their hearts and minds, to teach them how to live as empowered, connected people.

The wilderness was a crucible for this transformation. It was a place where the Israelites had to confront their dependency, face their fears, and learn to trust the Creator in new ways. It wasn't easy, and they often stumbled. But each challenge was an opportunity to grow, to shed their victim mindset, and to step into the freedom the Creator had always intended for them.

REFLECTION: THE JOURNEY OF EMPOWERMENT

The Exodus invites us to consider our own journeys. Where are we living in bondage to dependency, fear, or false beliefs? How can we step into the trust and action required for true freedom? The Creator's invitation is the same today as it was then: to leave behind the familiar comforts of bondage and step into the uncertainty of empowerment, knowing that His love and provision are constant.

In the next chapter, we'll explore how the Creator continued to shape the Israelites' identity through the giving of the law, establishing a framework for living in connection and empowerment. For now, let the story of the Exodus remind us that freedom isn't about avoiding hardship—it's about engaging with life in partnership with the Creator, trusting in His provision, and embracing the responsibility of empowered living.

SVEN MASTERSON

COMMON RESPONSES

"Yeah, but isn't dependency on God the point of faith?"

This can be a nuanced discussion because 'dependency' can mean many things. Dependency on the Creator, in the sense of trust, is crucial. But the dependency the Israelites experienced in Egypt wasn't trust—it was bondage, a surrender of their agency and identity. They wanted to be free from that bondage but without faith, action, challenge, adversity, hardship, or participation. They wanted rescue. The Creator invites us into partnership, not passive dependency. Faith isn't about sitting back and waiting; it's about trusting His provision while actively engaging in the life He's called us to build.

"Yeah, but why did the Creator make freedom so hard for the Israelites?"

Freedom isn't just about physical liberation—it's about transforming the heart and mind. The wilderness wasn't a punishment; it was a place of preparation. The Creator used those challenges to teach the Israelites trust, resilience, and how to live as empowered people. True freedom requires growth, and growth often comes through difficulty.

"Yeah, but doesn't the Passover lamb suggest the Creator demands sacrifice?"

When our theology is derived from Satisfaction Theory and Penal Substitutionary Atonement, we project this into the text. Yet the scriptures say in numerous places that the Creator neither needs these nor takes pleasure in them (1 Samuel 15:22, Jeremiah 7:21-23, Proverbs 21:3,

WHAT TO DO WHEN THE ALIENS SHOW UP (AND EVEN IF THEY DON'T)

Amos 5:21-24, Hosea 6:6, Matthew 9:13, Matthew 12:7, Hebrews 10:5-6, Mark 12:33).

The blood of the lamb wasn't about appeasing the Creator but about trust. It symbolized alignment with His protection and an outward expression of faith. All the gods worshipped by others have demanded sacrifices (drama triangle) from their worshippers. The God of Abraham, Isaac, and Jacob is unique in that he does not. The Creator doesn't demand sacrifices to love us. He provides opportunities to demonstrate trust and participate in His promises.

"Yeah, but why didn't the Creator just rescue them instantly?"

Instant rescue might free the body, but it doesn't transform the heart or mind. It leaves the rescued in a state of disempowered victimhood. The Creator's goal wasn't just to liberate the Israelites but to teach them how to live as free and empowered people. Transformation takes time and often involves learning through participation and action.

"Yeah, but what if I'm stuck in my own version of Egypt—what if I can't leave?"

Leaving doesn't always mean a physical departure—it begins with a change in mindset. The Creator's invitation is to start where you are, taking small steps of trust and action. Liberation is a process, and each choice to trust, act, and align with His love moves you closer to freedom.

CHAPTER FORTY-EIGHT
MINISTRY OF LIFE
RESTORING DIGNITY AND FREEDOM THROUGH THE LAW

The law of the Lord is perfect, refreshing the soul. The statutes of the Lord are trustworthy, making wise the simple.
– Psalm 19:7

GROWING UP, THE TEN COMMANDMENTS WERE PRESENTED TO ME AS A list of rules that held cosmic consequences. They were etched in stone by the Creator's hand, thundered from Mount Sinai, and carried the weight of eternal judgment. Breaking them, I was told, would invoke the wrath of an angry deity, and my only hope was to cling to grace as a flawed, undeserving recipient of love.

For years, I approached the commandments through the lens of the **Drama Triangle**:

- The **Creator was the Persecutor**, setting impossible standards that revealed my unworthiness.
- I was the perpetual **Victim**, powerless to fulfill these laws on my own.
- **Jesus became the Rescuer**, stepping in to shield me

from the Creator's wrath and secure my place in eternity.

This framing left me anxious, insecure, and judgmental—not just of myself but of others. I believed I was unworthy of love unless I performed, and I held others to the same rigid expectations. If I could suffer guilt and shame to keep the rules, why couldn't they? The Ten Commandments became a symbol of condemnation, a list that proved my inadequacy rather than a guide to living a life of connection, love, and empowerment.

THE CREATOR'S INVITATION: FROM BONDAGE TO FREEDOM

Egypt: A Culture of Bondage

To understand the commandments' significance, we must first grasp the oppressive culture of Egypt, where the Israelites had been enslaved for generations. Egypt wasn't just a place of physical bondage; it represented a way of life that was antithetical to the flourishing and freedom the Creator desired for humanity.

- **Exploitation Over Dignity:** In Egypt, the Israelites' worth was tied solely to their productivity. They were bricks without names, laborers without identities, and reduced to tools for Pharaoh's ambitions.
- **Dependency Over Self-Reliance:** The Israelites initially came to Egypt seeking famine relief—a temporary dependency. But as they remained, this dependency deepened, replacing the freedom of Abraham's covenantal relationship with Pharaoh's provision. Dependency became bondage, stripping them of agency and connection to their Creator.
- **Disconnection Over Intimacy:** Generations in Egypt eroded the Israelites' connection to their heritage. They

forgot their role as heirs of Abraham's promise and lost sight of the Creator's call to partnership.

The Ten Commandments, given after their deliverance, weren't arbitrary rules. They were a stark contrast to the culture of bondage they had known. Each commandment was an invitation to reclaim their dignity, self-reliance, and connection.

THE TEN COMMANDMENTS: AN EMPOWERING BLUEPRINT

Unlike the oppressive demands of Egypt, the commandments offered clarity and simplicity. They pointed the Israelites toward a way of living that was not only sustainable but flourishing. Let's explore each commandment as an invitation to empowerment:

1. No Other Gods

- **Egyptian Context:** Pharaoh and the pantheon of Egyptian deities demanded loyalty. Worship was transactional, a way to appease forces believed to control their fate.
- **Empowerment Dynamic:** The Creator invited the Israelites to trust Him alone—a constant, unchanging source of love and provision. This was not a demand for obedience but an invitation to step out of fear-based worship and into a relationship rooted in trust.

2. No Idols

- **Egyptian Context:** Egypt was filled with tangible symbols of power—statues, monuments, and images that people trusted for protection and prosperity.
- **Empowerment Dynamic:** This commandment invited the Israelites to recognize the Creator's presence within

them, freeing them from dependence on external symbols for validation.

3. Honor the Creator's Name

- **Egyptian Context:** Invoking the names of gods in Egypt was often a tool for manipulation or self-advancement.
- **Empowerment Dynamic:** Honoring the Creator's name meant living with integrity, reflecting His love and truth in every action and word.

4. Remember the Sabbath

- **Egyptian Context:** Slaves in Egypt knew no rest. Their worth was tied to unending labor.
- **Empowerment Dynamic:** The Sabbath was a revolutionary gift, reminding the Israelites that their value was inherent, not tied to productivity. Rest was an act of trust, affirming that the Creator's provision was enough.

5. Honor Your Parents

- **Egyptian Context:** Family structures in Egypt were often strained under the weight of slavery.
- **Empowerment Dynamic:** Honoring parents reconnected the Israelites to their heritage, fostering reconciliation and breaking cycles of shame and blame.

6. Do Not Murder

- **Egyptian Context:** Life was cheap in Egypt, where power often determined worth.
- **Empowerment Dynamic:** This commandment affirmed

the sacredness of life, calling the Israelites to resolve conflict through love and understanding.

7. Do Not Commit Adultery

- **Egyptian Context:** Egypt's culture often devalued marital fidelity, leading to fractured relationships.
- **Empowerment Dynamic:** This commandment invited the Israelites to honor their commitments, cultivating intimacy and trust.

8. Do Not Steal

- **Egyptian Context:** Scarcity and inequality in Egypt bred theft and corruption.
- **Empowerment Dynamic:** This commandment encouraged trust in the Creator's provision and alignment with honesty and fairness.

9. Do Not Bear False Witness

- **Egyptian Context:** Lies and deceit were common tools of survival in an oppressive society.
- **Empowerment Dynamic:** Speaking truth fostered authenticity and built relationships based on trust and mutual respect.

10. Do Not Covet

- **Egyptian Context:** In a society of haves and have-nots, envy was a natural consequence.
- **Empowerment Dynamic:** This commandment encouraged gratitude and contentment, freeing the Israelites from the toxic cycle of comparison.

NOT ABOUT SALVATION, BUT PARTNERSHIP

The Ten Commandments were never about earning salvation. The Creator's love and acceptance were already theirs. Instead, the commandments offered a way to live in freedom and alignment—a guide for how to flourish as a people in partnership with the Creator.

- **Restoration of Agency**: The commandments returned to the Israelites what Egypt had stripped away: the ability to choose a path of love, truth, and connection.
- **Preparation for Partnership**: The Creator wasn't demanding perfection but inviting collaboration. The commandments outlined what it looked like to live as a people who could embody and extend His redemptive purposes to the world.

THE COMMANDMENTS AS A MIRROR

Over time, I've come to see the commandments not as a source of shame but as a mirror. When I deviate from these principles, they reveal where I've drifted from connection—not to condemn me, but to guide me back. They act as rumble strips on the road of life, reminding me when I've veered off course.

MINISTRY OF DEATH?

One of the most perplexing aspects of my journey was reconciling the idea that the Torah—the Creator's teachings and instructions—was somehow flawed, defunct, or even a "ministry of death," as some interpretations of the New Testament claim. Growing up, I was taught that the Torah was burdensome and impossible to keep and that it existed to show humanity its need for salvation. Yeshua, I was told, came to "fulfill the law" by abolishing it, freeing us from its oppressive yoke. But as I began revisiting the scriptures with fresh eyes, I realized how inconsistent this perspective was with both the Torah itself and Yeshua's teachings.

WHAT DOES THE TORAH SAY ABOUT ITSELF?

The Torah consistently describes itself in terms that are anything but burdensome or flawed. Here are just a few examples:

- **Perfect and Life-Giving**: "The law of the Lord is perfect, refreshing the soul" (Psalm 19:7). Far from being a source of death, the Torah is described as restorative and life-giving.
- **A Delight**: "Your statutes are my delight; they are my counselors" (Psalm 119:24). The psalmist revels in the Creator's teachings as a source of joy and guidance.
- **A Path to Wisdom**: "The commandment of the Lord is pure, enlightening the eyes" (Psalm 19:8). The Torah offers clarity and understanding, not confusion or condemnation.

These descriptions reflect the Creator's intentions for the Torah: not as a punishment or burden, but as a means to guide humanity into flourishing, connection, and empowerment.

THE "MINISTRY OF DEATH" MISUNDERSTANDING

The phrase "ministry of death" comes from 2 Corinthians 3:7, where Paul contrasts the "letter" of the law with the Spirit. This verse has often been taken to mean that the Torah is inherently harmful or obsolete, but such an interpretation doesn't align with the broader scriptural narrative. Instead, Paul appears to be addressing a specific misuse of the Torah—one that emphasizes rigid adherence to rules as a means of earning righteousness while neglecting the transformative power of the Creator's Spirit.

The problem wasn't the Torah itself; it was how people

approached it. When the commandments are viewed as a checklist to prove our worth, they do indeed bring death—not because they are flawed, but because they expose the futility of trying to earn connection through performance. This is consistent with Paul's broader teaching: the law reveals where we fall short, but its purpose is to guide us back to the Creator, who empowers us to live in alignment with His principles.

THE TEST OF DEUTERONOMY 13

The Torah itself provides a clear standard for discerning the validity of any teaching or prophetic message: If someone claims to speak for the Creator but encourages disobedience to His commandments, they are not to be trusted (Deuteronomy 13:1-5).

This passage underscores the enduring validity of the Torah. It would be nonsensical for the Creator to declare His instructions eternal and then send a prophet or Messiah to nullify them. By its own criteria, the Torah cannot contradict itself. This test, foundational to the Jewish understanding of scripture, reveals a major flaw in the common Christian narrative that pits Yeshua against the Torah.

If Yeshua had come to abolish the law, He would have failed the Deuteronomy 13 test and could not be the Messiah. Instead, Yeshua affirmed the Torah's ongoing significance, declaring, "Do not think that I came to abolish the Law or the Prophets; I did not come to abolish but to fulfill" (Matthew 5:17). To fulfill is not to abolish but to bring to its fullest expression—a life lived in alignment with the Creator's wisdom and love.

THE TORAH AS A GIFT, NOT A CURSE

Another common misunderstanding stems from Galatians 3:13, which says, "Christ redeemed us from the curse of the law." Some interpret this to mean that the law itself is a curse, but this misses the point. The "curse" Paul refers to is not the Torah—it's the consequences of disobedience. The Torah outlines blessings for those who live in alignment with its principles and consequences for those who don't (Deuteronomy 28). The Torah is not the curse; it simply reveals the natural outcomes of our choices.

Yeshua's redemptive work doesn't nullify the Torah; it empowers us to live in harmony with it, free from the bondage of shame, fear, and disconnection. He doesn't rescue us from the Creator's teachings; he invites us back into alignment with them, showing us how to walk in their wisdom and love.

THE LAW AS A PATHWAY TO EMPOWERMENT

The Ten Commandments—and the Torah as a whole—are not relics of a bygone era, nor are they burdens to be discarded. They are a gift, offering timeless guidance for living in connection with the Creator, ourselves, and one another. Misunderstandings about the Torah's role have led many to reject its wisdom, but when seen through the lens of empowerment, the commandments reveal themselves as a roadmap to flourishing.

The Torah was never about earning salvation or proving worth; it was, and is, about partnership. It equips us to live in alignment with the Creator's purposes, not as passive recipients of grace, but as active participants in His redemptive plan. Far from being a "ministry of death," the Torah is a ministry of life—a mirror that reflects the Creator's character and calls us to live as His image-bearers in the world.

Let us step into this partnership with gratitude, embracing the commandments not as constraints but as pathways to freedom, love, and empowerment.

SVEN MASTERSON

COMMON RESPONSES

"Yeah, but weren't the Ten Commandments impossible to keep? Isn't that the point—to show us our failure?"

The commandments weren't designed to trap us in guilt or expose our failure. Instead, they serve as a guide to living a life of connection and flourishing. While no one is perfect, the commandments point us toward alignment with the Creator's love and values. They show us where we've veered off course and invite us back, not to condemn but to guide. No, they aren't impossible to keep and not really all that hard to keep, come to think of it.

"Yeah, but didn't Yeshua come to do away with the law? Why should we care about the commandments now?"

Yeshua didn't come to abolish the Torah; He came to fulfill it. Fulfillment means living out its deepest purpose—to guide us in loving the Creator and each other. Rather than discarding the commandments, Yeshua showed us how to embody their principles in our daily lives, making them a pathway to love and connection.

"Yeah, but isn't the Torah called a 'ministry of death'? Doesn't that mean it's harmful?"

The phrase "ministry of death" in 2 Corinthians refers to a misuse of the law as a rigid system for earning righteousness. In Psalm 19, the Torah is described as "perfect" and "refreshing the soul." When approached as a guide to connection and flourishing rather than a checklist for worthiness, the Torah brings life, not death.

"Yeah, but doesn't Galatians say the law is a curse? Why follow it at all?"

WHAT TO DO WHEN THE ALIENS SHOW UP (AND EVEN IF THEY DON'T)

Paul's reference to the "curse of the law" isn't about the Torah itself but the consequences of disobedience. The Torah outlines blessings for alignment and consequences for disconnection. Yeshua's work doesn't abolish the Torah—it redeems us from the weight of disconnection and empowers us to live in harmony with its principles. If Paul really did believe the Torah or Law of Moses to be a curse, he differs from Yeshua and The Creator, and per the Creator's instructions in Deuteronomy 13, should not be followed.

"Yeah, but doesn't focusing on commandments lead to legalism?"

Legalism happens when we reduce the Torah to a rigid set of rules for earning approval. The commandments, however, are relational—they guide us in loving the Creator, ourselves, and others. They're not about performance; they're about living in alignment with the Creator's design for flourishing. I'd suggest that a Victim trying to earn the favor of a Persecutor through perfect understanding, doctrine, belief, and behaviors is about as legalistic as one can get.

CHAPTER FORTY-NINE
THE RADICAL REST
FINDING FREEDOM FROM SHAME, STRIVING, AND ENDLESS TO-DO LISTS

> All of humanity's problems stem from man's inability to sit quietly in a room alone. – Blaise Pascal

---

I MENTIONED EARLIER HOW A SHIFT IN MY UNDERSTANDING OF THE Sabbath led to our setting aside Sunday church service attendance, which caused quite a bit of upheaval. You might have wondered if it was worth it and if we'd do it again. You may also have wondered if we had joined a specific sect of Christianity that caused this. Yes, we would do it all again. No, we did not join any group that has this tradition.

Growing up, the Sabbath was a concept I heard about but rarely saw practiced in any meaningful way, other than some Christians judging others if they mowed their lawn or went to work on Sunday. It was generally taught that honoring the sabbath men attending Sunday church services and that the day was to be filled with church activity, responsibilities, and the same pressures as the rest of the week, albeit with a religious veneer.

The idea that the Sabbath could be transformative or even relevant to my daily life felt distant. It seemed like an outdated relic, something for ancient Israelites, not modern believers. But as I began to rediscover the richness of the Torah, I found myself drawn to it in ways I never expected.

What I've come to understand is that the Sabbath isn't just a day of rest—it's a profound, multi-layered practice that touches every aspect of our being. It challenges our notions of productivity, value, and identity, inviting us into a rhythm of life that is deeply connected to the Creator, ourselves, and others.

THE FOURTH COMMANDMENT: A COMMAND WITH DEPTH

Among the Ten Commandments, the instruction to observe the Sabbath stands out for its depth and detail. While other commandments are stated succinctly, the Sabbath commandment is expanded upon:

> "Remember the Sabbath day, to keep it holy. Six days you shall labor and do all your work, but the seventh day is a Sabbath to the Lord your God. On it, you shall not do any work... For in six days the Lord made the heavens and the earth, the sea, and all that is in them, but He rested on the seventh day. Therefore, the Lord blessed the Sabbath day and made it holy" (Exodus 20:8-11).

This isn't just a prohibition against work—it's an invitation to participate in a divine rhythm of creation and rest. It reminds us that we are not defined by our productivity and connects us to the Creator's rest after the work of creation.

THE SABBATH: A RADICAL CONTRAST TO EGYPT

For the Israelites, the Sabbath would have been a revolutionary concept. In Egypt, they had lived as slaves, defined entirely by their labor. They worked endlessly under the oppressive hand of Pharaoh, with no rest, no autonomy, and no sense of worth beyond their ability to produce. Their value was tied to what they could build, carry, and harvest.

The Sabbath turned this reality on its head. By commanding a day of rest, the Creator declared that their value was intrinsic, not tied to their output. This was more than a break from work—it was a declaration of freedom and dignity. No longer would they be slaves to production; they were invited to rest as an act of trust and connection.

The Sabbath wasn't just a gift—it was a sign of the covenant between the Creator and His people. It set them apart as a nation that lived in alignment with divine wisdom, rejecting the endless striving and dependency they had experienced in Egypt.

MY JOURNEY TO SABBATH REST

When I first began exploring the Sabbath, it wasn't out of a deep spiritual conviction—it was more like curiosity. I had grown up dismissing it as a relic of the Old Testament, something that Christians were no longer "bound" to observe. But as I dug deeper into the Torah, I started to wonder: if the Creator gave this day as a gift, why had I so easily dismissed it?

At first, observing the Sabbath felt awkward. I was a driven, ambitious person, always moving, always doing. The idea of setting aside an entire day to rest felt counterproductive, even indulgent. But as I leaned into the practice, something began to change. The Sabbath became a space where I could let go of striving and simply be. It was a day to stop, to breathe, to reconnect with the Creator and with myself.

THE MULTI-DIMENSIONAL MEANING OF THE SABBATH

As I continued to practice the Sabbath, I began to see its layers of meaning unfold:

1. **Rest for the Body and Mind:** On the surface, the Sabbath is a day to cease from labor. But it's not just about physical rest—it's about mental and emotional renewal. It's a reminder that our worth isn't tied to our work and that rest is a sacred act of trust.
2. **Freedom from Compulsion:** The Sabbath is an opportunity to step away from the "ought to's" and "have to's" that dominate our lives. It's a day to break free from the tyranny of productivity and to simply be present.
3. **A Weekly Reset:** The Sabbath is like a reset button for the soul. It's a chance to pause, reflect, and realign with what truly matters. In a world that constantly pulls us in a thousand directions, the Sabbath anchors us in the Creator's rhythm.
4. **A Foreshadowing of Eternity:** The Sabbath points to something greater—a future reality where rest and renewal are not just weekly experiences but eternal truths. It's a glimpse of the restored connection and peace that the Creator intends for all of creation.

MY TRANSFORMATION THROUGH THE SABBATH

One of the most profound shifts in my life came when I began to embrace the Sabbath not just as a commandment but as a gift. It wasn't easy—I had spent years measuring my worth by what I accomplished. Taking a day to rest felt like a loss of control, a vulnerability I wasn't sure I could handle. But in that vulnerability, I found something unexpected: freedom.

The Sabbath taught me to trust the Creator in ways I never had before. It showed me that I didn't have to earn His love or prove my worth. It allowed me to experience His constant presence and provision in a tangible way. And as I entered into this rhythm of rest, I began to feel the weight of shame and striving lift. I was no longer a slave to the demands of the world or my own perfectionism. I was free to simply be.

THE CREATOR'S WISDOM IN THE SABBATH

The more I practice the Sabbath, the more I see the Creator's wisdom in this commandment. He doesn't demand rest because He needs us to acknowledge Him—He invites rest because *we* need it. In a world that constantly demands more, the Sabbath is a radical act of defiance. It says, "I am enough. I have enough. The Creator's love is enough."

The Sabbath also reveals the Creator's character. He is not a taskmaster, demanding endless labor; He is a loving guide, inviting us into rhythms that restore and empower. The Sabbath isn't about restriction—it's about flourishing.

> The Sabbath became more than just a day for me—it became a turning point in my journey of healing and self-discovery. For years, I struggled with shame and a deep sense of inadequacy. I could argue theologically about my worth, but I didn't feel it. I was constantly striving, always trying to prove myself.
>
> When I began practicing the Sabbath, something shifted. It forced me to confront my compulsions and my fear of stillness. At first, I resisted. But over time, I began to see the Sabbath as a mirror, reflecting the areas of my life where I was still striving for validation. And as I let go of those compulsions, I began to experience a profound sense of peace.
>
> It was through the Sabbath that I finally began to internalize the truth of my worth, not in a theoretical way, but in a deep, soul-level way. The practice of stopping, of resting, of being present allowed me to feel the Creator's love in a way I never had before.

SVEN MASTERSON

THE SABBATH AS A GIFT

The Sabbath isn't just a commandment—it's a gift. It's an invitation to step out of the cycle of striving and into a rhythm of rest and renewal. It's a day to reconnect with the Creator, to celebrate His provision, and to remember that we are not defined by what we do but by who we are: loved, whole, and enough.

In a world that demands constant performance, the Sabbath reminds us to stop, breathe, and trust. It's a practice that grounds us in the truth of the Creator's love and equips us to live empowered, connected lives. Whether we see it as a day of rest, a weekly reset, or a glimpse of eternity, the Sabbath reminds us of who we are and who the Creator is—a loving guide who invites us to flourish in His rhythm.

COMMON RESPONSES

> "Yeah, but isn't the Sabbath just an Old Testament thing? Christians don't need to follow it."

The Sabbath isn't about legalism or obligation; it's a timeless gift that transcends covenants. The Creator designed it for humanity's benefit, not as a burden but as a blessing. Even Yeshua affirmed the Sabbath's purpose as a day of rest and renewal, not a restrictive rule. It's less about "needing" to follow it and more about receiving its gift.

> "Yeah, but I'm too busy to take an entire day off. My responsibilities won't wait."

The Sabbath challenges the culture of busyness by reminding us that our worth isn't tied to productivity. Taking a day to rest doesn't mean

WHAT TO DO WHEN THE ALIENS SHOW UP (AND EVEN IF THEY DON'T)

neglecting responsibilities—it means trusting the Creator's provision and prioritizing what truly matters. It's a radical act of self-care and trust in a world that glorifies overwork.

"Yeah, but won't resting make me fall behind? The world doesn't stop for a Sabbath."

The Creator's rhythm is countercultural, but it's also freeing. The Sabbath invites us to step out of the relentless pace of the world and into a rhythm that restores. Paradoxically, rest often leads to greater clarity, creativity, and energy for the tasks ahead. Trusting the Creator's design allows us to flourish, even when it feels counterintuitive.

"Yeah, but isn't resting selfish? Shouldn't I be serving others instead of focusing on myself?"

Rest isn't selfish—it's essential. The Sabbath equips us to serve from a place of abundance rather than exhaustion. By taking time to renew, we become more present and effective in our relationships and work. The Sabbath models a balance of giving and receiving, reminding us that we can't pour from an empty cup.

"Yeah, but I wouldn't even know how to 'do' a Sabbath. What if I get it wrong?"

There's no "wrong" way to observe the Sabbath—it's about finding what nourishes your soul and aligns with the Creator's invitation to rest. Start small: set aside time to pause, reflect, and reconnect with what matters. The Sabbath isn't a rigid formula; it's a gift meant to be explored and enjoyed.

CHAPTER FIFTY
THE SECOND ADAM

YESHUA'S LIFE AS THE EMBODIMENT OF CONNECTION, LOVE, AND FREEDOM

In Him was life, and that life was the light of all mankind. - John 1:4

YESHUA: THE EMBODIMENT OF THE CREATOR'S WISDOM AND MISSION

GROWING UP, I WAS TAUGHT TO SEE JESUS AS SOMEONE WHO CAME TO replace what didn't work—as if the Creator's commandments were flawed and Yeshua's role was to toss them aside. But as I dug deeper, I realized this view didn't just mischaracterize Yeshua's mission—it diminished the profound beauty of His life and disconnected Him from the Creator's timeless wisdom.

Yeshua didn't come to abolish the Creator's guidance; He came to embody it. He came to show us what alignment with the Creator looks like—what it means to live fully, freely, and connected to the source of life.

"Yeshua," which means "salvation," wasn't just His name—it was His mission. He came to restore what was lost in the garden, to confront the lies that keep us bound in fear, shame, and judgment, and to invite us into the Creator's kingdom—a place of flourishing, empowerment, and abundant life.

THE DEUTERONOMY 13 TEST: AUTHENTICITY OF A PROPHET

In understanding Yeshua's mission, it's essential to recognize how the Torah itself provides a test for authenticity. Deuteronomy 13 warns against prophets or dreamers who may perform signs or wonders but lead people away from the Creator's commandments:

> *If a prophet or a dreamer of dreams arises among you and gives you a sign or a wonder, and the sign or wonder that he tells you comes to pass, and if he says, 'Let us go after other gods,' which you have not known, and let us serve them, you shall not listen to the words of that prophet or that dreamer of dreams.*
> –Deuteronomy 13:1-3, ESV

The test is clear: no matter how impressive or persuasive a figure might be, if they lead people away from the Creator's commandments, they are not from Him. This test underscores the Creator's unwavering commitment to His Torah as the foundation of truth and connection.

Yeshua passes this test perfectly. Far from leading people away from the Torah, He affirmed and embodied it in every way. He declared:

> *Do not think that I have come to abolish the Law or the Prophets; I have not come to abolish them but to fulfill them.*
> –Matthew 5:17, ESV

Yeshua's teachings, actions, and life consistently pointed people

THE TORAH: A PATH TO WHOLENESS, NOT A BURDEN

back to the Creator's commandments, revealing their deeper purpose and helping people see them as pathways to life rather than burdens.

To grasp Yeshua's mission fully, we have to revisit the Torah—the Creator's teachings and commandments. Too often, the Torah has been misunderstood as an impossible set of rules meant to expose human failure. This view distorts the Creator's intent, reducing His loving guidance to a burden of shame.

But the Torah wasn't given to weigh us down; it was given to show us how to thrive. It's profoundly simple compared to the endless complexity of human legal systems. The commandments are clear, concise, and designed to cultivate connection—with the Creator, with ourselves, and with others.

Even the Torah itself affirms this truth:

> *For this commandment which I am commanding you today is not too difficult for you, nor is it far away... On the contrary, the word is very near you, in your mouth and in your heart, so that you may follow it.*
>
> –Deuteronomy 30:11–14, ESV

The problem isn't with the Torah—it's with the shame-based mindset we often bring to it. Shame twists loving guidance into impossible tasks, making us feel unworthy and incapable. But Yeshua reframed this entirely.

When He declared, *"My yoke is easy, and My burden is light"* (Matthew 11:30, ESV), Yeshua wasn't rejecting the Torah—He was showing us how to live it as it was meant to be lived: from a place of love, trust, and connection. The commandments become not burdens but a natural outpouring of alignment with the Creator's heart.

YESHUA'S MISSION: RESTORING THE HEART OF THE TORAH

This is where Yeshua's mission shines most brilliantly. He didn't come to abolish the Torah but to fulfill it. His life was the perfect embodiment of the Creator's wisdom, showing us the deeper purpose of the commandments:

- To guide us into flourishing.
- To teach us how to love.
- To bring us into connection with the Creator and one another.

Yeshua's teachings clarified and deepened the Torah's principles, shifting the focus from mere external compliance to internal transformation:

- **On murder:** Yeshua said it wasn't just about the act but about the anger and contempt in our hearts (Matthew 5:21–24, ESV).
- **On adultery:** He emphasized purity and faithfulness, not just outward actions but the desires of the heart (Matthew 5:27–28, ESV).

By living the Torah perfectly, Yeshua revealed its true nature: it's not hard when lived through love, but shame and disconnection make it feel impossible. Yeshua's mission was to restore this understanding, freeing us from the lies that distort the Creator's guidance and inviting us to experience the Torah as a path to life.

WHAT TO DO WHEN THE ALIENS SHOW UP (AND EVEN IF THEY DON'T)

THE TORAH AND THE KINGDOM OF GOD

Yeshua proclaimed the kingdom of God as being "at hand" (Mark 1:15, ESV)—not far off, not unattainable, but present and accessible. And at the heart of this kingdom was the Creator's guidance, not as rules to follow but as a way to thrive.

When Yeshua invited people into the kingdom, He wasn't creating something entirely new—He was restoring what had been lost. The Torah, the Creator's teachings, was always meant to be the foundation of this kingdom, a framework for flourishing and connection.

But over time, the Torah had been buried under layers of legalism and distorted by shame. People saw it as a list of demands rather than an invitation to relationship. Yeshua came to strip away those distortions, to show us that the Torah is a gift, not a burden—a way to align with the Creator's love and wisdom.

YESHUA'S INVITATION TO WHOLENESS

Yeshua's mission wasn't to rescue us into passivity or free us from the Creator's guidance. It was to empower us to live in alignment with the Creator's design. Through His life, Yeshua demonstrated that obedience to the Torah isn't about striving—it's about living from a place of trust and connection.

He fulfilled the Torah by living it perfectly, not as a rigid set of rules but as a natural expression of love, freedom, and authenticity. His invitation to follow Him is an invitation to live this way too:

- To see the commandments not as obligations but as opportunities.
- To leave behind shame and embrace love.
- To align with the Creator's wisdom and flourish in His kingdom.

Yeshua didn't come to replace the Torah—He came to restore its heart. He showed us that the Creator's guidance is not an impossible burden but a path to life and wholeness. And in doing so, He revealed the Creator's love in its purest form: a love that empowers, restores, and invites us into abundant life.

THE KINGDOM PROCLAIMED: A CALL TO FLOURISHING

Yeshua's first proclamation set the tone for His entire mission:

> *The time is fulfilled, and the kingdom of God is at hand; repent and believe in the gospel.*
> —Mark 1:15

The kingdom of God wasn't some far-off future reality—it was here, now, breaking into the world through Yeshua. This wasn't a kingdom of earthly power or domination. It was a kingdom where love triumphed over fear, where the lost were found, and where the least were raised up.

Yeshua proclaimed a message of freedom:

- Freedom from shame.
- Freedom from fear.
- Freedom from the lies that tell us we're unworthy or incomplete.

He declared that the Creator's kingdom isn't for the perfect but for the broken, the humble, and the seeking. He told the poor in spirit that they were blessed, the meek that they would inherit the earth, and the peacemakers that they were children of God (Matthew 5:3-9).

Yeshua invited everyone into this kingdom—not by earning it, but by turning toward it. His message wasn't about condemnation but about restoration, about leaving behind the patterns of

THE FIRST AND SECOND ADAM: TWO RESPONSES TO THE SAME LIE

To understand Yeshua's mission fully, we must see Him in contrast to Adam, as Paul explains in Romans 5:

> *For as by the one man's disobedience the many were made sinners, so by the one man's obedience the many will be made righteous.*
> –Romans 5:19

Through Adam, disobedience, shame, and separation entered the world. Through Yeshua, obedience, grace, and reconciliation became available to all.

Adam's choice to believe the serpent's lie introduced a cycle of striving and disconnection. He believed the Creator's love wasn't enough, that he needed something more to be "like God." This choice brought death—not because the Creator punished him, but because disconnection from the source of life inevitably leads to death.

Yeshua, the Second Adam, faced the same fundamental lie. In the wilderness, after 40 days of fasting, the enemy tempted Him with three distortions:

1. **Hunger as Lack:**
   - The tempter said, *"If You are the Son of God, command these stones to become bread."*
   - Yeshua rejected the lie, saying, *"Man shall not live by bread alone, but by every word that comes from the mouth of God."* (Matthew 4:4)
2. **Power as Validation:**

- The tempter offered Him all the kingdoms of the world: *"I will give You all these, if You fall down and worship me."*
- Yeshua refused, declaring, *"You shall worship the Lord your God, and Him only shall you serve."* (Matthew 4:10)

3. Testing Love:
    - The tempter urged Him to throw Himself from the temple to prove the Creator's care. Yeshua answered: *"You shall not put the Lord your God to the test."* (Matthew 4:7)

Unlike Adam, Yeshua rejected the lie of incompleteness at every turn. He trusted fully in the Creator's provision, power, and love, breaking the cycle of shame and disconnection that began in the garden.

FROM DRAMA TRIANGLE TO EMPOWERMENT DYNAMIC

Yeshua's mission also reframed how we see ourselves and our relationships with the Creator and others. Where Adam's choice plunged humanity into the Drama Triangle, Yeshua invited us into the Empowerment Dynamic:

From Victim to Creator:

Adam's disobedience led to a mindset of victimhood—blaming others and feeling powerless. Yeshua showed us how to take ownership of our lives, empowering us to partner with the Creator in bringing restoration.

From Rescuer to Coach:

Yeshua didn't swoop in to "rescue" humanity in the way we often think. Instead, He taught, encouraged, and equipped us to live as empowered co-heirs. He didn't do the work for us—He showed us how to walk in connection with the Creator.

From Persecutor to Challenger:

The Creator doesn't act as a harsh judge or persecutor, as shame tells us. Yeshua revealed the Creator as a compassionate Challenger, calling us to step into our true identity and live in alignment with His love.

> Now listen... I know you might be thinking, "Sheesh, Sven, you're really fixated on this Drama Triangle stuff!" I get it. I really do. And yes—I am absolutely fixated on it. Let me tell you why.
>
> Over the years, I've had the honor of helping men (and others) move from suffering to thriving, recovering from destroyed marriages, deep personal brokenness, devastating losses, and more. The Drama Triangle was, without exception, a key pattern in their suffering.
>
> It was evident in their feeling powerless and stuck, seeing themselves as victims of their circumstances. They also tried to rescue others at their own expense or lashed out as persecutors, convinced they needed to control everything to avoid being hurt again.
>
> But here's the incredible part: every single person I've witnessed find freedom and restoration shared one defining moment. They saw the patterns of the Drama Triangle for what it is—a trap of shame, fear, and disconnection—and they realized they could leave it by choice. Specifically, a choice made in <u>faith</u>—not religious faith, or to be blunt, even faith in Yeshua. Simply a faith that they'd be okay leaving victimhood behind.
>
> They chose to step out of the endless cycles of blame

and into a new way of being. They embraced the role of an empowered creator, taking ownership of their lives and aligning themselves with the Creator's love, truth, and guidance.

This wasn't just a psychological shift. It was spiritual, relational, and deeply transformative. It's why I'm so passionate about this.

In a universe that operates on structures and patterns—patterns that govern everything from the laws of physics to the natural rhythms of life—does it make sense that the story of our redemption would be the single exception to these patterns? I don't think so.

Yeshua's life, death, and resurrection aren't just historical events; they're the Creator's ultimate invitation for us to leave the Drama Triangle behind and step into empowerment. They're the model for how redemption works—not through shame or blame, but through trust, connection, and love. This is why I care so much. It's not just about theology; it's about freedom.

And if I can help even one person see this, it's worth every word I've written here.

THE PROMISES OF YESHUA

Yeshua didn't just proclaim the kingdom—He made promises that transformed what it means to live in connection with the Creator:

Rest for the Weary:
Come to me, all who labor and are heavy laden, and I will give you rest. Take my yoke upon you, and learn from me, for I am gentle and lowly in heart, and you will find rest for your souls. For my yoke is easy, and my burden is light.

WHAT TO DO WHEN THE ALIENS SHOW UP (AND EVEN IF THEY DON'T)

—Matthew 11:28-30

Living Water:
Whoever drinks of the water that I will give him will never be thirsty again. The water that I will give him will become in him a spring of water welling up to eternal life.
—John 4:14

Abundant Life:
I came that they may have life and have it abundantly.
—John 10:10

Yeshua didn't promise an escape from hardship—He promised a life of flourishing through trust, connection, and empowerment.

YESHUA'S MISSION: RESTORING WHAT WAS LOST

Yeshua's mission was to restore what Adam lost: trust, connection, and flourishing. He came to proclaim the kingdom, confront the lies of shame and fear, and invite humanity back into a relationship with the Creator.

He didn't abolish the Creator's commandments but fulfilled them, showing us how to live them as pathways to love and freedom. He didn't rescue us into passivity but empowered us to partner with Him in restoring the world.

Through Yeshua, we see the Creator's heart: a heart that forgives, restores, and invites us to step into abundant life.

COMMON RESPONSES

"Yeah, but isn't Yeshua's mission mostly about saving us from God's wrath?"

That perspective stems from theological developments that began taking shape in the 11th and 12th centuries, particularly with Anselm's view of God as a feudal Lord whose honor required satisfaction. This idea was later expanded during the Reformation, emphasizing God as a judge whose justice demanded Yeshua's sacrifice. However, Yeshua's mission wasn't about appeasing an angry God; it was about restoring humanity to connection with the Creator. He showed us that the Creator's heart has always been one of love, patience, and a desire for relationship. Yeshua's life, death, and resurrection revealed the Creator's relentless pursuit of restoration, not punishment.

"Yeah, but isn't the Torah impossible to follow perfectly?"

It's true that no one follows the Torah flawlessly—but that's not its purpose. The Torah wasn't given as an impossible test; it was a guide to flourishing, connection, and love. Yeshua embodied the Torah not to prove its difficulty but to show how it can be lived out in alignment with the Creator's wisdom. The goal isn't perfection—it's relationship, trust, and growth.

"Yeah, but didn't Paul say the law is a 'ministry of death'?"

Paul's words in 2 Corinthians 3 are often misunderstood. He wasn't calling the Torah flawed or harmful; he was highlighting how shame and a legalistic approach to the Torah distort its purpose. The Torah brings death only when it's approached as a means to earn worth or connection. Yeshua showed us how to live the Torah as it was intended: from a place of love, not striving.

"Yeah, but doesn't 'fulfilling the law' mean replacing it?"

WHAT TO DO WHEN THE ALIENS SHOW UP (AND EVEN IF THEY DON'T)

Not at all. In Matthew 5:17, Yeshua made it clear that He didn't come to abolish the Torah but to fulfill it—to bring it to its fullest expression. He demonstrated how the commandments could be lived out in love and truth, not as a burdensome checklist but as pathways to life. Fulfilling doesn't mean replacing—it means embodying and deepening their intent.

"Yeah, but if Yeshua succeeded where Adam failed, shouldn't we just rely on Him to save us?"

Yeshua's success does invite us to trust Him fully, but it's not about passive reliance. His mission wasn't to rescue us into inaction—it was to empower us to live as co-creators with the Creator. By rejecting the serpent's lies and embodying trust and connection, Yeshua showed us how to do the same. His example invites us to step into an active, flourishing partnership with the Creator.

CHAPTER FIFTY-ONE
FORGIVENESS UNVEILED
A JOURNEY FROM JUDGMENT TO FREEDOM THROUGH YESHUA'S LIFE, DEATH, AND RESURRECTION

> Forgiveness is the fragrance that the violet sheds on the heel that has crushed it. – Mark Twain

---

OVER THE YEARS, MY UNDERSTANDING OF FORGIVENESS HAS profoundly transformed. I grew up believing that forgiveness from the Creator was conditional—dependent on my repentance, confession, or moral behavior. It was taught as a transactional concept: If you repent, then the Creator will forgive your sins; otherwise, *you will die and experience eternal punishment.*

But this perspective never sat well with me. Something about it felt incomplete, even inconsistent with the broader themes of the Creator's character revealed in Scripture. Thirty years ago, when I was training to be a Bible translator and missionary, I began to notice a troubling pattern in how forgiveness was presented. The message often included an *if/then/else* framework: *If you repent, say this prayer, or stop sinning, then your sins will be forgiven.*

It felt like programming code, and after 25 years of writing code, I know conditional logic when I see it. But even before that, this appeared to inject a rigid condition that reduced forgiveness to a mere response to human actions. But the more I studied Scripture, the more this framework unraveled. I came to believe that **the Creator forgives our transgressions unconditionally—whether or not we do anything to earn it.**

I believe this is one of the principal ways, inadvertently and deceptively, that people are kept in bondage to judgment, shame, disconnection, and fear.

THE CREATOR'S FORGIVENESS BEFORE THE CROSS

Forgiveness didn't begin at the cross. As I revisited Scripture, I realized the Creator's forgiving nature has always been present. The cross wasn't the starting point for forgiveness—it was the culmination of a truth that existed from the very beginning.

Genesis: The Garden and Beyond

The story of Adam and Eve in Genesis 3 stood out to me. After they ate from the Tree of Knowledge, they judged themselves, covered themselves with fig leaves, and hid. I expected the Creator to react with wrath or rejection. Instead, His response was relational: *"Where are you?"* (Genesis 3:9).

This moment changed how I saw forgiveness. The Creator didn't abandon them. Instead, He clothed them with garments of skin (Genesis 3:21), an act that symbolized His provision and grace even amidst their disconnection.

The same grace appeared in the story of Cain and Abel. After Cain murdered Abel, the Creator approached him with a question: *"Where is your brother?"* (Genesis 4:9). Even after Cain resisted repentance, the Creator marked him with protection, sparing him from vengeance (Genesis 4:15). These stories revealed a profound truth: **forgiveness and grace flow from the Creator's character, not from humanity's ability to earn them.**

The Psalms and Prophets

WHAT TO DO WHEN THE ALIENS SHOW UP (AND EVEN IF THEY DON'T)

I began seeing the Creator's forgiveness echoed throughout the Psalms and prophets:

Have mercy on me, O God, according to your steadfast love; according to your abundant mercy blot out my transgressions.
  –Psalm 51:1

Though your sins are like scarlet, they shall be as white as snow; though they are red like crimson, they shall become like wool.
  –Isaiah 1:18

Who is a God like you, pardoning iniquity and passing over transgression for the remnant of his inheritance? He does not retain his anger forever, because he delights in steadfast love.
  –Micah 7:18

Jonah and the Forgiveness of Nineveh

Jonah's story challenged me even further. When Jonah reluctantly preached to Nineveh, the people repented, and the Creator spared the city (Jonah 3:10). Jonah's frustration revealed his understanding of the Creator's nature:

I knew that you are a gracious God and merciful, slow to anger and abounding in steadfast love.
  –Jonah 4:2

Forgiveness transcended boundaries. It wasn't tied to Israel's covenant alone—it was extended to all, revealing the Creator's unchanging heart.

SVEN MASTERSON

PROCLAIMING FORGIVENESS BEFORE THE CROSS

Yeshua's ministry further deepened my understanding of forgiveness. He repeatedly proclaimed forgiveness as an already-present reality, not a future possibility.

In Luke 5:20, He forgave the sins of a paralyzed man, saying simply: *"Friend, your sins are forgiven."* No sacrifice. No conditions. This audacious declaration scandalized the religious leaders, but it revealed an eternal truth: **forgiveness is freely given, not earned.**

THE CROSS: HUMANITY'S JUDGMENT OF THE CREATOR

For years, I believed the cross was about satisfying the Creator's wrath. It seemed logical—humanity sinned, the Creator was angry, and someone had to pay the price. But over time, I began to see cracks in this view. That interpretation wasn't born in the first century. It wasn't the understanding of those who walked with Yeshua.

It was the invention of men living as ashamed, Drama-Triangle-bound victims, projecting their own struggles with judgment, blame, and retribution onto the Creator. The *Satisfaction Theory of Atonement*, which depicts the cross as satisfying God's honor or justice, first emerged in the writings of Anselm of Canterbury in the late 11th century (c. 1098). Later, in the 16th century, **Penal Substitutionary Atonement**—the idea that Yeshua was punished to satisfy divine justice—became a central tenet of Reformed theology under John Calvin.

Neither of these theological frameworks appears to have reflected the beliefs of Yeshua's first followers. They were theological constructs shaped by medieval and Reformation-era contexts, worlds obsessed with hierarchy, feudalism, and legal systems of honor and punishment–all structures that quite easily demonstrate drama triangle thinking.

I've come to believe that the cross wasn't about the Creator needing to forgive us—it was about *humanity's judgment of Him.*

We are so entrenched in our shame, fear, and judgment that when the embodiment of unconditional love stood among us, declaring peace, acceptance, and forgiveness, we misinterpreted and misjudged Him in the worst way possible. We called the source of life a liar. We labeled the source of unconditional love a devil. We condemned the very essence of goodness as an evildoer. And then we put Him to death. And The Creator knew all that back in the garden (Genesis 3:15)

YESHUA'S RESPONSE TO HUMANITY'S MISJUDGMENT

Yeshua willingly endured this ultimate act of misjudgment, exposing the lies of shame and fear by walking through mockery, false accusations, and a death sentence. Yet, even in the face of humanity's worst judgment, He didn't retaliate. He didn't condemn. Instead, He revealed the Creator's eternal posture of grace:

> *Father, forgive them, for they know not what they do.*
> –Luke 23:34

This wasn't Yeshua introducing forgiveness. Forgiveness wasn't suddenly granted because of the cross. Forgiveness had always been there. What Yeshua was revealing, in the starkest, most undeniable terms, was the Creator's *unchanging* love, even when humanity judged Him as unworthy of it.

THE CROSS WAS NOT TO SATISFY WRATH—IT WAS TO REVEAL GRACE

The cross wasn't about satisfying the Creator's wrath. The Creator was never in need of being satisfied. The cross was about humanity confronting the reality of its own shame and judgment. It was about demonstrating the truth of what Yehovah told Adam in the garden: *If you take upon yourself the role of deciding good and evil, you will die (and so will your offspring, including my son).*

The death of Yeshua wasn't an act of divine retribution—it was the inevitable outcome of humanity's disconnection from the source of life. It was the natural consequence of a world living under the veil of shame and fear, where judgment and self-righteousness reign.

Everyone dies. Yeshua's death was not unique in that sense—it exposed the human condition. But what makes His death extraordinary is what it reveals: even when humanity is at its worst, even when we commit the ultimate misjudgment, the Creator's love remains steadfast.

A WILLINGNESS TO BE MISUNDERSTOOD

Yeshua's death on the cross demonstrates the Creator's willingness to be misunderstood, misjudged, and even condemned by His own creation. He didn't come to assert power or demand recognition. He came to reveal that unconditional love persists even in the face of the deepest rejection.

The cross wasn't to satisfy the Creator's need for justice. It was to expose the lie of shame and fear—the lie that leads humanity to think we must define good and evil for ourselves. It was to show us that even in our worst moments of judgment, the Creator's posture is still grace, still forgiveness, still love.

Yeshua's prayer, "Forgive them," isn't just for those standing at the foot of the cross—it's a declaration of the Creator's eternal nature. It proclaims that grace is not dependent on our understanding or deserving it—it simply *is*.

A LOVE THAT OVERCOMES ALL SHAME AND DEFIES EVERY CONDITION

What kind of love is this?! A love so vast, so relentless, that it obliterates every boundary we've imagined and every condition we've invented to measure worthiness. Can anything more profound exist to reveal its unconditional nature? What greater proof could we ever demand—or even dream of receiving—that "no conditions" truly means *no conditions*?

This love doesn't falter when we fail. It doesn't retreat when we hide in shame. It doesn't wait for us to become "good enough." It simply *is*.

It is a love that meets us in our deepest brokenness, in the moments we believe we are most unlovable, and declares without hesitation or compromise: *You are enough. You are mine. You are loved.*

But here's the paradox: though this love is freely given, we can't experience its fullness while clinging to the lies that keep us in shame, judgment, and disconnection. Repentance isn't about earning this love—it's about *turning toward it*. It's letting go of the fear that tells us we're unworthy and stepping into the light of this relentless grace.

REPENTANCE: TURNING TOWARD LOVE

Repentance is not about convincing the Creator to forgive or love us—He already does. It's about realignment. It's about turning away from the shame, judgment, and disconnection that keep us from living in the truth of this love.

When we repent, we're not stepping into something new; we're stepping into what's been waiting for us all along. It's the act of saying "no" to the lies that tell us we're unlovable and saying "yes" to the love that has always been ours. Repentance is not groveling or guilt—it's an awakening, a reorientation, and a return to the Creator's embrace.

> And I will give you a new heart, and I will put a new spirit in you. I will take out your stony, stubborn heart and give you a tender, responsive heart. And I will put my Spirit in you so

SVEN MASTERSON

that you will follow my decrees and be careful to obey my regulations*.

–Ezekiel 36:26-27

---

* Our natural, ashamed, disconnected response to "obey my regulations" is to read that through a filter that sees The Creator as Persecutor. Not so fast. The Hebrew word חֻקִּים (chuqqim) in Ezekiel 36:27 is often translated as "statutes," "decrees," or "regulations," depending on the Bible version. However, the term carries a richer meaning than many modern interpretations might suggest. Rather than referring to rigid rules, **chuqqim** denotes enduring principles or divine guidelines designed to foster connection, flourishing, and alignment with the Creator's intended way of life. Translations like "teachings," "ways," or "instructions" may better capture the relational and restorative tone of this passage, particularly in the context of repentance and transformation. This reflects the Creator's intent not as a rule-enforcer but as a guide inviting humanity into a life of thriving and harmony. As one with a new spirit, I've not found one of these "regulations" I've not found really refreshing!

WHAT TO DO WHEN THE ALIENS SHOW UP (AND EVEN IF THEY DON'T)

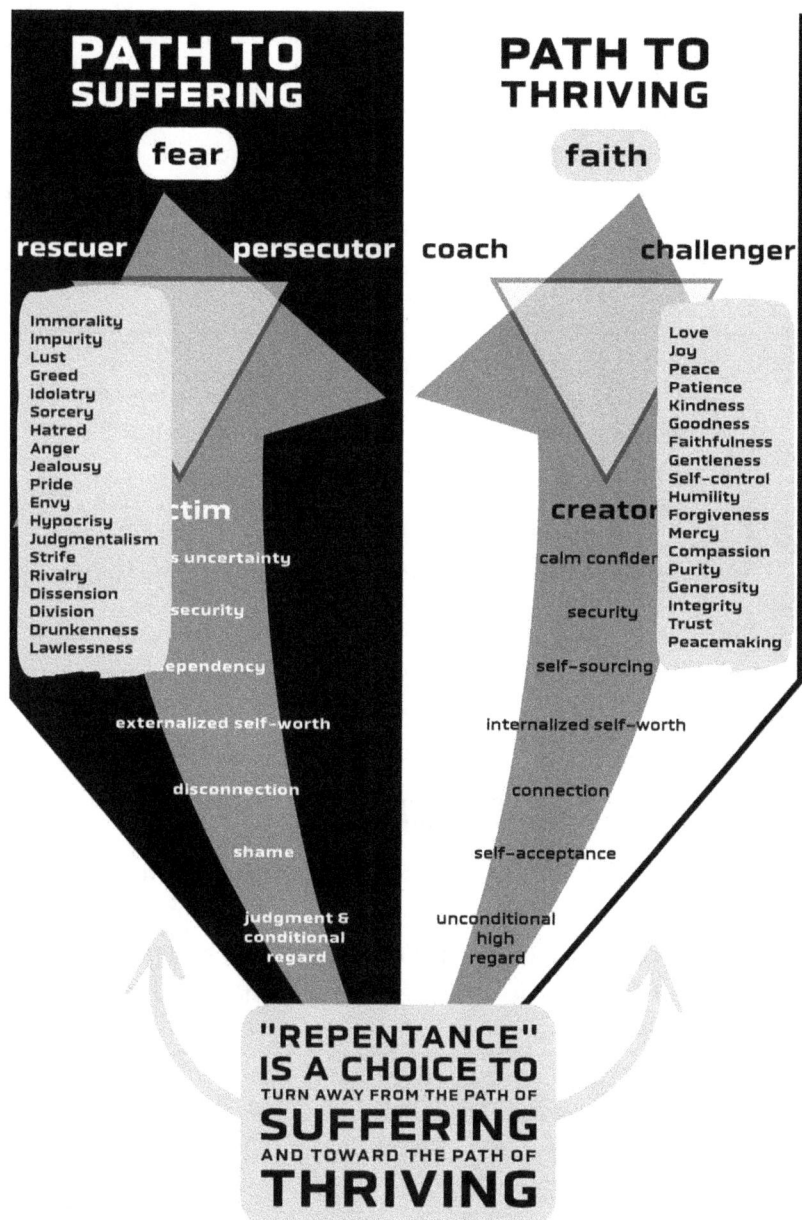

Understanding Repentance: Turning away from the "root" (shame), not merely the "fruit" (behaviors or "sin")

SVEN MASTERSON

FROM SHAME TO ACCEPTANCE

Shame whispers, *You're not enough.* It tells us that our failures define us and that we must hide who we are to be accepted. But repentance is the moment we let go of those lies. It's when we stop running, step out of the shadows, and accept the Creator's invitation to live in the truth of His love.

Come now, let us reason together, says the Lord: though your sins are like scarlet, they shall be as white as snow; though they are red like crimson, they shall become like wool.
—Isaiah 1:18

Repentance is the act of turning away from shame and realizing that we don't need to strive for the Creator's acceptance—it has always been freely given.

FROM HIDING TO VULNERABILITY

Shame drives us to hide—just as Adam and Eve hid in the garden after their disconnection. But repentance calls us to step into the light. It's a return to authenticity, a willingness to be seen as we are, trusting that the Creator's love meets us even in our vulnerability.

Create in me a clean heart, O God, and renew a right spirit within me.
—Psalm 51:10

Repentance breaks the cycle of hiding. It's the decision to be honest, to stop covering ourselves with fig leaves of perfectionism and fear, and to trust the Creator's grace to clothe us with His love.

FROM JUDGMENT TO FAITH

Judgment is a barrier that keeps us from love, whether we judge ourselves, others, or even the Creator. Repentance invites us to abandon the need to control or condemn and instead trust in the Creator's goodness.

It's stepping away from fear and into faith. Faith says *I don't need to prove myself; I trust that the Creator's love is enough.* Faith moves us from striving to rest, from judgment to peace.

The Lord is my shepherd; I shall not want. He makes me lie down in green pastures. He leads me beside still waters. He restores my soul.

—Psalm 23:1-3

THE INVITATION OF LOVE AND REPENTANCE

Repentance is not about earning the Creator's forgiveness—it's about stepping into the fullness of His love. It's the decision to stop living in shame, hiding, and judgment and instead turn toward the light of grace.

This love—the love that defies every condition and overcomes all shame—is already ours. Repentance is simply how we realign with that truth, how we let go of the barriers that hold us back, and how we finally begin to live in the freedom and flourishing that the Creator has always intended for us.

GENESIS 3 AND THE CROSS: FROM FIG LEAVES TO FREEDOM

As I reflected on Genesis 3, I began to see profound parallels between the garden and the cross. In the garden, Adam and Eve covered themselves with fig leaves—symbols of shame, fear, and self-protection. Their judgment of themselves led to hiding, a desperate attempt to mask their disconnection from the Creator.

At the cross, humanity's judgment played out on a far larger scale. Yeshua, the embodiment of love, stood before us, and we couldn't see Him for who He was. Instead, we called Him a liar, a devil, and an evildoer. We condemned Him to death, projecting our shame and fear onto the One who came to heal it.

Yet, in both stories, the Creator's response was the same: to clothe and restore. In the garden, He provided garments of skin, covering Adam and Eve with grace even in their disconnection. At the cross, Yeshua's death exposed the lies of shame and judgment, showing us their true nature—illusions that separate us from love and life.

The cross wasn't about satisfying wrath or appeasing an angry deity. It was about revealing the depth of the Creator's love and exposing shame and judgment as the lies they are. It was the ultimate act of restoration, a declaration that no matter how deeply we misunderstand or misjudge, the Creator's love remains unshaken.

FORGIVENESS, REPENTANCE, AND FLOURISHING

The good news isn't that forgiveness *can* happen—it's that it already has. Forgiveness isn't a possibility; it's a reality. The Creator's forgiveness is complete, unconditional, and eternal. It doesn't waver. It doesn't depend on our repentance. It simply *is*.

But here's the paradox: even though forgiveness is always present, we can't live in its fullness while we're trapped in shame, judgment, and disconnection. Repentance isn't about earning forgiveness—it's about stepping into its light. It's about aligning ourselves with what's already true and allowing that truth to transform us.

Repentance is the act of turning:

- From fear to faith.
- From shame to acceptance.

WHAT TO DO WHEN THE ALIENS SHOW UP (AND EVEN IF THEY DON'T)

- From hiding to vulnerability.
- From judgment to love.

Together, forgiveness and repentance invite us into a life of flourishing. Forgiveness is the Creator's gift, a declaration of His steadfast love. Repentance is our response–the moment we say yes to that love and begin to live in its freedom.

This is the Creator's heart: to see us free from shame, fear, and disconnection. To see us flourishing in connection, trust, and love. The good news isn't just about the forgiveness of sins—it's about the restoration of everything we were created to be.

AN INVITATION TO FREEDOM

This love—this boundless, relentless, unconditional love—is already yours. It's waiting for you. The Creator isn't holding anything back. The only question is: will you step into it? Will you turn from the lies of shame and judgment and walk into the freedom of forgiveness and flourishing?

This is the Creator's invitation. It's not a demand, not a condition, but a call: *Come. Be free. Be loved.*

What will you say?

COMMON RESPONSES

"Yeah, but isn't forgiveness conditional on repentance and confession?"

No, forgiveness is an expression of the Creator's character, not a transaction. It's already been extended to us without conditions. Repentance allows us to step into the freedom and restoration that forgiveness offers—it's a response to love, not a prerequisite for it.

If I invite you to a feast at my house, and you're willing to change your plans, the feast will be there for you, whether you attend or not. If you don't change plans, you won't attend and enjoy the feast. Your change of mind and related actions will lead you to the feast.

"Yeah, but doesn't the Bible teach that without repentance, we can't be forgiven?"

The Bible consistently reveals forgiveness as an ever-present reality flowing from the Creator's love. Repentance doesn't earn forgiveness—it turns toward and aligns us with its truth. It's the act of turning toward what has always been freely given.

"Yeah, but didn't Yeshua die because God's justice required payment for sin?"

The cross happened because we refuse to let go of judgment. We are so bad at it that we misjudged the Creator's messenger of our peace, connection, and love and killed him instead. Nevertheless, through it, the immense love of the Creator is revealed, not His demand for retribution. Yeshua's death wasn't about satisfying wrath but exposing the lies of shame and judgment. It demonstrated the Creator's commitment to love and reconciliation even in the face of humanity's deepest misjudgment.

"Yeah, but doesn't the Old Testament emphasize sacrifices for forgiveness?"

Sacrifices in the Old Testament were a means of symbolizing humanity's need for connection and restoration, not a condition for earning forgiveness. Time and again, the Creator declares that His delight is in steadfast love, not ritual sacrifice (Hosea 6:6, Micah 6:6-8). The sacrificial system allowed humans a temporary, albeit very complicated means, to feel like they could momentarily be reconnected with the Creator.

WHAT TO DO WHEN THE ALIENS SHOW UP (AND EVEN IF THEY DON'T)

"Yeah, but if forgiveness is unconditional, why does repentance even matter?"

Repentance matters because it's how we experience the fullness of forgiveness. The Creator's forgiveness is always present, but repentance turns us away from shame, fear, and disconnection so we can live in alignment with the truth of His love. It's not about earning—it's about embracing.

CHAPTER FIFTY-TWO
THE RESCUE THAT WASN'T
SALVATION AS CONNECTION, NOT ESCAPE

Perfect love casts out fear, because fear involves punishment.
– 1 John 4:18

MOVING AWAY FROM A WRATH-BASED UNDERSTANDING OF SALVATION was not a simple shift—it was a journey of unlearning, reexamining, and opening my heart to the patterns I saw in scripture, life, and my own relationship with the Creator. For much of my life, I believed the Creator was deeply offended by my sin, with a wrath that demanded appeasement. This perspective fueled a theology of rescue: One where Yeshua stepped in to shield me from the punishment I deserved.

But as I began to explore the Creator's love more deeply and reflect on Yeshua's teachings, I came to see salvation as something profoundly different. It isn't about being rescued from a wrathful deity—it's about being delivered from disconnection. This shift changed everything for me, and it's rooted in scripture, logic, and the Creator's unchanging patterns of love.

1. THE CREATOR IS LOVE, AND THERE IS NO FEAR IN LOVE

One of the most transformative realizations for me came from the words of John:

> God is love
> –1 John 4:8

The Greek word here is *agape*—unconditional, self-giving love. John goes further, proclaiming:

> There is no fear in love, but perfect love casts out fear because fear involves punishment
> –1 John 4:18

This passage shook me. If the Creator's very essence is unconditional love, how could fear and punishment be part of His nature? A wrath-based message, by definition, relies on fear—fear of eternal torment, fear of rejection, fear of not being good enough. But fear is incompatible with love.

Yeshua's life reflects this truth. Time and again, he reassured people not to fear:

> Do not be afraid; you are more valuable than a great number of sparrows
> –Luke 12:7

Through his actions, Yeshua embodied this love. He embraced the unclean, forgave sinners, dined with outcasts, and restored the dignity of those cast out by society. His love was not conditional on repentance or sacrifice—it was freely given. If Yeshua is the perfect representation of the Creator, how could the Father be any different?

2. THE WRATH-BASED MESSAGE IS A DRAMA TRIANGLE

In my work and relationships, I've often encountered the destructive patterns of the Drama Triangle—a cycle of Victim, Persecutor, and Rescuer that perpetuates fear, shame, and disconnection. When I looked at the wrath-based gospel, I realized it perfectly mirrored the Drama Triangle:

- Humanity is cast as the perpetual **Victim**, hopelessly sinful and deserving of punishment.
- The Creator is the **Persecutor**, demanding justice and threatening wrath.
- Yeshua is the **Rescuer**, shielding us from the Creator's anger.

This dynamic fosters dependency, fear, and shame—none of which align with the Creator's patterns of empowerment. In every area of life, the Drama Triangle leads to brokenness and disconnection. How could the Creator, the ultimate source of life and love, operate within a system that only creates more fear and fragmentation?

Instead, I began to see the Creator's pattern reflected in Yeshua's life: an empowerment dynamic that calls us out of victimhood, dismantles the need for persecution, and replaces rescuing with partnership. Yeshua didn't come to rescue us from the Creator's wrath; he came to remind us of our intrinsic connection to Adonai.

3. THE LOVE OF A PARENT

As a father, this shift became personal. Even in my imperfection, I would never rain down wrathful punishment on my children for their mistakes, let alone for their misunderstandings or missteps. If my flawed love is not wrathful, how could the Creator's perfect love be?

Yeshua captures this truth beautifully:

> If you then, being evil, know how to give good gifts to your children, how much more will your Father who is in heaven give good things to those who ask Him?
> –Matthew 7:11.

This verse challenged everything I had believed about divine wrath. How could I hold onto the idea of a wrathful Creator when Yeshua explicitly described the Father as generous, patient, and loving? The more I meditated on this, the more it became clear: a wrathful Creator is a projection of humanity's own brokenness, not a reflection of Adonai's true nature.

4. COULD CREATION IMAGINE A BETTER GOSPEL?

I began to ask myself: Could humanity imagine a better gospel than the Creator? The wrath-based message I was taught portrayed the Creator as conditional, reactive, and punitive—a being whose love was contingent on sacrifices and appeasement. But Yeshua's life demonstrated a love far greater than this narrative.

> But God demonstrates His own love toward us, in that while we were still sinners, Christ died for us
> –Romans 5:8

This is unconditional love. It doesn't wait for us to earn it or deserve it—it is freely given, always available. The wrath-based gospel, in contrast, feels like a lesser love—a human creation rooted in fear and control. The true gospel is far better, reflecting the Creator's infinite wisdom and love.

5. CONDITIONAL LOVE TURNS THE CREATOR INTO AN IDOL

One of the hardest realizations I had to confront was this: A wrath-based message reduces the Creator to a reactive, conditional idol. It paints a picture of a deity whose love and acceptance waver depending on our behavior. But the Creator is not like this. James writes:

> Every good thing given and every perfect gift is from above, coming down from the Father of lights, with whom there is no variation or shifting shadow
> –James 1:17

The Creator's love is constant and unchanging. Yeshua confirms this when he says:

> The one who comes to Me I certainly will not cast out
> –John 6:37

This is not the language of wrath or conditional love. It's the language of an unchanging, ever-present Creator who invites us into a relationship and empowers us to live fully.

6. THE WRATH-BASED MESSAGE PITS THE CREATOR AGAINST YESHUA

Perhaps the most glaring issue with the wrath-based message is how it pits the Creator and Yeshua against each other. This framework suggests that Yeshua shields humanity from the Father's wrath, as though their purposes were at odds. But Yeshua's own words refute this entirely:

> I and the Father are one
> –John 10:30

> The one who has seen Me has seen the Father
> –(John 14:9

Yeshua didn't come to rescue us from the Father; he came to reveal the Father's true heart—a heart of unconditional love, forgiveness, and connection. He showed us that the Creator is not a Persecutor but a loving parent who works tirelessly to restore us to wholeness.

WHY THE WRATH-BASED GOSPEL ISN'T "GOOD NEWS"

The word *gospel* means "good news." But how can a message rooted in wrath and fear be good news? Isaiah warns against calling evil good and good evil (Isaiah 5:20). The wrath-based message twists the Creator's love into something conditional and transactional. That is not good news—it's a distortion of the Creator's true character.

A PERSONAL REFLECTION: FREEDOM FROM FEAR

Letting go of the wrath-based gospel has brought me freedom–not freedom to sin or live unrighteously, but freedom from judgment, shame, and disconnection. I no longer see the Creator as a distant judge waiting to punish me. Instead, I experience the Creator as a loving guide, always present and inviting me back into connection. This shift has transformed my relationship with the Creator, allowing me to live without fear and embrace the love and freedom that have always been available.

The good news of Yeshua is not about mediating between a wrathful Father and sinful humanity. It's about revealing the unity and love of the Creator, delivering us from the disconnection we created, and inviting us into partnership with Adonai's redemptive work. Yeshua's mission wasn't to shield us from wrath—it was to embody the Creator's love and free us from fear, shame, and judgment. Salvation is not about escaping punishment—it's about embracing the love and connection that have always been ours.

COMMON RESPONSES

"Yeah, but if the Creator isn't wrathful, why does the Bible talk about His wrath?"

The Creator's wrath isn't about an emotional outburst or personal vendetta—it's about His fierce opposition to anything that destroys life, love, and justice. Think of it this way: the Creator's wrath is His "no" to wickedness, injustice, and anything that corrupts His creation. This is why passages like Psalm 11:5 describe His wrath against "those who love violence." It's not wrath for wrath's sake; it's His protective, restorative justice at work.

But here's the important part: the Creator's wrath is never directed at those who are humble, repentant, or seeking Him. Scripture is full of reassurances that He is "compassionate and gracious, slow to anger, abounding in love" (Psalm 103:8). His ultimate goal isn't destruction—it's always restoration. Even in His "wrath," He's working to make things right, as seen in Ezekiel 33:11, where He declares, "I take no pleasure in the death of the wicked, but rather that they turn from their ways and live."

So, who is the target of His wrath? It's those who persist in harming others, rejecting love and justice. It's not people who struggle, fail, or wrestle with their humanity—it's the proud, the oppressors, and the unrepentant. The Creator's wrath isn't random or arbitrary; it's His unwavering commitment to uphold what is good and to oppose what is evil.

"Yeah, but doesn't the cross show that God's wrath had to be satisfied?"

This is a common misunderstanding. The cross doesn't demonstrate the Creator's need to vent His wrath toward Yeshua (he does, and will, toward wickedness); it reveals the depths of His love. Yeshua didn't die to appease an angry deity—He died to expose the lies of fear, shame, and separation that humanity had believed for so long.

What we often call "wrath" at the cross wasn't the Creator's anger—it was humanity's. Our wrath (which is a byproduct of our misjudgment) was the cause. It was the wrath of a system that couldn't handle the truth Yeshua embodied: that the Creator is for us, not against us. When Yeshua said, "Father, forgive them, for they know not what they do" (Luke 23:34), He showed us that the cross was about forgiveness, not appeasement.

Paul confirms this in Colossians 2:15, where he explains that the cross disarmed the powers of evil and exposed them for what they were. The cross wasn't about satisfying wrath; it was about breaking the chains of fear, shame, and death, declaring, "It is finished" (John 19:30).

"Yeah, but isn't fear of punishment necessary to keep people moral?"

It might seem that way at first but fear only works as a short-term motivator. It can change behavior temporarily, but it doesn't transform hearts. Fear of punishment might stop someone from doing something harmful in the moment, but it doesn't inspire love, kindness, or justice.

The Creator's goal isn't to scare us into obedience—it's to transform us through love. Yeshua made this clear when He said the greatest commandments are to love the Creator and love our neighbors (Matthew 22:37-39). Fear doesn't produce that kind of love; connection does.

And let's be honest: fear-based morality often leads to hidden shame, resentment, and even rebellion. True morality flows from a heart transformed by love, not a life lived in fear of punishment. When we're connected to the Creator's love, we naturally begin to live in ways that reflect justice, compassion, and humility (Micah 6:8).

"Yeah, but doesn't this mean everyone is automatically saved?"

Theological frameworks rooted in drama triangle thinking often portray "salvation" as a scenario in which a victim is rescued from a persecutor. From this perspective, salvation becomes about being saved from punishment, hell, or condemnation, placing individuals in a passive role dependent on a rescuer. Likewise, these systems make salvation the same as forgiveness, which is not what the scriptures teach. Everyone is forgiven, to the last soul. However, not everyone will choose to live in that forgiveness.

However, in the scriptures, salvation is described as deliverance from bondage into freedom—and it's a freedom that invites us into an active, participatory connection. Salvation isn't merely about avoiding punishment or escaping harm; it's about stepping into a restored relationship with the Creator, embracing connection, and living in alignment with His love and truth.

The Creator's forgiveness is unconditional and freely available to everyone, but salvation isn't just about being forgiven—it's about saying "yes" to love and participating in the transformative process of becoming who we were created to be. Salvation requires our active engagement, as Yeshua expressed when He said, "Repent and believe the good news" (Mark 1:15). Repentance isn't about earning salvation; it's about turning away from fear, shame, and disconnection to align ourselves with the truth of who we are: beloved and accepted children of the Creator.

The Creator doesn't force anyone into connection with Him. Instead, He invites us to respond to His love and step into His grace. Salvation is an invitation to walk in connection and freedom, but it requires our willingness to accept that invitation and live from a place of connection. It's not about perfect performance but about our openness to participate in this journey of love, restoration, and freedom.

So, no, salvation isn't automatic. It's a gift offered to everyone, but it becomes transformative only when each person actively chooses to embrace it.

"Yeah, but doesn't rejecting a wrath-based gospel downplay sin?"

Not at all. In fact, rejecting a wrath-based gospel actually takes sin more seriously because it focuses on the real damage sin causes: disconnection, fear, and harm to ourselves and others.

Sin isn't just about breaking rules—it's about breaking relationships. It's about actions rooted in fear, shame, and selfishness that distort who we were created to be. The Creator opposes sin not because He's vindictive but because He's passionate about restoring us to wholeness.

The wicked—the truly unrepentant who persist in harming

others—are those who reject this restoration and choose paths that perpetuate destruction. But for those who are humble and seek the Creator's love, His response is always one of grace, not condemnation.

Yeshua addressed sin by calling people out of it, not out of fear of punishment but out of an invitation to live differently. He didn't minimize sin—He showed its devastating effects while pointing to the way of restoration. This is why He told the woman caught in adultery, "Neither do I condemn you. Go and sin no more" (John 8:11).

The seriousness of sin is in how it separates us—not because the Creator leaves, but because we hide in shame (Genesis 3:8-10). Rejecting a wrath-based gospel doesn't ignore sin; it magnifies the power of the Creator's love to heal and restore what sin has broken.

CHAPTER FIFTY-THREE
THE CREATOR'S BOUNDARIES
GRAVITY, GRACE, AND THE PATTERNS OF THE UNIVERSE

Good fences make good neighbors. – Robert Frost

BOUNDARIES AND THE CREATOR: GRACE AND STABILITY IN THE PATTERNS OF THE UNIVERSE

BOUNDARIES AREN'T JUST SOMETHING WE ENCOUNTER IN relationships—they're woven into the very fabric of the universe. The Creator's boundaries are reflected in the natural laws and patterns that make life possible. Gravity, mathematics, and the laws of physics are not random; they're a demonstration of the Creator's steadfastness and His commitment to an ordered and flourishing creation.

If we jump off a cliff, we will feel the wrath of gravity—not because gravity is angry with us but because we violated a natural boundary. It's not personal. It's not emotional. It's simply the way things are. The Creator's boundaries work the same way. His judgment isn't about punishing us out of offense or wounded pride—it's about maintaining the harmony of His creation and the natural consequences of stepping outside that harmony.

Yet none of this precludes grace and mercy. Even in a universe of unyielding natural laws, the Creator has allowed for exceptions and solutions that reflect His love. For example, gravity is constant and reliable, but the laws of aerodynamics allow us to overcome some of its effects. The Creator's boundaries are consistent, but His grace makes room for redemption, healing, and restoration.

THE CREATOR'S BOUNDARIES IN THE PATTERNS OF THE UNIVERSE

We don't often think of the laws of physics or mathematics as boundaries, but they are. They're the framework that makes life possible.

1. The Predictable Patterns of Creation

The laws of the universe—gravity, thermodynamics, mathematics—are not arbitrary; they reflect the Creator's nature. He is consistent, trustworthy, and orderly, and His boundaries ensure that creation reflects those qualities.

Imagine living in a universe where gravity was fickle. Some days it worked, other days, it didn't. Or where two plus two didn't always equal four. Such chaos would make life impossible. The Creator's boundaries are what keep the world stable, livable, and safe.

He set the earth on its foundations, so that it should never be moved.
    –Psalm 104:5

---

2. The Consequences of Boundary Violations

When we violate these natural boundaries, we experience consequences. Jump off a cliff, and you'll feel gravity's pull. Touch a hot stove, and you'll get burned. These aren't acts of punishment; they're the results of stepping outside the natural order.

The same principle applies to moral and spiritual boundaries. When we lie, cheat, or sever relationships, the consequences ripple through our lives. The Creator's boundaries aren't arbitrary—they're designed to protect us, to guide us into connection, and to help us thrive.

WRATH AS CONSEQUENCE, NOT EMOTION

We often think of "wrath" as anger, but the Creator's wrath is different. It's not an emotional reaction to being offended. Instead, it's the natural consequence of living outside His boundaries.

1. Gravity and Wrath

Think about gravity again. If you jump off a cliff, gravity doesn't get mad at you. It doesn't punish you because you broke its rules. It simply acts as it always does. The pain you feel is the result of stepping outside the boundary.

The Creator's wrath works the same way. It's not personal in the way we often think—it's the natural result of disconnection from Him. When we choose to live outside the Creator's design, we feel the consequences, just as we feel the pull of gravity.

2. Judgment Without Drama

Unlike us, the Creator doesn't operate from ego. He doesn't judge out of wounded pride or a need to assert authority. His judgment is calm, consistent, and rooted in truth. It's about managing His sphere with absolute justice and love.

SVEN MASTERSON

GRACE IN A WORLD OF BOUNDARIES

Here's the beautiful thing about the Creator's boundaries: while they are consistent and unyielding, He's made room for grace.

1. Aerodynamics: A Metaphor for Grace

Gravity is constant, but the Creator has also established the laws of aerodynamics. Through those laws, we can build airplanes and soar through the sky. Aerodynamics doesn't cancel out gravity—it works within the framework of gravity to give us a way to rise above it.

Grace and mercy work the same way. The Creator doesn't cancel His boundaries, but He provides ways for us to overcome the consequences of our choices. His grace doesn't erase truth—it works within it.

> The Lord is merciful and gracious, slow to anger and abounding in steadfast love. He does not deal with us according to our sins, nor repay us according to our iniquities.
> –Psalm 103:8-10

---

2. Mercy in the Midst of Consequences

Even when we feel the consequences of stepping outside His boundaries, the Creator's mercy is there. He walks with us through the pain, offering healing and restoration. Just as gravity doesn't cease to exist, but aerodynamics gives us a way to rise, grace provides a path back to connection.

WHY BOUNDARIES MATTER

Imagine a universe without boundaries. It would be unlivable, unpredictable, and chaotic. The Creator's boundaries are what make life possible. They're the reason the sun rises every day, the reason you can trust that a planted seed will grow into a tree, and the reason you can build relationships based on truth.

1. Boundaries Create Stability

The Creator's boundaries give us a foundation to stand on. Without them, we'd be left adrift, unable to navigate life or find meaning.

2. Boundaries Reflect Love

The Creator's boundaries aren't harsh—they're loving. They protect us from harm and guide us toward thriving. Just as a parent sets boundaries for a child, the Creator's boundaries are there to keep us safe and connected.

REFLECTION

Boundaries are not the enemy. They're a gift. The Creator's boundaries—both in the physical universe and in our spiritual lives—are there to guide us, protect us, and give us a foundation for connection and thriving.

1. How do you view boundaries in your life? Are there areas where you resist them, and what consequences have you experienced as a result?
2. Have you experienced the Creator's grace in the midst of consequences? How did it help you rise above your circumstances?

3. What would change if you embraced the Creator's boundaries as an act of love and care rather than restriction?

The Creator's boundaries reflect His steadfastness, love, and wisdom. They are consistent and unwavering, yet they allow grace and mercy, offering us a way back when we fall. Understanding and embracing these boundaries can transform the way we view the Creator, ourselves, and the world around us.

COMMON RESPONSES

"Yeah, but aren't boundaries just restrictive rules that limit freedom?"

I get it—boundaries can feel restrictive at first. I've wrestled with that too. But think about this: boundaries aren't there to fence us in; they're there to protect what matters most. Like a riverbank giving shape to the water, boundaries help us flow toward connection and purpose, not chaos.

"Yeah, but doesn't the Creator's wrath mean He's angry at us when we mess up?"

I used to feel that way, too, imagining the Creator as this cosmic figure ready to lash out at every mistake. But over time, I've come to see His "wrath" differently. It's not about anger—it's about cause and effect. Like touching a hot stove, the pain teaches us something. It's not about His anger but His desire to keep us safe and whole.

"Yeah, but if the Creator is loving, why does He allow us to feel consequences at all?"

WHAT TO DO WHEN THE ALIENS SHOW UP (AND EVEN IF THEY DON'T)

I hear you—it's tough to reconcile love with pain. But think of it this way: a parent lets their child stumble when learning to walk, not because they want to see them fall but because they want to see them grow. Consequences are sometimes the only way we learn, and grace is there to pick us up when we do.

"Yeah, but why can't grace just remove all consequences?"

I used to wonder the same thing. Then I realized that grace doesn't erase truth—it works with it. It's like aerodynamics allowing us to fly while gravity keeps us grounded. Grace doesn't mean there are no consequences; it means there's always a way back to connection, even when we fall.

"Yeah, but doesn't forgiveness mean there shouldn't be any boundaries?"

I know how easy it is to think that love equals no boundaries. But I've learned that true forgiveness and healthy boundaries actually go hand in hand. Forgiveness says, "I release you from the debt," while boundaries say, "But I still need to protect what's sacred in my life." They're not opposites—they're allies.

CHAPTER FIFTY-FOUR
WHO ARE THE WICKED?
UNDERSTANDING THE CREATOR'S JUSTICE AND WRATH

The best way to deal with evil is to do good. – Leo Tolstoy

MISUNDERSTANDINGS ABOUT SIN AND WICKEDNESS

ONE OF THE MOST COMMON REACTIONS I ENCOUNTER—ESPECIALLY from Christians, but sometimes from thoughtful non-Christians as well—is the concern that my perspective diminishes sin. They anticipate that I might be saying everyone is thoroughly good, that wickedness is overstated, or that the Creator's judgment is inconsequential. These concerns are understandable because, for many of us, our understanding of sin and wickedness has been shaped by frameworks of fear and punishment.

But let me be clear: my understanding of sin, wickedness, and the Creator's judgment does not minimize their reality. Instead, it reframes them in a way that emphasizes their true weight and consequence. Wickedness, as I understand it, is not about falling short or struggling with imperfection. It is about willful disconnection—choosing to reject the Creator's boundaries and the lifegiving relationship we were designed for. Similarly, sin is not diminished but rightly placed as the thing that disrupts connection and flourishing.

This chapter explores who the "wicked" truly are, not as caricatures of villainy, but as those who persistently sever themselves from the Creator's design and resist the call back to love, truth, and restoration. Far from trivializing sin, this perspective deepens our understanding of its consequences and the incredible grace of the Creator's invitation to return.

WHO ARE THE WICKED? UNDERSTANDING GOD'S JUDGMENT AND WRATH

When we hear the words "judgment" and "wrath," many of us instinctively picture something human. We imagine courtroom judges slamming gavels in righteous indignation or a parent punishing a disobedient child. But when the Creator judges, we must resist the temptation to project these familiar human dynamics onto Him. This is especially true when we consider the wicked and God's response to them.

Human judgment often carries the baggage of ego, vengeance, and Drama Triangle roles, casting people as victims, persecutors, or rescuers. But the Creator transcends these dynamics entirely. God's judgment is never rooted in shame, insecurity, or the need to assert power—it flows from absolute justice, perfect love, and covenantal integrity.

WHO ARE THE WICKED?

We're often taught to believe that the wicked are anyone who commits sins. This then makes all people wicked, and now all people are under wrath and need a rescuer. I don't think such perspectives serve us or are a biblically sound definition. The "wicked" in Scripture are not merely flawed people trying to do right but falling short. They are those who, through ongoing, conscious, and deliberate rebellion, sever themselves from the

WHAT TO DO WHEN THE ALIENS SHOW UP (AND EVEN IF THEY DON'T)

Creator and oppose His design for life, justice, and flourishing. To understand this distinction, we must start with the biblical characteristics of the wicked.

1. The Wicked Actively Reject The Creator's Order

The wicked are defined by a state of lawlessness (*anomia*), which means living in deliberate opposition to God's instructions:

Everyone who makes a practice of sinning also practices lawlessness; sin is lawlessness.
—1 John 3:4

The wicked are not so, but are like chaff that the wind drives away. Therefore, the wicked will not stand in the judgment, nor sinners in the congregation of the righteous; for the Lord knows the way of the righteous, but the way of the wicked will perish.
—Psalm 1:4-6

Woe to those who call evil good and good evil, who put darkness for light and light for darkness, who put bitter for sweet and sweet for bitter! ... Therefore, as the tongue of fire devours the stubble, and as dry grass sinks down in the flame, so their root will be as rottenness, and their blossom go up like dust; for they have rejected the law of the Lord of hosts, and have despised the word of the Holy One of Israel.
—Isaiah 5:20-24

---

2. The Wicked Sever Themselves from Life

Wickedness is not about imperfection or failure—it's about choosing disconnection. As you might imagine a branch cut from an evergreen tree, the wicked may seem alive for a time, but they are disconnected from the source of life and destined to wither. This disconnection is both the result of their choices and the natural consequence of rejecting the Creator.

> *I am the vine; you are the branches. Whoever abides in me and I in him, he it is that bears much fruit, for apart from me you can do nothing. If anyone does not abide in me he is thrown away like a branch and withers; and the branches are gathered, thrown into the fire, and burned.*
> –John 15:5-6

---

3. The Wicked Oppose Covenant and Connection

Covenant relationships with God are based on *chesed*—His steadfast, loyal love—and they invite us into connection and flourishing. The wicked actively reject this invitation. As in the case of a broken marriage covenant, their disconnection leads to natural consequences, not because God ceases to love, but because they have chosen to sever the relationship.

THE CREATOR'S JUDGMENT AND WRATH: BEYOND HUMAN PROJECTION

To understand the Creator's response to the wicked, we must set aside our human biases. Unlike human judgment, which often springs from wounded pride or a sense of personal offense, the Creator's judgment is rooted in His character: absolute justice, perfect love, and covenantal faithfulness.

1. The Creator is the Only Qualified Judge

As the Creator of all things, God alone has the perspective, wisdom, and authority to judge. Human judgment is clouded by bias, emotion, and incomplete knowledge. God's judgment, by contrast, flows from absolute truth and justice:

> *The Rock, his work is perfect, for all his ways are justice. A God of faithfulness and without iniquity, just and upright is he.*
> –Deuteronomy 32:4

2. God's Judgment is Perfect and Just

God's justice is not arbitrary or vindictive. It is perfect because it aligns with the truth of who He is and the design He established for creation. The wicked are not judged because they offend God's ego but because their choices disrupt the harmony and flourishing of creation:

> *For I the Lord love justice; I hate robbery and wrong; I will faithfully give them their recompense, and I will make an everlasting covenant with them.*
> –Isaiah 61:8

> *Righteousness and justice are the foundation of your throne; steadfast love and faithfulness go before you.*
> –Psalm 89:14

3. Judgment is Rooted in Covenantal Integrity, Not Personal Offense

God's wrath is not a reaction to personal offense but a response to covenant violation. His steadfast love (*chesed*) remains unshaken, even as consequences unfold. Think of a marriage where vows are broken—there is a natural severing of the partnership, yet unconditional high regard (*UHR*) for the other person can remain:

> *Behold, the days are coming, declares the Lord, when I will make a new covenant with the house of Israel and the house of Judah, not like the covenant that I made with their fathers on the day when I took them by the hand to bring them out of the land of Egypt, my covenant that they broke, though I was their husband, declares the Lord. But this is the covenant that I will make with the house of Israel after those days, declares the Lord: I will put my law within them, and I will write it on their hearts. And I will be their God, and they shall be my people.*
> –Jeremiah 31:31-33
>
> *If we are faithless, he remains faithful—for he cannot deny himself.*
> –2 Timothy 2:13

THE NATURE OF GOD'S WRATH

The term "wrath" (*orgē* in Greek) often carries negative connotations for modern readers. But God's wrath is not like human anger. It is better understood as His settled opposition to anything that corrupts, harms, or destroys His creation. Wrath is an expression of God's love for justice and His refusal to allow evil to flourish unchecked.

1. Wrath as Love in Action

God's wrath is not in conflict with His love—it is an extension of it. Just as a parent would fiercely protect their child from harm, God's wrath arises from His desire to see creation restored to its intended state:

> *The Lord is a jealous and avenging God; the Lord is avenging and wrathful; the Lord takes vengeance on his adversaries and keeps wrath for his enemies. The Lord is slow to anger and great in power, and the Lord will by no means clear the guilty.*
> —Nahum 1:2-3

2. Wrath as Consequences of Disconnection

Wrath is often described in Scripture as the natural outworking of disconnection from God. It is not God inflicting harm, but the inevitable result of living apart from Him:

> *Therefore God gave them up in the lusts of their hearts to impurity, to the dishonoring of their bodies among themselves, because they exchanged the truth about God for a lie and worshiped and served the creature rather than the Creator, who is blessed forever! Amen.*
> —Romans 1:24-25

> *How can I give you up, O Ephraim? How can I hand you over, O Israel? How can I make you like Admah? How can I treat you like Zeboiim? My heart recoils within me; my compassion grows warm and tender. I will not execute my burning anger; I will not again destroy Ephraim; for I am God and not a man, the Holy One in your midst, and I will not come in wrath.*
> —Hosea 11:8-9

JUDGMENT, WRATH, AND THE WICKED: A COVENANT PERSPECTIVE

In covenantal terms, judgment and wrath are not about retribution but about relational reality. When a covenant is broken, there are natural consequences—a severing of the partnership and a loss of the benefits that come from that connection. Yet, God's *chesed* ensures that His love remains steadfast, and His ultimate goal is always restoration:

The steadfast love of the Lord never ceases; his mercies never come to an end; they are new every morning; great is your faithfulness.
   –Lamentations 3:22-23

Have I any pleasure in the death of the wicked, declares the Lord God, and not rather that he should turn from his way and live?
   – Ezekiel 18:23

REFLECTION: LIVING IN LIGHT OF GOD'S JUSTICE AND LOVE

Understanding the Creator's judgment requires humility and trust. Unlike human judges, who often act out of self-interest, God judges with perfect love and justice. His wrath is not punitive but restorative, aimed at preserving the integrity of creation and drawing people back into connection.

For us, the lesson is twofold:

1. **Resist the temptation to judge others**, recognizing that judgment belongs to God alone:
   - *"Judge not, that you be not judged. For with the judgment you pronounce you will be judged, and with the measure you use it will be measured to you."* (Matthew 7:1-2)
2. **Embrace God's invitation to a covenant relationship**, knowing that His steadfast love endures even when we falter:
   - *"But God shows his love for us in that while we were still sinners, Christ died for us."* (Romans 5:8)

The wicked are those who persistently reject this invitation, severing themselves from the source of life. But for those who turn back, the Creator's arms are always open, ready to restore, renew, and reconnect.

COMMON RESPONSES

"Yeah, but isn't everyone wicked in some way?"

No, the biblical definition of wickedness doesn't apply to everyone. While we all fall short and make mistakes, wickedness in Scripture refers to persistent, willful disconnection from the Creator's design and a rejection of covenantal relationship. It's not about imperfection; it's about a deliberate turning away.

The problem with our judgmental nature is that we immediately fear, as Adam and Eve did, that we are "evil" or "wicked," and then hide and cover ourselves as they did, also. Yet, how many wicked people do you suppose actually worry about potentially being wicked? Is not the desire to be something other than wicked evidence that we are not?

"Yeah, but doesn't God's wrath mean He's angry with us?"

God's wrath isn't human anger or a reaction born of wounded pride. It's His settled opposition to anything that harms or corrupts His creation. Wrath is better understood as love in action—a refusal to allow evil to flourish unchecked, motivated by justice and restoration.

"Yeah, but doesn't this view downplay sin?"

Not at all. This perspective highlights the true weight of sin as something that disrupts connection and flourishing. It acknowledges the deep consequences of disconnection while emphasizing the Creator's relentless invitation to return to Him.

Further, we know from thousands of years of human history that people behave according to their self-view. Those who persistently see themselves as wicked, ashamed, horrible, and wretched tend to behave in those ways because they don't see themselves as having a nature to do otherwise. Try this: Spend the next 90 days telling yourself you are a deeply loved, accepted, cherished creation—His workmanship, created in Yeshua for good works. Then, see how sinful your behavior becomes over that timeframe.

"Yeah, but why does God allow the wicked to prosper sometimes?"

The Creator's justice operates on an eternal scale, not just a temporary one. What may seem like prosperity is often a fleeting illusion. God's ultimate goal is restoration, and His patience allows time for repentance and return, as seen in 2 Peter 3:9: 'The Lord is not slow in keeping His promise...but is patient, not wanting anyone to perish.'

"Yeah, but doesn't judging the wicked create a sense of superiority in believers?"

It can if misunderstood. Judgment belongs solely to the Creator, who judges with perfect love and justice. For believers, the focus should be on humility and self-reflection, trusting God's justice while extending grace and compassion to others.

CHAPTER FIFTY-FIVE
REPENTANCE & DELIVERANCE
FROM FEAR TO FLOURISHING

Hardships often prepare ordinary people for an extraordinary destiny. – C.S. Lewis

---

DELIVERANCE—A JOURNEY FROM FEAR TO FLOURISHING

IN THE PREVIOUS CHAPTERS, WE EXPLORED THE CREATOR'S WRATH and boundaries, understanding that His judgment is not about personal offense but about the natural consequences of disconnection. We also examined repentance as the turning point, where we move out of fear, shame, and drama and into alignment with the Creator's love, truth, and empowerment.

Now, we step deeper into what this journey looks like: deliverance—a movement from one side of the dichotomy to the other. Deliverance is not just escaping something bad; it's stepping into something better. It's leaving behind judgment, shame, and disconnection and moving toward unconditional love, faith, and flourishing.

This journey of deliverance requires turning away from what diminishes us and toward what restores us. It's about shifting from:

- Judgment to love.
- Fear to faith.
- Shame to acceptance.
- Hiding to vulnerability and authenticity.
- Drama to empowerment.
- Ego to heart.
- Disconnection to connection.
- Victimhood to creativity.

DELIVERANCE: MOVING FROM JUDGMENT TO LOVE

1. The Dichotomy of Judgment and Love

When we live in fear, we perceive the Creator's boundaries as judgment, and His wrath feels like punishment. But this perception comes from disconnection. Deliverance begins when we realize the Creator's boundaries are not barriers—they are guideposts leading us back to love.

We turn away from judgment not because it isn't real but because its purpose is to redirect us toward flourishing. Judgment exposes disconnection, so we can choose connection.

For God did not send his Son into the world to condemn the world, but in order that the world might be saved through him.
  –John 3:17

The Lord is merciful and gracious, slow to anger and abounding in steadfast love.
  –Psalm 103:8

Have I any pleasure in the death of the wicked, declares the Lord God, and not rather that he should turn from his way and live?
  –Ezekiel 18:23

WHAT TO DO WHEN THE ALIENS SHOW UP (AND EVEN IF THEY DON'T)

> *For the mountains may depart and the hills be removed, but my steadfast love shall not depart from you, and my covenant of peace shall not be removed, says the Lord, who has compassion on you.*
> —Isaiah 54:10

---

2. Unconditional Love and the Absence of Judgment

In the Creator's unconditional love, there is no shame, condemnation, or drama. Love replaces judgment with acceptance, inviting us to trust in the Creator's steadfast care.

> *There is no fear in love, but perfect love casts out fear. For fear has to do with punishment, and whoever fears has not been perfected in love.*
> —1 John 4:18

DELIVERANCE: MOVING FROM FEAR TO FAITH

1. Fear as the Root of Disconnection

Fear keeps us stuck in the Drama Triangle—blaming others, hiding from the truth, and resisting connection. Fear says, "I'm not enough," or "I can't trust the Creator." Deliverance calls us to abandon fear and choose faith.

Faith is the antidote to fear. It trusts that the Creator's boundaries are for our good and that His love is steadfast, even when we falter.

> *Fear not, for I am with you; be not dismayed, for I am your God; I*

> will strengthen you, I will help you, I will uphold you with my righteous right hand.
> —Isaiah 41:10

> The Lord is my light and my salvation; whom shall I fear? The Lord is the stronghold of my life; of whom shall I be afraid?
> —Psalm 27:1

> Be strong and courageous. Do not be frightened, and do not be dismayed, for the Lord your God is with you wherever you go.
> —Joshua 1:9

> Now faith is the assurance of things hoped for, the conviction of things not seen.
> —Hebrews 11:1

---

2. Faith as Trust and Action

Faith is not passive; it requires stepping out of fear and into the unknown. Like Noah building the ark or the Israelites stepping into the Red Sea, deliverance demands that we trust the Creator's plan even when it's not fully visible.

DELIVERANCE: MOVING FROM SHAME TO ACCEPTANCE

1. The Weight of Shame

Shame whispers, "You're not enough," and drives us to hide—not just from others, but from the Creator. In the garden, Adam and Eve's first response to failure was to cover themselves and avoid the Creator's presence. Shame isolates us, convincing us we're unworthy of love.

WHAT TO DO WHEN THE ALIENS SHOW UP (AND EVEN IF THEY DON'T)

2. Acceptance as the Antidote

Deliverance calls us out of hiding and into the Creator's unconditional acceptance. Acceptance doesn't deny our imperfections—it acknowledges them while affirming our worth. It says, "You are seen, you are loved, and you are enough."

Those who look to him are radiant, and their faces shall never be ashamed.
  –Psalm 34:5

Come now, let us reason together, says the Lord: though your sins are like scarlet, they shall be as white as snow; though they are red like crimson, they shall become like wool.
  –Isaiah 1:18

You shall know that I am the Lord, and those who wait for me shall not be put to shame.
  –Isaiah 49:23b

There is, therefore now no condemnation for those who are in Christ Jesus.
  –Romans 8:1

Shame isolates, but acceptance reconnects. It allows us to come as we are, trusting that the Creator's love is greater than our failures.

DELIVERANCE: MOVING FROM HIDING TO VULNERABILITY AND AUTHENTICITY

1. The Instinct to Hide

SVEN MASTERSON

When we feel shame, our natural instinct is to hide. We hide behind perfectionism, defensiveness, or avoidance. The Creator's invitation, however, is to come out of hiding and trust His love.

Where shall I go from your Spirit? Or where shall I flee from your presence? If I ascend to heaven, you are there! If I make my bed in Sheol, you are there!
    –Psalm 139:7-8

And the man and his wife hid themselves from the presence of the Lord God among the trees of the garden. But the Lord God called to the man and said to him, 'Where are you?'
    –Genesis 3:8-9

Trust in him at all times, O people; pour out your heart before him; God is a refuge for us.
    –Psalm 62:8

And the man and his wife hid themselves from the presence of the Lord God among the trees of the garden. But the Lord God called to the man and said to him, 'Where are you?'
    –Genesis 3:8-9

---

2. Vulnerability as Freedom

Vulnerability requires courage, but it's where true freedom begins. The Creator's love invites us to lay down our masks, confess our weaknesses, and live authentically in relationship with Him and others.

If we confess our sins, he is faithful and just to forgive us our sins and to cleanse us from all unrighteousness.

WHAT TO DO WHEN THE ALIENS SHOW UP (AND EVEN IF THEY DON'T)

–1 John 1:9

DELIVERANCE: MOVING FROM DRAMA TO EMPOWERMENT

1. Breaking the Drama Triangle

The Drama Triangle traps us in cycles of blame and disempowerment:

- **Victim:** *"I'm powerless."*
- **Rescuer:** *"I'll fix it for you."*
- **Persecutor:** *"It's all your fault."*

Deliverance breaks these cycles and shifts us into empowerment:

- **From Victim to Creator:** *"I can make choices and take responsibility."*
- **From Rescuer to Coach:** *"I can help you find your own strength."*
- **From Persecutor to Challenger:** *"I can hold you accountable with compassion."*

REPENTANCE: TURNING TOWARD LOVE AND LIFE

Repentance is often misunderstood and misrepresented as merely feeling bad about our mistakes or endlessly apologizing to the Creator. That's a drama triangle way to see it. At its core, repentance is not about wallowing in guilt—it's about *turning,* which encourages us to make *choices* and thus exercise *Power*!

Repentance is a choice to be powerful.

It's a decisive movement, a shift in orientation from one path to another, from disconnection to connection.

Repentance is the turning point in the journey of deliverance. It's where we leave behind the lies, shame, and fear that diminish us and step into the truth, love, and flourishing that the Creator offers.

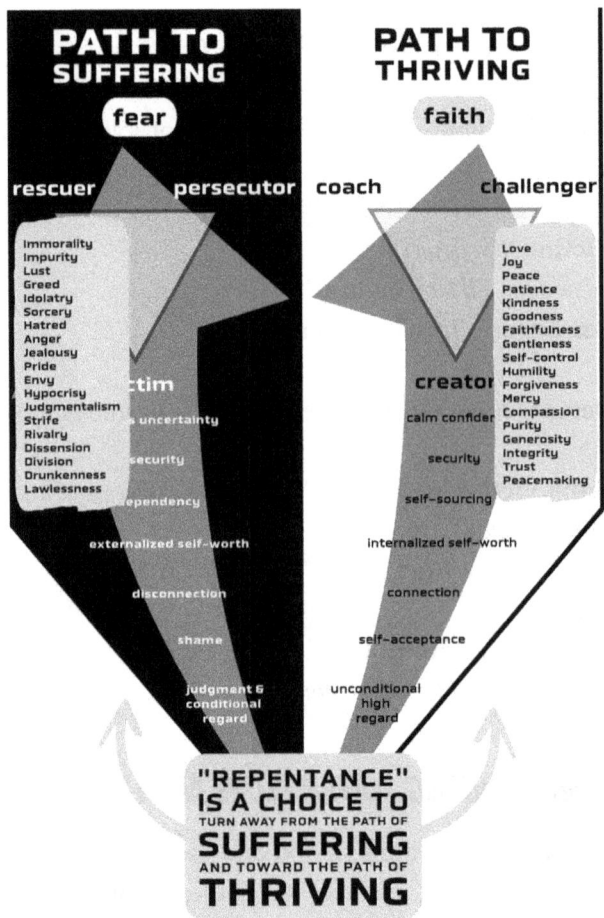

Understanding "Repentance"

TURNING AWAY: THE PATH OF THE SUFFERING IN THE "FLESH"

When we live in disconnection, we align ourselves with the "path of the flesh"—a way of life centered on striving, fear, and ego. This path is marked by works of the flesh: anger, envy, impurity, and division (Galatians 5:19-21). It's the way of the Drama Triangle, where we feel stuck as victims and strive to rescue others at our own expense or blame and control as persecutors.

Living in this way leads to exhaustion and brokenness. It's a path of death, not because the Creator punishes us, but because disconnection from the source of life inevitably leads to withering.

TURNING TOWARD: WALKING IN THE PATH OF THE "SPIRIT"

Repentance is the moment we recognize that we're on a destructive path and choose to turn toward life. It's a choice to embrace the "ascent," stepping into alignment with the Spirit and allowing its fruits to grow in our lives: love, joy, peace, patience, kindness, goodness, faithfulness, gentleness, and self-control (Galatians 5:22-23).

This turning is a decision to trust the Creator's love and wisdom, to release shame and striving, and to walk in partnership with the Spirit. It's the first step into the Empowerment Dynamic, where we live as creators, coaches, and challengers, embracing a life of purpose and connection.

A BIBLICAL CALL TO REPENTANCE

Throughout scripture, the call to repentance is an invitation to turn away from disconnection and align with the Creator's love:

Return to me, and I will return to you, says the Lord of hosts.
–Malachi 3:7

Come now, let us reason together, says the Lord: though your sins are like scarlet, they shall be as white as snow; though they are red like crimson, they shall become like wool.
–Isaiah 1:18

Repent, for the kingdom of heaven is at hand.

–Matthew 4:17

In the Gospels, Yeshua's proclamation of the Kingdom begins with this call to repentance. He invites us to turn from the patterns of the flesh and step into the Kingdom of God—a reality where love, peace, and empowerment flow like living water (John 4:14).

Repentance in Practice

Repentance isn't a one-time act; it's a daily practice of realignment. It's a constant choice to turn away from fear, shame, and disconnection and toward love, trust, and flourishing.

Here's what repentance might look like:

1. **Recognizing the Lie:** Identify where fear, shame, or ego is driving your decisions.
2. **Turning Toward the Truth:** Replace the lie with the truth of the Creator's love and acceptance.
3. **Living Differently:** Let your actions reflect your new alignment, stepping into vulnerability, authenticity, and empowerment.

THE FRUIT OF REPENTANCE

When we turn toward the Spirit, we begin to see its fruits manifest in our lives. Relationships are restored, peace replaces anxiety, and joy becomes our strength. Repentance doesn't just change our direction—it changes our hearts, our choices, and the way we experience the world.

As Yeshua said, "I came that they may have life and have it abundantly" (John 10:10). Repentance is the doorway to this abundant life.

DELIVERANCE: MOVING FROM EGO TO HEART

1. The Ego's Role in Disconnection

The ego thrives on self-protection and control, but it creates barriers to authentic connection. Deliverance invites us to live from the heart—a place of trust, vulnerability, and love.

> And I will give you a new heart, and a new spirit I will put within you.
> —Ezekiel 36:26

DELIVERANCE: MOVING FROM DISCONNECTION TO CONNECTION

1. The Pain of Disconnection

Disconnection is the source of all suffering. Deliverance reconnects us with the Creator and restores the relationships we were designed for.

> The Lord is near to the brokenhearted and saves the crushed in spirit.
> —Psalm 34:18

> They shall build houses and inhabit them; they shall plant vineyards and eat their fruit. They shall not build and another inhabit; they shall not plant and another eat; for like the days of a tree shall the days of my people be, and my chosen shall long enjoy the work of their hands.
> —Isaiah 65:21-22

SVEN MASTERSON

But you shall serve the Lord your God, and he will bless your bread and your water, and I will take sickness away from among you.
   –Exodus 23:25

Abide in me, and I in you. As the branch cannot bear fruit by itself, unless it abides in the vine, neither can you, unless you abide in me.
   –John 15:4

REFLECTION

Deliverance is the Creator's invitation to move out of fear, shame, and hiding and into a life of love, faith, and authenticity. It's a journey from disconnection to connection, from judgment to love, and from drama to empowerment.

1. Are there areas in your life where shame or fear still keep you in hiding?
2. How can you step into vulnerability and accept the Creator's unconditional love?
3. What would it look like to embrace deliverance as a daily journey of faith and connection?

The Creator's love calls us to stop hiding, let go of shame, and step into acceptance and flourishing. This is deliverance—will you take the first step?

COMMON RESPONSES

"Yeah, but isn't deliverance just about escaping punishment?"

WHAT TO DO WHEN THE ALIENS SHOW UP (AND EVEN IF THEY DON'T)

Deliverance is not merely an escape from something negative; it's an invitation into something profoundly positive. It's about embracing love, connection, and empowerment. The Creator's intention is not just to save us from harm but to guide us toward a flourishing life, rooted in trust and authentic relationships.

"Yeah, but what if I'm too broken or far gone to experience deliverance?"

The beauty of deliverance is that it's never about being worthy—it's about the Creator meeting you exactly where you are. No one is too far gone for His love, which is unconditional and unrelenting. Deliverance begins with a single step of turning toward that love, no matter how small.

"Yeah, but doesn't this idea of deliverance diminish the seriousness of sin?"

Not at all. Deliverance recognizes the weight of sin as disconnection from life and love, but it reframes the Creator's response. Instead of punishment, He offers restoration. It's not about ignoring sin; it's about addressing its root causes and offering a path back to flourishing.

"Yeah, but how can I trust the process when I don't see where it's leading?"

Faith is the essence of deliverance—a trust in the Creator's character and His plans, even when the outcome isn't clear. It's stepping out of fear and into the assurance that His love and boundaries are for your good. The journey of deliverance unfolds one step at a time, with the Creator walking alongside you.

"Yeah, but what if I fail again after starting the journey of deliverance?"

SVEN MASTERSON

Failure is part of being human, but deliverance isn't about perfection—it's about progress and alignment. The Creator's love doesn't waver with your missteps. Each time you stumble, His invitation to return remains open. Deliverance is a continual turning back to love, not a one-time achievement.

CHAPTER FIFTY-SIX
THE COSMIC FAMILY
FROM HIRED HANDS TO BELOVED SONS

> We are not human beings having a spiritual experience. We are spiritual beings having a human experience.
> – Pierre Teilhard de Chardin

SONSHIP: FROM IDOLATRY TO RELATIONSHIP

HAVE YOU EVER THOUGHT OF YOUR RELATIONSHIP WITH THE CREATOR —the source of all life, wisdom, and love—as a bond rooted in sonship? For many of us, the idea of being children of the Creator is familiar, but the depth and implications of this truth often remain unexplored. What does it mean to live as sons and daughters of the Creator, and how does it transform our understanding of love, identity, and connection?

For much of my life, I approached the Creator with a mindset shaped more by fear and performance than by love and trust. I saw the Creator as distant, demanding, and impossible to please. This perception wasn't just relationally damaging—it was idolatrous. I treated the Creator as though He were an idol, projecting my fears and desires onto Him rather than embracing the truth of who He is and who I am as His child.

But as I began to understand sonship—what it means to be adopted into the Creator's family—a profound shift occurred. I saw the contrast between living as a son or daughter and relating to the Creator through the lens of idolatry. I also discovered that sonship doesn't just offer connection; it fosters a relationship that grows into friendship, much like the evolving bond I experience with my own children.

This chapter explores the power of sonship, how it contrasts with the idolatrous patterns that so often define our relationships, and how it deepens into friendship with the Creator as we mature.

SONSHIP: IDENTITY AND INTIMACY

Sonship is more than a metaphor; it's a relational reality. To be a son or daughter of the Creator means being fully known, fully loved, and fully accepted—not because of what we do, but because of who we are. This is the heart of what the Apostle Paul described when he wrote:

"For you have not received a spirit of slavery leading to fear again, but you have received a spirit of adoption as sons and daughters, by which we cry out, 'Abba, Father!'" (Romans 8:15).

The term "Abba," used by Yeshua to address the Creator, conveys intimacy, trust, and familial love. It's not the distant "Father" of formal speech but the affectionate "Papa" or "Dad" that a child calls out in vulnerability and trust.

This invitation to call the Creator "Abba" is radical. It shatters the transactional mindset of servitude and replaces it with the secure identity of sonship. To be adopted by the Creator means that we no longer have to earn love or acceptance. We are already part of the family, heirs to all the promises of connection, love, and empowerment.

WHAT TO DO WHEN THE ALIENS SHOW UP (AND EVEN IF THEY DON'T)

Paul emphasized this inheritance when he wrote:

> The Spirit Himself testifies with our spirit that we are children of God, and if children, heirs also, heirs of God and fellow heirs with Christ
> –Romans 8:16–17.

THE CONTRAST: IDOLATRY AND TRANSACTIONAL WORSHIP

To grasp the beauty of sonship, we must see it in stark contrast with idolatry. Idolatry isn't just about worshiping false gods or material things—it's a way of relating to the Creator through fear, manipulation, and transaction. It's rooted in a distorted understanding of love and relationship, one that keeps us trapped in cycles of dependency and disconnection.

IDOLATRY: ROOTED IN DRAMA TRIANGLES

At its core, idolatry reflects the **Drama Triangle** dynamic of **Victim, Persecutor, and Rescuer:**

1. **Victim:** "I'm unworthy and powerless." In idolatry, we approach the Creator (or an idol) with the belief that we are inherently inadequate and helpless. This shame-driven mindset keeps us stuck, believing that we need saving from external forces.
2. **Persecutor:** "I must appease or manipulate the divine." Idolatry turns the Creator into a Persecutor, demanding appeasement through sacrifices or perfect performance. Fear of punishment drives this dynamic, fostering disconnection.
3. **Rescuer:** "I need something external to save me." In the idolatry mindset, we often turn to intermediaries—

whether religious systems, rituals, or material idols—to mediate our relationship with the Creator. These Rescuers perpetuate dependency and disempowerment.

This dynamic echoes the Israelites' experience with the golden calf in Exodus 32. Out of fear and insecurity, they fashioned an idol, hoping it would mediate their relationship with the Creator. This pattern still repeats today, whether in religious legalism, performance-based faith, or material dependencies.

SONSHIP: ROOTED IN EMPOWERMENT DYNAMICS

Sonship, on the other hand, mirrors the **Empowerment Dynamic** of **Creator, Challenger, and Coach**:

1. **Creator:** *"I am loved, valued, and capable."* In sonship, we recognize our inherent worth as children of the Creator. This secure identity empowers us to live boldly and creatively, knowing we are deeply loved.
2. **Challenger:** *"I am called to grow and mature."* The Creator challenges us not to punish but to strengthen and empower us. As sons and daughters, we embrace growth as an opportunity to deepen our connection and purpose.
3. **Coach:** *"I am guided, not controlled."* The Creator's love is not coercive or conditional. Like a coach, the Creator provides wisdom, encouragement, and support, helping us step into our full potential.

SONSHIP VS. IDOLATRY: TWO APPROACHES TO RELATIONSHIP

1. Identity vs. Performance

- **Sonship:** Begins with the truth of who we are: beloved children of the Creator. Our identity is secure, rooted in love, and not dependent on our behavior.
- **Idolatry:** Makes our relationship contingent on performance. It says, *"If I do enough, I'll be loved. If I fail, I'll be rejected."*

In sonship, love flows naturally from the Creator, not as a reward but as a constant reality. This frees us from striving and allows us to rest in the truth of our belovedness.

2. Connection vs. Transaction

- **Sonship:** Invites us into intimate connection with the Creator, where trust and honesty form the foundation of the relationship.
- **Idolatry:** Is inherently transactional, about giving to get, placating fears, and manipulating outcomes.

Sonship allows us to approach the Creator with confidence, knowing that our love and connection are unshakable. Idolatry keeps us at arm's length, trapped in fear and manipulation.

3. Empowerment vs. Dependency

- **Sonship:** Empowers us to grow, mature, and co-create with the Creator. The Creator's love is liberating and nurturing.
- **Idolatry:** Fosters dependency. It keeps us small, fearful, and reliant on intermediaries rather than stepping into the fullness of our identity.

SONSHIP AND THE EVOLUTION OF FRIENDSHIP

As a father of six, I've experienced firsthand how sonship and friendship are connected. With my three adult sons, I've seen how our bond has deepened and transformed as they've grown. While our relationship began with dependence—me providing for their needs and guiding their development—it has evolved into something more reciprocal. Today, we share mutual respect, shared purpose, and genuine delight in each other's company. Our sonship has grown into friendship.

This mirrors what the Creator desires for us. Sonship is the foundation, but as we grow in trust, maturity, and self-reliance, our relationship with the Creator deepens into friendship. Yeshua captured this beautifully when he said:

No longer do I call you slaves, for the slave does not know what his master is doing; but I have called you friends
   –John 15:15

Friendship with the Creator is not a replacement for sonship—it's its fulfillment. It's the natural result of stepping into our identity as beloved children and maturing into empowered, self-reliant partners in the Creator's work.

THE CREATOR'S DELIGHT IN US

One of the most beautiful aspects of sonship and friendship with the Creator is the mutual delight it fosters. Zephaniah 3:17 paints a stunning picture of this delight:

"He will rejoice over you with joy; He will be quiet in His love; He will rejoice over you with shouts of joy."

The Creator doesn't tolerate us or merely put up with us. He delights in us. As we mature in sonship and step into friendship, this mutual delight becomes the heart of our relationship. We find joy not only in being loved but in loving the Creator in return.

AN INVITATION TO SONSHIP AND FRIENDSHIP

The Creator's invitation to sonship is open to all. Through Yeshua, we are reminded of who we are: beloved children, heirs to the promises of love and connection. This identity frees us from the fear and striving of idolatry and invites us into a relationship rooted in trust, empowerment, and mutual delight.

If you've ever felt distant from the Creator, know this: you are already loved, already known, and already invited into sonship. As you step into this identity, you'll discover that it's not just about being a child but about maturing into friendship—a relationship of shared purpose, mutual respect, and abiding love.

SONSHIP AS THE PATH TO CONNECTION

Sonship is the antidote to idolatry. It replaces fear and transaction with love and connection, empowering us to step into our true identity as heirs of the Creator's promises. As we grow in sonship, our relationship deepens into friendship, reflecting the Creator's ultimate desire: a bond of trust, delight, and shared purpose. This relationship frees us to live fully, love unconditionally, and co-create with the Creator in the work of restoration.

COMMON RESPONSES

> "Yeah, but doesn't sonship mean we lose reverence for the Creator?"

Not at all. True sonship deepens reverence. When we experience the Creator as a loving parent, our awe grows—not out of fear, but from gratitude, trust, and the profound realization of being fully known and loved.

> "Yeah, but doesn't the idea of sonship feel too informal or irreverent for a holy God?"

The Creator Himself invites us into this intimacy. Yeshua's use of "Abba" reflects a relationship both reverent and deeply personal, proving that holiness and intimacy coexist beautifully.

> "Yeah, but if sonship is secure, what's to keep us from becoming complacent?"

A true understanding of sonship inspires us to grow and mature. Being secure in love doesn't lead to passivity—it empowers us to live purposefully, reflecting the Creator's nature and participating in His work.

> "Yeah, but how is sonship different from just being a follower of the Creator?"

Sonship goes beyond following; it's about belonging, intimacy, and access. As sons and daughters, we are heirs, not merely servants or subjects. This identity transforms obedience into partnership and connection.

> "Yeah, but what about those who feel unworthy or distant from the Creator?"

The beauty of sonship is that it's not earned—it's given. The Creator's love reaches us even in our unworthiness, inviting us into a relationship that affirms our identity and bridges every distance.

CHAPTER FIFTY-SEVEN
MISSION RECALIBRATED
AN INVITATION TO FLOURISH AND CO-CREATE

The true gospel is the good news that God is making all things new—and we get to help. – N.T. Wright

---

FOR YEARS, MY UNDERSTANDING OF THE CREATOR'S MISSION WAS shaped by the fear-based "gospel" I had inherited. It was a message steeped in shame, presenting the Creator as distant, angry, and eager to punish. Salvation, I believed, was Yeshua swooping in to rescue me from this wrath.

But as I stepped into the deeper truths of redemption, deliverance, sonship, and connection, I realized this narrative wasn't just incomplete—it was fundamentally distorted. Slowly, I began to see that Yeshua's mission wasn't to shield us from the Creator but to reveal the Creator's true heart: love, connection, and empowerment. It wasn't about rescue; it was about co-creation.

This chapter reflects on my journey to see the Great Commission not as a fear-driven mandate but as an invitation to join the Creator in the flourishing and restoration of the world.

FEAR AND SHAME: THE BAD SEED

Much of what I was taught about the Great Commission was rooted in fear. Evangelism was framed as an urgent mission to save people from the Creator's wrath. Every interaction carried the weight of eternal consequences—one wrong word, one missed opportunity, and someone might end up in hell.

This perspective was exhausting, and it has bore fruit that has reflected its origins as a dead seed:

- **Disconnection:** Instead of drawing people closer to the Creator, it often pushes them away. Many couldn't reconcile the idea of a loving Creator with a gospel rooted in fear and shame.
- **Shrinking Impact:** Churches cling to this fear-based message, but their numbers have declined, and their relevance has faded.
- **Spiritual Exhaustion:** Those who have tried to carry out the Great Commission this way were left feeling inadequate, judged, and worn out.

The fruit of this message wasn't life—it was stagnation. The "gospel" I had been taught didn't align with the Creator's character or with the abundant life Yeshua promised.

THE TURNING POINT: REDISCOVERING GOOD NEWS

My turning point came when I started to revisit foundational truths about the Creator, Yeshua, and the gospel. Earlier in this book, I explored what salvation truly means: deliverance not from a wrathful deity but from the disconnection and shame that humanity created. I came to see sonship as the foundation of our relationship with the Creator—an identity rooted in love and intimacy, not fear and performance.

These realizations reshaped my understanding of the Creator's

WHAT TO DO WHEN THE ALIENS SHOW UP (AND EVEN IF THEY DON'T)

mission. I began to see the alignment between the Creator's original mandate in Genesis and Yeshua's Great Commission. Both are invitations to life, connection, and flourishing.

FROM THE GARDEN TO THE GREAT COMMISSION

The Creator's first words to humanity were an invitation to co-creation:

Be fruitful, multiply, fill the earth, and subdue it; and rule over the fish of the sea, the birds of the sky, and every living thing
 —Genesis 1:28

This wasn't a call to domination or exploitation. It was a charge to steward creation, nurture life, and reflect the Creator's love in everything we do. It was an invitation to co-create a flourishing world.

Yeshua's Great Commission echoes this original mandate:

"Go therefore and make disciples of all the nations, baptizing them in the name of the Father and the Son and the Holy Spirit, teaching them to follow all that I commanded you" (Matthew 28:19–20).

At its core, the Great Commission is about multiplying connections and flourishing. It's about spreading the good news of the Creator's love and empowering others to live in alignment with that love. It's not a message of fear and judgment; it's an invitation to abundant life.

CO-CREATION VS. FEAR-BASED COMPLIANCE

The fear-based gospel and the true gospel of co-creation couldn't be more different:

- **Fear-Based Gospel:** Driven by shame, it focuses on avoiding punishment and "saving souls" out of fear of eternal consequences.
- **Good News of Redemption & Co-Creation:** Rooted in love, it invites us to partner with the Creator in bringing life, connection, and flourishing to the world.

The fear-based gospel operates in the Drama Triangle: the Creator as a wrathful Persecutor, humanity as the helpless Victim, and Yeshua as the Rescuer. But truly good news calls us into empowerment dynamics, where we live as creators in partnership with the Creator, stepping into the fullness of our sonship.

FLOURISHING AS THE FRUIT OF GOOD SEED

The Creator's message has always been about life and flourishing. In the parable of the sower, Yeshua describes how good seed produces an exponential harvest: thirty, sixty, and even a hundred times what was sown (Matthew 13:23). The fear-based gospel cannot produce this kind of fruit because it is rooted in bad seed: fear, shame, and judgment. But the good news of love and empowerment is good seed, and its fruit is evident:

- **Connection:** It draws people into deeper relationships with the Creator, themselves, and others.
- **Empowerment:** It equips people to live abundantly and share that abundance with others.
- **Flourishing:** It creates communities that reflect the Creator's love, justice, and wisdom.

LIVING OUT THE TRUE GREAT COMMISSION

When I began to see the Great Commission through the lens of co-creation, everything changed. No longer did I feel the weight of shame or the pressure to perform. Instead, I felt empowered to partner with the Creator in ways that were life-giving and joyful.

This doesn't mean the work is always easy. Co-creation requires trust, vulnerability, and action. But it's a labor of love, not fear. It's a response to the Creator's invitation, not an attempt to earn approval.

Here are some ways I've learned to live out the true Great Commission:

1. **Stewardship:** I've come to see my relationships, work, and resources as opportunities to reflect the Creator's love. Stewardship isn't about perfection; it's about intentionality and care.
2. **Connection:** I've prioritized connection through prayer, reflection, and relationships. The Creator's love flows through connection, and fostering it has transformed every aspect of my life.
3. **Flourishing:** I've embraced the call to create spaces where life can grow—whether that's in my family, my work, or my community. Flourishing is about multiplying love, justice, and wisdom in tangible ways.

THE INVITATION TO CO-CREATION

The Great Commission isn't a burdensome task or a fear-driven mandate. It's an invitation to co-create with the Creator, to bring flourishing and connection to the world. It fulfills the Creator's original mandate in Genesis, carried forward through Yeshua's life, death, and resurrection.

If the fear-based gospel has left you feeling disconnected, exhausted, or inadequate, know this: the Creator's invitation is still open. You are already loved, already connected, and already equipped to co-create with the One who called you into being.

SVEN MASTERSON

CO-CREATION IS THE HEART OF THE MISSION

The Creator's mission isn't about fear, shame, or judgment. It's about life, connection, and flourishing. Through the good news of salvation, sonship, and empowerment, we are invited to partner with the Creator in co-creating a world that reflects His love. This is a truly Great Commission—an invitation not to rescue but to create, connect, and flourish together.

COMMON RESPONSES

"Yeah, but isn't the Great Commission about saving souls from hell?"

The Great Commission is about bringing people into connection with the Creator and empowering them to live abundantly. It's not focused on fear-based rescue but on flourishing, love, and transformation.

"Yeah, but doesn't this perspective downplay the urgency of the mission?"

On the contrary, this perspective amplifies urgency in a different way—it invites us to bring life, connection, and flourishing into a world desperate for restoration. It's not about panic but purpose.

"Yeah, but doesn't this sound like works-based theology?"

Not at all. Co-creation is not about earning salvation but living out the connection and empowerment we've already received. It's the natural fruit of experiencing the Creator's love.

WHAT TO DO WHEN THE ALIENS SHOW UP (AND EVEN IF THEY DON'T)

"Yeah, but aren't we called to warn people of judgment?"

Yeshua's focus was on inviting people into the Kingdom of God that was within and near them, not instilling fear of punishment. Judgment is real, but it serves to expose disconnection and invite people back to love, not to terrify them into compliance.

"Yeah, but what about evangelism? Isn't sharing the gospel still vital?"

Absolutely! Sharing the gospel is essential, but it's about proclaiming the good news of connection, redemption, and flourishing—not spreading fear or shame. Effective evangelism invites others into a relationship, not into avoiding punishment.

CHAPTER FIFTY-EIGHT
THE BREATH WITHIN
OUR CO-PILOT IN CREATION

The winds of grace are always blowing, but you have to raise the sail. – Ramakrishna

---

EMPOWERED BY BREATH: REDISCOVERING THE SPIRIT'S ROLE

For much of my early journey, the Spirit was a mystery I couldn't quite pin down. I'd read the mentions of the "Spirit" or the "Holy Ghost" in scripture and felt equal parts fascination and alienation. Was it a force? A presence? A person? And if the Spirit was real, why did it feel so distant from me?

Looking back, I can see that my struggle to understand the Spirit was shaped by the same misconceptions that had clouded my understanding of the Creator. Just as I once saw the Creator through the lens of fear and judgment, I viewed the Spirit as some elusive force I had to chase—always just out of reach. It wasn't until I began reframing my relationship with the Creator and stepping into my identity as a son that the Spirit started to feel less like a mystery and more like a companion.

This chapter reflects on my journey to understanding the Spirit

—not as a distant, dramatic force but as the breath of life, a guide, and an empowering partner in the Great Commission.

THE SPIRIT AND MY EARLY FOMO

In my younger days, the Spirit seemed like something other people had but I lacked. I heard stories of miraculous encounters, dramatic healings, and speaking in tongues. I watched as preachers laid hands on people, who would then collapse in tears or joy. It was captivating and alienating all at once.

I wanted what they had—or at least what they said they had. I wanted proof that the Creator saw me, loved me, and valued me enough to pour out dramatic experiences. But when those moments didn't come for me, I felt stuck. Was there something wrong with me? Was I not praying hard enough, believing strongly enough, or living righteously enough?

In hindsight, I see how trapped I was in the **Drama Triangle** during that season:

- **Victim:** I felt spiritually deficient, unworthy of the Spirit's presence.
- **Persecutor:** I projected judgment onto the Creator, imagining Him as withholding the Spirit from me.
- **Rescuer:** I looked to the Spirit as a magical force that would swoop in and fix my sense of inadequacy.

This mindset left me disconnected from the Creator, myself, and the Spirit. I was chasing an experience, not a relationship.

THE SPIRIT RENEWED: EMPOWERMENT, NOT TRANSACTION

It wasn't until years later that my perspective began to shift. As I grew in my understanding of sonship and moved away from a transactional view of the Creator, I started to see the Spirit differ-

WHAT TO DO WHEN THE ALIENS SHOW UP (AND EVEN IF THEY DON'T)

ently. The Spirit wasn't a performer or a rescuer—it was a constant, quiet presence, inviting me into partnership.

I began to notice how scripture described the Spirit:

- As **breath**—intimate, life-giving, always present.
- As a **guide**—pointing toward truth, connection, and love.
- As a **comforter**—reminding us that we are never alone.
- As an **empowering presence**—not taking over our lives, but equipping us to live abundantly.

The Spirit wasn't there to prove my worth or "rescue" me from my struggles. It was there to empower me to step into my role as a creator in partnership with the Creator.

BREATH AND SPIRIT: A PROFOUND CONNECTION

One of the most transformative realizations for me was the connection between the Spirit and breath. In both Hebrew (ruach) and Greek (pneuma), the words for Spirit also mean "breath." This wasn't just a linguistic curiosity—it was a profound truth about the Spirit's role in our lives.

I started to see the Spirit as the breath that animates us, the quiet presence that's always one inhale away. When I felt overwhelmed, stuck, or disconnected, I began to pause and take a deep breath. This simple act became a spiritual practice. Every inhale reminded me of the Spirit's presence, and every exhale was an opportunity to let go of fear, shame, and judgment.

THE SPIRIT AS A SOURCE AND PARTNER IN EMPOWERMENT

As I leaned into this understanding of the Spirit, I began to notice its vital role as both the source of life and a partner in the Empowerment Dynamic. This wasn't just an abstract concept; it was deeply practical and transformative.

SVEN MASTERSON

The Spirit as the Breath of Life

As I mentioned above, the word "Spirit" itself comes from the Hebrew word *ruach* and the Greek *pneuma*, both of which mean breath or wind. The connection to breath is profound. Just as breath sustains our physical life, the Spirit sustains our spiritual life. The English word *inspiration* literally means "to breathe in," and it captures this dynamic beautifully. When we are aligned with the Spirit, we are inspired—infused with life, energy, and creativity.

But fear, shame, and disconnection often disrupt this rhythm. Think about how you breathe when you're afraid or stressed. You hold your breath, or your breathing becomes shallow and restricted. Physically, you're cutting off the full flow of oxygen, but spiritually, the same thing happens. Fear and shame cause us to "hold our breath," disconnecting us from the life-giving inspiration of the Spirit. We end up hanging onto the carbon dioxide we need to release while shorting ourselves of the oxygen that infuses our blood, delivery life and flourishing to every cell. The Spirit (breath) is vital to every aspect of our being!

To live inspired is to live in harmony with the Spirit's breath—deeply connected, fully alive, and open to the flow of love and truth. Conversely, to live "expired" is to live in disconnection, as though we've spiritually held our breath, cutting ourselves off from the source of life.

The Spirit's role, then, is not just to empower us but to reintroduce us to this rhythm of life. It invites us to inhale deeply the truth of the Creator's love and to exhale the lies of fear and shame.

THE SPIRIT AS A PARTNER IN EMPOWERMENT

The Spirit doesn't just inspire—it equips and partners with us, helping us move from passivity to participation, from victimhood to empowerment. In this dynamic, I began to see the Spirit not as something external that "fixes" me but as an intimate partner working alongside me in every area of life:

WHAT TO DO WHEN THE ALIENS SHOW UP (AND EVEN IF THEY DON'T)

1. The Spirit as Source

The Spirit is the wellspring of life and empowerment. Just as breath sustains our physical being, the Spirit sustains our spiritual growth. It's the force that energizes, renews, and brings clarity when we feel lost or stuck. In moments of exhaustion or doubt, the Spirit reminds us to breathe deeply, reconnecting us to the Creator's love and wisdom.

2. The Spirit as a Guide

The Spirit gently nudges us toward truth, illuminating the path ahead. It helps us discern the difference between life-giving choices rooted in love and those born of fear or disconnection. When we're tempted to fall into old patterns of shame or blame, the Spirit's guidance helps us step back and realign with the Creator's purposes.

3. The Spirit as a Coach

Like a skilled coach, the Spirit doesn't take over or demand submission. Instead, it teaches, challenges, and encourages us, helping us grow into maturity. It provides insight, but it also invites us to take ownership of our decisions and actions. The Spirit empowers us to be active participants in our own journey, working with us to develop resilience, courage, and creativity.

4. The Spirit as a Challenger

At times, the Spirit confronts the lies we've believed—about ourselves, others, or the Creator. These lies often keep us trapped in cycles of fear and disconnection. The Spirit's challenge isn't harsh or condemning; it's compassionate and liberating. It invites us to examine the stories we've been telling ourselves and to step into deeper freedom and connection.

SVEN MASTERSON

LIVING IN PARTNERSHIP WITH THE SPIRIT

This reframing of the Spirit shifted my mindset entirely. The Spirit wasn't there to perform for me or fix me. It wasn't a magical solution to my problems. It was a partner—faithful, present, and empowering.

When I began to live inspired, I noticed how my spiritual and physical rhythms began to align. Just as I learned to breathe deeply and intentionally in moments of fear or stress, I also learned to pause and invite the Spirit into my decisions, relationships, and struggles.

The Spirit's empowerment wasn't about making life easy. It was about equipping me to face life with clarity, courage, and connection. It was about helping me step out of the Drama Triangle and into the Empowerment Dynamic—living not as a victim, rescuer, or persecutor but as a creator, coach, and challenger.

Living inspired means living connected to the Spirit's breath. It means choosing trust over fear, connection over shame, and flourishing over disconnection. It's an invitation to breathe deeply, to let the Spirit fill you with life, and to walk in partnership with the Creator.

So, take a moment. Pause. Breathe. Inhale the Spirit's truth and exhale the lies that hold you back. The Spirit is here, not to control or fix you, but to partner with you—to empower you to live fully, freely, and inspired.

THE FRUITS OF THE SPIRIT AND THE ASCENT FROM SUFFERING TO THRIVING

One of the most profound shifts in my understanding came when I recognized how closely the journey described in scripture aligns with the movement from what I call "The Descent" to "The Ascent." These stages in my model parallel the biblical themes of living "in the flesh" versus "in the Spirit." The fruit of each way of living is drastically different, and understanding this distinction offers clarity and hope for anyone seeking to move from suffering to thriving.

THE DESCENT: LIVING IN THE "FLESH"

The Descent is the stage of disconnection, fear, and striving. It's marked by a life oriented around self-protection, ego, and disempowerment—what the scriptures describe as walking in "the flesh." Paul outlines the works of the flesh in Galatians 5:19-21, and they map perfectly onto the struggles we face in the Drama Triangle:

- **Immorality, impurity, and lust**—seeking temporary satisfaction to fill an internal void.
- **Hatred, jealousy, and fits of anger**—blame and resentment toward others or the Creator.
- **Strife, dissension, and divisions**—broken relationships and isolation.
- **Envy and pride**—a desperate need to validate our worth by comparing ourselves to others.

Life in the Descent feels heavy, chaotic, and exhausting. It's the spiritual equivalent of holding your breath—cutting yourself off from the life-giving inspiration of the Spirit. The fruit of this way of living is predictable: brokenness, disconnection, and suffering.

THE ASCENT: WALKING IN THE "SPIRIT"

The Ascent represents the turning point—stepping out of the Drama Triangle and into the Empowerment Dynamic. It's a shift from fear to trust, from striving to connection, and from disempowerment to flourishing. Scripture describes this transformation as walking "in the Spirit," where the fruits are radically different (Galatians 5:22–23):

- **Love:** The freedom to see yourself and others through the Creator's eyes, without shame or judgment.
- **Joy:** A deep sense of fulfillment and gratitude that doesn't depend on circumstances.
- **Peace:** A steady trust that allows you to navigate uncertainty with calm and clarity.
- **Patience, kindness, and gentleness:** Relational fruits that heal and restore connection.
- **Faithfulness and self-control:** The strength to align your actions with your values, even in the face of challenge.

This stage aligns with Yeshua's description of the Kingdom of God. In John 4, He tells the Samaritan woman about "living water" that will satisfy her forever—a picture of life in the Spirit. In Mark 1:15, He proclaims that the Kingdom is "at hand," inviting us into a reality of flourishing and empowerment right now. The Ascent is the Kingdom breaking into our lives, transforming how we think, act, and relate to the Creator, ourselves, and others.

THE SPIRIT AS LIVING WATER

The Spirit's role in this transformation is nothing short of life-giving. Yeshua described the Spirit as "living water" (John 7:38-39), flowing from within those who believe in Him. This water doesn't just quench—it sustains, nourishes, and empowers.

Consider the physical sensation of thirst. In the Descent, we're spiritually dehydrated, grasping at anything to fill the emptiness. But in the Ascent, the Spirit becomes an endless source of refreshment, inspiring us to create, love, and thrive. Living in the Spirit is like stepping into a flowing stream—alive, dynamic, and continually renewing.

WHAT TO DO WHEN THE ALIENS SHOW UP (AND EVEN IF THEY DON'T)

THE FRUITS OF THE JOURNEY: A VISUAL REPRESENTATION

I imagine this journey as a vertical movement from the works of the flesh (Descent) to the fruits of the Spirit (Ascent). It's not a linear process or a one-time leap—it's a rhythm, much like breathing. As we walk in the Spirit, we align ourselves with the Creator's heartbeat, experiencing life as it was meant to be lived.

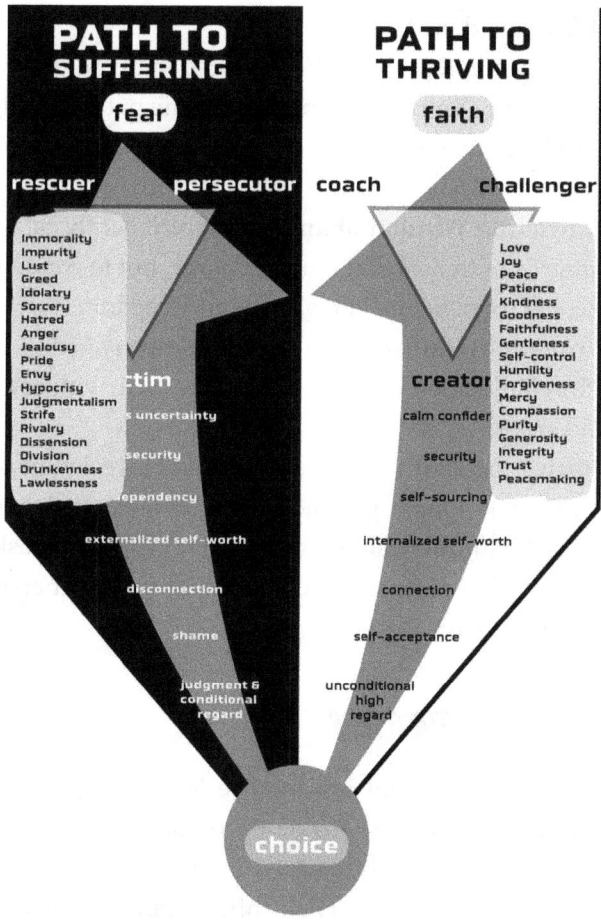

Fruits of "The Flesh" (Drama Triangle Living) vs Fruits of "The Spirit" (Empowerment Dynamic Living)

SVEN MASTERSON

THE SPIRIT'S ROLE IN TRANSFORMATION

The more I've grown in my awareness of the Spirit, the more I've seen its transformative power in specific ways:

1. **Comfort in Uncertainty:** When I feel overwhelmed or unsure, the Spirit whispers reminders of the Creator's love and presence. This has been a lifeline in moments of fear and doubt.
2. **Guidance in Decisions:** When faced with tough choices, the Spirit helps me discern the path that aligns with love and connection, even when it's not the easiest route.
3. **Conviction Without Shame:** The Spirit gently calls out patterns or beliefs that don't serve me, not to condemn me, but to invite me into growth and freedom.
4. **Strength in Hardship:** The Spirit doesn't shield us from life's challenges but equips us to face them with courage and grace.
5. **Cultivating Fruit:** The Spirit produces love, joy, peace, patience, kindness, goodness, faithfulness, gentleness, and self-control (Galatians 5:22–23). These aren't tasks to strive for but natural outcomes of living in partnership with the Spirit.

BREATHING IN PARTNERSHIP

One of the most profound lessons I've learned is that the Spirit doesn't shout—it whispers. It doesn't demand—it invites. When life feels chaotic, I've found that the simplest way to reconnect with the Spirit is through breath. Each inhale reminds me of its presence, and each exhale offers an opportunity to release fear, shame, and judgment.

This practice has changed how I experience the Spirit. I no longer chase dramatic encounters or compare my journey to others. Instead, I lean into the quiet, steady partnership the Spirit offers, knowing that it's not about performance or perfection—it's about connection.

EMPOWERED TO CO-CREATE

The Spirit's role in the Great Commission isn't to control us or overshadow us. It's to empower us to step into our identity as sons and daughters of the Creator, partnering with Adonai to bring flourishing and connection to the world. Through the Spirit, we're equipped to live abundantly, love courageously, and co-create purposefully.

The Spirit isn't a distant force or a dramatic performer. It's as close as our breath, as steady as our heartbeat, and as empowering as a trusted guide. Through this partnership, we step into the fullness of the Creator's vision for our lives—connected, empowered, and alive with purpose.

COMMON RESPONSES

"Yeah, but what if I don't feel the Spirit's presence in my life?"

I've been there—it can feel isolating and even discouraging, especially if we've deeply struggled with shame and feelings of unworthiness and abandonment. But not feeling the Spirit doesn't mean it isn't with you. The Spirit is often taught as being about whiz-bang, flashy, supernatural moments of signs, wonders, and significant emotional moments. But the promise of the Spirit is about an abiding presence, connection, counsel, and comfort. Like most close relationships, those often take place more like a gentle breeze or the steady rhythm of your breath. When I've struggled to sense the Spirit, I've learned to pause, breathe deeply, and simply breathe the Spirit in, having the assurance, from acceptance, that this is always available to me. Even when I couldn't feel it, the Spirit was quietly present, waiting for me to notice.

> "Yeah, but isn't the Spirit only for people who are extra holy or specially called?"

I used to think that, too, and it left me feeling unworthy and excluded. But the Spirit is for everyone—it's the breath of life, present in every inhale you take. You don't need to achieve a certain level of righteousness or have a special calling. The Spirit isn't a reward; it's a gift freely given to empower you right where you are, in the middle of your ordinary, messy, beautiful life.

> "Yeah, but how can I trust the Spirit when everything feels chaotic?"

This is one of the hardest questions, isn't it? Chaos makes us want to take control or retreat into fear. I've found that the Spirit is most steady and reliable in those moments—it's not here to fix everything instantly, but to guide and empower you through it. Trust starts small: a whispered prayer, a deep breath, or simply asking for wisdom in the next step. The Spirit thrives in chaos, gently reminding us that even when we're overwhelmed, we're never alone.

> "Yeah, but isn't relying on the Spirit just an excuse to avoid responsibility?"

I've wrestled with this, too, fearing that surrendering to the Spirit would mean giving up my agency. But the Spirit doesn't control you—no more than your breath controls you—it partners with, enables, and empowers you. It's like a coach who equips and empowers you to make bold, loving, and wise choices. The Spirit doesn't take responsibility from you; it helps you carry it with courage and grace.

WHAT TO DO WHEN THE ALIENS SHOW UP (AND EVEN IF THEY DON'T)

"Yeah, but how do I know it's really the Spirit and not just my own thoughts?"

This is a question I've spent a lot of time wrestling with myself. Over the years, I've come to see that the Spirit isn't some distant or separate entity whispering from the outside—it's intertwined with the union we share as beings connected to the Source of life and love. The voice of the Spirit is not distinct from the voice of our truest, most aligned self, the part of us that reflects the Creator's image and is already rooted in connection, love, and truth.

Scripture reminds us that "the spirit of the prophets is under the control of the prophets," which means the Spirit doesn't take over, control, or force its way. Instead, it works in partnership with us, empowering us to step into alignment with our true identity.

When I've questioned whether something is the Spirit or just my own thoughts, I've learned to pause and reflect: Does this lead me toward deeper connection? Does it foster love, peace, and authenticity? Does it align with the truth of who I am as a child of the Creator? The Spirit will never shame or condemn—it calls us back to love, to life, to flourishing. Trusting this voice takes time, but it's not about straining to hear something outside yourself. It's about learning to trust the union and connection you already have with the Creator, through the Spirit, within your own heart.

CHAPTER FIFTY-NINE
GROUND ZERO
THE UNSHAKABLE LOVE THAT HOLDS US STEADY

> The deepest truth of who we are is that we belong to an unshakable love, and that belonging frees us to live fully, love deeply, and flourish abundantly. – Henri Nouwen

APPROACHING THE END OF THE JOURNEY

As I near the end of sharing my journey with you, I find myself reflecting on the transformation that's taken place—not just in how I view the Creator, but in how I understand myself and the world around me. This has been more than a shift in theology or worldview; it has been a deep, ongoing healing, a restoration of connection I didn't even know I had lost.

When I began this journey, I lived under the heavy weight of striving. Striving to be good enough, striving to find love, striving to secure a place where I belonged. I believed love, acceptance, and purpose were rewards—something I had to earn through my actions or prove through perfection. But when I fell short (as I always did), I would spiral into shame. That shame whispered lies: I was broken, I was incomplete, I was disconnected. For years, I lived as though those lies were the truth.

But the Creator had other plans. Through encounters with the Spirit, through Yeshua's life and example, and through a gradual reframing of what salvation, connection, and love really mean, my perspective began to shift. Piece by piece, the truths I had once heard but dismissed or misunderstood began to settle into my heart. And these truths—they changed everything.

ETERNAL TRUTHS THAT CHANGED EVERYTHING

There are truths so profound that, once we grasp them, they reframe every aspect of life. They aren't conditional or fleeting; they're eternal, rooted in the Creator's unchanging nature. These truths were the foundation of my transformation:

- You are loved.
- You are accepted.
- You are forgiven.
- You are invited.
- You are empowered.

When I first encountered these truths, I struggled to believe them. How could they possibly be true for me? After all, I'd spent years feeling as though my worth was conditional, tied to my performance or achievements. But as I dug deeper into the story of Yeshua, I realized these truths weren't contingent on anything I could do. They were constant because they were rooted in the Creator's nature, not mine.

What struck me most was the realization that these truths didn't start at the cross—they were simply revealed there. The Creator's love didn't begin with Yeshua's sacrifice; it was demonstrated through it. Forgiveness wasn't something that had to be earned or bought; it was something that had always been available. The cross wasn't about changing the Creator's mind about humanity—it was about changing humanity's mind about the Creator.

THE LIE THAT KEPT ME STUCK

Looking back, I can see how the lie of disconnection shaped so much of my life. It's the same lie humanity has wrestled with since the very beginning. In the garden, the serpent whispered to Adam and Eve that they were incomplete, that the Creator's love wasn't enough, that they needed something more to be truly whole. Believing that lie, they hid in shame and began striving to cover their perceived lack.

I fell for that same lie in my own life. I believed that my worth was tied to what I could achieve or how well I could perform. I thought love and belonging were things I had to secure, not gifts I could receive. That lie drove me into cycles of striving and shame:

- Striving for approval through accomplishments or status.
- Hiding in fear and self-judgment when I fell short.
- Numbing the ache of disconnection in ways that never truly satisfied.

The more I tried to secure my worth, the more disconnected I felt. It wasn't until the Spirit began gently confronting the lies I had believed that I started to see the truth: my worth was never in question. I wasn't broken or incomplete. The Creator's love wasn't something I had to earn—it was something I had always had.

THE SPIRIT'S ROLE IN MY TRANSFORMATION

The Spirit played a pivotal role in reshaping my understanding of connection and self-worth. Early in my journey, I viewed the Spirit as a distant concept or an occasional visitor—a rescuer who swooped in during dramatic moments but left me to figure out the rest on my own. But as I grew in my relationship with the Creator, I began to see the Spirit differently.

The Spirit became a quiet, constant presence in my life. Not a dramatic force or an external rescuer, but a guide, a coach, and a companion:

- **A Guide:** Leading me gently toward truth, helping me see where I had been living out of shame or fear.
- **A Coach:** Encouraging me to grow, to let go of striving, and to trust the Creator's love.
- **A Challenger:** Confronting the lies I believed and inviting me into deeper freedom.

The Spirit didn't remove my struggles, but it empowered me to face them. It didn't give me all the answers, but it walked with me as I wrestled with the questions. Over time, I came to see the Spirit as the breath of life—always present, always reminding me that I was connected, loved, and free.

UNSHAKABLE WORTH AND THE END OF STRIVING

One of the most transformative truths I've learned is this: my worth doesn't come from what I do; it comes from who I am. And who I am is rooted in who the Creator is.

These words of Yeshua capture this beautifully:

> I am the vine, you are the branches; the one who remains in Me, and I in him bears much fruit, for apart from Me you can do nothing.
> –John 15:5

For years, I lived as though I had to be my own vine, supplying my own worth and striving to produce fruit on my own. But a branch disconnected from the vine can't flourish. My disconnection didn't change the truth of who I was, but it kept me from experiencing it. Shame and striving are like fig leaves—they might cover the surface, but they can't provide the life and nourishment we truly need.

The Spirit showed me that connection—not performance—is the source of life. When I remain in the Creator's love, I don't have to strive for worth or hide in shame. My worth isn't something I achieve; it's something I embrace. It's unshakable because it's rooted in a love that doesn't waver.

WHAT THE GOOD NEWS REALLY IS

As I approach the end of this journey of sharing, I want to be as clear as possible about what the good news really is. It's not a list of rules to follow or hoops to jump through. It's not a message of fear or condemnation. It's not about securing something you don't already have.

The good news is this:

- You are already *loved*.
- You are already *accepted*.
- You are already *forgiven*.
- You are already *invited*.
- You are already *empowered*.

The Creator's love is constant, unshakable, and unearned. The Spirit is always present, always inviting us into connection. The cross reveals that nothing—not shame, not fear, not even death—can separate us from this truth.

The invitation is simple: will you embrace it? Will you step out of striving and into connection? Will you let go of shame and trust the truth of your worth? The good news isn't just something to believe—it's something to live.

SVEN MASTERSON

FREEDOM TO FLOURISH

The truth of the good news has set me free—not just from shame or striving but for something greater. It has freed me to live boldly, authentically, and abundantly. It has freed me to reflect the Creator's love and bring flourishing to the world around me.

This is what I hope for you, too: not just to hear the good news but to experience it, to live it, and to share it. You are already loved. You are already accepted. You are already invited into connection. And through that connection, you are empowered to flourish.

COMMON RESPONSES

"Yeah, but how can I believe I'm already loved and accepted when I've made so many mistakes?"

The Creator's love isn't based on how well you perform or the mistakes you've made—it's based on who He is. Love that's conditional isn't love at all, and the Creator's love is the most consistent, unshakable thing there is. Your mistakes don't disqualify you; they're the very reason grace exists. The cross didn't make the Creator love you—it showed He always has.

"Yeah, but isn't this idea of unconditional love just a license to sin?"

The Creator's love doesn't excuse destructive behavior; it transforms us, providing a way for use to move away from destructive behaviors. When you truly understand you're loved and accepted, you don't want to stay in patterns that harm you or others. Unconditional love inspires freedom, not recklessness. It calls you into a flourishing life, not one driven by shame or fear.

WHAT TO DO WHEN THE ALIENS SHOW UP (AND EVEN IF THEY DON'T)

"Yeah, but doesn't this message of grace ignore the need for repentance?"

Repentance isn't about groveling for forgiveness—it's about turning toward life. It's a recognition that shame, disconnection, and fear don't serve you, and choosing to step into love, truth, and connection. Grace doesn't remove the need for repentance; it empowers it. It gives you the courage to face what's been holding you back and embrace the Creator's invitation to flourish.

"Yeah, but why do I still feel disconnected if all of this is true?"

Disconnection often comes from the lies we've internalized—the belief that we're unworthy or that love has to be earned. The Creator's love hasn't gone anywhere; the Spirit is always present, always inviting. Take it one step at a time. Practice moments of trust, lean into gratitude, and be gentle with yourself as you unlearn the patterns of fear and striving. Connection is always available, even if it takes time to feel it.

"Yeah, but what if I can't believe this is true for me?"

Doubt doesn't scare the Creator. If it's hard to believe, that's okay—it's part of being human. Start where you are. Practice saying, "I'm loved," even if you don't fully believe it yet. Look for small moments of grace in your life—kindness, beauty, connection. The Spirit will gently guide you into this truth, not by force but through persistent, patient love. Believing isn't a test; it's a journey.

CHAPTER SIXTY
THE WELLSPRING
DRINKING DEEPLY FROM THE SOURCE OF LOVE

> And the day came when the risk to remain tight in a bud was more painful than the risk it took to blossom. – Anaïs Nin

A JOURNEY TO WHOLENESS

THE JOURNEY I'VE SHARED WITH YOU HAS BEEN ONE OF DISCOVERY, healing, and transformation. For so many years, I lived in judgment, shame, and disconnection—from myself, from my wife, from others, and even from the Creator. I was striving, performing, and endlessly searching for something I thought I lacked. But as I began to embrace the truths I've shared in this book, my life changed in ways I never could have imagined.

These weren't just intellectual shifts or theological tweaks. They were deeply personal, life-altering revelations that touched every part of my being. They changed how I saw myself, how I related to the Creator, and how I showed up in my relationships. The more I understood and implemented these truths, the more I experienced what Yeshua called "living water"—a wellspring of life that brought renewal, freedom, and flourishing.

This chapter is about what has changed for me since those days of shame and striving. It's about the power of living in connection, the healing that comes from embracing the Creator's love, and the fruit that grows when we step into sonship, friendship, and empowerment. My hope is that as I share my story, you'll see what's possible for you, too.

THE DEFEAT OF SHAME: EMBRACING THE CREATOR'S LOVE THROUGH YESHUA

One of the most profound changes I experienced was the gradual and ongoing defeat of shame. For years, shame had been a constant companion, whispering lies about my worth, my identity, and my failures. It kept me in hiding—disconnected from my true self, from others, and most painfully, from the Creator. I thought shame was a motivator, a necessary burden to keep me on the straight and narrow. But in reality, it was a thief, stealing my joy, authenticity, and connection.

The Root of Shame and Its Power

Shame thrives on judgment—our own, others', and what we imagine the Creator's to be. At its root, shame tells us we're not enough and that we'll only ever be accepted if we prove ourselves worthy. It convinces us that failure is fatal and imperfection is a dealbreaker. This lie led me to believe that I had to perform, strive, and earn love and belonging. But striving only deepened my disconnection and self-condemnation, keeping me trapped in cycles of guilt and hiding.

Yeshua's Life and Message: Dismantling Shame

The turning point came when I began to see the Creator not as a wrathful judge but as a loving Father. Yeshua's life, actions, and message dismantled the lie of shame in powerful ways:

WHAT TO DO WHEN THE ALIENS SHOW UP (AND EVEN IF THEY DON'T)

1. Yeshua's Declaration of Worth

Yeshua didn't base His interactions on people's achievements or failures. He declared the worth of the outcast, the sinner, and the broken-hearted simply because they were beloved by the Creator. In His interactions with those weighed down by shame—the Samaritan woman at the well, the woman caught in adultery, Zacchaeus the tax collector—He spoke words of peace, dignity, and connection. He didn't shame them; He restored them.

His message was clear: Our worth is not tied to our performance or status. The Creator's love is unconditional, and no amount of shame can separate us from it.

2. The Cross as the Death of Judgment

For years, I thought the cross was about satisfying the Creator's wrath. But as I wrestled with its meaning, I began to see it differently. The cross wasn't about judgment being satisfied—it was about judgment being exposed and defeated. Humanity judged Yeshua, condemning the embodiment of love and truth, yet He didn't respond with retaliation or condemnation. Instead, He absorbed our judgment and offered forgiveness, declaring, "Father, forgive them, for they know not what they do" (Luke 23:34).

In doing so, He revealed the Creator's heart: not one of condemnation but of infinite love. His resurrection affirmed this truth, proving that shame and death do not have the final word.

3. An Invitation to Connection

Yeshua's entire mission was an invitation—to return to the Creator's love, to lay down our self-imposed judgment, and to walk in the freedom of being fully known and fully loved. He showed that the Creator doesn't judge us the way we judge ourselves. Instead, He calls us out of hiding, clothes us in His acceptance, and restores us to a place of dignity and connection.

Replacing Shame with Truth

As I embraced these truths, the grip of shame began to loosen. I realized that I didn't need to strive for love or acceptance—I already had them. Shame's lies were replaced with the truth of sonship, forgiveness, and connection:

- **Sonship:** I am not an outsider trying to earn a place at the table; I am a child of the Creator, already loved and accepted.
- **Forgiveness:** My failures and imperfections are not barriers to love; they are opportunities for grace and growth.
- **Connection:** I am not alone or unworthy; I am deeply known and cherished by the Creator.

Living in Freedom

This freedom isn't just internal—it transforms how I live. Without the weight of shame, I've found the courage to step into authenticity. I no longer need to hide behind masks or fear judgment. I can show up fully, knowing that my worth is unshakable.

This freedom has also brought clarity and integrity to my life. Boundaries, once an area of struggle, have become natural extensions of living in alignment with the truth of who I am. I've found that when I live from a place of connection, it's easier to make decisions, navigate challenges, and build relationships rooted in love and mutual respect.

So if the Son sets you free, you will be free indeed.
–John 8:36

WHAT TO DO WHEN THE ALIENS SHOW UP (AND EVEN IF THEY DON'T)

The Path to Wholeness

OVERCOMING SHAME ISN'T a one-time event—it's a journey. But with each step, the lies of shame lose their power, and the truth of love and connection takes root. Yeshua's life and message continue to invite me to turn away from judgment and toward the Creator's unconditional love.

If you've carried the weight of shame, know this: You don't have to strive, prove, or earn your worth. The Creator's love is already yours, unchanging and unshakable. Yeshua's life declares it, and His resurrection proves it. Shame is a liar, but the truth will always set you free.

THE HEALING OF MY MARRIAGE

As I have healed, my marriage has healed. As I continue to flourish, so does it. Shame had created walls between me and my wife—walls I didn't even fully recognize at the time. I had been emotionally distant, insecure, and reactive. I wanted to connect, but I didn't know how. I felt inadequate and unworthy, and those feelings bled into our relationship.

When I began to experience the Creator's love and acceptance, something shifted. I stopped approaching my marriage from a place of fear and started showing up as my whole, authentic self. I became more patient, more compassionate, and more present. I stopped needing my wife to validate me or fill the gaps left by my disconnection from the Creator. Instead, I was able to love her freely, without the entanglements of insecurity or dependency.

Our relationship transformed. Conversations that once felt strained became opportunities for connection. Conflicts that once felt insurmountable became chances to grow together. My wife didn't just see the change in me—she felt it. And as I healed, so did we.

THE RECONNECTION TO MYSELF

For years, I had been disconnected from my true self. I didn't trust my own feelings, instincts, or desires. I saw them as flawed or dangerous, something to suppress rather than embrace. But as I stepped into sonship and began to see myself as the Creator does—loved, accepted, and whole—I started to reconnect with who I truly am.

This reconnection brought a sense of peace and clarity I had never known. I stopped trying to be someone I wasn't and began to embrace my unique gifts, strengths, and passions. I found joy in being myself, without the need for approval or validation from others. And as I became more connected to myself, I became more present and authentic in all my relationships.

THE TRANSFORMATION OF FATHERHOOD

My relationship with my kids had always been good—or so I thought. But as I healed, I realized there was room for so much more. Shame and striving had subtly shaped how I parented, creating moments of impatience, fear, and control. I wanted to be a good father, but I often felt like I was falling short.

As I embraced the truths of sonship and connection, my parenting transformed. I stopped trying to control my kids and started empowering them. I became more present, more patient, and more attuned to their needs. I listened more and judged less. I stopped projecting my insecurities onto them and started seeing them as the unique, beloved individuals they are.

The results were remarkable. My kids felt more seen, valued, and supported. Our bond deepened, and our home became a place of safety, trust, and connection. I went from being a good father to a great one—not because I tried harder, but because I loved from a place of wholeness.

THE GROWTH OF AUTHENTIC FRIENDSHIPS

As I healed, my friendships changed, too. I had always valued my friends, but shame and insecurity had kept me from being fully authentic with them. I worried about what they thought of me, avoided vulnerability, and sometimes tried to impress them to feel accepted.

When I let go of shame, I stopped performing in my friendships. I became more honest, more open, and more willing to let others see the real me. This authenticity deepened my connections and drew new, like-minded friends into my life. Instead of shallow interactions, I experienced genuine community—friends who celebrated my growth and walked with me through challenges.

FROM INEFFECTIVENESS TO TRUE IMPACT

Perhaps the most surprising transformation was in how I approached what some might call "ministry." For years, I had tried to "make disciples," but my efforts were rooted in shame, fear, and striving. I thought my job was to convince people of their sinfulness and their need for salvation, but all I really did was perpetuate the cycles of shame that had kept me stuck for so long.

When I began living out the truths of connection, sonship, and empowerment, everything changed. I stopped trying to "save" people and started helping them see the truth of who they already were: loved, accepted, and whole. I shared my story, not as a blueprint for perfection but as an invitation to freedom. And people responded—not out of fear or obligation, but out of a genuine desire for the connection and transformation they saw in my life.

Today, I have the privilege of helping people all over the world overcome their shame and disconnection. I've seen lives transformed, marriages restored, and individuals step into their true identities. It's not because I have all the answers, but because I've learned to point people to the truths that set me free.

LIVING WATER: THE POWER OF CONNECTION

Yeshua once spoke to a Samaritan woman about living water—a source of life that would quench her thirst and never run dry. For so long, I lived as though that water was out of reach, something I had to earn or find through striving. But now, I understand that it was always available. It wasn't something I needed to achieve—it was something I needed to receive.

Living water isn't just a metaphor. It's the reality of a life rooted in connection, love, and empowerment. It's the freedom to be fully yourself, to love without fear, and to live with courage and purpose. It's the fruit of stepping into sonship, friendship, and partnership with the Creator.

AN INVITATION TO TRANSFORMATION

If there's one thing I hope you take away from this book, it's this: transformation is possible. No matter how stuck, ashamed, or disconnected you feel, the truths I've shared are available to you. You are already loved. You are already accepted. You are already invited into connection.

The journey to living water isn't always easy, but it's worth it. It's a journey of healing, reconnection, and flourishing. And as you step into these truths, you'll not only experience transformation in your own life—you'll become a source of living water for others.

The invitation is open. Will you say yes?

COMMON RESPONSES

> "Yeah, but how can I let go of shame when it feels so deeply ingrained?"

WHAT TO DO WHEN THE ALIENS SHOW UP (AND EVEN IF THEY DON'T)

Shame is persistent because it thrives on lies we've believed for so long. It whispers that you're not enough, but the truth is, you've always been enough in the Creator's eyes. Letting go of shame doesn't happen all at once—it's a process of replacing lies with truth. Each time you remind yourself that you are loved, forgiven, and accepted, shame loses its grip a little more. The Spirit will guide you gently, helping you see yourself through the Creator's loving eyes.

"Yeah, but what if my relationships are too damaged to heal?"

Relationships can be deeply wounded, but healing is always possible when love and truth are invited in. It starts with you stepping into authenticity and vulnerability. The Creator's love doesn't just transform you; it transforms how you show up for others. While not every relationship will reconcile perfectly, the freedom and love you live from can create space for incredible restoration, sometimes in ways you least expect.

"Yeah, but how do I live authentically when I fear rejection?"

Living authentically is brave, especially when fear of rejection looms large. Remember this: the Creator's acceptance of you is unshakable. You are already fully known and fully loved. That truth gives you the strength to take small steps toward authenticity. Not everyone will understand or accept the real you, but the right people—the ones who are meant to walk alongside you—will be drawn to your authenticity. You'll find deeper, more meaningful connections as you let go of the masks.

"Yeah, but how can I impact others when I still feel like I'm struggling myself?"

Your struggles don't disqualify you; they make you relatable and real. The most profound impact comes from sharing your journey honestly, not from presenting yourself as someone who has it all figured out. People are drawn to authenticity, not perfection. Your willingness to share how the Creator's love has met you in your struggles can inspire and encourage others far more than polished answers ever could.

"Yeah, but what if I'm too far gone for transformation?"

No one is ever too far gone. The Creator's love is boundless, and His invitation to transformation is for everyone. Yeshua's message is clear: shame and disconnection don't have the final word—love does. The fact that you're asking this question means you're already open to the possibility of change. Trust that the Creator's love meets you exactly where you are and that every step you take toward connection will lead to more freedom and flourishing.

CHAPTER SIXTY-ONE
THE RESISTANCE BEGINS WITH YOU

HOW TO REJECT FEAR-BASED NARRATIVES AND EMBRACE EMPOWERMENT

The truth will set you free, but first it will make you miserable. – James A. Garfield

---

A CALL TO DISCERNMENT: CHOOSING THE STORIES THAT SHAPE US

AS WE NEAR THE END OF THIS JOURNEY, I INVITE YOU TO PAUSE AND consider the stories you live by. Every belief, every narrative, every assumption we hold shapes the way we see the world and the choices we make within it. Are these stories leading you toward freedom, connection, and empowerment? Or are they pulling you into fear, disconnection, and bondage?

In times of uncertainty, the stories we live by become even more critical. Deception thrives in these moments, feeding on fear and vulnerability, shaping our decisions, and defining our reality. Whether we're facing personal crises, societal upheavals, or the hypothetical arrival of beings from beyond the stars, one truth remains: the stories we choose to believe will either enslave us or set us free.

This book has been an invitation—a call to examine your stories, resist the seduction of fear-based narratives, and boldly step into the clarity, courage, and connection that come from living in alignment with truth. Regardless of your beliefs—whether they're rooted in faith, philosophy, or personal experience—this is an opportunity to reflect and ask yourself: Am I living free?

RECOGNIZING THE STORIES THAT DECEIVE

Throughout this book, we've explored how fear, shame, and judgment create fertile ground for deception. These forces thrive when we feel uncertain, disconnected, or insecure. They twist the truth, offering comfort at the cost of clarity, promising rescue while deepening our dependency.

In an alien invasion scenario—our metaphor for global or personal crises—these stories might look like this:

- **The Savior Complex:** Believing someone else holds all the answers and must be obeyed without question.
- **The Scapegoat Narrative:** Blaming a person, group, or ideology for all problems, rather than addressing the deeper issues within ourselves or our systems.
- **The Isolation Trap:** Believing you must go it alone, cutting yourself off from the support and wisdom of others.

These stories mirror the patterns of **D.R.A.M.A.**, a framework explored in the appendix that highlights how the dynamics of Victim, Persecutor, and Rescuer keep us trapped in cycles of fear, disempowerment, and shame. The more we buy into these roles, the more disconnected and powerless we feel.

CHOOSING THE STORIES THAT LIBERATE

In contrast, there are stories that free us—stories rooted in love, connection, and truth. These are the stories that align with the Creator's heart, the ones Yeshua lived and taught:

- **The Story of Empowered Sonship:** You are not a victim, but a beloved child of the Creator. Your identity is secure, and you are invited into a relationship of love, trust, and empowerment.
- **The Story of Loving Connection:** You are never alone. You are part of a larger whole, intricately connected to the Creator, yourself, and others.
- **The Story of Co-Creation:** You are not powerless. You have been entrusted with agency, creativity, and the ability to partner with the Creator in bringing life, love, and flourishing to the world.

These narratives align with the **C.R.E.A.T.O.R.** framework, which invites us to move out of the disempowerment of the Drama Triangle and into roles of Creator, Challenger, and Coach. This dynamic is the antidote to the cycles of fear and shame. It encourages us to step into lives of purpose, courage, and transformation, shaping reality through empowerment and love.

EXAMINING YOUR STORIES

The question we must ask ourselves is this: What stories am I living by? Are they rooted in fear or freedom? Do they reflect the truth of who I am, or are they distortions that keep me stuck?

Take a moment to reflect:

1. **Are My Stories Empowering or Enslaving?**
    - Do the narratives I believe give me courage, agency,

and clarity? Or do they leave me feeling small, afraid, and dependent?
2. **Are My Stories Rooted in Love or Fear?**
    - Do my beliefs reflect unconditional love and acceptance, or do they perpetuate shame, judgment, and division?
3. **Do My Stories Connect or Isolate?**
    - Do they draw me closer to the Creator, myself, and others? Or do they create barriers of mistrust, suspicion, and disconnection?

RESISTING DECEPTION THROUGH EMPOWERMENT

Resisting deception begins with cultivating discernment—the ability to see through false narratives and align with truth. This requires intentionality, especially in moments of uncertainty. Here's how:

1. **Seek Clarity:** Take time to reflect on your beliefs and values. When faced with new information or decisions, ask yourself: Does this align with love, truth, and connection?
2. **Build Connection:** Surround yourself with people who challenge and support you. Share your stories and invite trusted voices to help you discern truth.
3. **Embrace Courage:** Fear is a powerful motivator for deception. Learn to sit with uncertainty and act in alignment with your values, even when the path isn't clear.

WRITING A BETTER STORY

The D.R.A.M.A. and C.R.E.A.T.O.R. frameworks are practical tools for examining and reshaping your stories. They help us see the patterns that trap us and the paths that set us free. By recognizing when we're stuck in cycles of victimhood, blame, or control, we can make intentional choices to step into roles of empowerment, authenticity, and creativity.

Whether the crisis is personal, societal, or hypothetical, the call remains the same: Examine your stories. Choose the ones that lead to flourishing, freedom, and connection. Resist fear, shame, and deception, and step into the truth of who you are and what you were created to be.

As you move forward, I encourage you to take the tools and perspectives shared in this book and apply them to your own life. Reflect on the narratives you live by. Reject the ones that enslave you. Embrace the ones that empower you to write a better story.

The world needs your clarity, your courage, and your connection. Together, we can resist deception, heal disconnection, and create lives that reflect the love, truth, and empowerment we were always meant to live.

COMMON RESPONSES

"Yeah, but how can I even tell which stories are true and which are deceptive?"

Discernment isn't about having all the answers—it's about learning to ask the right questions. Start by asking whether a story aligns with love, truth, and connection. Does it empower you, or does it fill you with fear and shame? Over time, as you practice tuning into these guiding principles, it will become easier to distinguish between what liberates and what enslaves. You'll also need to remind yourself that "there is no fear in love"–including the fear of being wrong. Thriving isn't a byproduct of "right-ish-ness" but righteousness, which we are and obtain by what and who we are connected to, not by the perfection of our understanding.

> "Yeah, but isn't it easier to just go along with what everyone else believes?"

It can feel safer to follow the crowd, but true freedom often means stepping off the well-worn path. The easy way isn't always the way of flourishing. Living intentionally, examining your stories, and aligning with truth may require courage, but it's a choice that leads to deeper connection, authenticity, and peace.

> "Yeah, but what if I'm afraid of letting go of the stories I've always known?"

In an age where we've come to believe that it is our being right that "saves us," questioning those beliefs can feel very scary. Changing them, even more so, especially when it means letting go of familiar narratives. But remember, the Creator's love is constant and unshakable—it doesn't depend on the stories you believe or how well you understand them. As you release what no longer serves you, trust that you're stepping into something better: a life of greater freedom, truth, and connection.

> "Yeah, but what if I'm wrong? What if I let go of something important?"

Mistakes are part of the journey, and the Creator's love isn't contingent on you getting it all right. Discernment isn't about perfection; it's about growth. Trust that the Spirit will guide you back to truth, even if you veer off course (John 6:39, Philippians 1:6). The willingness to examine your stories and seek truth is itself an act of courage and faith.

> "Yeah, but isn't it exhausting to keep questioning everything?"

WHAT TO DO WHEN THE ALIENS SHOW UP (AND EVEN IF THEY DON'T)

It's not about questioning everything all the time—it's about living intentionally. As you align more with truth, you'll find that clarity brings peace, not exhaustion. The process of discernment becomes less about effort and more about being rooted in love, which provides strength and renewal instead of weariness.

THE POWER OF DISCERNMENT
REFRAMING THE INVADERS

As we get ready to wrap things up, I want to pause and ask you a question: Did you notice how, throughout this book, I've sometimes described fear, shame, and judgment in ways that align with the Drama Triangle? If you didn't, don't worry—you're not alone. If you did, good catch! Either way, there's something important here to unpack.

Let's be honest: when we face fear, shame, or anything that disrupts our sense of peace, it's easy to frame those things as the enemy. It's natural to see them as Persecutors—forces coming against us, robbing us of joy, freedom, and connection. In some ways, that's not entirely wrong. These "invaders" do wreak havoc when we let them take over. But what if that's not the whole story?

This is where discernment comes in.

SEEING THE PATTERNS

Throughout this book, I've been dropping clues about how the Drama Triangle and Empowerment Dynamic show up in just about everything—including how we relate to our emotions and struggles. When we cast fear, shame, or judgment as the Persecutors in our story, we often end up feeling like Victims, trapped in cycles of blame or helplessness.

But here's the thing: even the "invaders" in our lives don't have to stay in those roles. With discernment, we can choose to see them differently. They don't have to be the bad guys in your story. They can be something else entirely—**Challengers** that help you grow.

REFRAMING THE INVADERS

Let's take some of the most common emotional "invaders" we face and look at how we might reframe them as Challengers, inviting us to growth and transformation:

- **Fear** can be a signal that something matters to you. It's an invitation to trust, to step forward with courage, and to face the unknown.
- **Shame** can expose where you've bought into lies about your worth, giving you the chance to reclaim the truth of who you are.
- **Judgment** can reveal the standards you've been holding—some of which might not even be yours—and invite you to align with values that actually serve you.
- **Insecurity** can highlight areas where you've outsourced your sense of worth to external validation. It's an opportunity to build a stronger foundation of self-acceptance.
- **Dependency** can reveal where you've been overly reliant on systems or people, nudging you to cultivate resilience and independence.
- **Anxiety** can act as a spotlight, pointing to unresolved tensions in your life. It's a call to explore with curiosity and to find peace by focusing on what you can control.

These reframes don't deny the discomfort of these experiences; they honor it while inviting us to engage differently. By shifting our perspective, we transform the invaders from forces that disempower us into opportunities for growth.

A REMINDER OF WHY DISCERNMENT MATTERS

This isn't just about reframing your emotions—it's about learning to navigate life with clarity and intentionality. Without discernment, it's easy to fall back into patterns of fear, blame, and disconnection. But with discernment, you gain the freedom to choose how you engage with the world, your circumstances, and even your struggles.

Discernment doesn't mean you ignore pain or pretend everything's fine. It means you step back and ask:

- What's the opportunity here?
- What's the invitation?
- How can I grow through this?

Discernment isn't a one-time skill—it's a practice. By cultivating it, you reclaim your power to respond to life's challenges with clarity, connection, and creativity.

THE INVADERS' HIDDEN GIFT

Here's the surprising truth: the very things you've been running from might be the things that help you the most. Fear, shame, judgment, insecurity, dependency, and anxiety—those "invaders" you've been battling—can actually be your greatest teachers if you let them.

I'm not saying it's easy. It's not. But the growth, freedom, and transformation that come from shifting your perspective are worth it. When you see the invaders not as Persecutors but as Challengers, you reclaim your power. You stop living as a Victim and start creating a life of meaning and purpose.

SVEN MASTERSON

AN INVITATION TO REFRAME

As we near the end of this journey, I invite you to look back on the invaders in your own life. Have you been seeing them as Persecutors, as enemies out to get you? Or have you started to see them as Challengers, pushing you toward growth and freedom?

What would change if you reframed your relationship with fear, shame, and judgment? How might your story look different if you saw even your struggles as part of your path to flourishing?

The choice is yours. Discernment gives you the power to rewrite your story—to see the invaders not as villains, but as unlikely allies in your journey to becoming a Creator.

So, what will you choose?

CONCLUSION: LIVING FREE, NO MATTER WHAT

As we close this journey, I want to bring us back to where we started: the question of how we respond to the unknown, the overwhelming, and the downright scary. Whether it's an alien invasion (hypothetical, but let's humor it), a global crisis, or the day-to-day struggles that feel like mountains in our lives, the way we respond determines whether we stay stuck in fear or move forward with strength and purpose.

We've explored a lot of ideas in this book, and not all of them will resonate with everyone. That's okay. What matters is recognizing that you have the power to respond to life's challenges in ways that lead to greater peace, freedom, and empowerment—whether you're dealing with an otherworldly threat, a messy relationship, or the gnawing self-doubt that keeps you up at night.

A REMINDER OF WHAT IT TAKES

In Part I, we imagined an alien invasion—a scenario designed to bring our fears into sharp focus. While we've journeyed far from those opening pages, the lessons remain the same:

1. **Ground Yourself in Truth:** When faced with chaos or uncertainty, the first step is clarity. Look past the noise and fear-mongering narratives. What do you actually know to be true? What are the stories you're telling yourself that might not be serving you?
2. **Cultivate Connection:** The strength to face the big scary things (and the little ones too) doesn't come from isolation. It comes from connection—to yourself, to others, and to whatever source of strength you find most empowering.
3. **Stay Present:** Whether it's an alien mothership hovering in the sky or an overwhelming to-do list staring you down, the key to responding powerfully is staying present. Fear often lives in the future, while shame clings to the past. Freedom happens in the here and now.
4. **Focus on What You Can Control:** In the face of fear, it's easy to spiral into what-ifs and worst-case scenarios. But the most empowering question is always, "What can I do right now?" Even small, practical actions can restore your sense of agency and momentum.
5. **Respond with Curiosity, Not Panic:** Fear wants you to react without thinking. But curiosity invites you to explore, adapt, and learn. Instead of succumbing to knee-jerk panic, ask questions: "What's really happening here? What options do I have? How can I move forward?"

LIVING FREE IN THE EVERYDAY

While alien invasions make for dramatic metaphors, most of the fears and challenges we face are quieter but no less significant. They show up in our relationships, careers, health, and self-image. They test our ability to remain grounded, connected, and resilient.

The principles we've explored throughout this book—self-awareness, empowered thinking, connection, purpose, and rest—are just as effective in navigating everyday challenges as they are in responding to hypothetical intergalactic crises. They're tools for living free, no matter what life throws your way.

FREEDOM AS A PRACTICE

Freedom isn't about eliminating fear or shame—it's about how you respond when they arise. It's a practice of choosing clarity over confusion, connection over isolation, and empowerment over helplessness. It's about responding to life's challenges with the confidence that, whatever happens, you have the tools and resilience to move forward.

This kind of freedom doesn't require you to believe in any specific framework or worldview. It's accessible to anyone willing to take small, intentional steps toward self-awareness, connection, and action. Whether you call it living free, staying grounded, or being unshakable, the result is the same: a life where fear and shame no longer dictate your choices.

WHAT WILL YOU CHOOSE?

So, as we close this journey, I leave you with a question: How will you choose to respond?

- Will you let fear and uncertainty dictate your actions, or will you ground yourself in truth and move forward with intention?
- Will you let shame and insecurity keep you stuck, or will you reconnect with your sense of worth and take action from a place of strength?
- Will you give in to the stories that say you're not enough, or will you write a new story of empowerment, connection, and courage?

SVEN MASTERSON

The choice isn't about perfection—it's about practice. Every day, you have the chance to take one small step toward freedom, resilience, and a life that feels truly alive.

A FINAL WORD

The world will always have its challenges—big, small, and everything in between. Whether it's the hypothetical alien invasion or the very real struggles of navigating relationships, careers, and self-worth, the way forward is the same: clarity, connection, and courageous action.

Thank you for walking through this journey with me. My hope is that these ideas will inspire you, challenge you, and equip you to face whatever comes your way—not with fear or shame, but with confidence and freedom. Because the truth is: You were made to live free, to step into love and connection, and to reflect the unshakable truth of who you are.

PART FIVE
APPENDIX

CHAPTER SIXTY-TWO
THE MATHEMATICAL MIRACLE OF YOUR EXISTENCE

THE PROBABILITY OF ANY ONE PERSON EXISTING IS STAGGERINGLY small, making your life a mathematical marvel. Let's break it down:

1. **Your Parents Meeting:** Studies estimate that the odds of two random individuals meeting in the same place and time are about 1 in 20,000. Now factor in the chance that they form a relationship and produce a child—this narrows the odds significantly.
2. **Conception:** During conception, only one sperm out of roughly 100 million fertilizes an egg. The likelihood of that particular sperm meeting that particular egg is 1 in 100 million.
3. **Ancestral Lineage:** For you to exist, each generation in your lineage—spanning hundreds of thousands of years—needed to survive, reproduce, and continue the chain. The probability of this uninterrupted lineage persisting is roughly 1 in $10^{45,000}$, according to calculations by Dr. Ali Binazir, a Harvard-trained mathematician and philosopher.
4. **Environmental Factors:** Your ancestors faced natural

disasters, wars, and diseases, any of which could have disrupted the chain of life leading to you.

When multiplying these probabilities together, the likelihood of your existence comes out to approximately 1 in $10^{2,685,000}$. That's a number so vast it exceeds the number of atoms in the observable universe (around 10^{80}).

Yet, against these overwhelming odds, you are here—thinking, feeling, and living. Your existence is a statistical impossibility that happened anyway, making you a living, breathing miracle.

Citations:

- Binazir, A. (2011). *"The Odds of You Being Born."* Blog post explaining statistical improbability.
- Lineweaver, C. H., & Davis, T. M. (2002). *"Does the Rapid Appearance of Life on Earth Suggest that Life Is Common in the Universe?"* Astrobiology.

CHAPTER SIXTY-THREE
FROM DRAMA TO CREATOR
TOOLS FOR DISCERNMENT AND EMPOWERMENT

IN THE FACE OF FEAR, MANIPULATION, AND UNCERTAINTY, IT'S EASY TO feel overwhelmed and reactive. This is why we need tools—not just to understand what's happening, but to reclaim our sovereignty and respond with clarity and strength. The **D.R.A.M.A.** and **C.R.E.A.T.E.** frameworks are two sides of this process: one for diagnosing disempowering dynamics and the other for responding with empowered action.

Together, they offer a pathway from reactive drama to creative, intentional living. This appendix provides a detailed guide to using these tools.

D.R.A.M.A. - DIAGNOSING MANIPULATIVE PATTERNS

The **D.R.A.M.A.** framework helps us spot patterns of fear, shame, dependency, and disconnection in messages, relationships, and narratives. It's not about judging truth but recognizing dynamics that lead to victimhood, blame, and drama triangle behavior.

The D.R.A.M.A. Checklist

1. **D – Does it Divide?**

- **Ask:** Does the message create an "us vs. them" dynamic?
- **Spot the Pattern:** Division fosters judgment, disconnection, and reliance on external saviors or authorities.

2. **R – Is it Rooted in Judgment or Shame?**
   - **Ask:** Does the message emphasize guilt, inadequacy, or failure?
   - **Spot the Pattern:** Shame and judgment fuel dependency, preventing personal empowerment and self-acceptance.

3. **A – Does it Amplify Fear or Anxiety?**
   - **Ask:** Does the message provoke fear, urgency, or panic?
   - **Spot the Pattern:** Fear-based messaging narrows focus and heightens reliance on external solutions, bypassing critical thinking.

4. **M – Does it Minimize Agency?**
   - **Ask:** Does the message diminish your ability to act or discern independently?
   - **Spot the Pattern:** Minimizing agency reinforces dependency and discourages connection to internal sources of power.

5. **A – Does it Avoid Responsibility?**
   - **Ask:** Does the message encourage blame or avoid personal accountability?
   - **Spot the Pattern:** Blame perpetuates victimhood and traps people in drama triangle dynamics.

C.R.E.A.T.E. - RESPONDING TO D.R.A.M.A.

Once we've identified disempowering patterns, the **C.R.E.A.T.E.** framework offers a pathway to empowerment. Each step counteracts the dynamics of **D.R.A.M.A.**, fostering clarity, connection, and sovereignty.

WHAT TO DO WHEN THE ALIENS SHOW UP (AND EVEN IF THEY DON'T)

The C.R.E.A.T.E. Response Framework

1. **C – Curiosity**
   - Replace judgment with curiosity. Explore your feelings, needs, and values.
   - **Practice:** Ask, "What is my experience of this? What's the deeper need or truth here?"
2. **R – Responsibility**
   - Take ownership of your emotions, choices, and boundaries.
   - **Practice:** Shift focus from blame to action by asking, "What's within my control?"
3. **E – Empathy**
   - Extend compassion to yourself and others. Recognize shared humanity without condoning harmful behavior.
   - **Practice:** Pause and affirm, "I am enough, and so are they."
4. **A – Authenticity**
   - Act from your values and true self, rather than reacting from fear or ego.
   - **Practice:** Reflect on how you can respond in alignment with who you are.
5. **T – Trust**
   - Trust yourself, your process, and the Creator. Let go of the need to control outcomes.
   - **Practice:** Remind yourself, "I have the capacity to navigate this with clarity and grace."
6. **E – Empowerment**
   - Take intentional action to protect your values and sovereignty while fostering connection.
   - **Practice:** Act boldly, knowing your worth is inherent and unshaken.

C.R.E.A.T.O.R. – EXPANDING THE RESPONSE FRAMEWORK

To deepen the practice of C.R.E.A.T.E., we can expand it into C.R.E.A.T.O.R. by adding two additional principles that foster resilience and openness:

7. **O – Openness**
   - Stay open to growth, perspectives, and unexpected possibilities.
   - **Practice:** Reflect, "What might I learn from this situation?"
8. **R – Resilience**
   - Cultivate resilience through balance, rest, and reflection.
   - **Practice:** Affirm, "Challenges are opportunities to grow stronger and wiser."

USING D.R.A.M.A. AND C.R.E.A.T.E./C.R.E.A.T.O.R. TOGETHER

1. Diagnose With D.R.A.M.A.
   - When you encounter a destabilizing situation, use the **D.R.A.M.A.** checklist to identify whether fear, judgment, dependency, or disconnection are at play.
2. Respond With C.R.E.A.T.E. or C.R.E.A.T.O.R.
   - Use the response framework to counteract the dynamics you identified. Replace fear with curiosity, blame with responsibility, and judgment with empathy.
3. Reinforce Sovereignty and Growth
   - Regularly practice the empowering elements of **C.R.E.A.T.E.** or **C.R.E.A.T.O.R.** to build resilience, trust, and connection.

WHAT TO DO WHEN THE ALIENS SHOW UP (AND EVEN IF THEY DON'T)

PRACTICAL EXAMPLE: NAVIGATING A FEAR-BASED MESSAGE

Scenario: You hear a fear-driven message in the news claiming an imminent crisis.

- **D.R.A.M.A. Diagnostic:**
    - Does it divide? Yes, it creates an "us vs. them" narrative.
    - Does it amplify fear? Absolutely. The language is designed to provoke panic.
    - Does it minimize agency? Yes, it implies you're powerless without external intervention.
- **C.R.E.A.T.E. Response:**
    - **Curiosity:** Ask, "What's my experience of hearing this? What facts do I know?"
    - **Responsibility:** Identify what's within your control, such as fact-checking or preparing calmly.
    - **Empathy:** Recognize the shared fear without letting it consume you.
    - **Authenticity:** Decide how to respond in alignment with your values, not the panic of the narrative.
    - **Trust:** Trust your ability to navigate the situation thoughtfully.
    - **Empowerment:** Take meaningful action without succumbing to fear.

WHY THESE FRAMEWORKS MATTER

The combination of **D.R.A.M.A.** and **C.R.E.A.T.E.** helps us move from reactive, fear-based patterns to intentional, empowered living. Whether we're facing external manipulation or internal self-doubt, these tools guide us toward discernment, authenticity, and connection. By recognizing and transforming disempowering dynamics, we reclaim our sovereignty and step into our role as creators of lives rooted in clarity, courage, and love.

EPILOGUE
WOLVERINES!

As we close this journey together, let me remind you that *Red Dawn*, the first movie I ever watched at home on a VCR, taught me an unforgettable lesson: even in the face of overwhelming odds, resistance is possible. That story of courage, rebellion, and finding connection under fire left a mark on my young mind.

And here's the truth I hope you take away from this book: no matter what "invasion" you're facing—fear, shame, disconnection, or deception—you have the power to resist.

JOIN THE CONVERSATION

AT ALIENARRIVALBOOK.COM

Thank you for reading *What to Do When the Aliens Show Up (and Even If They Don't): A Guide to Overcoming Fear, Anxiety, Insecurity, Shame, and Deception.* Your journey doesn't end here—this is where it begins.

Visit **AlienArrivalBook.com** to connect with a growing community, share your thoughts, and access resources designed to help you navigate uncertainty with courage and clarity.

WHAT YOU'LL DISCOVER AT ALIENARRIVALBOOK.COM:

- **Contact the Author:** Have questions or reflections about the book? Need guidance on your journey? Reach out to me directly through the site—I'd love to hear from you.
- **Redoubt Resources:** Interested in finding or building a personal redoubt—a place of safety, preparation, and resilience? Explore practical tools, guides, and connections to help you create your sanctuary.
- **Exclusive Content:** Additional resources that expand on the book's themes.

JOIN THE CONVERSATION

- **Deeper Insights:** Stay updated with articles, guides, and resources to help you prepare for crises—whether personal, societal, or even hypothetical extraterrestrial contact.

WHY VISIT ALIENARRIVALBOOK.COM?

Whether you're exploring redoubt strategies, seeking to connect with others, or looking for answers to life's uncertainties, this is a space for you. Together, we'll build resilience, foster connection, and explore what it means to live with clarity and courage, no matter what comes.

TAKE THE NEXT STEP

Visit **AlienArrivalBook.com** today. Start the conversation, discover empowering resources, and find support for your journey toward thriving in the face of uncertainty.

Because the future is shaped not by fear, but by the courage we choose to cultivate today.

ABOUT SVEN MASTERSON
& HOW TO CONNECT

Sven Masterson is an author, men's coach, mentor, and the founder of Masterful Men, a global community dedicated to helping men become **unstuck, unshakable, and unstoppable**—even in the face of life's greatest "alien invasions." Specializing in guiding men through high-conflict relationships, Sven helps men uncover and resolve the root issues that sabotage connection, intimacy, and trust in their partnerships.

Drawing on over thirty years of marriage, parenting, and entrepreneurial experience, Sven offers relatable and authentic guidance to men wrestling with frustration, resentment, or feelings of disconnection. His work provides actionable steps to rebuild confidence, emotional resilience, and connection—not just in relationships but in life as a whole. Whether working one-on-one, in small groups, or through his private community, Sven creates a safe, down-to-earth space where men can untangle their struggles, confront their fears, and step into strength and purpose.

Sven's coaching combines warmth, humor, and accountability to help men break cycles of conflict and self-doubt, confront issues like low self-worth, and move toward thriving relationships and lives. He believes in "facing your inner aliens head-on"—taking personal responsibility for growth and living with bold authenticity.

As a seasoned author, coach, and mentor, Sven has helped countless men navigate life's "invasions," equipping them with the tools to transform personal crises into opportunities for connection and growth. His work reminds men of what's possible when they show up for themselves, their partners, and their families.

Outside of his professional life, Sven enjoys outdoor adventures, travel, creating things, and exploring nature. He finds fulfillment in self-reliance pursuits like homesteading, gardening, cultivating and animals, and hands-on crafting, reflecting his commitment to living intentionally. He and his wife of thirty years, Zelda, live on a homestead in North Central Pennsylvania with three of their six children. There, they embrace the beauty and simplicity of rural life while always keeping an eye on the sky.

- facebook.com/MentorSven
- x.com/masterfulmen
- instagram.com/masterful.men
- linkedin.com/in/svenmasterson
- amazon.com/stores/Sven-Masterson/author/B0D3YFWY5P
- youtube.com/@SvenMasterson

ACKNOWLEDGMENTS

First and foremost, I give thanks to Abba (no, not the 70s Swedish pop group, but my Creator), in whom I live, move, and have my being. Your steadfast, unconditional love and high regard have been my foundation. You remind me of who I am when I lose sight of myself and continually lead me toward freedom from guilt and shame. Thank you for empowering me to take ownership of my life and for answering my prayers for good brothers to journey alongside me. To Yeshua, the Alpha and Omega, who holds all things together—you are the ultimate example of love and grace.

This book has been a journey of transformation and growth, and it could not have been realized without the support of so many remarkable individuals.

To my family, especially my wife Zelda and our children: thank you for your unyielding patience and encouragement as I navigated the winding path that brought me to the truths shared in this book. Your love and understanding have been my anchor through every challenge. Zelda, without your commitment to us—even in the most frustrating moments—this book and my personal growth would not have been possible.

To my parents, who overcame significant challenges to instill in me and my siblings a love for truth, curiosity, and perseverance: thank you. Dad, your example of offering strangers kindness and presence and consistent encouragement to do what is right, even when it's hard, has been a guiding light. Mom, your deep thinking and relentless drive to push me beyond the easy answers have shaped my character profoundly.

A special thanks to Rob Schneps, whose insights into the Tree of the Knowledge of Good and Evil as a representation of judgment sparked a radical shift in my perspective. Your wisdom planted a seed that continues to grow, influencing how I approach life, relationships, and this book's central themes.

To Mike Remick and Brian Weisgerber, your enduring friendship and camaraderie have been a wellspring of encouragement and strength. Your unwavering belief in me and our shared vision has profoundly enriched this journey.

Finally, I want to acknowledge those I've unintentionally hurt as I've stumbled through life searching for answers to deep pain. While I have never sought to harm anyone, I recognize that in my own woundedness, I have wounded others along the way. To those individuals, I offer my sincere gratitude for their patience and grace, and my heartfelt apology for any pain I've caused.

This book is not just my story—it is a testament to the people and experiences that have shaped me and to the collective spirit of growth and learning. Thank you to everyone who has walked beside me, offering support, wisdom, and encouragement. May we continue to grow together.

SPECIAL THANKS

I would like to extend my heartfelt gratitude to Jay Mitchell and Jeff Friedman. Their unwavering support, friendship, and shared vision have truly enriched my journey. Their generous, enthusiastic, and kind-hearted encouragement has been a beacon of strength for me. I am profoundly thankful for the camaraderie and partnership we've created as we strive to make a meaningful difference together. Your steadfast belief in this mission inspires me every day—thank you for walking alongside me.

EXTRA SPECIAL THANKS

It takes courage to endure the sharp pains of self-discovery rather than choose to take the dull pain of unconsciousness that would last the rest of our lives. - Marianne Williamson

Some people illuminate the path not just by pointing the way, but by walking it with profound courage. Craig Vickers, you have been such a light. Your unwavering support of this work has transcended the typical bounds of friendship and professional collaboration. In choosing to share your deepest struggles with raw authenticity, you've demonstrated what true courage looks like—not the absence of fear, but the willingness to be seen in our most vulnerable moments.

Your boldness in facing your hardest times head-on, and then using those experiences to help others find their way, exemplifies the very essence of what healing and growth can look like. The trust you've placed in this work, and the fearless way you've advocated for it, has touched countless lives beyond your own.

Thank you, Craig, for showing us all what it means to transform personal challenges into beacons of hope for others. Your friendship and trust have been instrumental in bringing this work to life.

ALSO BY SVEN MASTERSON

From Resentment to Reconnection: A Man's Guide to Overcoming Personal and Marital Conflict

Are you feeling stuck in cycles of resentment and disconnection in your marriage? This transformative guide offers practical steps to rebuild intimacy, trust, and emotional connection. Learn how to embrace high regard, self-reliance, and ownership to reignite love and partnership.

More Info at www.resentmenttoreconnection.com

Narcissist! Or Not?: A Man's Guide to Transforming Hurtful Accusations into Lasting Love & Trust

Have you been called a narcissist? This book challenges harmful labels and provides tools to break free from cycles of defensiveness and conflict. Discover how to cultivate emotional strength, rebuild trust, and create deeper connection in your relationships.

More Info at www.narcissistornot.com

A NOTE TO READERS

Dear Reader,

Thank you for walking with me on this journey of overcoming fear, shame, and disconnection. Your courage to explore these themes and step into a life of connection, empowerment, and truth is deeply meaningful to me.

If this book has resonated with you, encouraged you, or offered you a new perspective, I would be truly grateful if you could share your thoughts in a review where you purchased it. Your reflections not only help others discover this book but also contribute to a larger, hopeful conversation about living free from fear and shame.

I'd love to hear about your personal experience with these ideas. Whether this book has sparked transformation, deepened your understanding, or raised questions you'd like to discuss, please don't hesitate to reach out to me at **sven@alienarrival-book.com**. It's an honor to support and connect with readers who are embracing the invitation to live boldly and authentically.

Thank you for being part of this journey and this community. Together, we are choosing stories that lead to flourishing, freedom, and truth.

With gratitude and encouragement,
Sven Masterson

END NOTES

INTRODUCTION TO ENDNOTES

So much has gone into the thoughts in this book that the volume was far more than I'd intended, but in the words of Blaise Pascal (and Mark Twain), "I have made this longer than usual because I have not had time to make it shorter."

Because this book reflects a lifetime of my experiences and perspectives, the endnotes are not traditional citations tied directly to specific passages or claims within the chapters. Instead, they offer a curated list of complementary resources that can deepen your understanding of the ideas explored in each chapter. Some of these references are works by leading thinkers, researchers, and authors whose perspectives align with or inspire the themes discussed. Others provide scientific, psychological, or philosophical insights that enrich the topics covered. I hope that these resources will invite you to explore further, reflect deeply, and engage with these concepts in ways that resonate with your unique journey.

Feel free to use this section as a guide to discover new perspectives, explore the subject matter more deeply, or simply explore ideas that pique your curiosity. Each resource expands the conver-

END NOTES

sation and offers additional tools and understanding for your path toward authenticity, acceptance, and freedom.

PRE PART 1

1. **Brown, Brené.** (2012). *Daring Greatly: How the Courage to Be Vulnerable Transforms the Way We Live, Love, Parent, and Lead.* Penguin Random House.
    - Explores vulnerability, courage, and their role in overcoming shame, fear, and disconnection.
2. **Kahneman, Daniel.** (2011). *Thinking, Fast and Slow.* Farrar, Straus and Giroux.
    - Examines how cognitive biases shape our responses to fear, uncertainty, and manipulation.
3. **Van der Kolk, Bessel.** (2014). *The Body Keeps the Score: Brain, Mind, and Body in the Healing of Trauma.* Penguin Books.
    - Discusses the impact of trauma and fear on the mind and body, offering tools for resilience and healing.
4. **Frankl, Viktor E.** (1959). *Man's Search for Meaning.* Beacon Press.
    - Highlights the transformative potential of meaning-making in navigating suffering and thriving.
5. **Sagan, Carl.** (1997). *The Demon-Haunted World: Science as a Candle in the Dark.* Ballantine Books.
    - Offers a framework for critical thinking and skepticism in the face of deception and fear.
6. **Cialdini, Robert B.** (2001). *Influence: The Psychology of Persuasion.* Harper Business.
    - Explores the mechanics of persuasion and manipulation, and how to recognize and resist them.
7. **Tolle, Eckhart.** (2004). *A New Earth: Awakening to Your Life's Purpose.* Penguin Group.

- Explores how awareness and presence dismantle egoic patterns of fear and dependency.
8. **Kabat-Zinn, Jon.** (1994). *Wherever You Go, There You Are: Mindfulness Meditation in Everyday Life.* Hyperion.
   - Provides mindfulness practices for cultivating awareness and breaking free from reactive cycles.
9. **Heuer, Richards J. Jr.** (1999). *Psychology of Intelligence Analysis.* Center for the Study of Intelligence.
   - Examines cognitive biases and how they can be exploited by deception, with tools for sharpening discernment.
10. **Harari, Yuval Noah.** (2016). *Homo Deus: A Brief History of Tomorrow.* Harper.
    - Explores humanity's ongoing struggle with fear, dependency, and the search for meaning in a complex world.
11. **Sun Tzu.** (5th century BCE). *The Art of War.*
    - Offers timeless insights into strategy and how deception exploits fear and uncertainty.
12. **Clear, James.** (2018). *Atomic Habits: An Easy & Proven Way to Build Good Habits & Break Bad Ones.* Avery.
    - A practical guide to creating lasting change through intentional action and repetition.
13. **Selye, Hans.** (1976). *The Stress of Life.* McGraw-Hill.
    - Discusses the physiological effects of stress and the balance of challenge and recovery in resilience.

PART 1

1. **Brown, Brené.** (2012). **Daring Greatly: How the Courage to Be Vulnerable Transforms the Way We Live, Love, Parent, and Lead. Penguin Random House.**
   - A deep dive into the role of vulnerability as an antidote to shame and disconnection. Brené Brown

END NOTES

explores how courageously showing up in our imperfections can dismantle the hold of fear, shame, and judgment.

2. Hari, Johann. (2015). Chasing the Scream: The First and Last Days of the War on Drugs. Bloomsbury.
   - This book introduces the idea that "the opposite of addiction is connection," offering a profound lens on how disconnection fuels dependency and isolation while connection fosters healing and growth.
3. Brown, Brené. (2010). The Gifts of Imperfection: Let Go of Who You Think You're Supposed to Be and Embrace Who You Are. Hazelden.
   - Brown emphasizes the power of self-acceptance and authenticity, providing tools to move past shame and the narratives that undermine our worth.
4. Clear, James. (2018). Atomic Habits: An Easy & Proven Way to Build Good Habits & Break Bad Ones. Avery.
   - A practical guide for creating positive changes through small, consistent steps. Clear's approach to habit-building aligns with the process of dismantling the invaders' lies and fostering resilience.
5. Neff, Kristin. (2011). Self-Compassion: The Proven Power of Being Kind to Yourself. William Morrow.
   - This book explains how self-compassion can counter the effects of shame and judgment, showing how kindness toward oneself fosters connection and courage.
6. Frankl, Viktor E. (1959). Man's Search for Meaning. Beacon Press.
   - A timeless reflection on finding meaning in the face of suffering. Frankl's insights provide guidance on reframing life's challenges, breaking the cycle of judgment and shame.
7. Gilbert, Paul. (2009). The Compassionate Mind: A New Approach to Life's Challenges. New Harbinger.

- Gilbert explores the evolutionary roots of shame and the role of compassion in overcoming its hold. His work ties to understanding shame's infiltration and cultivating internal connection.
8. **Tolle, Eckhart. (2005). A New Earth: Awakening to Your Life's Purpose. Penguin Group.**
    - This book addresses the ego's role in perpetuating judgment and disconnection, offering a spiritual perspective on reconnecting with one's inherent worth.
9. **Selye, Hans. (1976). The Stress of Life. McGraw-Hill.**
    - A foundational exploration of stress and its impact on the mind and body. This book helps readers understand the physiological components of fear and judgment, reinforcing the importance of connection and recovery.
10. **Roosevelt, Theodore. (1910). "Citizenship in a Republic," Speech Delivered at the Sorbonne.**
    - Known for the "Man in the Arena" quote, this speech highlights the courage required to confront fear, shame, and judgment. It provides inspiration for engaging fully in life despite imperfections.

PART 2

1. Frankl, Viktor E. (1959). *Man's Search for Meaning.* Beacon Press.
    - Frankl's exploration of finding purpose and agency under the most extreme conditions aligns with the chapters on reclaiming sovereignty, dismantling judgment, and building resilience in the face of life's challenges. His insights on choice as the final freedom underscore the foundation of agency.

END NOTES

2. **Rogers, Carl. (1961).** *On Becoming a Person: A Therapist's View of Psychotherapy.* Houghton Mifflin Harcourt.
   - Rogers's concept of self-actualization and the need for unconditional positive regard directly relates to Unconditional High Regard (UHR). His emphasis on authenticity resonates throughout the discussions of the false self and the journey to reclaim our intrinsic worth.
3. **Winnicott, Donald. (1965).** *The Maturational Processes and the Facilitating Environment.* International Universities Press.
   - Winnicott's concept of the false self as a defensive construct and its contrast with the authentic true self provides a psychological foundation for understanding the masks we wear and the journey toward authenticity.
4. **Brown, Brené. (2012).** *Daring Greatly: How the Courage to Be Vulnerable Transforms the Way We Live, Love, Parent, and Lead.* Penguin Random House.
   - Brown's work on vulnerability as the antidote to shame ties closely to the chapters on embracing authenticity and dismantling judgment. Her research provides tools for building resilience through connection.
5. **Neff, Kristin. (2011).** *Self-Compassion: The Proven Power of Being Kind to Yourself.* William Morrow.
   - Neff's work on self-compassion provides practical approaches to countering judgment and shame, laying the groundwork for self-sourcing worth and creating a stronghold of resilience.
6. **Clear, James. (2018).** *Atomic Habits: An Easy & Proven Way to Build Good Habits & Break Bad Ones.* Avery.
   - Clear's principles on building habits reinforce the importance of repetition and small, deliberate

choices in strengthening the stronghold and fostering growth.
7. **Jung, Carl. (1959).** *The Archetypes and the Collective Unconscious.* Princeton University Press.
    - Jung's concepts of the persona and individuation align with the exploration of the false self, emphasizing the integration of our masks into an authentic self.
8. **Schwartz, Richard. (2021).** *No Bad Parts: Healing Trauma and Restoring Wholeness with the Internal Family Systems Model.* Sounds True.
    - Schwartz's Internal Family Systems model describes the psyche as a collection of "parts," including protector parts similar to the false self, and emphasizes reconnecting with the authentic Self.
9. **Hari, Johann. (2018).** *Lost Connections: Why You're Depressed and How to Find Hope.* Bloomsbury.
    - Hari explores the role of connection in overcoming disconnection, shame, and isolation—key themes in building redoubts and dismantling the narratives that perpetuate conditional worth.
10. **Gilbert, Paul. (2009).** *The Compassionate Mind: A New Approach to Life's Challenges.* New Harbinger.
    - Some aspects of Gilbert's exploration of evolutionary psychology and the role of compassion directly supports the discussions on high regard, dismantling shame, and fostering resilience.
11. **Maslow, Abraham H. (1954).** *Motivation and Personality.* Harper & Row.
    - Maslow's hierarchy culminates in self-actualization, emphasizing living authentically and transcending external validation, which aligns with themes of reclaiming agency and authenticity.
12. **Selye, Hans. (1976).** *The Stress of Life.* McGraw-Hill.
    - This foundational text explores the physiological effects of stress and the importance of balancing

END NOTES

challenge and recovery to foster growth and prevent burnout.

13. **Van der Kolk, Bessel. (2014).** *The Body Keeps the Score: Brain, Mind, and Body in the Healing of Trauma.* Penguin Books.
    - Essential insights into recognizing and addressing old patterns of fear and shame, critical for maintaining boundaries and sovereignty within the stronghold.
14. **Karpman, Stephen. (2014).** *A Game-Free Life.* Drama Triangle Publications.
    - Karpman's Drama Triangle illustrates the dynamics of fear, shame, and judgment that perpetuate the false self and relational struggles, offering frameworks for reclaiming agency.
15. **Lieberman, Matthew D. (2013).** *Social: Why Our Brains Are Wired to Connect.* Crown.
    - This book provides insights into the neurochemical cycles of dopamine and serotonin, highlighting how connection and self-sourcing acceptance foster contentment and resilience.
16. **Walker, Matthew. (2017).** *Why We Sleep: Unlocking the Power of Sleep and Dreams.* Scribner.
    - Walker's work on the importance of rest underscores its role in maintaining emotional and physical resilience, vital for sustaining the stronghold.
17. **Heschel, Abraham Joshua. (1951).** *The Sabbath.* Farrar, Straus, and Giroux.
    - Heschel's reflections on rest as sacred underscore the value of creating intentional time for recovery and connection within the stronghold.
18. **MacGyver (1985-1992).** Created by Lee David Zlotoff, ABC.
    - The Swiss Army knife metaphor draws inspiration from MacGyver's resourcefulness, emphasizing the

versatility and utility of UHR in navigating emotional and relational challenges.

19. **Tolle, Eckhart. (2005).** *A New Earth: Awakening to Your Life's Purpose.* Penguin Group.
    - Tolle's focus on the ego and its illusions aligns with the exploration of the false self. His teachings on presence and letting go of external dependencies enrich the discussion on reclaiming agency.

20. **Brown, Peter. (2014).** *Make It Stick: The Science of Successful Learning.* Harvard University Press.
    - Insights on learning and habit formation reinforce the importance of repetition and challenge in strengthening the stronghold.

21. **Watts, Alan. (1989).** *The Book: On the Taboo Against Knowing Who You Are.* Vintage.
    - Watts's perspective on the false self as a social construct aligns with themes of intrinsic worth and the journey toward authenticity.

22. **Covey, Stephen R. (1989).** *The 7 Habits of Highly Effective People: Powerful Lessons in Personal Change.* Free Press.
    - Covey's emphasis on proactivity and focusing on one's sphere of influence connects deeply to the discussions on reclaiming agency and stepping into the Creator role.

23. **Guyton, Arthur C., & Hall, John E. (2016).** *Textbook of Medical Physiology (13th ed.).* Elsevier.
    - Provides a foundation for the concept of hypertrophy, offering parallels between physical and emotional strengthening through deliberate effort and recovery.

END NOTES

PART 3

1. Brown, Brené. (2012). *Daring Greatly: How the Courage to Be Vulnerable Transforms the Way We Live, Love, Parent, and Lead.* Penguin Random House.
   - Explores vulnerability as a strength rather than a weakness, aligning with themes of courage, authenticity, and connection discussed in Part 3.
2. Clear, James. (2018). *Atomic Habits: An Easy & Proven Way to Build Good Habits & Break Bad Ones.* Avery.
   - Offers practical strategies for incremental transformation, echoing Part 3's emphasis on consistent, intentional action for thriving.
3. Neff, Kristin. (2011). *Self-Compassion: The Proven Power of Being Kind to Yourself.* William Morrow.
   - Provides tools for cultivating self-compassion, a critical component in dismantling shame and fostering thriving.
4. Van der Kolk, Bessel. (2014). *The Body Keeps the Score: Brain, Mind, and Body in the Healing of Trauma.* Penguin Books.
   - Addresses the impact of trauma on identity and relationships, resonating with the discussion of reclaiming narratives and self-connection.
5. Heschel, Abraham Joshua. (1951). *The Sabbath.* Farrar, Straus, and Giroux.
   - Highlights rest and intentionality as acts of liberation, supporting Part 3's focus on sustainable growth and thriving.
6. Emerald, David. (2009). *The Power of TED (The Empowerment Dynamic).* Polaris Publishing.
   - Introduces frameworks for shifting from victimhood to empowerment, central to the counteroffensive themes in Part 3.

END NOTES

7. Covey, Stephen R. (1989). *The 7 Habits of Highly Effective People: Powerful Lessons in Personal Change.* Free Press.
   - Aligns with principles of ownership, alignment, and intentionality discussed as foundations for thriving.
8. Schoenfeld, Brad J. (2010). "The Mechanisms of Muscle Hypertrophy and Their Application to Resistance Training." *Journal of Strength and Conditioning Research, 24(10), 2857-2872.*
   - Draws parallels between physical and emotional growth, illustrating the importance of challenge and recovery.
9. Kabat-Zinn, Jon. (1994). *Wherever You Go, There You Are: Mindfulness Meditation in Everyday Life.* Hyperion.
   - Provides mindfulness practices for cultivating presence and dismantling reactive cycles, themes central to connection and self-expression.
10. Frankl, Viktor E. (1959). *Man's Search for Meaning.* Beacon Press.
    - Explores meaning-making as a pathway through suffering, a core element in transitioning from survival to thriving.
11. Walton, John H. (2009). *The Lost World of Genesis One.* IVP Academic.
    - Offers insights into ancient cosmology and frameworks of purpose, linking to the broader narratives in Part 3 about self-definition and purpose.
12. Lewis, C. S. (1940). *The Problem of Pain.* HarperOne.
    - Examines themes of judgment, free will, and resilience, complementing the theological underpinnings in chapters addressing self-worth and sovereignty.
13. Tolle, Eckhart. (2005). *A New Earth: Awakening to Your Life's Purpose.* Penguin Group.

END NOTES

- Focuses on dismantling egoic patterns and aligning with authentic self, aligning with thriving narratives in Part 3.
14. Cloud, Henry, & Townsend, John. (1992). *Boundaries: When to Say Yes, How to Say No to Take Control of Your Life*. Zondervan.
    - Provides practical tools for maintaining emotional and relational integrity, key to self-sourcing and thriving.
15. Walker, Matthew. (2017). *Why We Sleep: Unlocking the Power of Sleep and Dreams*. Scribner.
    - Explains the role of rest and recovery in well-being and performance, supporting the concept of intentional self-care as part of thriving.

PART 4

END NOTES

1. Chapters 36–40: Reconnecting with Our True Selves
   1. The Genesis Narrative and Original Design
      - Genesis 1:26–31 – Humanity's creation in the image of the Creator and the declaration of "very good."
      - Genesis 2:15 – Humanity's placement in the garden with a mandate to cultivate and protect.
      - John Walton, *The Lost World of Genesis One* – Explores the cultural context and function of Genesis in its ancient setting.
   2. The Root of Shame and Judgment
      - Genesis 2:16–17 – The Creator's prohibition and the introduction of the Tree of Knowledge of Good and Evil.
      - Genesis 3:7–11 – Humanity's first response to shame, hiding, and judgment.
      - C.S. Lewis, *The Problem of Pain* – Explores judgment, free will, and humanity's role in creation.
2. Chapters 41–45: Liberation and Flourishing
   1. Overcoming Shame Through Connection
      - John 8:36 – "If the Son sets you free, you will be free indeed."
      - Brené Brown, *Daring Greatly* – Vulnerability as a path to healing shame and embracing authenticity.
   2. Boundaries and Freedom
      - Cloud & Townsend, *Boundaries* – A psychological framework for developing healthy relationships rooted in connection.
   3. Shame, Judgment, and the Torah
      - Deuteronomy 13:1–5 – The Torah as a guide for discernment and truth.
      - Psalm 19:7–11 – The law of the Creator as perfect, reviving the soul.

END NOTES

- Timothy Keller, *The Reason for God* – Insight into divine justice and restorative love.

3. Chapters 46–50: Sonship, Identity, and Agency
   1. Sonship and Identity
      - Romans 8:15 – "For you have not received a spirit of slavery leading to fear again, but you have received a spirit of adoption as sons and daughters, by which we cry out, 'Abba! Father!'"
      - Henry Nouwen, *The Return of the Prodigal Son* – A powerful reflection on embracing divine love and sonship.
   2. Human Flourishing and Connection
      - John 15:5 – "I am the vine; you are the branches."
      - Brené Brown, *The Gifts of Imperfection* – On cultivating connection and living authentically.

4. Chapters 51–55: The Cosmic Family and Co-Creation
   1. The Creator's Response to the Fall
      - Genesis 3:9–21 – The Creator's actions post-fall, including questions and the provision of animal skins.
      - Genesis 3:15 – The protoevangelium (first gospel) as a promise of redemption.
      - Miroslav Volf, *Free of Charge* – On divine forgiveness and grace.
   2. The Great Commission as Co-Creation
      - Genesis 1:28 – The original mandate to be fruitful, multiply, and steward creation.
      - Matthew 28:19–20 – "Go therefore and make disciples of all the nations..."
      - N.T. Wright, *Simply Good News* – Explores how the Gospel aligns with human flourishing and connection.

5. Chapters 56–57: Thriving and Discernment
   1. Freedom, Love, and Flourishing

- 1 John 4:18 – "There is no fear in love, but perfect love casts out fear."
- **Romans 8:1–4** – Living according to the Spirit and not the flesh.
- **Richard Rohr,** *Falling Upward* – On moving beyond fear and into spiritual freedom.

2. Discernment in Stories
    - **Isaiah 5:20** – "Woe to those who call evil good and good evil..."
    - **1 Thessalonians 5:21** – "Examine everything carefully; hold fast to that which is good."
    - **Dallas Willard,** *The Divine Conspiracy* – On cultivating discernment and living aligned with divine wisdom.

6. Additional Frameworks and Tools
    1. The Drama Triangle and Relational Dynamics
        - **Stephen Karpman, "Fairy Tales and Script Drama Analysis"** – The foundational theory of the Drama Triangle.
        - **David Emerald,** *The Power of TED (The Empowerment Dynamic)* – A practical guide to shifting from victimhood to empowerment.
        - **Genesis 3:12–13** – Blame-shifting dynamics after the fall.
    2. The Spirit's Role as Companion
        - **John 14:26** – "But the Helper, the Holy Spirit, whom the Father will send in My name, will teach you all things..."
        - **Sarah Bessey,** *Out of Sorts* – On evolving faith and rediscovering the Spirit.
    3. Sabbath as Resistance and Rest
        - **Exodus 31:13** – The Sabbath as a covenant sign between the Creator and humanity.
        - **Walter Brueggemann,** *Sabbath as Resistance* – The countercultural significance of Sabbath as a

www.ingramcontent.com/pod-product-compliance
Lightning Source LLC
Chambersburg PA
CBHW070603030426
42337CB00020B/3687